D0947286

Rethinking Rental Housing

TEMPLE UNIVERSITY PRESS  PHILADELPHIA

RETHINKING RENTAL HOUSING

John I. Gilderbloom | Richard P. Appelbaum

Temple University Press, Philadelphia 19122
Copyright © 1988 by Temple University. All rights reserved
Published 1988
Printed in the United States of America

Library of Congress Cataloging-in-Publication Data

Gilderbloom, John Ingram.
  Rethinking rental housing.

  Bibliography: p.
  Includes index.
  1. Rental housing—Government policy—United States.
2. Housing policy—United States. I. Appelbaum,
Richard P. II. Title.
HD7288.85.U6G55 1987   363.5'8   87-1958
ISBN 0-87722-498-6 (alk. paper)

FOR PATRICIA AND KAREN

ACKNOWLEDGMENTS

We would like to thank a large number of people and organizations who were helpful in putting this book together over the past six years.

For financial support, we thank the following: Shalan Foundation, Seed Fund, Sunflower Foundation, National Science Foundation, California Policy Seminar, Social Science Research Council, W. H. Ferry, Stanley Sheinbaum, Mary Ann Mott, Katherine Tremaine, California State Department of Housing and Community Development, California Senate Rules Committee, City of Orange (New Jersey) Housing and Community Development Program, City of Los Angeles Rent Stabilization Division, City of Madison (Wisconsin) Planning Department, University of Houston Department of Sociology, University of Houston Office of Sponsored Programs Research Initiation Grants, University of California Social Process Research Institute, University of California Academic Senate, and University of California Department of Sociology.

The following people read the entire manuscript and offered invaluable suggestions: Michael Ames, Jennifer French, Roger Friedland, Joe Feagin, Tina Mougouris, Patricia Gilderbloom, Dennis Keating, Barbara Lees, Richard Rich, Mark Rosentraub, Peter Marcuse, and Annette Pierson. Portions of this book were also reviewed by William Bielby, Richard Berk, Janet Chafetz, Richard Flacks, Harvey Molotch, Allan Heskin, Derek Shearer, Chester Hartman, Peter Dreier, Russell Curtis, Helen Rose Ebaugh, William Simon, and Nestor Rodriguez. Essential computer assistance was provided, at various stages, by Joan Murdoch, David Romero, James Stimson, Simon Gottschalk, Jin Jin He, Todd Glasser, and John Richardson. Patricia Gilderbloom, Tina Mougouris, and Annette Pierson were instrumental in organizing and checking the bibliography. Data for this project were collected, again at various stages, by John Richardson, Anthony Gressinger, John Gartland, Ross Follett, Miriam Baker, Dede Boden, Gale Trachtenberg, Neal Linson, Kevin Hunter, Nancy Desser, Annette Allen, and Patricia Gilderbloom. Special thanks to Karen Shapiro for technical and spiritual assistance. Mimi Hinnawi and Susan Erwin expertly read the page proofs. Finally, we wish to express our gratitude to Temple University Press for design, production, and editorial assistance.

Chapter 5 is partially adapted from Gilderbloom (1985c) and Gilderbloom and Appelbaum (1987). Chapter 8 is partially adapted from Appelbaum (1985b and 1986d). Chapter 9 is based on a National Comprehensive Housing Program that was drafted over a three-year period by the members of a national task force on housing policy, working under the auspices of The Institute for Policy Studies' Alternative Program for America Project (see Appelbaum et al. 1986). Task force members include Emily Paradise Achtenberg, Richard P. Appelbaum, John D. Atlas, Art Collings, Peter Dreier, Bob Goodman, Chester Hartman, Jackie Leavitt, Dan Lindheim, Peter Marcuse, Christine Minnehan, Carole Selter Norris, Mike Rawson, Florence Roisman, Joel Rubenzahl, and Michael Stone. Richard Appelbaum took overall responsibility for final drafting of the program, although key components were initially drafted by other task force members, in particular Emily Achtenberg, Peter Dreier, Chester Hartman, Jackie Leavitt, Peter Marcuse, Christine Minnehan, Carole Selter Norris, and Michael Stone. The task force was funded by grants from the Shalan Foundation, Sunflower Foundation, and Seed Fund. The version in this chapter departs in some significant ways from the original program, and is of course the full responsibility of the authors of the present volume.

Both authors made equal contributions in the research, writing, and production of this book. The order of their names was randomly determined. The authors alone bear responsibility for the book's contents.

CONTENTS

FOREWORD by Joe R. Feagin

Rethinking Rental Housing is a path-breaking analysis. It is a refreshing sign of new times in the social sciences in the United States, and raises a host of significant questions about how housing markets operate in cities and offers answers that regularly conflict with conventional social science wisdom. For too long, urban social scientists in the United States have used their sophisticated research techniques to "prove" the conventional wisdom of powerful elites. Freely functioning private markets, for example, have been "proven" by the mainstreamers to be the best possible way of allocating space and housing in cities. As Gilderbloom and Appelbaum point out, one dominant and prevailing view is that inter- and intracity rent differentials are almost entirely the result of supply and demand factors—a view found not only in the popular press and among the business elites but also in the urban social sciences. Policy conclusions flow from this neoclassical housing and rental analysis: let the market operate unconstrained, let the developers produce more apartment units, unhampered by "big government," and the national housing crisis will be solved.

Remarkably, this naive neoclassical view of the U.S. housing market has been characteristic of urban social science for many decades. Market-oriented urban social scientists, particularly the ecologists, have long dominated the sociological and geographical debates on cities. The first major burst of energy in urban sociology occurred in the 1920s and 1930s at the University of Chicago, where urban ecological researchers such as Robert Park and Ernest W. Burgess drew on nineteenth-century theorists, especially Herbert Spencer, in crafting an ecological framework for viewing urban development. Park and Burgess derived their concept of competitive relations between human groups from the Spencer tradition: competition "invariably tends to create an impersonal social order in which each individual, being free to pursue his own profit . . . invariably contributes . . . to the common welfare."[1] Together with geographers, mainstream urban sociologists viewed this individualistic and group competition in urban land and other markets as resulting in regularities in urban land-use patterns and, thus, as generative of a reasonable milieu for urban life. For mainstream ecologists and sociologists today, competition, conflict, and accommodation still take place within a "framework of rules approximately the same as those advocated by Herbert Spencer —with room for social evolution, enterprise, and the survival of those most fit to survive."[2]

A string of important books and articles from the 1950s to the 1970s established the dominance of the urban ecological paradigm in the United States. Although the ecological paradigm has been radically challenged in European scholarly circles since the early 1970s, it has remained strong in the United States.

The basic arguments and assumptions of the mainstream urban social science framework include an uncritical acceptance of a self-regulating market system, viewed as operating for the public good; a pervasive technological determinism; emphasis on regional convergence and the filtering of growth down urban hierarchies; neglect of the role of the capital-supportive state, routine downplaying of inequality; and a structuralist approach deemphasizing powerful, profit-seeking actors and class-motivated protest action. These assumptions and arguments are clearly those of the dominant business elites at the city and national levels.

Note, too, what is missing from this mainstream analysis. For example, in a 1984 reader, titled *Sociological Human Ecology,* numerous prominent ecologists, including urban ecologists, review the question of how humans adapt to their environments, but with no serious discussion of capitalism, development capital, mechanisms of housing production, poverty, inequality, or urban conflict.[3] It would appear that much urban social science, including urban ecology, has been little more than a class-biased exercise in gathering sophisticated data "proving" that what the powerful wish the public to believe is true.

Many urban social scientists, including the urban ecologists, accept the capitalistic market system and processes of capital accumulation uncritically. For example, in an important 1980 article on urban development in Sunbelt and Frostbelt cities, John Kasarda views profit-seeking entrepreneurs, operating in a self-regulating market, as a wise guiding force in city development.[4] From this perspective, capitalists follow the allegedly beneficent profit logic of a capitalistic market system that develops "good business climates" like those in Sunbelt cities, "climates" with low taxes, limited public services, low wages, and pro-business governments. Market-centered competition is a key idea for the ecologists. Mainstream analysis tends to view spatial inequities in land use and in housing as an inevitable consequence of competition for the highest and best use of space and of functional differentiation.

Given this preoccupation with the private, self-regulating market, it is not surprising that mainstream urban analysts have given limited attention to the role of government in buttressing and supporting the capitalistic processes of urban development. For example, mainstream analysts such as Berry and Kasarda only briefly note that in market-directed societies, particularly the United States, the role of the state has been primarily "limited to combating crises that threaten the societal mainstream," that state involvement tends to be incremental, and that state actions tend to follow rather than lead private enterprise.[5] As Gilderbloom and Appelbaum show, this is an incomplete view of the pervasive influence of local and national government on the development of the housing stock and housing patterns of cities.

In the last decade, the dominance of an urban sociology rooted in the ideas of Herbert Spencer has been challenged by a more critical power-conflict paradigm substantially influenced by a sophisticated reading of Marx, Weber, and more recent European theorists such as Henri Lefebvre, David Harvey, and Manuel Castells. By the early 1970s, a number of European social scientists, including David Harvey and Manuel Castells, had published critical assessments of the mainstream market-centered paradigm. And in the next decade numerous urban scholars in the United States began to build a new urban paradigm grounded to a substantial degree in the work of leading European thinkers.[6] The new paradigm accents the importance of analyzing capitalism, class conflict, and the unequal distribution of resources in assessing urban life, space, structure, and change. Among the central assumptions of this power-conflict perspective are the following:

- To understand how cities are created and how they operate, one must carefully examine the underlying political-economic system, which in the case of the United States means a careful analysis of the capitalistic system.
- Various types of powerful capitalistic actors shape the land and building environments of cities, including housing patterns. Developers, finance capitalists, contractors, and apartment companies play a central role in the growth and decline of cities. And these powerful actors develop and circulate their own legitimating ideology for how this urban development process works.
- In U.S. cities, the role of the state in supporting urban development and redevelopment must be examined, particularly in relation to the structure and changes in market and capital investment operations.

The contrast with mainstream Spencerian analysis is clear. From this critical power-conflict perspective, society is characterized by antagonistic class relations that generate change, but not as the mainstream ecologists would have it, by an equilibrium upset only by outside social influences such as new technologies. A modern city is many things: a set of corporations and complex labor markets, a spatially segregated complex of rental and homeowner communities, a complicated land and building environment of productive and consumption facilities, and a class-structured social milieu in which various classes contend for space and for control of the state. Much pressure for change flows out of the contradictions of a conflict-ridden capitalistic system.

The power-conflict analyses tend to pay more attention to the concrete actors in the urban drama. Cities reflect human choices and decisions. Who decides how cities are developed? Who decides where the apartment buildings are located and constructed, and where the residential houses-centered suburbs are situated? Who decides to put workers in glassed-in office towers? Do all the people residing in cities contribute equally to their growth, development, and decline? Mainstream social scientists have argued that everybody makes cities, that first and foremost the choices and decisions by large groups of consumers, demanding housing in the form of apartments and detached houses, lead to the distinctive ways cities are built. But this is not accurate. Developers, landlords, apartment-owning firms, land speculators, bankers, industrial executives, and their allies build cities, although they often run into conflict with ordinary urbanites over their land and construction actions. Development projects in capitalistic cities are structured and built to maximize the profits of real estate investors, banking capitalists, and industrial corporations, not necessarily to provide decent and livable environments for all urban residents.

Elsewhere, I have suggested that the major categories of decision making in regard to urban development are as follows:

1. Industrial and commercial location decisions
   Industrial companies
   Commercial companies
2. Development decisions
   Development companies and developers
   Land speculators
   Landlords and landowners
3. Financial decisions
   Commercial banks
   Savings and loan associations
   Insurance companies
   Mortgage companies
   Real estate investment trusts
4. Construction decisions
   Architectural and engineering firms
   Construction companies[7]

In assessing the housing crisis in U.S. cities, it is necessary to give particular attention to the second and third categories of decision making (above).

In this book, Gilderbloom and Appelbaum develop their own approach to the analysis of housing. Many of their arguments are grounded in the emerging power-conflict paradigm. Theirs is a critical and probing stance toward the "free market" and "supply and demand" assumptions of much mainstream research on housing. It is surprising that mainstream urban sociology, for all its concern with urban growth, filtering, and development, has for several decades all but ignored the housing questions so ably discussed here. Social scientists have long neglected those involved with the taking and paying of rents—of the rental housing market and the renters who make up the great mass of urbanites in most central cities. This was not the case with early urban sociologists, as Gilderbloom and Appelbaum make clear. The reason for this neglect of "shelter matters" seems to lie in another mainstream sociological bias, a bias in favor of research questions that seem more "scientific" than research on urban social problems.

The origin of U.S. sociology in the late 1800s and early 1900s lies to a substantial degree in the exploration of and remedying of urban social problems. The 1940s–1960s generation of prominent sociologists at the major universities decided to break with that applied and problem-oriented tradition and to make sociology into more of a "science." In practice, this strategy meant an emphasis on research topics without an applied focus (or, if applied, within the sphere of government-funded research concerns), on atheoretical survey research and demographic techniques, on the latest statistical procedures, or on a certain type of structural-functional theorizing that accepted the existing political-economic system as basically healthy.

Gilderbloom and Appelbaum herein return sociological analysis to its important roots, to the analysis of the fundamental urban issue of housing. The housing crisis they discuss leaps out from the pages of our newspapers. There is the unforgettable case of the homeless man in Chicago who spent his nights sleeping in a trash compactor that was broken, until one day the compactor was fixed, without his knowledge, and he was dumped—and crushed—along with the trash.

That an affluent society cannot provide enough decent housing for its citizens is symbolized by the growing millions of Americans, including an increasing number of families with children, who are homeless, as well as the tens of millions who cannot find shelter that is affordable. The number of homeless and otherwise poorly housed Americans grew during the late 1970s and 1980s, in part because the Reagan administration was dominated by development-oriented business leaders with little interest in renters. The multifaceted U.S. housing crisis indicates that something is fundamentally wrong, and the inequitable operation of housing markets is basic to this housing crisis. Not enough capital is flowing into the kinds of housing that tens of millions of Americans need. The real estate industry tends to blame the government for this crisis, for too much regulation or too much taxation. Gilderbloom and Appelbaum, knowledgeable and experienced housing researchers, take issue with the real estate industry's perspective on the housing crisis. They provide the reader an intensive analysis of the rental housing crisis in the United States.

How does rental housing development proceed? The first step is the decision of employers, who select locations inside and outside the central cities for their workplace site. Then apartment construction follows the location of the workplaces. Some apartment development projects involve small-scale developers or landowners, while other types of projects are very large scale. Gilderbloom and Appelbaum are lucid in discussing the role of large-scale landlords' taking control of existing apartment projects in cities. They also demonstrate how governmental programs have an impact on the urban rental housing scene.

Another important feature of this book is its discussion of tenant movements. For the most part, residential housing, and thus residential communities of ordinary urbanites, are created in a way that is consistent with real estate capitalism. The spatial separation of workplaces in cities is thereby joined with the spatial separation of consumption spheres such as residential apartment buildings and detached homes for purchase. But it is also in these developer- and landlord-created residential spaces that a neighborhood and family force, antagonistic to the power of development and other aspects of real estate capital, is created. "Community building" means that family and neighborhood values do, on occasion, take precedence over the values of capital.

By deifying the private property principle, capitalism creates its own nemesis: people want to defend their life spaces, their use-value concerns, and thus stand in the way of capitalism's restless appropriation of urban space. Gilderbloom and Appelbaum give substantial attention to the tenant movements that have tried to implement the values of community in opposition to the values of development and landlord capital. Because of its thorough attention to these movements and to housing strategies developed in European countries like Sweden, this book is strong on the key public policy issues involved in solving the persisting housing crisis in the United States.

Critical to the health and progress of U.S. society have been certain basic social and cultural arrangements: stable neighborhoods and communities, dependable social relationships, and a sense of the limits to destructive capital investments. Yet these family-home arrangements are being destroyed by the operation of modern corporate capitalism.

Sociologists with an interest in applied urban problems have some difficulty getting their important work published in the mainstream social science journals, such as the *American Sociological Review*. It is very unfortunate for the state of sociology in the United States that research like that reported in this book often cannot get published in the mainstream journals. In contrast, in the urban planning profession in the United States or in the sociological profession in Europe, this type of research and analysis, with its immediate policy implications, is much more likely to be welcomed—in the European journals as well. The fact that it is policy oriented would be considered a virtue. Yet this type of urban research is particularly important for the development of a social science that is relevant to the needs of U.S. society.

Gilderbloom and Appelbaum should be congratulated for providing the kind of research that can guide progressive policymakers, should they arise in local communities, in taking the actions necessary for the solution of the housing crisis. Moreover, their work shows the value of a broad sociological approach to urban problems, one that takes into account not only the basic economic dimensions of the urban crisis but also the social and political dimensions.

THE
CRISIS
IN
RENTAL
HOUSING

Part I

1
Introduction and Overview

One of the most serious domestic problems facing America today is the ongoing and seemingly intractable crisis in rental housing. The proportion of income going into rent has reached record levels, with one-half of the nation's renters paying rents that are unaffordable by government standards. Between 1970 and 1983, median rents *tripled,* with the growth in renters' income lagging far behind. Waiting lists for public housing have grown dramatically, forcing more than two-thirds of the nation's cities to close their lists to new applicants. These unfortunate conditions have been instrumental in creating an estimated million or more homeless persons in America—perhaps the greatest shame of the richest nation in the world. We believe that as our nation moves into the next decade, the crisis will only worsen.

While rents have been rapidly rising, President Reagan has slashed housing assistance funds by more than 85 percent during his administration. These deep budget cuts are "justified" with the assertion that, in reality, no rental housing crisis exists. In fact, the President's Commission on Housing optimistically concludes that "Americans today are the best-housed people in history, with affordability problems limited to the poor" (1983:xvii, 9–11).

This hopeful picture is grounded in traditional economic theory, which has dominated and guided housing policy for both Democratic and Republican administrations for years. Such theory, which holds that home prices and rents are the straightforward result of marketplace supply and demand factors, has

3

never been convincingly challenged, either by economics itself or by other disciplines in the social sciences. We believe that sociologists can offer valid insights into the limitations of the conventional economic approach and we seek, therefore, to develop a sociological understanding of rental housing markets, with a corresponding analysis of American housing policy. In doing so, we hope to launch a new debate on how housing should be produced and allocated.

This book, accordingly, systematically critiques the conventional assumptions concerning the provision of decent and affordable housing in America. Our viewpoint is unique in that it combines institutional and market analyses —sociology and economics. We challenge many widely held beliefs about housing market dynamics, and consequently question policies that are widely believed to be appropriate. Our research indicates, for example, that rental housing markets are far from competitive, though this is widely assumed; rather, they pose significant institutional barriers to supply-side responses to changes in demand.

We have found very little empirical support for conventional theories purporting to explain market dynamics. As a consequence, policies aimed only at increasing housing supply will not necessarily result in lowered rents or prices. We argue, in fact, that neither the conventional market-driven response (build additional housing) nor its opposite (control rents) are likely, by themselves, to do much toward solving the rental housing crisis. We argue that government cannot rely on the "unregulated marketplace" to supply decent and affordable housing. Instead, we believe, a comprehensive national housing policy, along the lines pioneered by Sweden, is badly needed to combat the housing crisis.

Housing as a field of sociological research is rooted in the works of such prominent sociologists as Louis Wirth, Robert Merton, and Herbert Gans. Wirth argued that sociology is the best-equipped discipline to study housing. As president of the American Sociological Association, Louis Wirth in 1947 sought to promote "housing as a field of research," because "as sociologists we have the skills and the insights, the systematic framework and the background by virtue of our scientific training to view the problem in the perspective of a systematic science." Wirth further argued that, as an important social problem, the analysis of housing would reveal "a great deal concerning the role of norms, the complexity of the factors and the method of analysis of social problems in general" (1947:142). Merton concurred with Wirth's sentiments, arguing that "housing has a short, inglorious past and, I believe, a long productive future" (1948:163). Despite these pleas, American sociologists have for the most part ignored housing markets and policy as an area of inquiry, leaving the field to economists.

In Europe, on the other hand, sociologists play a leading role in the study of housing allocation and policy. Led by neo-Weberians such as Rex and Moore

(1967) and Pahl (1975), and neo-Marxists like Castells (1983) and Harloe (1977), housing analysis tends to be dominated by sociologists. In Europe, according to English sociologist Peter Saunders, "housing has always been a central concern of urban sociology, largely because it has posed important questions for both Weberian and Marxist analyses of class struggle in capitalist societies." Urban sociologists, in particular, have made housing a major concern of inquiry (Saunders 1981:232).

British sociologist Ray Pahl, in his book *Whose City?* (1975), argued that urban sociology was slowly dying and needed a new direction that went beyond the traditional Chicago School of urban ecology. He pointed out that much of the current work in urban sociology is redundant, and has failed to make a major advance beyond the traditional concerns of patterns of city growth and urban culture. Urban sociology, according to Pahl, was disappearing from introductory sociology and theory courses, as well as sociological course offerings. This decline in urban sociology occurred despite the fact that eight out of ten citizens in industrialized countries live in urban areas. Indeed, Saunders' words echo Pahl's concerns:

> For many years following the Second World War, urban sociology was unmistakably in decline as it became increasingly isolated from developments within the discipline as a whole. Following the demise of Chicago ecology and the lingering but finally inevitable collapse of the rural-urban continuum, urban sociology staggered on as an institutionally recognized sub-discipline within sociology departments, yet its evident lack of a theoretically specific area of study resulted in a diverse and broad sweep across a range of concerns that shared nothing in common save that they could all be studied in cities. . . . The "urban" was everywhere and nowhere, and the sociology of the urban thus studied everything and nothing. [Saunders 1981:110]

Pahl argued that urban sociology must redefine its intellectual mission in order to legitimate its continued existence as an area of inquiry. The central concern of urban sociology is to develop an understanding of the social and spatial constraints on scarce basic necessities such as housing, jobs, health care, and transportation. The urban sociologist should attempt to understand how access to these fundamental needs varies among urban areas and identify why certain urban places have problems allocating necessities while others do not. Pahl argued that "access to such resources is systematically structured in a local context" (1975:203). In terms of housing, urban sociologists should focus on the key actors who manage the urban housing system (owners of property) and the recipients of their housing (tenants—"those who must rent") (Pahl 1975:244–46). According to Pahl,

> It is evident that I have taken as my starting point the fact that the whole society is urban, but that, since people's life chances are constrained to a greater or lesser degree by the non-random distribution of resources and facilities, urban sociology is concerned with the understanding of the causes

and consequences of such distribution for relevant populations. The values and ideologies of the distributing, organizing and caretaking professions, or the relations between the formal and informal patterns of social relationships, are of central concern to urban sociology. [1975:206]

Pahl's argument that urban sociologists should attempt to explain the "causes and consequences" of resource allocation provides a new direction and meaning for urban sociology. An urban sociologist, according to Pahl, examines only those resources that are "fundamental" and have a "spatial" dimension: "Housing and transportation are elements in my view of the city, family allowances and pension schemes are not" (1975:10). Pahl argues that since the allocation of space is inherently unequal (no two persons can occupy the same space), urban sociology must examine how these spatially derived resources are distributed. The urban sociologist should also focus on the "gatekeepers" and "urban managers" as conscious social forces molding the urban environment, and abandon the human ecology assumption of subsocial urban forces competing against one another.

A final important implication of Pahl's approach is that the unequal distribution of scarce and vital resources creates conflict among social classes: "Fundamental life chances are affected by the type and nature of access to facilities and resources and this situation is likely to create conflict in a variety of forms and contexts" (1975:204). Inequalities within the urban system help to foster urban movements.

Instead of drawing from a simple Marxist model of a two-class society based on relations of production, Pahl refers to the work of Weberians Rex and Moore (1967), who argued that the working class could be further broken down by market relations, including housing—revealing fundamental conflicts over the allocation of housing between tenants and landlords. If the distribution of jobs and wage rates is the primary focus of much Marxist scholarship, the allocation of housing and housing costs is also of concern to Weberians. Inequalities do not only exist in the workplace, but in the consumption of basic necessities as well. For Pahl, a framework for a revived urban sociological analysis must "examine three elements—spatial constraints on, social allocation of, and conflict over, the distribution of life chances in the urban system" (Saunders 1981:118). Pahl argues that "urban problems are too big to leave to traffic engineers, economists and what have you" (1975:200). Urban sociology can play a vital and progressive role in affecting how the means to fulfill fundamental needs are allocated within the urban system.

In this spirit, our work has attempted to add a sociological contribution to the study of housing. In what ways does housing impact individuals from a social, psychological, and economic perspective? What are the sociological factors that influence the variation in rents from one housing market to another? What kinds of constraints exist on both the local and national level that prevent communities from providing affordable housing? Given these constraints, what kind of policies should cities pursue? How significant is the power relation between landlords and tenants in determining rents? Can housing conditions be significantly improved?

A review of conventional urban sociology indicates that these questions are not presently a concern. While a healthy pluralism of diverse methodological and theoretical perspectives exists among European urban sociologists, the concerns of American urban sociology have been limited in scope and definition.[1] The revival of American urban sociology rests upon a considerable broadening of its theoretical and analytical framework.

A sociological view of housing brings such a framework to housing policy, shedding new light on some of the simplified assumptions of traditional economic analysis. We argue throughout this book that conventional economic explanations for explaining rising rents are incomplete in that they ignore important social and institutional factors. Following a suggestion by Pahl (1975), we have focused on some of the *social* constraints placed upon the distribution of housing in different urban areas, looking at the providers as well as consumers of housing. In that spirit, we have sought to understand the institutional framework of landlording, on the one hand, and the role of the tenant movement on the other.

Our book draws on research we have been conducting, jointly and separately, over the past several years, and it is organized into three areas of emphasis. In Part I we argue that a sociological analysis can shed light on how housing is produced and allocated. We summarize the dimensions of the present housing crisis, examining the impact of housing both on individuals and the larger society. In Part II we examine the institutional structure of rental housing markets: the social and political framework that both constitutes and is constituted by economic activity in the area of housing. In separate chapters, we consider the "frictionless" market assumptions underlying conventional economic theory, the role of the federal government, the social organization of landlording in terms of its influence on market allocation, and the impact of local governmental restrictions on housing supply. In Part III we turn to the future of national housing policy. In successive chapters, we consider the significance of the tenants' movement in reshaping national debate, the lessons of postwar European housing policy, and some suggestions for a comprehensive national U.S. housing program.

PART I
THE CRISIS IN RENTAL HOUSING

In his previously mentioned remarks to American sociologists, Wirth asserted that "civilization can be judged, at least to some extent, by the minimum housing conditions which a society will tolerate for its members" (1947:139).

The home is the cornerstone of the American Dream. It is a sanctuary from the pressures of work, a haven from the intrusions of government, the place where the rewards of private life are to be enjoyed, secure from all outside pressures. Housing is much more than shelter. It provides social status, access to jobs, as well as education and other services. Yet, despite the importance of housing and its relationship to an individual's quality of life, some have far more difficulty finding adequate housing than others. Notwithstanding the fact that for many low- and moderate-income persons housing is a major concern, very little sociological work has been done that defines the housing needs and problems of the disabled, homeless, and poor.

Part I attempts to redress this deficiency. In Chapter 2 we examine the scope of the housing crisis, its historical development, and its impact upon individuals. Briefly, we document the development of homeownership as the dominant form of tenure in the United States, examining the policies that have made widespread ownership possible. The marginalization of low-income groups from this ideal will be considered. Past trends and short-term demographic projections, in light of current and forecast supply, will be analyzed to shed some light on both shortage and "affordability" issues.

We will then turn to an analysis of the psychological and sociological ramifications of poor housing conditions. While we will consider low-income homeowners as well as tenants, our analysis will primarily focus on the latter. We contend that rent levels have played a major historical role in the lives of tenants. Rent payments can influence household size, immediate social relations, school and job opportunities, and access to health care and other services and amenities that are spatially segregated by economic level. When rents rise, tenants have few choices but to pay, move, or double up. Each of these alternatives has potentially negative social and economic consequences for tenants. Under extreme conditions, discontent over housing can contribute to violence, as occurred in many of the nation's ghettos in the sixties (Friedland 1982).

PART II

THE STRUCTURE OF RENTAL HOUSING MARKETS

Over the years, a small number of well-known American sociologists have sharply criticized the neoclassical economic model of a free and unorganized land market, and have called for an analysis of land markets grounded in a sociological framework. In a pioneering work criticizing both Adam Smith's and human ecology's theories of urban land markets, William Form argued passionately for a "sociological analysis of economic behavior":

> It is apparent that the economic model of classical economists from which
> these processes are derived must be discarded in favor of models which

consider social realities. . . . The reason for this is that the land market is highly organized and dominated by a number of interacting organizations. Most of the latter are formally organized, highly self-conscious, and purposeful in character. [1954:317]

Despite Form's call for a sociological analysis of urban land markets, very little research has been conducted on the processes by which rents are determined. Feagin raised this issue when he argued that urban sociology can contribute to "a more realistic framework" for understanding the operation of urban land markets. According to Feagin, a major weakness of the human ecology paradigm was that it "assumed a free market in land without much analysis of that market." He suggests that the inability of city planning to solve urban problems has been caused by its failure to develop a "broader theoretical understanding of urban structure and process" (1986b:117).

These arguments complement Randall Collins' essay on the future direction of sociology. Collins declares that a sociological examination of markets and networks would be a fruitful area of inquiry, which would yield both "creative work" and "fireworks" (1986:1336).

In Chapter 3 we consider the prevailing economic view that intercity rent differences are solely the outcome of supply and demand interactions in nearly perfect competitive markets. This conception of rent determination is accepted by the popular press, lawmakers, real estate interests, and even most tenant groups. The acceptance of this theory entails a simple policy prescription for all housing problems: Let the marketplace operate in an unconstrained fashion, while developers are encouraged to build more housing. The construction of more housing, according to this view, will result in higher vacancies and, eventually, lower rents. Government plays an important role in this process, primarily by helping the various parties in this process secure profitability. Thus, local government should encourage growth, provide urban infrastructure, and avoid excessive taxation, while the federal government provides favorable tax and monetary policies, along with interest subsidies and federal assistance for urban development programs of various sorts.[2]

We begin Chapter 3 by enumerating the conditions that economists assume must exist in order for rents to respond in a straightforward fashion to changes in supply and demand. Then we subject each condition to a detailed examination in light of our own and others' work on the institutional organization of rental housing markets. We believe that the conventional analysis is only a partial explanation of the dynamics of rent. While we do not deny that rent is in part a function of such demand factors as unit size and quality, location, neighborhood amenities, and access to jobs—as well as the relative supply of rental housing—we also believe that rent is determined by nonmarket forces that are best understood sociologically.

We argue that there are numerous interferences in free or "frictionless" market operation. These include the concentration of rental housing ownership;

formal and informal networks among providers of rental housing that operate at local, state, and national levels; the "professionalization" of landlording, particularly as it affects rent-setting practices; and the effects of government policies. With regard to the latter, we examine local regulatory policies, on the one hand, and national credit and tax policies on the other, since the latter are extremely influential in determining the attractiveness of rental housing as a short-term investment.

In Chapter 4 we examine the importance of federal tax and monetary policy in shaping local housing markets, before turning to a brief consideration of the effectiveness of federal housing programs. Although the former is not explicitly targeted at housing, we believe that it is far more important than the latter (indeed, than any other set of factors) in determining housing supply and demand, prices, and rents. We will look at the significance of tax policies on speculation, and the relationship between speculation and prices. The counter-cyclical function of housing in the larger credit economy will also be considered as a source of the "boom or bust" quality of the housing cycle. We conclude the chapter with a consideration of the limitations of current governmental programs, the Reagan administration's severe low-income housing cutbacks, and the probable short-term effects of the 1986 Tax Reform Act on rental housing.

In Chapter 5 we offer an empirical analysis of the failure of market allocation, in light of the conditions discussed in the previous chapter. Statistically examining the determinants of intercity rent differentials, we find that, contrary to conventional explanations, neither high vacancy nor large volumes of new construction result in lower rents, once other supply and demand characteristics of cities are taken into account. Instead, we find that the degree of landlord professionalization in a housing market has a major impact on overall rents.

We follow up these insights with a more qualitative analysis, focusing in detail on those factors that we believe influence different classes of landlords in setting rents. We seek to demonstrate that *social relations* characterize most housing markets, both among landlords and between landlords and tenants. Rents, as a result, become in part socially defined and constructed as a by-product of these interactive processes. We argue, for example, that landlords are often organized into groups that exist, in part, to undermine individual competition in setting rents. The overall effect of such social factors is to foster cooperation in the face of competition. Through interviews and other materials, we seek to show that rent-setting strategies differ between small-scale, amateur landlords and large-scale, professional ones. The latter, in particular, are likely to regard rental housing strictly as an investment, rather than at least partly providing an essential service, and as a consequence make financial decisions in terms of short-run gains and losses relative to other investment possibilities.

Chapter 6 examines the belief that lack of competition in rental housing markets is due in large part to unwarranted interferences by local government. According to the *overregulation hypothesis,* city and county governments have placed unwarranted restrictions on the ability of builders and developers to respond to market demand. Ordinarily, the reasoning goes, rising prices and rents trigger a supply-side response that restores market equilibrium. If the market is not functioning as theory would predict, it is because of local restrictions of various sorts. These so-called restrictions include zoning and land-use controls, building code requirements, environmental requirements, growth-control measures, and—in some places—rent controls. We carefully review the evidence for this argument in Chapter 6, and find it unconvincing.

Numerous studies indicate that local regulations have, at best, a minimal effect on supply and prices. An analysis of two California housing markets —one highly regulated, the other pro-development—indicates that local restraints had a marginal effect on supply and no effect on prices or rents. We believe this seemingly counterintuitive finding results from two factors. First, in the vast majority of housing markets, annual *flows* in new housing are small relative to the *stock* of existing housing. That means that the marginal effects of even severe limitations on new construction, at least in the short run, are bound to be minimal. Second, and more importantly, we found that local markets are far more influenced by national trends in credit and construction starts than by purely local conditions.

This supports our earlier conclusion, in Chapters 3 and 4, that federal tax and credit policy are the principal determinants of local supply and demand, prices, and rents. Local factors have to be understood as operating within a context that is highly structured by national policy; and within that context, institutional factors, such as the social organization of landlording, play a pivotal role.

PART III
THE FUTURE OF NATIONAL HOUSING POLICY

If our analysis is correct, housing conditions for low- and even moderate-income Americans will further deteriorate over the next few years, thereby initiating a renewed debate over the adequacy of U.S. housing policy. In Part III we consider several aspects of such a debate.

Chapter 7 focuses on tenants—a group that has been virtually ignored since the founding of American sociology, so that surprisingly little is known about renters as agents of social change: "In many ways tenants and homeowners are socially distinct categories. It is surprising, therefore, that within sociology tenants are almost invisible as a group. Indeed this neglect has a long history . . . [and] is reflected in the leading textbooks in urban sociology and urban politics" (Dreier 1982b:179). Duncan voices the same concern: "Our understanding of the effects of housing reform on social relations and political consciousness is left notably deficient. We are unable to say much about political action or even about class conflict on the economic level" (1981:251). We begin Chapter 7 with a discussion of efforts by renters to obtain more favorable housing conditions in the face of perceived governmental indifference at the federal level. Such efforts have focused on rent control as the chief policy objective, and have contributed to some empowerment of tenants as a political force in a number of cities and several states. During the seventies and early eighties, tenants began to organize for rent control in a number of communities across the United States. Rent control emerged as the principal organizing strategy of most tenants' unions.

The past few years have witnessed the creation of hundreds of locally based tenants' unions; statewide organizations in California, Michigan, Massachusetts, New Jersey, Texas, and Illinois; and a National Tenants' Organization (see Dreier et al. 1980). Roughly 200 cities and counties in the United States have some form of rent regulation. Most of these cities enacted controls in the early seventies, including more than 100 communities in New Jersey, as well as cities and counties in Massachusetts, New York, Virginia, Maryland, Alaska, Connecticut, and California. It is estimated that approximately 10 percent of the nation's rental housing stock is covered by some form of rent control (Baar 1983:725).

Chapter 7 documents the recent resurgence of the tenants' movement nationwide, before turning to an assessment of its principal demand: local rent controls. We review in detail the impact of controls on construction, maintenance, abandonments, tax base, and rent levels, drawing upon numerous studies, including our own. Our recent research—which focuses on New Jersey's rent controlled cities, Santa Monica (which has the nation's strictest rent control law), Berkeley, and West Hollywood—shows that rent control has led neither to a decline in the quantity or quality of the housing stock nor, in most instances, to appreciably lower rents. Rent control laws in the United States have served primarily to avert large rent increases, protect tenants against certain classes of evictions, and provide landlord and tenant alike with relatively clear-cut guidelines concerning future rent increases.

The chapter concludes with a consideration of equity and efficiency surrounding the use of rent control as an organizing strategy for tenants in the 1980s. Rent control has proven to be neither disaster nor panacea, contrary to the claims of landlords and tenants.

The struggle for rent control has played a major role in politically empowering tenants in places where they are in the majority. It has helped to build tenants' organizations in numerous cities and states, while to some extent educating renters on the inner workings of rental housing markets. It has also helped to empower tenants in nonhousing arenas, including, in some instances, local government. Insofar as tenants have historically been marginal to the political process, such empowerment has occasionally resulted in a greater political sensitivity to their needs and interests. Whether or not the tenants' movement will continue to grow in the future—and will continue to focus on rent control as its central issue—will depend in large part on the future of rental housing under the Reagan and subsequent administrations.

Although the United States has never had a national housing policy, this is not true of other Western industrial nations. In Chapter 8 we take a look at the postwar housing policies of a number of West European nations in hopes of deriving some insights from their successes and failures. The countries we examine have pursued aggressive housing policies that include large-scale public housing programs, nonprofit cooperative housing, extensive housing allowances, and strict local regulations (including tenant eviction protections and rent controls). In one country, Sweden, all of these policies have been adopted; moreover, the "Swedish model" is generally regarded as one of the most successful among major industrial nations in terms of securing decent and affordable housing for all social segments.

For these reasons we take an in-depth look at Swedish housing policy in particular. We believe that as housing conditions continue to deteriorate in the United States, policymakers will increasingly look beyond debates over free markets versus rent control to some of the more imaginative solutions that have been tried elsewhere. Sweden, with a mixed socialist-capitalist economy, has gone far to assure that all its residents are decently housed. It is virtually a slumless society; housing standards are high; an impressive array of planned, high-density, new suburban communities has been developed; and housing is subsidized to ensure universal affordability. Sweden's approach has combined nonmarket (nonprofit) financing with private financing, and involves extensive regulation of investment, development, and management in the private housing market. Housing production goals and plans, land-use planning, extensive public financing, and reinvigoration of local housing authorities were the basic methods. A long tradition of democratically controlled cooperative housing has been a central element, employing national-level financing (at attractive terms) and technical assistance on the behalf of local tenant-owner associations created by the national cooperative organizations. Although Sweden differs in many crucial ways from the United States, it is our belief that there is much we can learn from her successes and failures.

In Chapter 9 we turn to suggestions that have recently been formulated for a comprehensive U.S. housing policy. Drawing on materials from the previous chapters, we offer a program we believe is suited to conditions in the United States. Specifically, we argue that a "third stream" of nonmarket housing should be developed, alongside private ownership and rental housing, to serve the increasing number of persons whose needs are not met by the present system. While we propose some regulation of existing rental housing to help secure affordability, we focus primarily on nonmarket alternatives. These include federal, state, and local programs designed to promote the construction, rehabilitation, and conversion of housing to nonmarket forms (for example, community-owned housing, public housing, and tenant-owned, equity-controlled cooperatives).

Reforms of national credit and tax policies are proposed that would make the federal role more effective and efficient, while discouraging the speculative practices that presently help fuel housing inflation. We also discuss the role of local planning, and suggest local initiatives that might be pursued to meet supply and affordability objectives.

We begin Chapter 10 with a discussion of the need for a more sociological approach to the study of rental housing markets, taking account of institutional as well as market features. After summarizing the principal findings of the previous chapters, we present a formal model of the institutional structure of rental housing markets, discussing the chief actors at the federal, state, and local levels. We conclude by reconsidering alternative solutions to the rental housing crisis, reiterating our call for a comprehensive national housing program that treats housing as a right for all persons, regardless of their ability to pay.

2
Economic, Social, and Political Dimensions of the Rental Housing Crisis

Housing is more than shelter. In the American mind, housing represents home and community as well as physical structure. The house that is the American Dream is more than four walls and a roof: it combines shelter with the promise of security, peace, and independence. The American Dream is of comfortable living space for children and couples and older people; it entails growth and nurturing, refuge and support.

Sociologists and psychologists have long recognized that the house is an important symbol of self, reflecting the status of an individual:

> The house as symbol-of-self is deeply ingrained in the American ethos (albeit unconsciously for many), and this may partly explain the inability of society to come to grips with "the housing problem"—which is quite within technological and financial capabilities to solve and which [society] persistently delegates to a low level in the hierarchy of budgetary values. America is the home of the self-made man, and if the house is seen (even unconsciously) as the symbol of self, then it is small wonder that there is a resistance to subsidized housing or the State providing housing for people. The frontier image of the man clearing the land and building a cabin for himself and his family is not far behind us. To a culture inbred with this image, the house–self identity is particularly strong. Little wonder then that in some barely conscious way, society has decided to penalize those who, through no fault of their own, cannot build, buy or rent their own housing. They are not self-made men. [Cooper 1971:12]

Housing provides a framework for the structuring of economic, social, and political relationships. Inequality and segregation in housing limits educational and employment opportunities for low-income and minority families, even as it forces them to pay more of their income for declining services. Housing design and locational patterns reinforce the traditional division of labor within the male-dominant family, foster unpaid work in the home, and restrict opportunities for female labor-force participation (Saegert 1981; Hayden 1984; Rothblatt et al. 1979). In this way, housing reinforces and perpetuates economic and social divisions that exist within the larger society.

For the last fifty years, for most middle-class Americans, the promised security of homeownership appeared to be a realistic expectation—a part of the middle-class American Dream. The rapid development of suburban, detached dwellings; the availability of federally insured long-term mortgage financing; and the postwar rise in average real income all contributed to that expectation. For over half a century the proportion of renters steadily declined, so that by 1980 two out of every three American households could boast of homeownership.

The poor never shared in the American Dream. For minority households; for elderly renters, living on fixed incomes; for female-headed households; and for a significant number of working-class white families, ownership was at best a distant promise, a vague hope for one's children. Yet so long as most middle-class Americans felt secure in the dream, national policy was able to ignore the needs of those who were denied it.

The American Dream has become a national problem. This was first acknowledged at the end of the previous decade, in a report by the U.S. comptroller general, appropriately titled *Rental Housing: A National Problem that Needs Immediate Attention* (1979). During the past ten years, significant numbers of middle-income Americans have seen the dream recede, particularly those seeking first-time homeownership. It is no longer possible to provide decent, secure, and affordable housing to the majority of young Americans as if it were their birthright. Partly, this is because of the economic conditions of the post–Vietnam War period: chronic inflation, increases in long-term unemployment, growth stagnation, and recurrent cycles of deep decline and recovery. These conditions have resulted in a steady erosion in living standards for many middle-class Americans while, at the same time, reducing the number of affordable housing units.

DIMENSIONS OF THE HOUSING PROBLEM

President Carter's Task Force on Housing Costs forcefully argued that

the high cost of housing is now a major problem for millions of American families. Costs of acquiring or occupying decent housing have increased dramatically in recent years. . . . The high cost of shelter is not merely serious, it is too often an insurmountable crisis. The housing cost problem is nationwide. It is not limited to a few cities or regions. When so many families cannot afford to fulfill so basic a human need as shelter, it is clear that the country has failed them. All Americans are entitled to enjoy housing that is decent, sanitary, and safe—and affordable—as a matter of right. [1979:1]

Over the past decade, the supply of available housing has decreased relative to need. For homeowners, the vacancy rate has remained consistently low, under 1.4 percent, while for renters it declined from 6.6 percent in 1970 to 5.1 percent in 1980. No significant numbers of apartments were being built at the end of the 1970s, leading the U.S. comptroller general (1979) to characterize rental housing as an "endangered species." It is estimated that approximately 2.4 million housing units must be constructed each year to keep pace with demand (COIN 1979:56). That figure has not been realized since 1974, and in the highly cyclical building industry, annual production has frequently been half that amount (U.S. Bureau of the Census, 1983b:Table 1.1).

Unemployment in the construction industry has paralleled declining construction, reaching a high of 22 percent by the end of 1982 (U.S. Department of Labor 1982). Although construction recovered somewhat during 1985 and 1986, most observers believe the recovery is partly a short-term response to anticipated changes in the tax laws, which will remove many tax shelters from real estate. During 1984 and the first quarter of 1985, apartment starts fluctuated widely, from a seasonally adjusted eleven-year annual high of 650,000 units to a low of under 400,000 units (*Business Week* 1985:124–25).

Quality of Housing

By most criteria, the average quality of American housing meets the highest standards in the world. Since 1940, moreover, there has been a sharp reduction in the number of units that are overcrowded, lack plumbing, or show signs of structural dilapidation (Hartman 1983:17). According to the President's Commission on Housing,

> an even more pronounced rate of progress has occurred in the physical quality of the housing stock. By traditional definition, a housing unit was considered substandard if it was in poor structural condition ("dilapidated" or "needing major repairs"), or if it lacked complete plumbing. Almost half of the United States' housing stock was classified as substandard according to the criterion in 1940; by 1970, the fraction had dropped to less than 10 percent. Because of difficulties in identifying precisely which housing units were "dilapidated," the traditional quality measures were discontinued after the 1970 Census, but the number of units without complete plumbing has continued to fall, declining from 6 percent of the stock at the beginning of the decade to less than 3 percent by 1970. [1981:12]

This view is also held by low-income housing consultant and activist Cushing Dolbeare, who states that (among other things) less than 5 percent of the nation's housing stock is of poor quality: "Twenty years ago the problem was so many people living in substandard housing. That has now changed. The problem now is a shortage of housing people can afford. And that is just the tip of the iceberg" (Herbers 1985:1).

This increase in overall quality led the President's Commission on Housing to claim that "Americans today are the best-housed people in history" (1983:xvii). The President's Commission explains record rent levels as a direct result of the improvement in that quality; in fact, the Commission argues that "adequate rental housing has become more affordable over the past three decades" (1983:10). Citing a monograph from Rand economist Ira Lowry (1981a), the Commission states that between 1950 and 1980, median income for renters increased by 257 percent—in contrast to a 200 percent increase in the rent index. However, the Commission fails to point out that affordability actually worsened between 1970 and 1979, as rents rose 81 percent while renters' incomes rose only 59 percent.[1]

Lowry does not adequately explain (1981a, 1981b) that most of the improvements in the quality of the housing stock occurred between 1940 and 1960, with only marginal changes between 1960 and 1980; yet, as we shall see, rents increased most rapidly during the latter period (see Table 2.1). For example, the percentage of housing units that were dilapidated or in need of major repair fell from 18.1 percent in 1940 to 9.1 percent in 1950 to 4.6 percent in 1960, and to 3.7 percent in 1970. Similar patterns are observed with respect to overcrowding and adequacy of plumbing. In fact, during the periods of most dramatic improvements in quality, affordability also increased, as we indicate below.

TABLE 2.1
HOUSING INADEQUACY, TENURE, AND RENT, 1940–80

Characteristics	1940	1950	1960	1970	1980
Lacking all or some plumbing	55.4%*	34.0%	14.7%	5.5%	2.6%
Dilapidated or needing major repairs	18.1%	9.1%	4.6%	3.7%	—
Overcrowded (more than 1.5 persons per room)	9.0%	6.2%	3.8%	2.0%	1.4%
Overcrowded (more than 1 person per room)	20.0%	18.0%	13.0%	9.0%	5.0%
Doubling up (married couples)	6.8%	5.6%	2.4%	1.4%	1.8%
Owner-occupied unit	43.6%	55.0%	61.9%	62.9%	64.4%
Median rent (per month)	$18	$36	$58	$89	$198

*Percent of occupied housing
Source: U.S. Census of Housing, 1940–1980, as reported in Weicher (1979).

TABLE 2.2
CHARACTERISTICS OF RENTAL HOUSING 1983 AND 1970

Characteristics	ALL		BLACKS		HISPANICS	
	1983	1970	1983	1970	1983	1970
Lacking some or all plumbing	3%	8%	5%	18%	2%	7%
Incomplete bathroom	4%	9%	6%	19%	3%	—
Incomplete kitchen	2%	5%	4%	12%	2%	—
Median no. of rooms	4	4	4.1	4	4	3.9
Inadequate heat	1%	1%	2%	1%	5%	—
Overcrowded (1+ person per room)	5%	10%	9%	22%	19%	28%

Source: U.S. Department of Housing and Urban Development (1983a).

The Annual Housing Survey's indicators concerning housing quality offer additional insight, beyond the Census indicators of Table 2.1, and Table 2.2 presents these measures. The data show that between 1970 and 1983 there was some improvement regarding plumbing, kitchen facilities, bathrooms, and overcrowding, while heating and number of rooms showed no improvement. The improvements in the quality of rental housing during the 1970s and early 1980s represent only a small proportion of the stock and are not of sufficient magnitude to account for the sharp increase in rents.

Another argument, frequently made by economists, is that affordability is not a function of the quality of the unit, but the result of individual shortcomings such as divorce or inadequate income (Weicher et al. 1982; see also Myers and Bailargeon 1985:66). Thus the housing crisis is seen as a personal problem rather than a social one. Economists also argue that ''affordability'' is a subjective notion that should be eschewed in favor of more objectively measureable ones, such as quality (see Myers and Bailargeon 1985:66). According to this reasoning, no support can be found for the existence of a rental crisis because of the steady improvement in the quality of the housing stock (Hendershott 1981; Lowry 1981a, 1981b; Clemer and Simonson 1983).

Myers and Bailargeon astutely point out that the rising-quality argument is irrelevant in light of a government mandate that all housing have adequate plumbing, heat, running water, toilet facilities, and so forth.

Local housing codes and federal policies have strived to increase the quality of our housing stock, while poor renters occupy the most affordable housing still left. Unless it can be shown that large numbers of lower quality units have been left vacant by renters seeking luxuries elsewhere, and such is not the case in most cities, then it must be concluded that renters are forced to pay higher rents in a market with few lower-cost opportunities. In this view, unless we decide it is good for lower-income households to carry excessive rent burdens, the appropriate policy choice is to either solve the affordability problem or else lower quality again. [1985:66]

Even though housing quality has in the aggregate improved, this improvement is not shared equally by all consumer groups. According to Figure 2.1, the incidence of housing in need of rehabilitation[2] is 13 percent for renters, compared to only 4 percent for homeowners. The problem of inadequate housing is highest among very low income renters (19 percent) and black households (19 percent), followed by Hispanic households (12 percent). In 1979, according to the U.S. Census, 24 percent of renters and 19 percent of homeowners had insufficient heat. Thirty-two percent of all rental units and 10 percent of all owner-occupied homes were considered by their occupants to be in only fair or poor condition (U.S. Bureau of the Census 1982b:Tables A-2, A-3).

The problem of housing abandonment is a growing one in many large cities, particularly in the Northeast. New York City alone loses 30,000 units a year (Marcuse 1979:70; Stegman 1982:181). New homes are smaller, as builders

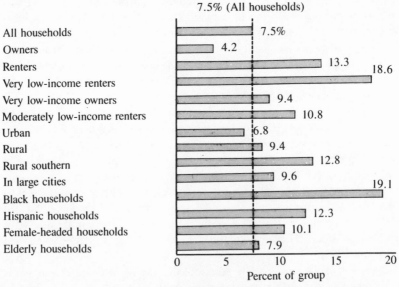

FIGURE 2.1
DEFICIENT HOUSING AMONG VARIOUS GROUPS, ACCORDING TO
CONGRESSIONAL BUDGET OFFICE DEFINITION (1977)
Source: U.S. Bureau of the Census (1977).

seek to cut costs in hopes of attracting middle-class buyers. Between 1979 and 1981 the average newly constructed home had declined 7 percent in floor area (U.S. Bureau of the Census 1983a:Table 21).

The most serious deficiencies are found not with individual units, however, but neighborhood quality. In 1979, for example, 73 percent of all renters and 62 percent of all homeowners found their neighborhoods to be deficient with respect to noise, litter, crime, street repair, or lighting (U.S. Bureau of the Census 1982b:Tables A-2, A-3).

Rising Cost of Rental Housing

Today, as we have seen, the quality of rental housing can be classified as decent for at least 90 percent of the nation's renters, yet unaffordable—even by government standards—for over half.[3] The chief problem now faced by government is how to avoid making a tradeoff between quality and affordability. This is especially difficult for lower-income households, among whom the poorest-quality housing stock is found, who nevertheless pay the highest proportion of their income into rents.

TABLE 2.3

INCREASES IN MEDIAN RENT AND TENANT INCOME, 1970 AND 1983

	MEDIAN RENT (PER MONTH)			TENANT INCOME		
	1970	1983	Increase	1970	1983	Increase
United States						
Total	$108	$315	192%	$6,300	$12,400	97%
Central City	107	308	188	6,100	11,500	89
Northeast						
Total	110	316	187	6,900	12,400	80
Central City	106	302	185	6,600	11,200	70
Midwest						
Total	110	286	160	6,700	11,800	76
Central City	108	276	156	6,300	10,200	62
South						
Total	93	304	227	5,400	12,400	130
Central City	97	308	218	5,500	11,700	113
West						
Total	119	362	204	6,500	13,500	108
Central City	118	359	204	6,000	12,600	110

Source: U.S. Department of Housing and Urban Development (1983a: tables A-2, D-2, A-10, B-2, E-2, F-10, C-2, A-8, F-4, F-5, F-8).

For renters, most of whom are of low to moderate income, housing costs are increasing almost twice as fast as incomes. Although rental housing became more affordable between 1950 and 1970, this trend has subsequently reversed itself. According to Table 2.3, between 1970 and 1983 median rents in the United States rose an average of 192 percent, while renters' incomes rose only 97 percent (U.S. HUD 1983:a). This divergence is partly due to the greater ability of higher-income renters to become homeowners over the period, leaving lower-income households to dominate rental housing markets increasingly. The disparity held for all regions of the country and for central cities considered alone, although income gains were largest in the South, reflecting its changed role in the American economy over the period.

In Table 2.4 we see that between 1970 and 1983 the rent-to-income ratio increased from one-fourth to one-third for the average renter in the United States.[4] Again, this is true of all regions and central cities considered separately. According to Table 2.5, 36 percent of all renter households paid at least 25 percent of their income for housing in 1970, and 23 percent paid at least 35 percent. But in 1983, the proportion paying 25 percent or more had increased to 55 percent, and 35 percent paid more than 35 percent—some 2

TABLE 2.4

GROSS MEDIAN RENT AS PERCENTAGE OF INCOME, 1983 AND 1970

Region	1983	1970
United States		
Central city	31	21
Total	32	23
Northeast		
Central city	30	20
Total	29	20
Midwest		
Central city	31	21
Total	28	20
South		
Central city	29	22
Total	27	20
West		
Central city	32	24
Total	30	22

Source: U.S. Department of Housing and Urban Development (1983a: tables A-8, B-2, F-10, C-2, F-8, D-2, A-2, A-10, E-2); U.S. Department of Housing and Urban Development (1983c: tables A-2, A-7, A-9, B-2, B-7, B-9). Figures compiled by research assistants John Gartland and Anthony Greisinger.

million renters. An astonishing 22 percent of renter households in 1983 devoted at least one-half of their income to housing. Again, the pattern holds for all regions, although affordability problems are slightly greater in the West and in central cities.

Needless to say, problems of affordability are felt most acutely by low-income households. In 1983, for example, 89 percent of all households earning less than $10,000 paid 25 percent or more of their incomes for housing, while only 3 percent of those with incomes of $50,000 or more paid this much (U.S. HUD 1983a:C:A-1). Between 1978 and 1983, median rents for the very poorest households—those with median incomes under $3,000—increased 82 percent; the corresponding figures for all renter households was 51 percent (U.S. HUD 1983a:C:A-1). Consequently, the rent/income ratio for those

TABLE 2.5
PERCENTAGE OF HOUSEHOLDS THAT PAY EXCESSIVE
RENTS, 1983 AND 1970

Region	Excessiveness of Rent	1983	1970	1983	1970
		Total		Central City	
United States	25*	55	36	60	40
	35*	35	23	40	26
	50	22	NA	25	NA
	60	16	NA	19	NA
Northeast	25	56	36	59	37
	35	37	23	40	24
	50	23	NA	26	NA
	60	17	NA	19	NA
Midwest	25	54	36	60	39
	35	35	23	41	26
	50	22	NA	27	NA
	60	17	NA	21	NA
South	25	50	35	56	40
	35	31	22	37	25
	50	18	NA	22	NA
	60	14	NA	17	NA
West	25	60	41	65	45
	35	38	26	41	29
	50	23	NA	26	NA
	60	17	NA	20	NA

*25 corresponds to percentage of households that pay 25 percent or more of their income into rent; 35 corresponds to percentage paying 35 percent or more of their income into rent; etc.
Source: U.S. Department of Housing and Urban Development (1983a: tables A-2, D-2, A-10, B-2, E-2, F-10, C-2, A-8, F-4, F-5, F-8).

TABLE 2.6
PROPORTION OF INCOME PAID FOR RENT,
BY INCOME AND RACE, 1983

Income	All	Black	Hispanic
$3,000 or less	60%	60%	60%
3,001–6,999	55	50	60
7,000–9,999	39	36	44
10,000–14,999	31	29	31
15,000–19,999	24	24	24
20,000–24,999	21	19	20
25,000–34,999	17	17	17
35,000–49,999	14	13	14
50,000–74,999	12	—	—
75,000 or more	10	—	—

Source: U.S. Department of Housing and Urban Development (1983a: tables A-1, E-1, F-9, B-1, A-9, F-7, C-1, A-7, D-1).

earning less than $3,000 is 60 percent (Table 2.6). It is estimated that fewer than half of these poorest households are able to find rental units that cost 25 percent or less of their income (Dolbeare 1983:33). In fact, by the 25 percent standard, it is estimated that nationally there is a shortage of some 1.4 million rental units for households earning less than $3,000, and a shortage of 4.1 million units for those earning under $7,000 (U.S. HUD 1983a: Table 2.4).

Table 2.6 shows that only when renters' incomes are above $15,000 a year, the rent/income ratio begins to fall below 25 percent. However, it should be noted that most tenants' incomes are below $15,000, at a 1983 median of $12,400. Black and Hispanic renters' incomes are lower than even the median, with the consequence that they are especially hard hit by high rents. Black renters, for example, had a median 1983 income of only $8,900 (72 percent of the national median), and Hispanics' income was $11,100 (90 percent). Table 2.7 shows that 40 percent of white renters earn less than $10,000 a year, while 45 percent of Hispanic renters' and 54 percent of black renters' incomes were below $10,000. For black and Hispanic tenants alike, rents between 1970 and 1983 increased at a rate twice their incomes in most regions of the country—except in the Midwest, where the disparity was considerably greater (Table 2.8).

Low-income households tend to fall into one or more of the following categories: female-headed, elderly, minority, and/or farmworker. For example, 10 percent of female-headed households live in housing that is officially rated inadequate, compared to 7.5 percent of all households (President's Commission on Housing 1982:9). Low-income, minority, and female-headed households are more likely than other households to be displaced; moreover, their housing options are more limited (U.S. HUD 1981:38).[5]

TABLE 2.7
TENANTS BY INCOME AND RACE, 1983

Income	All	Black	Hispanic
$3,000 or less	8%	14%	8%
3,001–6,999	21	28	23
7,000–9,999	11	12	14
10,000–14,999	18	17	21
15,000–19,999	13	11	12
20,000–24,999	9	7	8
25,000–34,999	11	7	9
35,000–49,999	6	3	3
50,000–74,999	2	1	1
75,000 or more	1	0	0

Source: U.S. Department of Housing and Urban Development (1983a: tables A-1, E-1, F-9, B-1, A-9, F-7, C-1, A-7, D-1).

According to the U.S. comptroller general (1979), the problem of rental housing affordability has reached such a crisis that in some cities virtually no housing exists for low-income persons. Similarly, Bradford Paul, executive director of the North of Market Planning Coalition in San Francisco, said that "in the Tenderloin, that last low-income area downtown, the rents at a residential hotel—this is for a 10 by 8 foot room with a sink—used to be $125. Now, it's $250 a month. The alternative is a studio apartment which rents between $350 and $450" (Thorsberg 1985:22).

Many experts predict that rents will climb even higher in the 1980s. Richard Garrigan, formerly a researcher for the Federal Home Loan Bank Board, said in the Fall 1982 issue of Real Estate Review:

TABLE 2.8
INCREASE IN MEDIAN RENT AND TENANT INCOME AMONG BLACKS
AND HISPANICS, 1970–83

Region	BLACKS		HISPANICS	
	Rent	Income	Rent	Income
United States total	199%	105%	217%	91%
Northeast total	171	76	196	50
Midwest total	171	45	152	43
South total	200	149	293	127
West total	228	127	234	111

Source: U.S. Department of Housing and Urban Development (1983a: tables A-2, D-2, A-10, B-2, E-2, F-10, C-2, A-8, F-4, F-5, F-8).

It is likely that in the near to intermediate future, rents will increase at a faster rate than the rate of increase in personal disposable income. . . . Married couples will seek rental housing because of their diminished ability to purchase homes. It follows that the large numbers of unmarried persons (one-income households who tend to have less than married couples) also will be unable to purchase homes. . . . The demand for rental housing will probably soar in the 1980s. [*Rocky Mountain News*, Sept. 4, 1982, 19-H]

Another prediction, from Lewis Bolan, vice president of Real Estate Research Corporation, claims that "renters who have grown used to spending less than 25 percent of their income for housing may find that percentage heading up toward 30" (Currier 1983:A-10). Melvin J. Adams, the 1985 president of the National Association of Housing and Redevelopment Officials, predicts that by 1990 every large U.S. city will have a crisis in providing low-cost housing. According to Adams, "The stage has been set for a major rental housing crisis . . . the shortage looms everywhere" (*Houston Post* 1985:14C). The 1986 Tax Reform Act will further fuel this crisis (see below).

THE CONSEQUENCES OF RAPIDLY RISING RENTS

To the extent that sociologists have looked at housing at all, they have largely concerned themselves with the impact of rental costs on individuals and groups. They have concluded that rent levels exert a major impact on the lives of tenants. High rents are a major source of "shelter poverty," since they can influence the size of households, immediate social relations, schools, job opportunities, health care access, and other needs that are spatially diverse. When rents rise, tenants have few choices but to pay, move, or double up. Each of these alternatives has potentially negative social and economic consequences for tenants.

"Shelter Poverty"

What is meant by "affordable" housing? At what point is a tenant paying "too much" for rent? Obviously, any standard is somewhat arbitrary, depending on such factors as income, expenditures on food, health, and other necessities, as well as expectations concerning living standards. Typically, government policy has been to define "overpayment" as anything in excess of a specified percentage of household income—a standard followed by the banking industry, as well, in determining loan eligibility for home mortgages. Until recently, that percentage was fixed at 25 percent, although it now stands at 30 percent.

When a low-income tenant is paying a large portion of his or her income into rent, cutbacks often have to be made on other basic necessities, such as food, medical care, clothing, and transportation. Stone (1980a) describes this as "shelter poverty," whereby the high cost of housing makes it impossible to afford other basic necessities of life. He offers this definition in lieu of the conventional "percentage of income" approach, on the grounds that, for many low- and moderate-income persons, paying even 1 percent of one's income into housing might be too great if it means forgoing other basic necessities.

The Bureau of Labor Statistics calculates a minimum budget necessary to afford "non-shelter necessities at a minimum level of adequacy" that allows one reasonably to calculate how much a person can afford for shelter as a percentage of income (Stone 1983:103–5). Using the Bureau of Labor Statistics minimum budget for a family of four, Stone estimates that for an average tenant family of four, if household income was less than $11,000 a year, basic nonshelter necessities would preempt all disposable income. Only when family income reaches $17,500 or more is enough money left to cover all basic "low" budget items, after paying one-quarter of one's income into rent.

Stone reports that a six-person household would need a total income of more than $30,000 to afford paying 25 percent on rent. He also finds that 95 percent of families of four, earning less than $15,000 a year, are shelter poor, and he estimates that 32 percent of all households in the United States were shelter poor in 1980, including 43 percent of all tenant households. Moreover, Stone calculates that the number of shelter-poor households increased during the 1970s by 6.4 million households, or 34 percent (1983:105).

Public opinion polls reveal that a majority of tenants feel rents are too high and that, consequently, the cost of housing is widely perceived as a major problem. For example, in a Los Angeles Times Poll (August 13, 1980), housing was viewed as one of the "worst" problems that affected people in Los Angeles, ranking only behind violence (see Table 2.9). The poll found that housing was considered a greater problem than schools, taxes, or police protection. A poll of Santa Barbara (California) residents found that 53 percent

TABLE 2.9
LOS ANGELES TIMES POLL OF ISSUES CONSIDERED
MOST DIFFICULT (1980)*

Issues	Latinos	Whites	Blacks
Violence	56%	43%	49%
Housing	47	38	34
Job opportunities	21	9	35
Transportation	19	37	16
Police protection	15	12	24
Taxes	12	14	13
Schools	7	24	10
Places to shop	0	1	2

*A representative cross-section of Los Angeles adults was read a list of situations that people sometimes say are difficult in Los Angeles and they were asked: "Which one or two do you think are the worst?" These are the results.
Source: Los Angeles Times, (1980).

TABLE 2.10
MERVIN FIELD POLL OF CALIFORNIA RESIDENTS' VIEWS ON RENT

Population	Higher than Called for	About Right	Lower than Called for	No Opinion
Statewide	60%	24%	2%	13%
Homeowners	47	31	3	19
Renters	81	14	2	3
Los Angeles/Orange Co.	60	20	4	16
Other Southern California	59	28	2	9
San Francisco Bay Area	67	19	1	12
Other Northern California	51	37	0	12

Source: San Francisco Chronicle (1979).

of the renters felt their landlords' profits were too high, and 44 percent felt their own rent was too high (Appelbaum 1980). Mervin Field (1979) found in a poll of California residents that 81 percent of renters felt that rents are "higher than called for" (see Table 2.10). As a result, 56 percent of the total population supported rent control, including 73 percent of the tenants (Table 2.11). In a poll of 1,007 Americans by Yankelovich, Clancy, and Shulman (1986:35) for *Time* magazine, 70 percent of those surveyed, between 30 and 40 years of age, felt they were "worse off" than their parents in terms of the price of housing.

Overcrowding

High rents can also contribute to overcrowding.[6] Nearly 3 million households were reported living in overcrowded conditions (1.01 or more persons per room) in the 1983 *Annual Housing Survey*, with 700,000 in conditions of

TABLE 2.11
MERVIN FIELD POLL OF CALIFORNIA RESIDENTS' ATTITUDES TOWARD
RENT CONTROL

Population	In Favor	Opposed	Depends	No Opinion
Statewide	56%	31%	4%	9%
Homeowners	47	38	3	12
Renters	73	20	4	3
Los Angeles/Orange Co.	61	26	4	9
Other Southern California	44	42	6	8
San Francisco Bay Area	62	26	3	9
Other Northern California	51	37	2	10

Source: San Francisco Chronicle (1979).

extreme overcrowding (1.51 or more persons per room). As to be expected, overcrowding is more common among lower-income renters. For renter households with incomes under $3,000 a year, nearly 10 percent were overcrowded, and among renter households with incomes of $3,000 to $6,999 a year, nearly 18 percent were overcrowded. Ten percent of New York's public housing tenants are illegally doubling up (Hartman 1983:24). In Heskin's study of Los Angeles County tenants (1983:128), 31 percent of the Spanish-speaking Latinos lived in overcrowded units, a condition that obtained for only 1 percent of black and white tenants and 5 percent of English-speaking Latinos. Studies of overcrowding in the United States indicate that adverse social, physical, and psychological consequences can result.

Pynoos, Schafer, and Hartman (1973:4) report that "overcrowding may lead to increased stress, poor development of a sense of individuality, sexual conflict, lack of adequate sleep leading to poor work and school performance, and intrafamilial tensions." Schorr (1963) argues that overcrowding is responsible for more health problems than the actual quality of the unit. Baldassare's national survey of metropolitan areas (1979:110) found that overcrowding can lead to poor marital relations.

Of all the studies done to date, the most methodologically sound is the work of sociologists Gove, Hughes, and Galle (1979:59–80). Using regression techniques to control for intervening variables, they find that overcrowding within the home is "strongly related to poor mental health, poor social relationships in the homes, and poor child care; and [is] less strongly but significantly related to poor mental health, poor social relationships outside the home." They further note that, taken together, the three crowding variables explain more of the variance than the combined impact of sex, race, education, income, age, and marital status. Research by Booth and Edwards (1976:308) finds that "household congestion" has a small positive impact on the incidence of sibling quarrels and the number of times parents have hit their children.

Disruption of Social Networks

According to recent government estimates, 600,000 to 850,000 households —some 1.7 to 2.4 million persons—are forced to move each year because of private-market activity. Over 40 percent of such moves are attributable to increased housing costs, with sale of the in buildings accounting for another 23 percent (U.S. HUD 1981:25–26). While tenants are most vulnerable to being forced out of their homes, homeowners are increasingly threatened by mortgage foreclosures and loss of home. Residential mortgage delinquencies have reached a postwar high, with an estimated 140,000 homes in the process of foreclosure in 1982 (Brooks 1982). In the first half of 1982, one of every 400 mortgages was foreclosed (Gulino 1983; Mariano 1983), while for the first quarter of 1985, 6.2 percent of all mortgage loans in the nation were 30 days or more past due—the highest rate since this information was first recorded in 1953 (see Bratt et al. 1986:xvii). Foreclosures, of course, reflect regional economic conditions as well as the national business cycle and, therefore, are considerably higher in high unemployment areas such as the Midwest, where the rate was 7.8 percent in 1985.

A person who is forced to move from his or her neighborhood can undergo considerable psychological stress from the loss of community or reference groups (Harvey 1973:82–86; Fried 1963; Wechsler 1961). Depression is correlated with sudden shifts or changes in social support networks, and this may be particularly true for lower-income groups. According to Harvey (1973:85), "low income groups . . . often identify closely with their housing environment and the psychological costs of moving is to them far greater than it is to the mobile upper middle class."

Fried (1963:151) reports that a person's mental health is threatened, if not adversely affected, when an individual is forced to move from his or her dwelling unit; and he catalogs such threats: "the feeling of painful loss, the continued longing, the general depressive tone, frequent symptoms of psychological or social or somatic distress, the active work required in adapting to the altered situation, the sense of helplessness, the occasional expressions of both direct and displaced anger and tendencies to idealize the lost place." He found that 46 percent of the women he interviewed and 38 percent of the men gave evidence of a fairly "severe grief reaction or worse." In his interviews with displaced residents, Fried reports the following remarks: "I had a nervous breakdown . . . I threw up a lot . . . I felt like taking the gas pipe. . . ."

Depressive disorders might result when an individual is forced to leave the community or home through which he or she acquires a sense of self-esteem. According to Angrist (1974:499):

> This critical link between relationships with people and well-being is also substantiated in other ways. Social interaction may be considered a pervasive source of reinforcement, and in situations relatively free of constraints, sustained interaction over time among one or more persons indicates satisfaction. . . . When moving disrupts patterns of interaction, the result is a decline in satisfaction and hence in well-being.

Impact on Family Formation

As the cost of housing and rentals rises, along with cutbacks in government aid, family size and work force participation will be affected. Hohm (1984) argues that high housing costs increasingly require two incomes in order to afford homeownership. Consequently, many young couples are choosing to limit the size of their families, or to forgo having children altogether. Using Annual Housing Survey data, Myers (1983) finds that, despite high housing costs, American families were able to maintain the high rate of homeownership by full-time employment of the wife and reduced fertility rates (see also Rudel 1984). Hohm's (1984) survey of San Diego State University students found that 48 percent indicated they would limit fertility in order to attain home-ownership. High housing costs also force many young adults to live longer with their parents than in the recent past (Heer, Hodge, and Felson 1985). Also, urban places with high housing costs are having trouble attracting top-rank faculty members ("a college brain drain") to their universities (Carroll 1981:23).

Homelessness

The number of homeless has grown in recent years, and is currently the largest since the Depression. In 1986, an estimated 55 homeless people died on the streets of San Francisco—a significant increase over the previous year (Butler 1986:1). According to one recent study of New York City's homeless (Freeman and Hall 1986:14), "homelessness appears to be a long-term state for large numbers," with "causes going far beyond the economic recession" (26). According to this and numerous other studies,[7] homelessness is the extreme outcome of the combined effects of several factors, in which the shortage of affordable rental housing plays a large and possibly growing role. This same study concludes, for example, that the increase in homelessness during the 1983–85 economic recovery was the result of "the concordance of increased poverty and income inequality with housing market developments deleterious to the poor," the latter including rising rents and diminishing low-income housing supply (20–21).

In a similar vein, Robert Hayes, an attorney who currently (1986) heads the New York City–based National Coalition for the Homeless, argues that "the housing availability for the poor is going from bad to worse. The housing availability for the very poor is nonexistent" (Herbers 1985:11). In a detailed study of Los Angeles' single-room-occupancy hotels (SROs), Ropers (1986) concludes that the homeless are increasingly comprised of racial minorities, families, and middle-aged individuals—a significant departure from skid row stereotypes and, according to Ropers, evidence of the growing importance of economic dislocation and rising housing costs.

Precise estimates of the number of homeless are difficult to come by. Actual counts have been done in only a few places, including parts of downtown Boston (Boston 1983), Phoenix (Consortium for the Homeless 1983), and Pittsburgh (Winograd 1982), although even the authors of such studies acknowledge the impossibility of adequately defining and subsequently locating homeless people. Does one count only street people and those living in shelters among the homeless? What of persons forced to live temporarily with friends or relatives? Persons living in cars or vans? There are many homeless who are not readily visible, including the hard-core, who simply want to be left alone; the homeless, who seek to avoid authorities, such as undocumented workers; and most of those who have "lost" their housing, for whatever reason, and wind up sleeping in cars or abandoned buildings, or on friends' sofas.

Earlier studies have estimated as many as 50,000 homeless in New York City and 30,000 in Los Angeles alone (U.S. HUD 1984:Table 1), with a national figure as high as 2.2 million (Hombs and Snyder 1982:vi). On the other hand, a recent study by HUD (1984) suggests a national "reliable range" of only 250,000–350,000 homeless—about one-seventh the previously cited number.[8] Since federal funding is in part tied to federal estimates of need, HUD's relatively low figures caused considerable interest among policymakers and advocates. It has been alleged that they significantly underestimate the number of homeless, since a subsequent examination of the study revealed methodological flaws that led HUD researchers to overlook a sizable portion of the homeless population.[9] Additionally, the "invisible homeless" (mentioned above) did not figure into HUD's estimation procedures, although they may well constitute the majority of the homeless population in some places.

We have noted that the problem of homelessness has worsened considerably in recent years, a trend that can be expected to continue. Displacement, shortages of affordable rental housing, sluggish economic growth, and the deinstitutionalization of mental patients[10] all contribute to the worsening problem. It is estimated that a "clear majority of the homeless are chronically disabled" by mental illness, alcoholism, or a combination of the two (HUD 1984:24), with the remainder suffering from temporary personal distresses that include loss of employment, eviction or other loss of housing, and marital distress. In general, the homeless are younger and more likely to be in families than was the case two decades ago. Families, in particular, represent a growing aspect of homelessness, having experienced the largest increase in the past two years of any homeless category (Freeman and Hall 1986:12). Overwhelmingly, such families tend to be female-headed, black, and young (13; see also Stoner 1986, and Stone 1986).

The homeless also face significantly greater health problems. According to a New York City study by the National Ambulatory Medical Care Survey (*USA Today* 1985:9A), the homeless suffer from a considerably higher incidence of virtually all forms of ailments (see Figure 2.2). For example, in comparison with the general population, the homeless experience:

- Twice the number of traumatic injuries (fractures, wounds, cuts)
- Four times the number of colds
- Five times the number of lung disorders
- Fifteen times the number of limb disorders
- Three times the number of skin problems
- Six times the number of nerve disorders
- Four times the number of nutritional disorders

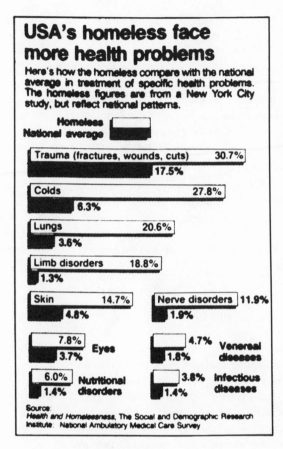

FIGURE 2.2
HEALTH PROBLEMS AMONG THE HOMELESS

From *USA Today* (1985). Copyright, 1985 USA TODAY. Reprinted with permission.

It is estimated that over half of the homeless suffer from some form of mental illness, and an estimated 25 to 33 percent of the homeless who use shelters have been in a psychiatric hospital at least once (Walsh 1985:3). A recent survey of studies provides the following summary (ibid.):

* In Philadelphia, of 179 shelter users given psychiatric examinations, 40 percent were found to have major mental disorders.
* In Washington, D.C.'s House of Ruth shelter for women, 48 percent needed psychiatric treatment.
* Community Service Society studies of New York homeless in 1981 and 1982 indicated that as many as half had serious psychiatric disorders.

- In San Francisco, a study of 103 homeless people found that 57 "could recall" at least two visits to psychiatric hospitals or mental health facilities.
- In Phoenix, two studies of homeless food-line patrons found that 30 percent had at one time lived in mental institutions.
- In Boston, a study of Shattuck Shelter by Harvard Medical School professor Ellen Bassuk found that 40 percent suffered from psychotic mental illness, and 33 percent had a history of psychiatric hospitalization. Bassuk termed the shelters "open asylums," or substitutes for the mental hospitals of old.

In the face of increasingly adverse housing conditions, combined with the declining federal role in assuring the availability of affordable housing (see below, and Chapter 4), we expect the homeless situation to worsen in the immediate future. To an extent, the number and plight of the homeless serve as a barometer of the health of the low-income housing economy in general in the United States.

Social Unrest

Severe shortages in affordable low-income housing can lead to "violent confrontations between citizens and authorities, and even revolutions" (Rosentraub and Warren 1986). This is persuasively demonstrated in Friedland's (1982) comprehensive study of black urban riots in the sixties, during which 100,000 were arrested, 10,000 were injured, and 300 were killed. Friedland found that "local public policies played an important role in conditioning the city's level of black political violence." He also found that when other factors were statistically controlled, the amount of urban renewal and the lack of available low-rent housing were significant determinants of riot severity (p. 162). Between 1949 and 1974, urban renewal demolished a half-million low-income housing units, of which only one-fifth were replaced, primarily with middle-income units (Shipnuck, Keating, and Morgan 1974). Even traditionally conservative observers anticipate "a major housing calamity," as Preston Butch, former co-chair of the National Multi-Housing Council and one of the rental housing industry's most prominent spokesmen, put it (quoted in Betz 1981:23). During the late 1970s and early 1980s, riots broke out over the lack of decent, affordable housing in West Germany, Holland, Switzerland, and England (Hall 1981:15–16; Glen and Shearer 1980).

Arson for Profit

Indirectly related to soaring rents has been an increase in arson for profit. This has become a significant and growing problem, causing death and injury while destroying a portion of the low-income housing stock. Between 1951 and 1977, arson increased *thirty-two* fold, from 5,600 incidents to over 177,000 (Carter 1980:41). In 1964, arson was responsible for an estimated 3 percent of all fire losses (Carter 1980:40), but by 1977 this figure had risen to 40 percent (Boudreau et al. 1977:5; *Economist* 1977:11). Brady's research on arson (1983:3) which is the most thorough account, provides a summary of the grim toll exacted by deliberately set fires:

> In 1981, 6,700 civilians died in burning buildings in the United States (Karter, 1982: 68), three times more than the number killed by handguns (LeBlanc and Redding, 1982: 50). Arson accounts for an increasing proportion of these fire deaths. During each year between 1977 and 1980, about one thousand civilians and 4,000 firefighters were injured (Carter, 1980; Fire and Arson Investigator, 1981: 14). These statistics understate the seriousness of the situation.

Brady's important sociological account of arson for profit demonstrates how the practices of inadequate law enforcement, financing, organized crime, and a few unscrupulous landlords contribute to the problem (see also Gilderbloom 1985c:166). According to *Dollars and Sense,* arson for profit typically involves the following scenario:

> [Real estate speculators] begin by selling property back and forth between combinations of associates, family members, and even loyal secretaries, at gradually rising prices. This allows the property to be insured each time at a higher value, and ultimately at a level considerably above its true market value. (Dummy corporations are sometimes employed to further obscure the nature of these sales.) While all this is going on, landlords will "milk" the building, putting off needed repairs and neglecting to pay taxes. This causes the true value of the building to deteriorate further below the insured value and make life miserable for the building's tenants. When the building is torched, the profit will be considerable. [Quoted in Hartman et al. 1981:43]

RENTING AND HOMEOWNERSHIP

Although there is a significant and growing disparity between renters' and homeowners' incomes, the latter have also experienced serious affordability problems. Between 1970 and 1980, the median sales price of existing homes increased by a factor of 2¾, from $23,400 to $64,400 (U.S. Congressional Budget Office 1981); by 1985, the price had risen to $88,900 (Longman 1986:11). During the same time, mortgage interest rates on conventionally financed single-family homes rose by over half, from 8.4 to 12.7 percent. Based on a conventional 30-year loan for 80 percent of the sales price, a typical monthly mortgage payment would have *quadrupled* over the ten-year period: from $140 to $558. Sixty percent of this increase can be attributed to the increase in sales price, and the remaining 40 percent is due to the rise in mortgage interest rates. During the same ten-year period, median homeowners' incomes rose only 104 percent (U.S. Bureau of the Census 1982a).

In 1981, first-time home buyers represented only 13.5 percent of the sales market, compared with 36 percent in 1977 (U.S. League of Savings Associations 1982). Among homeowners with mortgages, 31 percent currently pay more than one-quarter of their income on housing-related expenses, while 21 percent pay more than 35 percent (U.S. Bureau of the Census 1981a:Table A-1). According to the Urban Institute, the percentage of income for mortgage payments has gone sky high. In 1959, 16 percent of a household's income went to the mortgage, rising to 21 percent in 1973, and doubling to 44 percent in 1983 (Urban Institute 1986). These growing costs of homeownership have placed an additional burden on the already limited rental housing stock.

Research by Henretta (1984:131) suggests that a caste system might be evolving in terms of attaining homeownership. Using data from the Panel Study of Income Dynamics, Henretta finds that the probability of children owning a home has a strong positive correlation with parental ownership (133). The impact of parental ownership as a prerequisite for their children's eventual homeownership has become even stronger since 1974, when housing costs began to rise (134). Charles Hohm (1984) has argued that "very few owners of homes (especially the expensive variety) today could buy the homes they are living in if they had to pay the present market value and finance the property with current mortgage rates." High housing costs also mean higher rent levels. According to Jay M. Kaplan, executive vice president of Consolidated Capital Corporation in Emeryville, California, "People who can't buy houses are going to be renters and that's good for owners of apartment buildings" (Kinchen 1982:30).

While during the 1950s approximately 70 percent of all American families could afford to purchase an initial single-family home, today this figure has fallen to less than 15 percent (Hartman, Keating, LeGates 1981:13). According to David Maxwell (1986:15), chairman of the board of Federal National Mortgage Association (FNMA),

> There has been a precipitous decline in housing opportunities for first-time homebuyers. In constant dollars, family income remained flat from 1973 to 1984. But during the same period housing prices rose so swiftly that the median-priced house came to absorb more than twice as much of the median family income. That represents a very substantial hurdle for the first-time homebuyer who, unlike those who already own their own homes, has not built up equity during the escalation of housing prices over the past decade. At the same time, down payments are increasing—another reason for the affordability gap. And jobs are moving to the suburbs, where housing is considerably more expensive.

From 1940 to 1980, homeownership rates soared, from 44 percent of all households to 66 percent (Dreier 1982b:182–85), although ownership was concentrated disproportionately among whites and higher-income households, with other categories remaining overwhelmingly tenant. Evidence now indicates that this trend is beginning to reverse itself. According to the most recent figures available, the percentage of U.S. units owned has fallen from a high of 65.6 percent in 1980 to a twelve-year low, of 64.1 percent, in 1985 (Brown and Yinger 1986:7). The homeownership rate for households headed by persons under 35 has fallen from 41 percent in 1977 to 34 percent in 1983 (Longman 1986:18). These trends have been exacerbated by national policies affecting housing and interest rates. According to Jack Carlson, vice president and chief economist of the National Association of Realtors, the Reagan administration's policies have resulted in 4 million fewer households attaining homeownership during the past five years than would otherwise have been the case (Kinchen 1985:1). However, this figure might understate the growing percentage of renters in the U.S. because of "doubling up."

The decline in homeownership may be further accentuated by a shrinking middle class and growing poverty. To the extent that the United States has shifted from an industrial base (manufacturing) to a lower-level service economy (janitors, "fast food," and clerical employees), the incomes of workers have fallen. Sociologist Stephen Rose estimates that the number of persons in the middle class declined from 55 percent in 1978 to 42 percent in 1983 (*Minneapolis Star and Tribune* 1983:4A). The numbers below the poverty line are the largest since 1965 (Moberg 1984:6). Future employment trends suggest a boom in low-wage jobs and a virtual halt in the growth of high-wage jobs, suggesting a movement to a bipolar income distribution (Thurow 1984; Harrison and Bluestone 1984:1–29). Jobs paying annual wages of less than $13,600 (in 1980 dollars) had the biggest increase in employment opportunities, while jobs paying annual salaries of more than $20,250 a year (mostly in manufacturing) grew the least.

Adjusted for inflation, the average annual earnings for all men at age 30 fell from $23,580 in 1973 to $17,520 ten years later (Harrison and Bluestone 1984:1–29). In terms of housing affordability, these declining incomes have been partially mitigated by an increase in the number of households with two wage earners, as women have entered the labor force in increasing numbers in recent years. But the inability of working wives to fully offset rising housing costs is seen in the previously cited statistics on declining affordability.

Los Angeles is illustrative of the difficulties in becoming a first-time home buyer.[11] A report commissioned by Los Angeles Mayor Tom Bradley on the future of housing in Los Angeles declared:

> Many renters must accept the hard reality that they will, of necessity, remain tenants, never being able to afford the substantial down payment and increasing high mortgage payments that homeowners require. Future homeowners, likewise, must accept smaller sized units in higher density lots, often in multiple-story developments. Los Angeles' housing profile in the 1980s will be basically that of a rental community, with ownership options for new owners being available in large part in higher density projects. [Boyarsky 1980:3]

Other California areas, including such counties as Orange, Santa Barbara, San Francisco, and Marin, have even higher median home prices than Los Angeles. In San Francisco, the average price for a single-family home had climbed to $147,000 by 1982 (*Chicago Tribune* 1982:3–19). On average, a 2,000–square foot, three-bedroom, two-bath dwelling unit in San Francisco now commands a price of $325,000 (Turpin 1985a:1). The median home price in California stood at $112,093 in 1985, with banks requiring an annual income of $42,804 for mortgage payments. Since the median household income in the state was only $29,784, there was a shortfall of more than $13,000 between the median home price and the amount that the median household could afford to pay (Inman 1985:20).

This reality stands in stark contrast to the homeownership aspirations of most tenants. Heskin's exhaustive survey of Los Angeles County tenants found that for those under 40, two-thirds expected to buy a house some day (1983:184). Hohm's survey (1984) of over 1,000 San Diego State University students (a lower middle-class "commuter university") indicated that 94 percent felt they "will purchase a home sometime in the future," and 69 percent expected it to be a detached, single-family home.

Tenants' income appears to have little to do with these expectations. According to Heskin (1983:186), for tenants under 30 there is little difference in the homeownership expectation between those making less than $15,000 (76 percent expect to own their home) and those making more than $25,000 (81 percent). Similar conclusions have been made by Morris, Winter, and Sward, who show that homeownership is a "widespread cultural norm" regardless of one's income (1984:87). According to their research, age and household size are the best predictors of desire for homeownership.[12] Dreier's review of research on the status of tenants points to the negative social and cultural images of being a renter in America (1982b:183):

> Tenants are viewed as the opposite of homeowners. They "lack a stake in the community" that makes one a "better citizen." They are transient and don't care about or become involved with civic, social, and voluntary activities. Tenants lack the sense of "responsibility" . . . [are] less "family oriented" and less concerned about the well being of children. . . . And tenants lack the ambition, enterprise, skill, or other character traits necessary to achieve homeownership.

The "stigma" of being a renter seems to be a major force for the strong desire of homeownership. An opinion survey by the Department of Housing and Urban Development (1978b) shows that 85 percent of the American population prefers owning a home over renting, if given a choice.

Economics is another major reason that is cited for wanting to buy a home. Indeed, the economic benefits of homeownership are substantial. Most obvious, of course, is the opportunity to build equity over time and thereby realize significant appreciation. Of equal significance, however, are the tax benefits that accrue to homeownership, particularly for those in relatively high marginal tax brackets. Homeowners, in contrast with tenants, can deduct the interest and property taxes they pay from their taxable income. Such deductions, which were estimated to total as much as $60 billion in 1985 (Dolbeare 1983:66), amounted to a substantial subsidy for middle- and upper-income homeowners. According to Table 2.12, in 1980 less than 5 percent of the value of these deductions went to homeowners earning less than the median income. In fact, only 26 percent of all taxpayers claimed such deductions at all, suggesting that for the approximate two-thirds of all taxpayers entitled to the homeowner's deduction, only about 40 percent claimed it. The average tax savings for a homeowner making between $5,000 and $10,000 was $172. This contrasts sharply with homeowners earning over $100,000, who saved an average of $3,320 (Dolbeare 1983:68).

Beyond economic considerations, there are important individual and social advantages to owning a home. The home "furnishes symbolic evidence of social status; it encourages the private pursuit of one's activities; it permits one to make independent decisions about one's house and its furnishings; and it fosters an identification with one's own home" (Foley 1980:474). Homeown-

TABLE 2.12
REVENUE COST OF ALLOWING HOMEOWNERS'
DEDUCTIONS FOR MORTGAGE INTEREST AND REAL ESTATE
TAXES (1979 LAW, 1979 LEVELS)

Expanded Income Class (Thousands)	RETURNS WITH TAX SAVINGS		Average Tax Savings (Returns with Savings)	Total Revenue Cost (Millions)	Revenue Cost as Percent of Total Tax Paid by Members of Class
	Number of Returns (Thousands)	Percent of All Returns Filed in Class			
Under $5	83	0.4%	$ 104	$ 9	*
5–10	1,083	5.8	172	187	2.8%
10–15	2,553	17.6	254	649	3.7
15–20	3,955	33.3	331	1,310	5.4
20–30	8,153	51.7	536	4,369	8.3
30–50	5,924	73.9	1,023	6,058	11.9
50–100	1,658	82.9	2,048	3,395	11.0
100+	375	85.6	3,320	1,245	4.2
Total	23,785	25.6%	$ 724	$17,221	8.1%

Note: Details may not add to totals because of rounding.
*Total tax paid by members of this class is a negative amount.
Source: U.S. Department of Housing and Urban Development (1980).

ers also experience a greater sense of "community," which is associated with lower levels of crime. Renters, on the other hand, experience what Marcuse (1975:183) calls "residential alienation," which is "the condition of estrangement between a person and his/her dwelling." He argues that this estrangement is a major cause of landlord/tenant conflict. As Foley (1980:474) notes, "a renter lacks control over what he can do to and with his housing; he lacks the opportunity for self-expression through his housing." Many renters have little or no command over the policies that govern their apartments, including paint color, selection of furnishings, and landscaping.

Relatively secure tenure is another major benefit of homeownership. Apart from nonpayment of mortgage or property taxes, homeowners seldom face the threat of eviction. Renters, on the other hand, are typically subject to eviction for a variety of reasons, or for no reason at all. Evictions occur because of poor tenant behavior, lateness in rental payment, or failure to pay rent. They also occur because the landlord wishes to rent to higher-income tenants or relatives, because of too-frequent tenant complaints about building conditions, and occasionally because of participation in tenant unions or other activities perceived as threatening to the landlord. Less than 10 percent of all renters are covered by some form of just-cause-eviction legislation, which typically limits eviction to failure to pay rent, vandalism, or unlawful activity.

It is for these reasons that tenants have been labeled "second-class citizens" (Heskin 1981b:95). According to Dreier,

> prejudice against tenants has long-standing national roots, beginning with the first European settlers in North America. The stigma is based on the central importance of property ownership in U.S. ideology and values. The achievement of property ownership is believed to bestow on individuals, or be evidence of, certain character traits highly valued in U.S. culture. Despite changes in social structure and values since colonial times, the virtues attached to property ownership (and property owners), and the presumed absence of such virtues among propertyless tenants, have remained remarkably similar over the years. It is one of the few core values that has persisted throughout the more than two centuries. [1982b:181]

FUTURE PROSPECTS FOR RENTAL HOUSING

Certain features of the housing delivery system can be expected to impact the marketplace in the near future. While an exhaustive analysis is not possible in this book, some general observations can be made.

During the 1980s, some 42 million people will reach age 30, compared to only 30 million during the last decade. This growth will be reflected in a corresponding increase in housing demand. According to Sternlieb and Hughes' detailed study of "the future of rental housing" (1981), there will be an estimated increase of some 4.1 million renter and 12.6 million homeowner households over the 1980s—approximately 15 percent and 24 percent respectively. Among renter households, however, there will be a substantial shift in composition, with traditional male-female households declining by some 2.9 million and single-parent households increasing by 7.0 million (7). This compositional shift will be reflected in a greater relative poverty among renters, as higher-income renting families are "creamed off" into homeownership.

During the 1970s, growth in the supply of housing did not proceed at the same pace as demand, particularly housing destined for lower-income households. Sternlieb and Hughes (1981:9) characterize the seventies as the decade during "which the house buying power of all Americans came under sustained pressures of erosion." We have seen evidence of this earlier in this chapter, in statistics that indicate that all population groups spent growing proportions of income on housing. Inflation in home purchase costs have led would-be purchasers to regard housing more as an item of investment than consumption, fueling the "post-shelter society" (Sternlieb and Hughes 1980a), while freezing lower-income households into semipermanent renter status. Such renters have confronted a shrinking rental market that is characterized by rising operating costs. These two factors have combined to place considerable upward pressure on rents. Yet, as Sternlieb and Hughes note (1981:12), "The limitations on expanding rents are severe . . . [due to] the increasing paucity of rent paying capacity among the primary consumers of rental housing." Under such conditions, landlords have sought to raise rents at rates far in excess of the increase in tenants' incomes; renters have responded by sinking deeper into shelter poverty, doubling up, and pressing for local rent controls (see Chapter 7). This highly volatile combination, under present market conditions, could be expected to discourage future investment in rental housing, thereby gradually worsening the problem.

In fact, however, current government housing and tax policies will likely combine to produce a dramatic worsening in market conditions, with extremely adverse consequences for renters. While the role of the government will be considered in some detail in Chapter 4, the results of that analysis can be summarized as follows:

- Drastic cutbacks in all low-income housing programs since 1981, with the expressed intent of getting the federal government out of housing altogether
- Return of a large number of public housing and other assisted units to the private marketplace
- Eventual elimination of all low-income housing programs and their replacement by a single program of income supplements for low-income households, which could prove highly inflationary for rental housing
- Virtual demise of apartment construction, particularly for lower-income renters, as the 1986 Tax Reform Act removes the few remaining tax incentives for rental housing investment; and as a direct consequence thereof

• Strong pressures for nationwide rent increases, averaging as much as 25 percent above the rate of inflation, over the next few years

The prognosis for rental housing is bleak, although—if these predictions prove correct—the federal government may eventually be forced to develop a coherent national housing policy. We shall take up the possible elements of such a policy in Chapter 9, meanwhile noting that we are in agreement with housing economists William Apgar and Arthur Doud, who wrote: "If our assessment . . . is correct, Congress will be forced to return in the near future to the issue ignored today: how to develop a stable long term national housing policy that addresses the needs of the nation's growing number of homeless and poorly housed families" (n.d.:1).

SUMMARY

In this chapter we have attempted to show that high rents play an important role in the lives of tenants. For low- to moderate-income households—the vast majority of renters—housing has become a significant problem over the past decade. During the late seventies and early eighties, rents increased more rapidly than tenants' incomes, resulting in shelter poverty, overcrowding, displacement, psychological problems, and (for some) homelessness.

High rents may also make it harder for renters to buy a home, because they make it difficult for tenants to save enough money for a down payment and because rising rents have been associated with even more rapidly rising home prices and interest rates. Even middle-class renters have come to feel that homeownership, under present economic conditions, is no longer a realistic possibility. For such renters, this spells serious short- and long-term economic loss. Homeownership affords considerable income tax savings, as well as substantial equity appreciation, and thus has traditionally served as the principal long-term form of investment for retirement. Moreover, security of tenure is more tenuous for a renter than a homeowner.

Earlier, we reviewed much of the sociological literature showing how housing impacts patterns of behavior. Housing affects economic, social, and political relationships. It is a deep aspect of social status; it is a symbol of self. The economic literature, on the other hand, has generally concerned itself with treating housing as a dependent variable—for example, predicting rents through hedonic price equations. If sociologists have ignored the economic factors in housing market operation, economists have ignored the institutional factors. It is this imbalance that we seek to address in the chapters that follow.

THE STRUCTURE OF RENTAL HOUSING MARKETS

Part II

3
The "Frictionless" Market: Conventional Explanations of the Determinants of Rent

Why are rents high in some places and low in others? Most economists view intercity rent differences as the outcome of supply and demand interactions that, together, determine the price of housing (Beyer 1966; Niebanck 1976). In the short run, under relatively fixed supply conditions, rents will rise according to the elasticity of the demand curve. In simpler terms, to the extent that renters see themselves as having little choice with regard to available housing, landlords can raise rents without producing a decline in demand and a resulting loss of revenues. Under such conditions, rents are said to be relatively *inelastic* with respect to demand. Conversely, if renters are able to find many substitutions for a given unit, any increase in rents will result in a loss in demand for the units on which rents are raised; total revenues will decline as a result. Under this circumstance, rents are said to be *elastic* with respect to demand.

In the long run, if revenues in a given housing market exceed costs by a sufficient margin, the resulting profits will attract additional capital. This, in turn, will increase the supply of rental housing: new units will be constructed, or non-rental units (such as detached homes) will be converted to rentals. Economic theory holds that this *supply-side response* will have the effect of reducing the rate of rent increase, or, in extreme cases, of lowering rents altogether, as landlords compete for the limited pool of tenants. Eventually, in the absence of barriers to the free flow of capital, this increase in supply will result in the reestablishment of an equilibrium rent. That rent will be roughly equal to the after-tax cost of providing rental housing, plus a profit margin equal to that in similar investments of comparable risk.

In the final section of this chapter we formally present the assumptions on which the model of the perfectly competitive, or *frictionless*, market is based; then we ask some questions concerning its adequacy for rental housing markets. After considering the role of the federal government in the next chapter, we return to an examination of the "frictionless" market in Chapter 5, reporting some evidence bearing on its actual operation. In the next three sections of this chapter we examine the role of demand, then supply, and then the most commonly used indicator of the relative balance between the two: the rate of vacancy in the rental housing market.

DEMAND-SIDE EXPLANATIONS OF MARKET DYNAMICS

Demand for rental housing is a function of a number of factors. Conventionally, economists focus on the attributes of the unit, including its location, physical characteristics, and quality. In this section we briefly review these arguments and conclude that, by themselves, they are insufficient to account for rental housing demand. We then look at another component of demand, tenants' incomes. We argue that, despite rent increases that have greatly outstripped tenants' income gains in recent years, rents have not risen sufficiently to sustain profitability by themselves. We conclude this section by examining the central importance of inflation and speculation in sustaining profitability, in the face of flagging income-generated demand.

Housing Attributes, Quality, and Demand

Demand for rental housing is treated by economists as largely determined by the preferences of tenants for characteristics of the unit and its surrounding environment. These traits are usually examined on an *intraurban* basis, because the relevant data are both more readily available and precise within cities than between cities. Attributes of a property that are important in determining rent include size and condition, number of bedrooms and bathrooms, and such internal amenities as security, management services, swimming pools or other recreational facilities, and planned residential space. Such determinants enhance the attractiveness of a unit and hence increase its rent. According to Appelbaum (1978:112), rent can be affected by "the advantages of a piece of property [depending] upon its internal organization and the benefits of coordination or communication this confers upon its occupants."

Just as rent varies according to the amenities within the rental unit, it is also affected by the characteristics of surrounding properties. An apartment's location and neighborhood can entail advantages or disadvantages with respect to transportation costs, quality of life and job opportunities, schooling, access to shopping and recreational activities, and security for oneself and one's family. Burgess, echoing the findings of the early economic geographers, was among the first sociologists to argue that rents are highest in the center of the city because the "economic, cultural and political life enters here" (1925:40). These attributes attract population to the city center, resulting in greater demand and, consequently, higher rent levels. Similarly, urban economists Alonso (1964) and Muth (1969) argue that, as a result of central-city concentration of employment, a downward-sloping rent gradient exists from the center of the city to its outskirts. Rent is higher in the center of the city because the costs of transportation to work are lower and a tradeoff effect occurs between transportation and housing expenditures.

Location confers advantages or disadvantages on a particular rental unit and, therefore, is a prime determinant of rents. These advantages often take the form of externalities that result from both private investments, such as shopping malls and office buildings, and public investments such as parks, hospitals, and redevelopment projects. In either case, they allow the landlord to charge higher rents if his or her units offer ready access to such external amenities. While these advantages cause rents (and hence profits) to increase, the costs of such externalities are rarely borne by the apartment developer or owner, but rather by other private investors or by the general public. Urban growth is a common source of such externalities, resulting in generally increased land values and higher rents (Molotch 1976; Appelbaum 1978). Rent can be affected by *anticipated* use of surrounding neighborhood properties, as well as by *actual* use.

The few studies that have examined rent differentials *between* cities have found that rents are correlated with a variety of environmental, political, and economic characteristics that affect the demand for rental housing in a particular city. Wheeler (1974) and Fitch (1977), for example, report that rent varies according to the kinds of business activity within a city. Wheeler found that rents tend to be higher in cities with corporate headquarters than in cities that are mostly industrial. Both Appelbaum (1978:29–37) and Hoch (1972:315–17) found that the price of housing increases as the population rises. Appelbaum (36–37) also finds, in his study of 115 urban places, that rents in the United States are positively correlated with population growth rate, median family income, and location—outside the South. Conversely, he found that rents are negatively correlated with city age and percentage of units in single-family structures.

Ball (1973:226) classifies demand variables into three categories: (1) locational advantages, such as the distance from home to work or school; (2) house characteristics that measure internal attributes; and (3) environmental aspects that measure the quality of the area—population density, green belts, pollution, crime, and architecture. According to Ball (213), "If one house has more desirable attributes than another, this higher consumer valuation will be reflected in a higher market price."

Most studies on the determinants of rent focus exclusively on such demand-side attributes of rental housing as location and internal amenities. Ball (1973:231), in his review of empirical studies on the determinants of housing costs, argues that these studies focus exclusively on such variables, with total unconcern for the effect of income on demand or factors governing supply. These studies (Wabe 1971; Evans 1971; Apps 1971; Cubbin 1970; Wilkinson 1971; Lane 1970; Kain and Quigley 1970; Ridker and Henning 1967; Massell and Stegart 1971; Brigham 1965; Anderson and Crocker 1971) agree that houses with higher market values are those with more desirable attributes. The explained variance of these independent variables on the dependent variable (housing price) reveals a high degree of fit. Of the ten studies listed above, eight have an explained variance (multiple R square) above 0.70. Despite the high degree of fit, Ball argues (1973:231–32) that using these explanatory variables alone is "at best a poor procedure of approximation and at worst may promote misleading conclusions" since variations in supply, which exert a significant impact on the cost of housing, can seriously bias the coefficients.[1]

As we saw in the previous chapter, the overall quality of housing in the United States, including rentals, has improved during the postwar period. In terms of crowding, number of rooms, dilapidation, adequacy of plumbing, or such amenities as heat and air conditioning, renters are on the average better housed than twenty or thirty years ago. Such an increase in quality should produce a corresponding increase in demand and, hence, at least partly explain the increase in rents over the period. But changes in housing characteristics account for only a small part of the increased demand for rental housing that, under given supply conditions, accounts for rising rents. Several other sources of demand are of equal or greater importance, although they are often neglected in studies of the relationship between demand and rents. These include increases in tenants' income, speculative returns on the resale of rental property during inflationary periods, and the impact of federal income tax laws.

Renters' Incomes and Demand

Between 1970 and 1983, median renters' incomes increased 97 percent, considerably less than the overall Consumer Price Index for the period (157 percent) and almost exactly half the increase in rents (192 percent; see Chapter 2, Table 2.3). This partly indicates the extent to which higher-income renters have become homeowners over the period, with rental housing confined increasingly to lower-income households. This is one reason why renters' incomes have not kept pace with homeowners' income. In 1970 the median income of renting households was 65 percent that of homeowning households; by 1980 the ratio had declined to 54 percent (Dolbeare 1983:32), a trend that is partly due to the increasing impoverishment of renters as a group and partly to the fact that the more affluent renters had become homeowners. Renters' incomes fell far short of keeping up with inflation over the decade, increasing only about half as much as the Consumer Price Index (67 vs. 113 percent) (U.S. Bureau of the Census 1982c:Table A-2; Downs 1983:30).

Rental Housing as an Investment

How can profits for apartment builders and landlords be maintained in the face of sluggish growth in renters' incomes, when construction and maintenance costs, interest rates, and land costs have grown much faster? The answer, in part, is that profits haven't: profits in rental housing *from ordinary cash-flow alone* have declined (Downs 1983:Chapter 6). Downs (109–13) notes that the return on invested equity in rental housing remained strong because of four interrelated factors: leveraging, tax shelter, low real interest rates (relative to the rate of inflation), and high expected appreciation.[2] A complete explanation of the persistent attractiveness of rental housing as an investment must take into account other factors than rental income and current expenses.

"Leveraging" in real estate refers to the practice whereby a small down payment conveys full title to a property, with the difference between invested equity and market value covered by a mortgage lien. This has two consequences for calculating return on investment. First, it greatly enhances the value of real estate as a tax shelter, since the Internal Revenue Code permits income property owners to depreciate the full purchase value of the physical structure, even though their invested equity is typically only 20–30 percent of that value, and may be considerably less in the case of low-income housing syndications or HUD-subsidized construction. The 1981 Tax Act (effective at the beginning of the 1982 tax year) generally strengthened the appeal of real estate as a tax shelter, since it reduced the depreciation period to fifteen years while permitting up to 41 percent of tax writeoffs during the first five years.[3]

Leveraging not only enhances the value of accelerated depreciation to real estate investors; it also considerably increases the return on investment resulting from inflationary expectations, a factor of considerable importance during the late 1970s and early 1980s. A low-equity investment can leverage control over a very large property value that is subject to inflation, resulting in substantial profit which is realized when the property is sold—often to an investor with similar expectations of inflation-induced returns. Such purchases are best characterized as speculation, and profits result exclusively from inflation, rather than from productive investments that enhance the quality of the property. During the 1970s, apartment prices kept pace with common stocks, while rising much more quickly than bonds, as domestic and foreign investors bought American real estate as a hedge against inflation (Downs 1983: 111–12). Purely speculative returns cannot continue forever—eventually the bubble must burst; for a time, however, anticipation of appreciation can be a self-fulfilling prophecy.

Finally, interest rates play a key role in determining the return on highly leveraged investments, since interest rates that are high, relative to the rate of inflation, can result in carrying costs that offset inflationary gains. Although nominal interest rates rose substantially between the mid-1950s and the mid-1970s, real (that is, inflation-adjusted) rates declined, and after-tax real interest rates were actually negative for investors in high tax brackets (Downs 1983:47). During a period of rising inflation, long-term fixed-interest loans contribute substantially to the return on real estate investment.

The combined result of these factors has diminished the importance of actual net rental income (and therefore renters' incomes) in many landlords' rate-of-return calculations. That is why investment in rental housing remained strong until the late 1970s, even though landlords widely agreed that rents were too low to cover operating, maintenance, and financing costs,[4] particularly on newly constructed (or recently purchased or refinanced) properties with high mortgage payments. Downs (1983:100–109), in a model that simulates investment profitability of rental units under various assumptions, concludes that "rents would have had to be 86 percent higher in 1980 than they actually were to sustain the same real market value that the average rental unit had in 1960," or 37 percent higher to sustain 1970 real values (105–6).[5] Downs concludes (106–7) that "the real value of residential rental properties sustainable from their rents has declined sharply in the past fifteen years. . . . Rapid increases in operating costs and interest rates, plus lagging rents, have wiped out much of the real value of the nation's rental housing inventory over the past two decades."

Since 1980, high real interest rates[6] and a decline in inflation have reduced the attractiveness of rental housing investment, although in comparison with other forms of investment it remains relatively strong.[7] Many lenders have switched from long-term, fixed-interest loans to variable rate or renegotiable instruments that more closely track the real cost of money. The revisions of the 1986 Tax Reform Act will further adversely affect real estate investments, by further lowering the top tax bracket, by extending depreciation schedules, and by eliminating many of the sheltering provisions that extend to real estate tax syndications (see discussion at the end of Chapter 4). The 1984–85 boom in rental housing investment was widely attributed to anticipation of possible tax law changes, as investors sought to take advantage of existing provisions before the changes were made (*Business Week* 1985:124–25).

We may conclude, therefore, that on the demand side the value of rental housing has been sustained by a number of conditions that operated independently of renters' incomes and, indeed, have enabled rents to be significantly lower than would otherwise be necessary to maintain return on investment. Given the reduced demand stemming from renters' low incomes and the fact that conditions are changing in a manner adverse to the return on rental housing, we can anticipate a further erosion in the value of rental housing investment. It remains to be seen whether the market compensates by driving rents sharply upward—as is widely predicted—or by deflating the value of land, which would reduce mortgage costs and, eventually, restore market equilibrium at lower value levels (see the discussion at the end of Chapter 3).

SUPPLY-SIDE EXPLANATIONS OF MARKET DYNAMICS

Most economists regard rental housing markets as highly competitive with respect to supply. Mills (1972:164), for example, declares that the "supply of both new and used housing is competitive. . . . There is no substantial concentration of ownership in used housing. [While] comprehensive data are not available on the ownership of rental housing . . . there is no evidence of monopoly power in urban areas." Ingram, Leonard, and Schafer (1976:11) argue that the "housing market has much in common with the idealized competitive market portrayed in microeconomic theory. For example, the market is not concentrated and a large number of buyers and sellers participate in any metropolitian market."

Under the assumptions of a perfectly competitive or frictionless rental housing market, given a fixed level of demand, the effect of increased supply should be to lower rents, since tenants will have a wider range of equivalent units to choose from. In the long run, it should not matter which end of the market receives the increase in supply; rents will be affected throughout by a process termed "filtering." According to this concept, to lower the price of housing, one builds new housing in the "high end of the spectrum" (Mandelker and Montgomery 1973:225). This causes the supply of such housing to expand, thereby lowering its price (Gordon 1977:465), as high-income people vacate their old housing for newer residences, thereby easing demand at the lower market levels (Beyer 1958:45). Persons with slightly lower incomes are then able to move into this newly vacated housing and this, in turn, slackens demand for their units, forcing these housing prices down. This results in a greater ability of people of still lower income to afford better-quality housing. The process continues until it reaches the lowest-income families, allowing them to abandon their low-quality housing for more suitable places (Gordon 1977:465; Beyer 1958:45; Grigsby 1973:227). Eventually, if enough housing is built at the high end of the spectrum, even slums will—theoretically—disappear. The important assumption is that as a result of "filtering," new construction benefits everyone, even if it is directed at the wealthy. The end result is a larger supply of housing, higher vacancy rates, and consequently lower rent levels. New housing units may be built because of technological obsolescence, changes in style preferences, or quality deterioration (Lowry 1960:100)—or because shortages have resulted in profit margins that are favorable with regard to other investment opportunities (Olsen 1973).

In sum, theorists who emphasize the role of supply argue that rent is largely determined by the overall quantity of housing. Quantity affects return on investment; return influences the quality of the unit; and supply and quality, together, are reflected in the rent.

THE BALANCE BETWEEN DEMAND AND SUPPLY: THE SIGNIFICANCE OF VACANCY

The relationship between demand and supply factors is reflected in the vacancy rate, an index that most economists regard as the best single predictor of overall rent levels. This assumption has its roots in traditional economics (Ferguson and Maurice 1974; Beyer 1966; Pennance 1969; Kent 1978; Olsen 1973; Grigsby 1973; Smith 1973). Beyer (1966:133) makes the following argument in this regard:

> Although there is usually a close relationship between price of housing and costs of construction, price in the local market is a direct reflection of the relationship between supply and demand. As stated earlier, if the supply is large, relative to demand, the price of dwelling units (including rents) will tend to be lower; conversely, if the demand is large, relative to supply, house prices will tend to be higher. For older houses, current price levels are more important than cost of construction. . . . The most common measure of the degree of balance between supply and demand, both quantitatively and qualitatively, is the *number* and type of dwelling units that are vacant and available.

According to convention, whenever the vacancy rate is below 5 percent, a shortage is held to exist, reducing competition among landlords and thereby causing rents to be "excessively" high (see, for example, California Housing Task Force 1979:9; Lett 1976). On the other hand, when vacancy is above 5 percent, the market is assumed to be competitive. Under the assumptions of the frictionless market, when landlords are in competition with one another, rents will drop to reflect their costs, plus a rate of return comparable to similar investments. Such a return is held to be "reasonable" with respect to costs and risks, even though rents may be high in terms of tenants' ability to pay.

Following this line of reasoning, courts have generally ruled that a "housing emergency" can exist only when a municipality's vacancy rate falls below 5 percent. This view is shared by government officials, builders, bankers, landlords, and tenant activists. For example, tenants' rights lawyers Myron

Moskovitz, Ralph Warner, and Charles Sherman (1972:10) made the following argument in their widely circulated *California Tenants' Handbook:*

> It has to be said somewhere where it will stand out, so why not here: The heart of the tenant's problem is not the laws and regulations (imperfect though they may be), nor the goodness or badness of landlords (for they, like you, are but human)—no, the heart of the problem is with the supply of housing. It is drastically short.

When passing rent control laws, cities have generally cited a low vacancy rate as evidence that a housing emergency exists. For a city to use its police powers to enact rent control, it has usually had to establish a vacancy rate under 5 percent. Niebanck (1976:5), for example, in testifying to the existence of a housing emergency in Miami Beach, Florida, argued that: "five percent is a kind of turning point under which you would seriously consider rent control as a device. That is consistent with the law in existence in New York and the general figure that has been used nationwide."

In 1982, when the Los Angeles city council was debating whether its rent control ordinance should be extended, much of the discussion centered around the city's rental housing vacancy rate. Opponents and proponents had different sets of statistics to prove their cases. According to the *Los Angeles Times* (1982: II):

> The differences [in vacancy statistics] are important to a climactic battle scheduled at the City Council today over the future of rent control. Landlords and tenants have been taunting each other during months of public hearings, with each side citing its favorite statistics. . . . The different figures have been used by one side to argue that Los Angeles renters face an extreme housing crisis that is critical for low-income residents, and by others to show that the market is only slightly tighter than the national average. The whole ballgame in rent control is measuring the vacancy rate.

The courts have usually ruled that a city must have a low vacancy rate in order to validate the existence of rent control (Baar and Keating 1975; Lett 1976). Baar and Keating (1975) have found, in a survey of twelve selected rent control statutes, that all but one cite "housing shortage" as a justification and reason for enacting rent control. The Santa Monica rent control law, known as the most restrictive in the nation, states the conditions under which a housing emergency exists:

> A growing shortage of housing units resulting in a low vacancy rate and rapidly rising rents exploiting this shortage constitute a serious housing problem affecting the lives of a substantial portion of those Santa Monica residents who reside in residential housing. . . . If the average annual vacancy rate in any category, classification, or area of controlled rental units exceeds five (5) percent, the Board is empowered, at its discretion and in order to achieve the objectives of this Article, to remove rent controls from

such category, classification or area. . . . If units are decontrolled pursuant to this subsection, controls shall be reimposed if the Board finds that the average annual vacancy rate has thereafter fallen below five (5) percent for such category, classification or area.

Similar provisions are contained in other rent control ordinances. The state legislature of New York has declared that a municipality can only enact rent control when the vacancy rate is under 5 percent (Lett 1976; Baar and Keating 1975). There have been a few cases where the vacancy rate was set at 3 percent in order to justify rent control (Lett 1976:36). Baar and Keating (1975) have found only one case where supply factors are left completely out of the rent control laws' emergency criteria. In this case, the city (Fort Lee, New Jersey) cited rent increases, safety and general welfare, and tenant hardship as justification for enacting controls.

Given the pervasive assumption that vacancy is the best predictor for rent control, it is useful to examine the evidence for this assumption. In fact, little empirical work attempts to measure the relationship between rents, supply, and vacancy (Ball 1973; Smith 1976). Ball (1973:231), in his review of empirical work on the determinants of housing price, concludes that "researchers have ignored supply factors (the principal problems being a total absence of data and the difficulty of fitting meaningful supply equations)." Ignoring factors of supply "can generate serious biases in the coefficients, and differences in supply between cities make inter-city comparison very difficult." According to Ball, the differences in demand coefficients between cities are in part the result of variations in income and supply, and such variations have an important impact on the cost of housing. This suggests that housing analysts should include measures of supply when calculating the impact of demand variables.

Perhaps the best-known and most frequently cited evidence that rents will rise when vacancy rates fall is the early work of Blank and Winnick (1953). Based on an examination of rents in thirty-four large cities in the United States between 1930 and 1938, they argue that rents will rise when the vacancy rate reaches a certain "critical zone" (189). This "critical zone" will vary from city to city, with a range from 1 to 7 percent. Overall, rents appear to rise steadily, according to their data, when the vacancy rate drops below 6 percent. Conversely, when vacancy rates are above 9 percent, rents slide downward. Rents appear to be relatively stable when the vacancy rate is between 6 and 9 percent. Rents, however, will only fall to the point that they equal total costs; if total rents fall below this level, the units would be withdrawn from the market. Blank and Winnick report that in "reality even in the worst depression days, rents will never fall below operating costs and complete withdrawal of structures from the market has never been of any importance" (190).

Blank and Winnick's work, however, has a number of methodological problems that render their evidence suspect. While they state that their "data are quite crude," they maintain that their results are "still significant" (Blank and Winnick 1953:192). Among the problems they cite is that vacancy rate data are "subject to significant margins of error." The vacancy measuring variable is for *all* dwelling units, instead of just rental units. The selected cities do not necessarily represent self-contained housing markets, since many are located *within* large housing markets. Furthermore, no rationale or explanation is given as to why they chose a subsample (six cities) of the initial thirty-four cities for more detailed examination, and based most of their conclusions on this subsample.

These problems are important; however, Blank and Winnick made even more serious errors in their data analysis, principal among which is the failure to consider other factors that might affect the relationship between vacancy rates and rents. Their most important omission in this regard was any indicator to measure the impact of the 1929–33 Depression, which cut per capita incomes by nearly half (U.S. Bureau of the Census 1975:241). In fact, changes in rents closely track changes in per capita income for the thirty-four cities during the 1930s, allowing for a slight time lag, as Table 3.1 indicates.[8] Blank and Winnick did not take this relationship into consideration when they interpreted their data. They report that rents dropped sharply from 1930 to 1934, then leveled off, and then began to climb slowly, attributing these variations to vacancy rate alone. The relationship of vacancy rate to rent in this case is more likely the result of the relationship of both measures to income. This would seem plausible since, in reducing incomes, the Depression resulted in many evictions, while forcing other families and individuals to double up. Both factors undoubtedly resulted in an increase in the vacancy rate.

More recently, Rydell (1977) reports that despite sharply contrasting

TABLE 3.1
HISTORICAL RELATION BETWEEN RENT, VACANCY RATE,
AND PER CAPITA INCOME

Year	Per Capita Income	Rent Index	Vacancy Rate
1930	$625	137.5	8.4%
1931	531	130.3	9.1
1932	401	116.9	9.8
1933	374	100.7	10.8
1934	427	94.4	9.7
1935	474	94.2	8.3
1936	535	96.4	7.2
1937	575	100.9	6.6
1938	526	104.1	6.4

Source: Blank and Winnick (1953:194); U.S. Bureau of the Census (1975:225).

vacancy rates in two distinct housing markets, rents were almost the same. Rydell's conclusions are based on an examination of two housing markets: Brown County, Wisconsin, with a market vacancy of 5.1 percent (a "tight" market), and central South Bend, Indiana, with a rental vacancy rate of 12.3 percent (a "loose" market). Rydell estimates that when differences in housing services and age are controlled, the long-run equilibrium rents are almost the same in both markets, despite their widely differing vacancy levels. On the other hand, net operating income (rent revenues less operating and maintenance expenditures) is much less in the "loose" housing markets (central South Bend) than in the "tight" housing market (Brown County). This difference is due partly to the higher vacancy losses in the former area, and partly to higher maintenance and replacement expenditures. This evidence runs counter to the conventional assumption that, as a result of low net operating income, landlords will react by *cutting* maintenance expenditures and lowering rent levels to fill vacant units.

The major drawback with Rydell's study is that it is based on just two housing markets, rendering further generalization problematic. Moreover, Rydell should have attempted to control for other variables that might have affected the relationship between vacancy and rent, including income, population size and increase, and race.

Dreier, Gilderbloom, and Appelbaum's study (1980) of the impact of vacancy rates on rents examined 150 randomly selected California cities, utilizing data from the 1970 Census. Cities were categorized as either high or low vacancy, depending on whether their vacancy rates exceeded 5 percent. Overall, they found that median rent levels were 12 percent higher in low vacancy cities, although this relationship appeared to be partly mediated by city size; in medium-size municipalities (10,000–50,000 people), rents were 20 percent lower in the low vacancy cities, but this relationship disappeared in smaller and larger places. In fact, city size and growth in the rental housing stock were both found to be more significant determinants of rent than vacancy. Small cities, on the average, had rent levels that were 56 percent lower than large cities. At the same time, fast-growing places (those with a 1960–70 increase in the number of rental units exceeding 60 percent) had rents that were 27 percent higher than slow-growing places. When the effect of growth was examined while controlling for size, it was found that, within each of the three size categories, rents were consistently higher in municipalities that had high rates of rental construction. These results suggest that a municipal strategy of promoting growth in order to lower prevailing housing costs will not be effective.

A number of problems with Dreier, Gilderbloom, and Appelbaum's analysis prevent them from coming to any firm conclusions about the effect of supply on rents. While the sample size is relatively large (150 cities), the cities themselves do not constitute self-contained housing markets. In fact, many of them lie

within larger market areas and are therefore not free from external distur-
bances. Dreier, Gilderbloom, and Appelbaum note that they should have
attempted to choose cities that were isolated from other cities, so that housing
market operations could have been studied independently of such exogenous
effects. Their study also failed to control for additional variables that might
affect the rent levels, such as income, population increase, race, or quality of
the housing stock. These deficiencies provided the impetus for the analysis we
shall present in Chapter 5.

ARE RENTAL HOUSING MARKETS COMPETITIVE?
SEVEN NECESSARY ASSUMPTIONS

Conventional assumptions of how housing markets operate, rarely challenged
in the past, have recently come under attack on both theoretical and empirical
grounds (Gilderbloom 1982; Mollenkopf and Pynoos 1973; Appelbaum and
Glasser 1982; Linson 1978; Feagin 1983; Vaughan 1972; Cherry and Ford
1975; Cronin 1983). Squires (1981:756) argues that conventional supply and
demand models leave out institutional factors that can interfere with the
workings of the idealized market. In this section, we shall carefully examine
the underlying assumptions of the purely competitive or frictionless market
model. Then, in Chapter 5, we shall examine the extent to which rents can be
predicted as purely unconstrained market effects.

Olsen's work (1973) has been widely cited by other theorists for laying out
the basic assumptions of the competitive housing market (for example, Lett
1976:31; Stegman and Sumka 1976:117; Solomon and Vandell 1982). Olsen
(228–29) lists the following conditions as necessary for perfect competition to
occur:

1. both buyers and sellers of housing service are numerous;
2. neither buyers nor sellers collude;
3. entry into and exit from the market are free for both producers and
   consumers;
4. both producers and consumers possess perfect knowledge about the
   prevailing price and current bids, and they take advantage of every
   opportunity to increase profits and utility respectively;
5. no artificial restrictions are placed on demands for, supplies of, and prices
   of housing service and the resources used to produce housing service;
6. housing service is a homogeneous commodity; and
7. the sales or purchases of each individual unit are small in relation to the
   aggregate volume of transactions.

As Olsen points out (229), these conditions are seldom fully realized in most
housing markets. In the pages that follow, we shall examine each of these
conditions in turn. We are not interested in simply examining the extent to

which actual housing markets are likely to depart from the perfectly competitive model, but, more specifically, in hypothesizing how such departures are likely to influence rents.

Both Buyers and Sellers Are Numerous

The relationship between buyers and sellers of rental housing is asymmetrical. Tenants, typically, are numerous; consume single units of housing; and, depending on local conditions, may be in strong competition with one another for the units they consume. These conditions need not obtain for the sellers of rental housing, however. While rental housing market structure is a largely neglected topic of study, those few studies that examine market share concur that the ownership of rental housing tends to be concentrated in a relatively small number of hands. Mollenkopf and Pynoos (1973:55), for example, found that in the early 1970s a small proportion of the population owned the rental housing stock in Cambridge, Massachusetts. They estimated that 60 percent of the rental housing units were owned by just 6 percent of the city's population. Mollenkopf and Pynoss further estimated that 90 percent of the city's apartment owners belonged to the local property owners' association (a political action group of 700 members). Within this association, 20 members owned 40 percent of the rental housing.

More recently, Marcuse (1986) reports that, in New York City, some 975 owners (4.7 percent) account for 56.4 percent of all rent-stabilized units. Appelbaum and Glasser (1982:Table 5) report a strikingly similar finding in the largely student community of Isla Vista, California. By examining tax assessor rolls, they found that twenty-seven owners (5.8 percent) accounted for over 50 percent of the rental housing stock. Similarly, Linson (1978) found that half of the multifamily housing in Santa Barbara (California) was owned by just sixty individuals, with a total of 687 persons owning the entire rental stock. Moreover, seven landlords were found to own fully 20 percent of the rental housing. In a study of Orange, New Jersey, Gilderbloom and Keating (1982) document that just ten owners or companies controlled close to one-third of the rental housing stock. In Thousand Oaks, California, a single owner accounts for fully one-third of all rental units.[9] Cronin, in his study of rental housing submarkets in the Virginia suburbs of Washington (1983:366), found that, on average, one firm owned 70 percent of all rental units within each submarket. The average proportion of rental units controlled by the two largest firms was estimated to be 86 percent.

There is some evidence that rental housing ownership is becoming increasingly concentrated. According to Krohn, Fleming, and Manzer (1977:x), future rental housing will be marked by "increases in scale and specialization" that result from a shift toward large-scale "professional" landlords (see also Feagin 1983). These arguments are backed up by recent trends deduced from U.S. Census of Housing reports, which show steady growth in the construction of large apartment complexes as smaller ones are demolished or abandoned (Dreier 1982a:190; see our discussion in Chapter 5). This suggests that rental housing will be increasingly controlled by a smaller percentage of large owners who operate according to "professional" real estate standards. We shall explore the implications of this more fully in Chapter 5.

Absence of Collusion

Again, the relationship between landlords and tenants appears to be asymmetrical. Historically, tenants have been unorganized, leaderless, and "second class citizens politically" (see Heskin 1981b: 95–106). Rent strikes have proven to be generally unsuccessful in the United States (Marcuse 1981a; Lipsky 1970). Beginning in the early 1970s, however, a tenants' movement began to emerge, with renters demanding controls on rents, adequate living conditions, eviction protections, and political participation (Heskin 1981b; Lowe and Blumberg 1981). The success of this movement in achieving its objectives is a matter of considerable debate and controversy (see Gilderbloom 1981b; Lett 1976; Marcuse 1981a; Lowe and Blumberg 1981; Dreier and Atlas 1980; Mollenkopf and Pynoos 1973; Shulman 1980).[10] Whatever the actual success of the tenants' movement in organizing renters into a cohesive force, it seems plausible that fear of rent control might persuade some landlords to limit their rent increases (Grant 1976).

While tenants are seldom organized as a cohesive force, several recent studies have shown that landlords often explicitly or implicitly cooperate with one another in setting rents through a variety of social networks. "Social networks" are defined by Koenig and Gogel as a "system through which common norms, values and a sense of 'weness' can flow" (1981:37). According to Kadushin (1976:1), social networks operate to provide "evaluation, knowledge, prescriptions and opinion, influence and power." The social networks of landlords are particularly important in constructing a cooperative attitude out of ordinarily competitive behavior. According to Koenig and Gogel (45), most businesses in fact operate to foster cooperative values:

> Values are thus passed through the network. The simple reading of the daily newspaper leads one to suspect that one principal ethical value is to not go beyond certain boundaries in hurting business peers. Such a value is reinforced by the fact that all out battles with competition are "bad business," since they cut into profits as the attacked firm fights back on many fronts.

Through the social organization of landlords, the goal becomes increasing rents that are "below market." Landlords may achieve this goal through formal organizations or informal networks. The formal organization might be a local landlords' association that suggests a minimum rent increase for its members. The informal networks are characterized by conversations among landlords in which rents are compared and mutual determinations made.

If the local apartment owners' association is unfamiliar with some local conditions or rates, it may refer inquiries to large-scale owners of real estate or to members of the local board of realtors to get an idea of "how much the market will bear." "Pulling up" rents that are "below market" is a recurrent concern in both organizational and informal network contacts; for example, the landlords' association will, upon request, suggest an annual minimum rent increase to its members. Informal pressure may also be brought to bear through conversations among landlords in which rents are compared and "acceptable" increases identified.

During the period of double-digit inflation in the late 1970s, the most popular guide or formula for adjusting rents upward was to tie rent increases to changes in the regional consumer price index. Raising rents by an amount equal to the full index increase for a given year was the implicit "norm" of many local and statewide apartment owner groups, which often published yearly consumer price indexes in their newspapers in order that members could "use those numbers to help them calculate their percentage rent increase" (Gilderbloom 1985c:171–72). In *Real Estate Review,* for example, Richard Garrigan (1978:40–44) suggested that landlords raise rents 15 percent a year through 1982—a figure well over the annual Consumer Price Index for that period.

The national Consumer Price Index (CPI) became the standard for apartment owner groups in the late 1970s, because rents had historically lagged behind it. Rent increases, tied to the index, were thus seen by most landlords and many tenants as a reasonable way to "keep up" with inflation. Kelley (1975), for example, argued that rents had lagged behind increases in the Consumer Price Index and increases in wages, whereas they should "keep up with the economy. . . . The most common accepted index is the U.S. consumer price index." Since the index has fallen below 4 percent in the mid-1980s, however, its use as a guide for establishing annual rent increases has diminished considerably.

Apartment owners' associations may occasionally pressure members to avoid excessive rental increases, although it cannot be determined with accuracy how effective such pressures are. For example, an association may inform landlords that raises equal to the Consumer Price Index increase are more likely to be held in compliance with a state law that prohibits "unconscionable" rent increases. Owner groups might fear that raising rents *more* than the CPI could foment demands for local rent controls; therefore, they discourage members from seeking large increases. According to one landlord: "Have an indication of what other rentals are. Landlords do this by discussing it or looking in the paper. At the apartment owner meetings we will talk about it sometimes. Fear of rent control keeps rents reasonable and fear of losing a good tenant keeps rents down" (Gilderbloom 1985c:172).

By organizing themselves on the national, state, and local levels, landlords can provide formal guidelines for the determination of rents. On the national level, real estate house organs and literature provide the rationale and guidelines for increases. The Institute of Real Estate Management (IREM) of the National Association of Realtors is the largest and most influential landlord organization in the United States. Its principal function is to provide educational courses, publications, and designations (for example, "Certified Property Manager," "Accredited Management Organization"). It provides over 100 different publications and cassettes to "educate landlords" on how to operate rental property most profitably. IREM instructional materials include books, articles, cassette tapes, and workbooks.

Of particular interest is an IREM reprint of an article, "How to Get Your Manager to Raise Rents" (Kelley 1975), that first appeared in the Institute's *Journal of Property Management*. In this article, some owners are criticized for not raising rents sufficiently: "[They] have done the real estate industry tremendous damage." Kelley urges property managers to "act together," and he concludes with the following advice:

> Here's a tip: *When you raise rents, send a notice to your competition.* It's the best mail they'll get all day. Everyone is afraid to be the first to increase rents. *Once your competition sees you doing it, they'll very likely follow suit, thus making the rent increase a fact of life for all tenants.* The need to make rent adjustments to restore or safeguard the return on your investment should be very clear. Your manager must be made aware of what *your goal is: it is not occupancy levels, but money in the bank.* [Emphasis added]

In this same publication, IREM recommends that rent increases be made on January 1, because the holidays and poor weather make it difficult for tenants to relocate. Furthermore, the article notes, January 1 is desirable because "the news media spends a lot of time reporting spiraling costs toward the end of the year. This coverage will help substantiate the need for more rent."

In California, statewide apartment owner groups have urged landlords to raise rents according to annual increases in the all-items Consumer Price Index (Dreier, Gilderbloom, and Appelbaum 1980). Such guidelines are discussed in meetings and in real estate newsletters. In Santa Barbara, California a meeting conducted by the local apartment owners' association instructed the membership in "where, when, how and what dollar amount to raise rents" (*Santa Barbara News-Press*, Dec. 3, 1978). At that meeting, association officers recommended that rents be raised according to the full CPI, which was running at 8–10 percent annually.

There is some evidence that the nature of formal and informal ties among landlords differs according to the landlords' scale of operation. We shall consider this below and again in Chapter 5, when we look at the differences between "amateur" and "professional" landlords.

Freedom of Entry and Exit

Landlords face few restrictions on their ability to rent, sell, or otherwise dispose of rental units. In most jurisdictions, landlords retain the right to convert rental units to condominiums or nonresidential uses, to demolish units, and to make capital improvements that permit a retargeting of rental units from one market segment to another. Landlords in non–rent controlled cities are free to evict tenants without cause, to raise rents by any amount, and to choose freely among various categories of tenants. Landlords are likely to experience considerable freedom in markets where the ownership or management of rental property is concentrated in a few hands.

For tenants, on the other hand, severe limitations characteristically exist in terms of both entry and exit. Most obvious are discriminatory practices of various sorts, which often close off large segments of the rental housing market to families with children, racial minorities, and the poor in general. Tenants are essentially trapped by the marketplace. Harvey argues (1973:61–63) that as a result of cultural needs, job requirements, zoning restrictions, and limited housing availability, low-income persons (usually minorities) are forced to "locate in the relatively high priced inner cities." According to Vaughan (1972:82), low-income tenants are trapped within particular areas, conferring on the landlord a "virtual monopoly of power in the relationship." The only leverage a tenant has, Vaughan asserts (82), is to move:

> While they [tenants] carry the threat out with considerable frequency, this maneuver is relatively weak and both they and the owners know it. With their limited resources, they cannot hope to do appreciably better. The mobility is largely restricted to the immediate area. Even where it is a renters' market, the tenant would still operate at a structurally induced disadvantage.

As a result, rent for low-income tenants is related more to income than quality (81).

Muth's early research indicates how higher profits provide institutionalized pressure for racial segregation (1969:107–8):

> A much more reasonable explanation for residential segregation is that whites have a greater aversion to living among Negroes than do other Negroes. If so, whites would offer more for housing in predominantly white neighborhoods than would Negroes. . . . The failure of landlords to rent to or real estate agents to deal with Negroes is also readily understandable in terms of this explanation. The landlord's refusal may be interpreted as based upon a desire to avoid the loss of white tenants, the real estate agent's, similarly, on the desire to avoid the loss of future business—even if the white seller for whom he is acting as agent has no aversion to selling to a Negro buyer.

Rich (1984:32, 39) reports on the rationales and mechanisms used to maintain the racially segregated housing market of East Orange, New Jersey, where

> racial prejudice may . . . cause the value of land to increase with distance from the black neighborhood because white consumers are willing to pay a premium for physical distance from blacks in spite of the extra cost of

commuting to the CBD [Control Business District] . . . blacks have been dissuaded from moving into the area by a local vigilante organization and overt expressions of racial prejudice.

Shlay, using a survey research methodology (1983:27), finds that the racial composition of a neighborhood is one of the most important predictors of a person's assessment of residential satisfaction. She finds that while whites will tolerate "inclusion of several black residents" in a neighborhood, with no apparent impact on the neighborhood's perceived desirability to other whites, "nonetheless, each additional proportion of blacks causes the neighborhood to appear less and less desirable" (17).

Similar barriers exist for families with children. As recently as the late 1970s, surveys of apartment listings in California newspapers revealed that 70 percent of the available housing explicitly excluded families with children (Ashford and Salmonsen 1978:36). In Denver, 80 to 85 percent of the apartment buildings were for adults only (Groller 1978).

Housing is a basic necessity, a fundamental requirement for survival, and this has two implications for tenants' freedom of entry to and exit from rental housing units. First, most cities have vagrancy laws that prohibit overnight sleeping in parks and cars. As a consequence, most tenants cannot "simply do without" shelter if the price is too high; they must find somewhere to live, whatever price is asked. Second, even in the absence of antivagrancy regulations, few people feel they have a choice of real alternatives to whatever rental units are offered. Because of its importance, housing is strongly regulated by zoning ordinances and building codes, and tenants are not free to erect temporary units or convert garages into rental units. There are few substitutes for the existing stock. If the price of steak is too high, one can always switch to hamburger; most tenants, however, cannot always switch to another housing product or brand.

Furthermore, even when units are available on the market, moving entails significant costs for most tenants. The *economic* costs of moving include a finder's fee, moving company charges, security and cleaning deposits, and connection charges for telephone, gas, and electricity. Additionally, in many rental markets tenants must pay the first and last months' rent, and make a security deposit. In tight housing markets, such as those in California, these costs often total several thousand dollars. Moving entails significant *noneconomic* costs as well, as community attachments and social relations are lost (Fried 1963; Harvey 1973). Senior citizens, in particular, have great difficulty with moving, which is one of the reasons why landlords generally prefer to rent to the elderly (Stegman and Sumka 1976:99). Families with school-age children also suffer, if they are compelled to move into another school district or neighborhood.

When ownership costs are high, tenants' mobility is further limited by their inability to afford the cost of a home or condominium. In California, for example, the State Department of Housing and Community Development estimated that, in the mid-1970s, 90 percent of the state's renters could not afford to purchase the median-price home (California Housing Task Force 1979; California Department of Housing and Community Development 1977). Since the cost of homes affects the decision to buy, it serves as a rough ceiling on the amount tenants are willing to pay in rents, but this "ceiling" rose dramatically during the 1970s as the cost of homes climbed. Rents appear to vary directly with the cost of homes, leading some to conclude that this is a major reason why rents increased so rapidly during this period.

Knowledge of Market Conditions

Tenants are seldom in a position to devote much time to the systematic study of rental housing markets. As a result, they often "make do" with whatever information is readily available, particularly if units are scarce. Newspaper ads and word of mouth are the two principal means by which most tenants locate rental units, but this approach for determining rent levels often works to their disadvantage. Rents listed in the newspaper are generally higher than average rents, creating an upward bias in the perceptions of both landlords and tenants. Thus tenants become willing to pay more, and landlords end up charging more. For example, Robert Bruss, writing in his nationally syndicated real estate column, recommends to landlords: "To find out what rent to charge, shop comparable rentals through newspaper want ads for house rentals" (1979:3).

Large-scale owners, on the other hand, are likely to approach housing as short-term investors. Because of their financial stake, market control, and professional orientation, they are usually well informed on rent structures. Indeed, in some cases the largest owners will conduct market surveys to provide direction in the setting of rents (Dreier, Gilderbloom, and Appelbaum 1980:16). Also, as we have noted, a variety of formal and informal mechanisms facilitates the exchange of information among owners.

Not all landlords, however, determine rent levels according to newspaper ads. Manzer and Krohn's study (1973) of housing markets in Montreal found that rent is structured according to the kind of owner in the market: professional or amateur. For the latter, who generally rents out to friends and family, "the rational side of real property ownership, such as the calculations of the return to equity, of the consequences of financing for 'cash flow' and tax planning is completely missing. . . . We find that residential and other small owners supply better housing to tenants at lower rents than professional investors" (1–6). Besides, "amateur" landlords often develop personal relationships with their tenants, and to the extent that this happens, they may be willing to negotiate rents, and rents in their units may, as a result, be low. Landlords who reside on the premises will normally set rents on the basis of personalistic considerations, as a result of continual face-to-face interaction with tenants.

Other studies have also found rents to be lower in owner-occupied units—for example, in nonmetropolitan North Carolina cities of less than 50,000 (Stegman and Sumka 1976) and in Orange, New Jersey (Gilderbloom and Keating 1982). The latter study observed substantial differences in rents between owner-occupied apartments and other units. According to an annual survey of rents by Orange's tax assessor in 1982, the rent for an average 4 1/2-room apartment was $325 when one of the units was owner occupied, but $450 for a similar but nonowner-occupied unit. According to the tax assessor, the owner-occupied apartments were frequently rented out to close friends, relatives, or immediate family.

Detailed information on prevailing rent levels is limited to large owners of rental properties, who sometimes raise rents on the basis of professional surveys of comparable apartments in the region (*Los Angeles Times* 1979:3). Such surveys, which also try to evaluate whether current tenants will accept additional rent increases, are therefore used by builders and mortgage lenders to determine whether market conditions warrant the construction of new rental housing. Such information is not available for either tenants or smaller owners.

In sum, tenants and small landlords are similarly disadvantaged in making pricing decisions on the basis of market considerations, because of the difficulty in obtaining detailed knowledge of market conditions. Larger landlords, on the other hand, often approach this problem in a professional fashion, and through surveys and other studies are able to determine what rent levels the market will bear.

Absence of Artificial Constraints on Demand,
Supply, and Price

Local housing markets encounter two principal forms of artificial constraints, both affecting supply and price.[11] First, there are local regulations and restrictions of various sorts that impede a frictionless market response to changes in demand and, therefore, potentially add to housing prices and rents. Such regulations typically include zoning ordinances, health and safety regulations, and land-use planning. Additionally, many cities enact regulations in the form of architectural guidelines, growth controls, housing supply ordinances (such as inclusionary zoning), and tenant protections (such as rent control and just-cause eviction ordinances). We shall examine these sorts of constraints in some detail in Chapter 6; for the present, we can summarize that discussion by stating that a comprehensive review of studies linking local restrictions and high housing prices suggests that the latter are an extremely minor cause of the former.

The second—and in our view more serious—form of constraint stems from governmental involvement in the national housing economy. Housing markets are hardly unfettered entities in which consumer demand and producer response determine price. Rather, housing markets are very much creatures of federal policies, foremost among which are national monetary and tax policies. These policies strongly influence the profitability of housing and, hence, investment; the cost of construction, as well as mortgage finance; and the rate at which property is resold for tax-sheltering purposes. It is our belief that credit and tax policies are largely responsible for local fluctuations in supply and price. Because of the importance of these arguments, we shall return to them (separately) in Chapter 4.

Rental Housing as a Homogeneous Product

As Olsen (1973:229) concludes: "Most scholars would probably find [homogeneity] to be the least plausible assumption." A house is unique because of its amenities, size, architecture, age, quality, and neighborhood, as well as its location within a neighborhood. It would be next to impossible to find an exactly equal substitute for any particular house (this is less true, however, for apartments). To deal with this problem, housing economists typically redefine housing as a composite package of goods that together provide a calculable "housing service." Each dwelling (or housing) unit is presumed to yield some quantity of this service during each time period, and that quantity can be predicted and measured as a composite of each unit's attributes. In this approach, consequently, there is no distinction between the quantity and quality of a dwelling unit, as these terms are customarily used. Stegman and Sumka (1976:119), for example, argue that by breaking down the physical characteristics of each housing unit, the researcher can measure the contribution of each characteristic to determine the total cost of the house. Thus, while heterogeneity is seemingly observed on the aggregate level, homogeneity can in fact be found on the dissaggregate level, by examining individual attributes as equivalent substitutes. Housing price then becomes the sum of the quantity of services or attributes offered, which is often estimated through hedonic price analysis. However this approach entails numerous difficulties (Olsen 1973: 229).

Small Individual Transactions Relative to Total Market

This condition (above) is usually true for tenants and landlords, except when owners divest their large holdings at one time for, say, large-scale condominium conversions. At present, such large-scale transactions are probably infrequent and therefore not disruptive of most housing markets.

SUMMARY

Earlier in this book we said that the study of rent is largely neglected as an important topic for sociological study. We indicated that rent plays an important role in the lives of many tenants, consuming an ever-increasing proportion of income in recent years, thereby resulting in cutbacks on expenditures for other basic necessities while producing overcrowding and displacement. Sociologists and other social scientists have played a significant role in beginning to document the major social and economic impacts that rent can have on people's lives.

On the other hand, examining the determinants of rent has generally been the concern of economists. In the words of Stegman and Sumka (1976:115), "Market price is the summary measure which describes the ultimate outcome of supply and demand interaction in the housing market." In theory, availability of housing units plays an important role in the determination of housing prices, but this variable has been largely ignored in empirical studies of the housing market. Instead, research has focused on demand variables within the intraurban context.

Thus within the supply and demand equation, economists have attempted to account for the variation in rent, but they have been only partially successful. Much is known about the impact of demand variables, but little is known about the supply aspect. In fact, as we have seen, there are strong reasons to conclude that the requisite assumptions concerning market operation are imperfectly met in many housing markets.

The irony is that, despite this dearth of knowledge concerning the influence of supply on market rents, the preferred solution to high rents still emphasizes supply-side factors. Acceptance of a simple supply/demand paradigm as a model for how the housing market works entails its own solution to rising rents: increase the supply of housing while shoring up flagging demand.[12] We do not believe such an approach addresses the underlying causes of the rental housing crisis, as we shall argue in detail in Chapter 4.

4
The Federal Government and National Housing Policy

The federal government influences housing demand and supply, and thereby prices and rents, through monetary and tax policies, on the one hand, and through low-income housing programs on the other.[1] The former are seldom concerned directly with housing objectives *per se,* although small changes in interest rates or income tax deductions can have far-reaching consequences for housing investment. The latter, though the most visible vehicle for directly realizing low-income housing objectives, is relatively minor in impact. In fact, it can be argued that any federal impact on housing is to a large extent the indirect result of tax laws and monetary policy, and only to a small degree the consequence of explicit policies aimed at addressing national housing needs.

Historically, housing policy has been organized in a piecemeal fashion by banking and development interests, whose first priority is to maximize profit rather than provide necessary shelter. In our view, the principal reason our society is unable to provide adequate, affordable housing for everyone is that housing—a necessity of life—is treated not as a community good, but as a commodity. Housing in our society is produced, owned, operated, and sold in ways designed to maximize profits, rather than to provide needed shelter. The consequence is waste and inefficiency in production and allocation; a highly volatile housing economy; chronic shortages, particularly among low-income households; and a growing gap between income and housing costs.

Whatever the merits of profit-driven market allocation in the housing economy, it cannot be denied that profits at all levels add considerably to the cost of housing, since they are cumulated throughout the production, sales, and consumption process as each participant seeks to maximize his or her return. These participants, typically, include the owner of the land on which the unit is built, who may realize a speculative gain; the financial institutions that make the construction and mortgage loans, and whose profits are included in the interest charges; the general contractor and subcontractors, during the construction phase; the building material providers, which are frequently large corporations with few incentives for cost control; and each successive owner, who hopes to realize a profit every time the property is sold.

In this chapter we examine these issues. We first consider the role of federal credit and tax policy, and then turn to a brief examination of low-income housing programs. We conclude with the likely effects of the 1986 Tax Reform Act on housing investment over the next few years.

THE IMPORTANCE OF FEDERAL CREDIT AND TAX POLICY

Credit, Interest Rates, and Housing Prices

Since virtually all housing construction and purchase is financed through private credit, residential mortgages are a significant portion of private debt in the United States, averaging around one-third of the total debt over the past fifteen years. In 1980, residential mortgages exceeded $1 trillion. At the same time, overall indebtedness has increased, with the result that residential mortgage debt in 1980 stood at 41 percent of Gross National Product—a substantial increase from the 36 percent ratio ten years earlier, and three times the post–World War II ratio of 13.5 percent (Stone 1983:Table 4.3).[2]

This heavy dependence on private-debt financing renders housing costs and starts highly susceptible to fluctuations in credit markets. It also siphons credit from industry and other productive uses, and rechanels it into inflated and speculative housing markets, thereby depriving the national economy of needed investment capital (Downs 1980). Finally, debt financing threatens overall economic stability since, during a deep recession, significant numbers of mortgage failures threaten banks and affect the entire financial structure.

Rising interest rates push rents up substantially. Even a small increase in the interest rate can mean a substantial increase in total mortgage payments, an increase that is passed along to tenants. According to Stone (1975:23–37), between 1964 and 1975 mortgage costs increased more than any other landlord cost. This is especially significant since landlords' mortgage payments constitute 40 to 50 percent of their total costs (Sternlieb 1974, 1975). As a result, if a landlord were to refinance a loan from a 10 percent interest rate to 15 percent, assuming that 50 percent of the rent initially went to paying the mortgage, a rent increase of at least 22 percent would be needed for the landlord to maintain his level of return from rents.[3]

While higher payments may have a dampening effect on demand and hence inhibit price increases, this effect is small in comparison with the higher financing costs. Interest rates also add directly to the cost of construction, sales prices, and other consumer credit (Janczyk 1980). In the early 1980s construction loan interest was one of the two most rapidly rising components of housing production costs; and the other was land (see President's Commission on Housing 1982:181).

From the perspective of the local housing economy, interest rates are an *exogenous* constraint: they do not reflect local supply and demand conditions; rather, they reflect national and international credit markets and federal monetary policy. Local interest rates do not fall if demand slackens as a consequence of higher prices. While high mortgage interest rates may dampen demand for owner-occupied dwellings, this demand is simply transferred to the rental sector, where it helps to push rents higher. Since the Federal Reserve System uses high interest rates and credit control as its chief means of fighting inflation, housing consumers suffer greatly during times of anti-inflationary monetary policy, confronting high interest payments and a scarcity of credit.

The highly cyclical nature of housing production is the direct result of reliance on private credit. Another result has been significant impairment of the long-run productive capacity of the housing industry (see President's Commission on Housing 1982:xxi, 182; Solomon 1981:200). The cost of idle plant and construction equipment during slack times is recaptured in higher prices of those housing units that are built. Construction workers require higher wages to offset those periods when they will be unemployed. Builders face high risks, which they cover through higher profit margins, a cost that is passed on to consumers. Estimates of increased production costs resulting from cyclical instability run as high as 15 to 20 percent (COIN 1979:57).

Interest rates are determined in large part by the politics of the administration in office. Thurow (1982:3) argues that interest rates remain high, by historical standards, because of the monetarist policies of the Federal Reserve, large (and growing) federal budget deficits, and stringent restrictions on the money supply. To lower interest rates, Thurow says, these policies have to be reversed. Michael Sumichrast, chief economist for the National Association of Home Builders, notes that the conventional mortgage market follows the interest rates set by the Federal Housing Administration and the Veterans Administration, which in turn reflect rates set by the Federal Reserve.[4] The cost of housing tracks the cost of money in general, as rising interest rates have become a significant component of rising housing costs in recent years. The substantial increase in average rents during the 1970s has to be attributed in large part to rapidly rising interest rates.

Federal Tax Policy and Speculation

The effect of federal tax laws on housing costs is equally significant. Tax policies contribute both to artificially high housing demand and speculation —the buying and selling of property for short-term profit, resulting from inflation. Speculation can result in significant short-term price increases. Moreover, it is wasteful and inefficient, and can be extremely damaging to low-income neighborhoods, whose residents can be quickly priced out of the housing market.

For homeowners, the pre-1987 federal income tax deductions for interest and property taxes encouraged the purchase of more expensive housing than would otherwise be affordable (U.S. Congressional Budget Office 1981). For owners of income property, the ability to depreciate the purchase value of a structure over relatively short periods encouraged its resale as soon as the bulk of depreciation benefits was exhausted—under pre-1987 tax laws, usually five or six years. This, in turn, contributed to the treatment of rental property as a speculative investment, on which returns were calculated in terms of short-term yield rather than long-term income potential. The 1986 Tax Reform Act, in hopes of discouraging speculative buying and selling, extends depreciation terms while reducing acceleration.

According to a study by the U.S. Congressional Budget Office (1981:xii), income tax policies have had a substantial effect on homeownership:

> One study [Hendershott and Hu 1980] suggests that as much as one-third of the owner-occupied housing in the United States as of 1976–1977 would not have been built if tax benefits had not lowered the after-tax cost of buying a house far below the cost of other investment assets. Other research [Rosen 1978; Rosen and Rosen 1980] suggests that the fraction of homes that are owned by their occupants would be four to five percentage points less without the mortgage interest and property tax deductions, and without the exclusion of net imputed rental income. Studies also indicate that households would buy less expensive houses in the absence of tax subsidies, and that housing prices might be lower.

Federal tax laws favoring homeownership indirectly create class differences. As inflation pushes householders into higher tax brackets, homeowner deductions acquire increased importance, encouraging higher-income households to become homeowners. As a consequence, the remaining renters are of relatively lower income and, therefore, unable to afford the higher rents that are necessary to induce investment in rental housing. Apartment owners often respond by converting rental units to more profitable condominiums (U.S. Congressional Budget Office 1981:32–36).

Together, federal tax laws and high interest rates compound the problem of housing costs, since the former encourage rapid turnover of rental property and the latter often results in refinancing at more than the original interest rates.

Rapid turnover of property is associated with higher housing costs (see, for example, CALPIRG 1980; COACT 1979; Appelbaum 1980; Appelbaum and Glasser 1980; Molotch and Kasof 1982). Prior to 1987, before the 1986 tax reform took effect, rapid turnover was encouraged by the Internal Revenue Code (especially, accelerated depreciation allowances), which optimized investment returns with a four- to seven-year turnover period. This was because, under the previous tax laws, almost half of the value of the apartment unit could be depreciated as a business expense during the first five years of ownership. Such deductions were intended to encourage new investment in housing rental, but they did so at the cost of encouraging rapid turnover of properties and, thereby, higher average rent levels.

In housing, speculation is also furthered by a mortgage financing system that permits a small down payment to leverage control over a substantial investment. It is difficult to estimate the impact of speculation on housing prices, since the relationship between speculation and inflation is "circular": inflationary expectations contribute to speculative buying and selling, while speculation fuels inflation by artificially stimulating demand.

One way to isolate the effects of speculation is to compare the rate of price increase of rapid-turnover properties with the price increases of properties that are bought and sold infrequently. Appelbaum and Glasser (1980) made such a comparison in two very different housing markets—Santa Barbara, California, and Madison, Wisconsin. The former was one of the most inflationary locales in the nation during the 1970s, with home prices increasing 355 percent between 1970 and 1980—from an average of $31,000 to $141,000.

Looking first at the Santa Barbara metropolitan area, Appelbaum and Glasser examined all sales of rental property in the board of realtors' Multiple Listing Service between January 1972 and May 1980. During that period, approximately 1,700 different properties were sold in approximately 2,250 separate sales transactions. The sales price of rental properties increased an average 35 percent annually during the late seventies.[5]

To gauge the effect of rapid turnover on sales price, they isolated all properties that had been sold at least once since the beginning of 1978. They then examined two groups of such recently sold properties: those with at least two sales in a 24-month period, and those with two sales at least 36 months apart. All prices were deflated to constant dollars by controlling for changes in the average price for all income-property sales in the metropolitan area during that period. In this fashion, Appelbaum and Glasser hoped to separate the effects of rapid turnover from those of general inflation in the housing market.[6]

Large and statistically significant differences were found in the rate of inflation between slow and rapid turnover properties. While the former exhibited annual increases only 1 percent greater than the general rate of housing inflation, the latter appreciated at an annual rate 10 percent higher. This is a substantial difference, particularly when one bears in mind that 18 percent of all apartments in Santa Barbara in 1980 had been sold within the past year, 34 percent within the past two years, and almost half (46 percent) within the past three years (Glennon and Appelbaum 1980:7).

In Madison, Wisconsin, the rate of real estate turnover was considerably lower than in Santa Barbara during the same period. It was found, for example, that in seven selected neighborhoods in 1979, only about one-fifth of all rental units had been sold at least once during the previous two years, while only about two-fifths had been sold within the previous six years (Appelbaum 1981:3–4 and Table 3C). A comparison was made between slow- and rapid-turnover of two- to four-unit rental properties, analogous to the study for Santa Barbara.[7] All prices were deflated to constant dollars, using the overall rate of sales price inflation. It was found that slow-turnover rental properties appreciated at an annual rate 1.8 percent above the overall rate of inflation, while rapid-turnover properties increased approximately 11 percent annually (ibid.: 4 and Table 4). These figures were virtually identical to Santa Barbara's, despite the vast differences in the two housing markets. (It is interesting to note that some of the highest rates of inflation in *non-rapid* turnover property occurred in neighborhoods that were experiencing the highest turnover rates, suggesting that speculation has a "ripple" effect even on properties that are not "hot" [ibid.:Table 6].)

Speculation both fuels and responds to rising prices. On the one hand, speculators are attracted to rapidly inflating markets in hopes of making a quick profit on their investment. At the same time, their infusion of capital helps to drive prices up by creating an artificial demand for housing—based not on the need for shelter but on the desire for profit. During the late 1970s, housing was an extremely profitable investment in Southern California, with substantial amounts of money flowing into the regional housing market in search of quick, relatively safe profits, and bidding up the price of housing as speculation drove up the price of gold and silver during the same period. While speculative bursts are necessarily short term, they can have significant adverse consequences for the neighborhoods that are affected, pricing residents out of the housing market.

FEDERAL LOW-INCOME HOUSING PROGRAMS

Having considered what we regard as the strongest federal government influence on private-housing investment decisions, we shall now discuss federal programs that are aimed specifically at low-income housing needs. These are programs that seek to compensate for the failure of the private market to address the housing needs of special populations adequately, particularly the poor. In general, such programs seek to do so by buttressing private market activity (Starr and Esping-Anderson 1979). Presupposing that a competitive market exists, in which rent is determined by the interaction of supply and demand, Washington has funneled billions of dollars into subsidized rehabilitation programs, affordable mortgage supports, attractive capital gains structures, and generous accelerated depreciation allowances to encourage more housing construction and rehabilitation. As a result, most government housing programs are organized to benefit bankers, builders, and landlords. According to Starr and Esping-Anderson (1979:15),

> it is hardly a secret—although it is often forgotten by those eager to blame government for all of life's misfortunes—that public policy in America rests on the accommodation of private interests. To secure social programs as well as other legislation, reformers commonly find they have to offer inducements for cooperation of the most powerful interests. . . . Housing policies have had to accommodate the interests of banks and other finance institutions, builders and developers. The pattern has been to leave the interests of these parties at the very least unimpaired, while pumping in money through expanded insurance subsidies or credit.

The role of government has thus been to repair or boost the workings of the private market, largely by creating a profitable investment climate so that supply will be increased. As previously noted, federal housing programs have tended to be of minor influence, especially in comparison with the more powerful effects of federal credit and tax policy.

An Overview of Federal Housing Programs

Federal housing programs date back to the Depression, and over the years have included low-interest loans, mortgage interest subsidies, rent supplements, publicly owned low-income housing, and—in the case of military housing —direct public financing as well as ownership. Many programs have been targeted to specific groups, such as the elderly, rural households, or very low income households. However, federal programs have never reached more than a small fraction of those in need, because housing has never been regarded as an entitlement in the United States. In fact, the largest federal subsidies for housing have gone to upper middle-class homeowners, in the form of deductions for mortgage interest and property taxes, which are estimated to have cost the Treasury close to $70 billion in 1984. Sixty percent of these deductions go to taxpayers in the top 10 percent of the income range (Dolbeare 1983:Figure 2.1).

Public housing and rent supplements are the two principal programs that in recent years have been targeted at low-income populations. Public housing originated with the National Housing Act of 1937 as a pump-priming public works program, serving the needs of "submerged middle-class" families hit by the Depression. It wasn't until the massive urban renewal and slum clearance programs of the 1950s that public housing became identified exclusively with low-income populations. As large public projects became "last resort" housing for the economy's cast-offs, the program suffered from official neglect in the form of chronic underfunding, poor maintenance, and bureaucratic management. While there are many examples of well-constructed, attractive public housing units across the country, projects too often were poorly designed and cheaply built, fostering rapid deterioration. Many large projects lacked landscaping, adequate public transportation, and access to shopping areas and social services. All too frequently, jail-like architecture stigmatized residents.

While public housing is owned by public agencies (usually local housing authorities), it is built by private contractors and financed with bonds, and its costs thus reflect both private profit maximization and the instabilities of the private credit markets. Currently, some 3.5 million people live in approximately 11,000 public housing projects in over 3,300 localities (Hartman 1986:363).

Public housing is, for the most part, repressive. Typically, the residents have little control over the basic decisions that affect their lives, and consequently feel little personal identification with their homes. Restrictions on visitors, interior design, and choice of residence affords public housing tenants very little control over their living space. This often leads to a negative view of their homes, contributing to a pervasive alienation that is reflected in poor home maintenance, rent delinquency, and even vandalism. One comprehensive HUD study (U.S. HUD 1977, 1978a) found that on-site management, arbitrary tenant screening and evictions, and substandard maintenance were the three principal difficulties faced by large, multifamily projects. As a National Housing Law Project study concluded "One can think of few industries where the needs and desires of the consumer are so little recognized" (1981).

Since the 1960s, public housing has been replaced by a variety of mortgage, rental, and tax-shelter subsidy programs intended to stimulate the production of low- and moderate-income rental housing by private developers. These programs have also been designed to maximize profits and minimize risks for private owners and lenders, at the expense of long-term affordability and project viability. As a result, more than one-quarter of the subsidized housing inventory is in various stages of mortgage default, assignment, foreclosure, or resale by HUD, posing substantial risks to its tenant population. Many viable projects in "gentrifying" markets are approaching the point where their mortgages can be prepaid without restriction, jeopardizing their future use as low- and moderate-income housing (Achtenberg 1985).

During the past decade, the federal government's chief low-income housing program has consisted of providing direct rental subsidies to private landlords under Section 8 of the National Housing Act. Various programs fall under this category, including those that provide for the construction or rehabilitation of units destined for Section 8 occupancy, as well as those that provide rent supplements for existing rental units. Under these programs, participating private landlords agree to charge qualifying tenants "fair market" rents, which are based on prevailing rent levels as determined by HUD. The government then makes up the difference between the fair-market rent and the tenant's rent payments, set at 30 percent (formerly one-quarter) of monthly income. At a time when rents are skyrocketing, this program is highly inflationary, with the direct subsidy cost for a new unit of Section 8 housing estimated at $4,000–$5,500 per year (U.S. HUD 1982). Currently, some 3.5 million people are housed in Section 8 subsidized rental units (Hartman 1986:364).

With regard to neighborhood impact, the federal role is well known. Urban renewal enhanced opportunities for profit in the development of prime innercity real estate while fostering business and institutional expansion. In the process, at least 1 million low-income and minority households were uprooted and their communities destroyed (Gans 1982:385–86). In the 1960s, with the growing threat of social disorder in the cities, outright "slum clearance" efforts were replaced with more discreet attempts at housing rehabilitation and, ultimately, with the neighborhood-oriented Model Cities and Community Action programs of the Great Society. Then, in the mid-1970s, as the problems of the economy worsened and the protest of the poor seemed to weaken, Community Development Block Grants provided a vehicle through which funds for neighborhood programs could be drastically cut, in exchange for increased local political control over resource allocation. Currently, block grants provide little more than a limited form of revenue sharing to offset the impact of local "fiscal crisis" cutbacks, and an arena in which neighborhood groups are pitted against one another in the battle for diminishing resources.

Direct federal budget outlays for housing and community development have not kept pace with inflation. When all low-income housing programs are considered together, some 4.5 million units received some form of direct subsidy in 1981, of which 3.4 million were in urban areas administered by HUD, with the remainder in rural areas administered by the Department of Agriculture's Farmers' Home Administration (FmHA). The HUD-administered units included 1.2 million units of public housing, with about 1.3 million households receiving Section 8 payments (Dolbeare 1983:Table 2.6).

The Reagan Administration and Low-Income Housing

As long as economic growth resulted in a better standard of living and sustained business growth at the same time, improvement in housing was possible. But as major U.S. corporations have been increasingly threatened by foreign competition and Third World resistance to U.S. business interests, business has demanded, and gotten, a larger slice of the pie. Housing could be easily targeted for attack—precisely because of the wasteful way it has been produced, financed, and owned in our society.

President Reagan's supply-side strategy to bolster corporate profits is made possible by tax cuts and deregulation, combined with massive cuts in social spending and even larger increases in military outlays. While rents have

TABLE 4.1
CHANGES IN BUDGET AUTHORITY IN MILLIONS OF
CONSTANT 1987 DOLLARS (SELECTED YEARS) FOR MAJOR FUNCTIONS
AND SELECTED PROGRAMS

Functions/Programs	1981 Actual	1987 Estimate	1988 Proposed	1981–88 CHANGE	
				Dollars	Percent
National defense	$229,753	$292,927	$301,280	$71,527	31.1%
	25.4%	26.8%	27.3%		
Community/regional development	10,257	6,071	5,084	(5,173)	−50.4
	1.1%	0.6%	0.5%		
Housing assistance	32,881	10,709	7,123	(25,758)	−78.3
	3.6%	1.0%	0.6%		
Low income subtotal*	86,404	65,077	64,837	(21,567)	−25.0
	9.5%	5.9%	5.9%		
Total budget authority	904,878	1,093,933	1,103,051	198,173	21.9

*Includes social services, medicaid, subsidized housing (except public housing loans), food/ nutrition, and other income security.
Source: LIHIS (1987: table 8). Courtesy of LIHIS.

reached their highest level in recent history, housing assistance has been severely cut. In Table 4.1 we see that during the first seven years of the Reagan presidency—if the administration has succeeded in getting its 1988 budget proposals adopted—military expenditures will have increased by almost a third, from $230 billion to $301 billion (in constant 1987 dollars). During the same period, total housing assistance will fall by 78 percent, from $33 billion to only $7 billion. Put somewhat differently, defense will have grown from 25.4 to 27.3 percent of the budget, while housing assistance will have dropped from 3.6 to 0.6 percent. By 1988, the United States will be spending over 42 times as much on defense as on housing (in 1981 it was spending 7 times as much).

Table 4.2 provides a more detailed analysis of the fate of low-income housing programs under the Reagan administration. Between 1981 and 1988—again assuming the proposed 1988 budget has been adopted—total Section 8 housing expenditures will have declined by 82 percent, from $19 billion to $3.5 billion. Within the Section 8 appropriation, however, the two chief programs, new construction and existing allowances, will have been severely slashed. New construction will decline from $10 billion to only $276 million, a drop of 97 percent. Existing Section 8 allowances will have been eliminated altogether. Public housing will have suffered similar cutbacks, with expenditures projected to decline 85 percent, from $7 billion to only $1 billion. Loans for elderly and handicapped housing will also have dropped by

TABLE 4.2
HIGHLIGHTS OF SELECTED HUD LOW-INCOME HOUSING PROGRAMS,
1988 COMPARED TO EARLIER YEARS

Selected Programs	1981 Actual	1987 Estimate	1988 Proposed	1981–88 CHANGE	
				Dollars	Percent
Section 8	$19,357	$5,453	$3,495	($15,862)	−81.9%
New construction	10,245	1,372	276	(9,969)	−97.3
Existing	5,791	791	0	(5,791)	−100.0
Public housing	7,332	1,673	1,129	(6,203)	−84.6
Elderly/handicapped loans (Section 202)	873	593	131	(742)	−85.0
Home ownership (Section 235)	1,650	4	0	(1,650)	−100.0
Total budget authority	32,201	7,201	4,624	(27,577)	−85.6

Source: LIHIS (1987: table 1). Courtesty of LIHIS.

85 percent, from $873 to $131 million. And appropriations for low-income home ownership programs will have been eliminated altogether.

New housing construction for all HUD low-income housing programs dropped from 183,000 units in 1980 to only 28,000 in 1985 (Hartman 1986:364). Federal assistance for operating subsidies was projected to decline from $1.6 billion in 1984 to $1 billion in 1986 (365–66). HUD hopes to sell or demolish 100,000 public housing units over the next five years, and commitments for some 250,000 low-income units have been cancelled. Recipients of rent supplements will also be required to devote a higher proportion of their income to housing, even though public housing tenants must now pay 30 percent of their incomes on rent. Barry Zigas, president of the National Low Income Housing Coalition, estimates that under President Reagan only 25 percent of the nation's renters who qualify for Section 8 assistance are receiving aid (Gilderbloom, Rosentraub, and Bullard 1987). This estimate, however, might be overly optimistic. According to Gilderbloom, Rosentraub, and Bullard (1987), only 6 percent of persons qualifying for Section 8 assistance in Houston get government help, including 9 percent of the qualifying disabled and 5 percent of the qualifying elderly. Cities across the country have witnessed a dramatic increase in their waiting lists for public housing. According to a 1984 study by the U.S. Conference of Mayors, over two-thirds of all cities have closed their waiting lists to individuals seeking public housing (Maxwell 1986:15). Gramm-Rudman–mandated budget cuts will have a massive effect on other important housing subsidies, such as public housing modernization and operating funds and Community Development Block Grants.

Some segments of the housing industry have suffered as public and private resources have been reallocated to bolster the profitability of powerful corporate interests, but others have continued to prosper, particularly developers and investors who shift their capital to luxury housing or downtown office, commercial, and retail construction. Housing consumers—especially renters—are paying the *real* price, in the form of reduced housing options, less stability, and higher costs. Under the Reagan administration, the government's previous commitment to adequate housing for all segments of society has all but been abandoned. Moreover, the fundamental problems of the U.S. economy, which are the root of today's housing crisis, are likely to continue well beyond the Reagan administration. At stake, politically, is how the economy (including the housing sector) will be restructured in the long run to respond to these conditions, and in whose interest the restructuring will occur.

To the extent that the Reagan administration envisions any federal role at all in low-income housing programs, it is to buttress the marketplace by enhancing consumer demand, rather than continuing to subsidize housing structures. This is to be achieved by a new housing allowance or "voucher" program, which, like food stamps, would be spent by participating low-income households in the newly deregulated marketplace. We can summarize the results of a decade of experimentation with housing allowances (see Hartman 1986:369–71; also USGAO 1986:3–5):[8]

* relatively small percentages of eligible households actually participated in voucher programs (participation ranged from a quarter to about 40 percent of eligible households, and were lower for poorer, minority, and larger households)
* participation was significantly lower when recipients in substandard housing were required to meet a minimum quality standard either by making repairs or moving (this was particularly true among poorer, minority, and large households)
* where recipients were allowed to choose between spending their allowances either on improving their housing conditions or on non-housing expenditures, only one-quarter of total payments were used on the former; the large majority chose instead to alleviate their poverty (an average of 40 percent of pre-allowance household income was spent on shelter)
* the increased consumer spending on housing, made possible by providing allowances, did not result in either new construction or rehabilitation of substandard units

In view of these results, it seems likely that a housing allowance program with minimum quality standards will not reach those who most need it; it will, especially, discourage the participation of the large majority of low-income tenants who live in substandard housing. Nor will it necessarily result in an upgrading of substandard units, or the construction of additional rental units. A program sufficiently large to reach a sizable proportion of eligible households, however, may well result in higher rents, as the additional money available for housing expenditures stimulates demand and thereby bids rents up.[9] Indeed, as one researcher concluded,

> a full-scale earmarked allowance program might cause significant rent increases for both recipients and nonrecipients, and the [National Bureau of Economic Research] simulations pointed out the possibility that such a program might trigger large price declines and extensive abandonment in the worst neighborhoods. [John Kain, cited in Bradbury and Downs 1981: 358–59]

THE 1986 TAX REFORM ACT

In late 1986, Congress passed the Reagan administration's tax reform program, which took effect in the 1987 tax year. The expressed purpose of the Act was to simplify the Internal Revenue Code by reducing the number of personal tax brackets to two, while shifting the burden of taxation from individuals and families to businesses. The top personal marginal tax rate was reduced from 50 percent to 28 percent over a two-year period. Additionally, many tax shelters, which had previously enabled taxpayers to reduce or avoid paying taxes altogether, were eliminated; notable among them was a large number that impacted rental housing investment. The major provisions (or lack thereof) affecting housing[10] were:

- A rescheduling of rental housing depreciation to 28 years. Previously,[11] market rentals had been depreciated over an 18-year term, while low-income rentals were depreciated over 15 years. At the same time, accelerated depreciation was greatly reduced. The net effect was to markedly reduce the annual depreciation amounts that could be deducted from income, particularly in the early years of ownership.
- The provision that losses from "passive investments" (property that owners do not actually manage) could only be deducted against other income from similar investments.[12] This is expected to discourage future investment by wealthy individuals and syndications that had previously relied on paper losses from real estate and other investments to offset income from other sources.
- Elimination of the tax status of Industrial Development Bonds, making them considerably less attractive to wealthy investors. These bonds had previously been used by state and local housing finance agencies to provide below-market financing for as much as 20–30 percent of all rental units (Apgar et al. 1985:1).

- Elimination of interest deductions for most types of loans (including credit-card financing), with the exception of home mortgages, thereby— in the eyes of some analysts—greatly increasing pressures for home ownership, since home refinancing would provide a potential source of deductible loans for consumer purchases.
- No provision for "grandfathering" investments that would be adversely affected by the new legislation. Existing benefits were to be phased out over five years. A "transition rule" was, however, enacted to grandfather investors in low-income housing projects, due largely to the lobbying efforts of such low-income housing advocates as the National Low Income Housing Coalition.
- Inclusion of a tax credit for investors in housing projects that serve many low- and very-low-income tenants, which further limits rents to a fixed percentage of the qualifying income for the unit. Although only authorized through 1989, this provision may raise as much as $9 billion in federal tax subsidies to encourage low-income housing development. A minimum of 10 percent of the credits must be sponsored by nonprofit organizations. Again, this provision is largely the result of lobbying efforts by low-income housing advocates (Zigas 1987).

It is difficult to predict the long-term effects of this legislation, although most short-term predictions anticipate extremely adverse consequences. We argued in the previous chapter that, in much rental housing, cash flow does not provide an adequate return on investment and that, in the absence of tax- and inflation-generated returns, average rents would have to rise by as much as one-quarter to make rental housing as profitable as other investments of comparable risk. It is therefore not surprising that most analysts predict a reduction in the value of income property by some 20 percent (Furlong 1986:16), creating pressures for an increase in average rents of 20 to 24 percent above the rate of inflation by 1991 (Apgar et al. 1985:1), with even greater increases at the lower-income range (Apgar and Doud n.d.:2). Were such rent increases to occur, any personal income tax savings due to the tax reform would be more than offset, particularly for low- and moderate-income households. For example, if rents were to rise by 10 percent, only those with incomes above $23,000 would benefit from the new legislation, while if rents rose by 20 percent, the breakeven point would be approximately $45,000 (Apgar et al. 1985:1).

Whether or not landlords are able to raise rents by an amount sufficient to recoup their lost tax benefits depends on local conditions—in particular, on the competitiveness of the local rental housing market and the willingness of tenants to pay significant rent increases. In highly overbuilt markets and in places that enact (or already have) rent control, increases will be somewhat lower and the value of rental property will decline accordingly. Eventually, in such market areas, profitability will be restored at lower market values. On the other hand, where landlords are able to raise rents by substantial amounts, some tenants will respond by doubling up: one study predicts some 150,000 additional doubled-up households per year, or 1.4 million by 1994 (Apgar et al. 1985). This will (1) result in a loss in housing quality and (2) exacerbate the long-term trend of declining affordability we outlined in Chapter 2.

Eventually, of course, doubling-up could increase vacancies to a point where it would be difficult for landlords to continue to raise rents (although, as we demonstrate in the next chapter, a high level of vacancy may be necessary for this to occur). If this happens before rents have risen to the point where profitability is restored, a compensating erosion in market values could be expected. Which of these responses will occur will depend on local circumstances.

The Tax Reform Act is expected to have a very chilling effect on investment in rental housing, at least in the short run. Private real estate syndications are expected to decline from $4.7 billion in 1985 to less than $1 billion in 1987 (Furlong 1986:16). At the same time, the capital cost of conventionally financed rental housing is expected to rise by 44 percent (Apgar et al. 1985:1). The aggregate effect on rental housing construction, according to some predictions, is likely to be severe; the National Association of Home Builders, for example, anticipates a 50 percent drop in apartment construction in the first year of tax reform (Furlong 1986:16), while some market simulations predict an annual reduction in multi-unit construction of 160,000, or some 1.4 million units by 1994 (Apgar et al. 1985:1).

Total housing construction, for homeownership and rental, could decline by as much as 200,000 units per year, reaching a total of 1.9 million units by 1994 (Apgar et al. 1985:1) and causing at least one investment counselor to conclude: "The private market is for all intents and purposes dead."[13] In the face of chronic sluggishness in economic recovery, it is even possible that such large declines in multifamily construction could precipitate a recession in the construction industry, which, in turn, could trigger another national recession, resulting in housing foreclosures and insolvency for lending institutions that have heavily invested in real estate (Furlong 1986:16).

5
The Failure of Market Allocation: Causes of High Housing Costs

In Chapter 3 we examined the limitations of conventional explanations concerning the determinants of rent. In this chapter we address a related question: why the market has proven unable to provide adequate housing at prices affordable by all segments of the population. We begin with a study of the institutional structure of rental housing, looking particularly at the rent-setting practices of different types of landlords. This analysis offers additional evidence that large, professional landlord-investors are more likely to determine rent structures independently of short-run changes in supply than are small landlords. We then present an empirical study of the determinants of rent in 140 U.S. housing markets in 1980, as a preliminary way of suggesting some answers to this question and to related questions as well.

THE SOCIAL ORGANIZATION OF LANDLORDING

In Chapter 3 we concluded that rents fail to respond to changes in supply, and sought an explanation in the institutional structure of the rental housing industry. Specifically, we suggested that social networks among landlords can

This chapter is partially adapted from Gilderbloom (1985c) and Gilderbloom and Appelbaum (1987).

serve to reduce competition and, hence, market responsiveness to changes in supply. We argued that this would likely be particularly true in highly professionalized housing markets, in which ownership is concentrated in relatively few hands.

In this section we initiate an examination of the social organization of landlording, a neglected topic in the sociology of housing. In particular, we will examine the distinctive practices of two categories of landlords: *professional* landlords, with large holdings, and *amateur* landlords with relatively few units. Following the lead provided by studies such as Feagin (1983), Susser (1982), Clark, Heskin, and Manuel (1980), Lawson (1980), Vaughan (1972), Stegman and Sumka (1976), Krohn, Fleming, and Manzer (1977), and Stegman (1972), we will identify and analyze a variety of social factors that influence a landlord's behavior in calculating rent increases in the process of actually operating housing units. Although there is no clear-cut line between professional and amateur landlords, it is customary to identify the former as owning five or more units, while the latter ("mom and pop" landlords) own four or fewer.[1]

Professional Landlords

RENTAL HOUSING AS A SHORT-TERM INVESTMENT

Professional landlords are relatively sophisticated investors who approach rental housing much as they would any business investment. For a number of reasons (which we shall examine below), the rents they charge tend to be higher than those of amateur landlords. In their analyses of five neighborhood housing markets, Krohn, Fleming, and Manzer (1977) indicate the ways in which the operating and investment decisions of professional landlords tend to push up the cost of rental housing. Similarly, Feagin (1983:60) argues that when professional landlords dominate the market, rent increases will be 10 to 40 percent higher. And according to Stegman, the degree of professionalism varies with the scale of the operation (1972:29–30):

> Sophistication and permanence of operations increases with size of holdings. . . . Another way of looking at the importance of scale is to identify that point at which an investor must cease being a part-time landlord and concentrate full-time on his holdings, lest he lose control of his operation. While the point is realistically a range, one cannot very well manage more than 75 units on a part-time basis, unless most of the units are in contiguous buildings. Similarly, market conditions are such that it would be extremely difficult to earn even a modest living through owning and managing much less than 50 low-income units.

One reason professional landlords often charge higher rents is because they regard their units as part of a short-term investment portfolio, rather than as a long-term source of income. This, in turn, requires that rent/cost ratios be high, if the property is to command a high sales price. It also creates strong pressures to turn over rental property frequently. Rental units are acquired or liquidated on the basis of calculations that take into account a large range of alternative investment opportunities, along with expected resale value and tax sheltering. Actual cash flow, in some circumstances, may be a minor consideration. Professional landlords thus pursue the highest rate of return in economically rational terms (see, especially, Stegman 1972; Krohn, Fleming, and Manzer 1977; Feagin 1983). This often involves speculation—the rapid resale of units for short-term profit, based purely on appreciation and tax writeoffs for depreciation. As a consequence, professional landlords almost always face high mortgage payments, which increases their costs.

The professional landlords' business costs are high for a second reason: the scale of operation often mandates hiring a work force to manage and repair the units. Professional landlords, therefore, may depend on management and maintenance services, although the form of such service varies with the scale of operation. Large-scale professional landlords, for example, typically have at least one full-time person in management, with a part-time crew of carpenters, plumbers, and electricians. Smaller-scale professional landlords, on the other hand, typically hire maintenance personnel on an as-needed basis, and often at higher wages (Stegman 1972:29).

LANDLORD–TENANT RELATIONS

In a study of landlords in Orange, New Jersey, one of the authors (Gilderbloom 1985c) found that professional landlords tend to have impersonal, businesslike relationships with their tenants. (According to their own reports, they were concerned that personal ties with tenants could result in strong pressures for lower rents.) Many employed intermediaries—usually apartment managers or rental management companies—to handle all direct relations with tenants. On the other hand, a number of landlords reported that prior personal ties with some tenants were important considerations in setting rents. In some cases, even landlords who employed intermediaries would sometimes grant rent decreases for certain "hardship cases." For example, one large-scale landlord reported that he rescinded a rent increase after his manager informed him of a long-term tenant's financial difficulties.

The study found that professional landlords were primarily concerned with getting tenants who they felt would be able to pay the rent on time and who were unlikely to "skip out." As a way of determining this, some landlords refused to rent to tenants below specific income levels; others employed the rule of thumb that prospective tenants should spend no more than 25 percent of their income on rent. (Income thus becomes the criterion for assessing the credit worthiness of the tenant.) According to one large-scale professional landlord, "We try to screen tenants based on the following: (1) how long they have worked; (2) income to pay for rent; (3) previous landlord and credit report" (Gilderbloom 1985c:162).

Such landlords used several methods to determine the suitability of tenants. Some conducted full inquiries into prospective tenants' backgrounds, examining their credit records, employment, monthly income, and years of residence in the city. Such inquiries often included recent rental histories, in hope of identifying tenants who had reportedly been late in paying rent, or been "disruptive," or had sued their former landlords (for any reason). In some cases, professional landlords would rely on professional tenant-screening services for such investigations, while others would conduct the inquiries themselves. "Good" tenants, in these terms, were not only preferred, but were sometimes granted a reduction in rent as an inducement to move into a unit:

> I set rents according to a person's income. I look at the application and I look to see if he has been employed all his life and has stayed with the same employer all his life, a bank account, has credit, not divorced, semi-professional, no children . . . these are the qualities of a model tenant. I then tell him the rent. If he wants [to pay] less, I might even give it to him if he's good [reduce the rent]. It's the quality of the tenant that matters. [Gilderbloom 1985c:163]

Professional landlords expressed the belief that tenants with suitable jobs and adequate incomes would be more likely to get along with other tenants in the building. Conversely, they feared that "riffraff" in a building would frighten other tenants into moving away, producing a long-term loss in rental income. Some professional landlords contended that a few "bad tenants" would attract others like themselves, leading to a long-term decline in upkeep as well as a deterioration in relations among residents. On the other hand, some landlords contended that "the neighborhood" often precluded "good tenants," no matter what rent they charged or whom they sought as tenants. According to one landlord, "Class of tenants determines rents. We could raise rents if we had a higher class of tenants. Because of the neighborhood we could never attract tenants into the area and bring in new tenants" (ibid., 163).

Tenants with a high income are desirable not only because of lower risk, but also because they are able to bear a rent increase more easily than those who can barely afford the current rent. This consideration is especially important to professional landlords, who generally raise rents on a regular basis. Large-scale landlords, in particular, expressed awareness of the social and economic costs of moving, and the resulting constraint on tenants to absorb rent increases. According to one large-scale owner, "tenants will pay any rent you ask, you can get any rent you want with good management."

FORMAL AND INFORMAL NETWORKS AND THE
SETTING OF RENTS

Most professional landlords belong to local apartment owners' associations, while some of the large owners belong to statewide and national landlord groups as well. As we have seen, such organizations provide informal and formal networks that are important in promoting cooperation in the setting of rents. Yet landlords are differentially involved in these networks, depending largely upon the style and scale of their operations. Small-scale professionals rely heavily upon informal contacts, and secondarily upon local apartment owners' associations, in determining rental levels. Large-scale professionals tend to give less weight to local rental contacts and practices, but are involved in formal landlord associations on the local, state, and even national levels.

All the small-scale professional landlords interviewed by Gilderbloom (1985c) relied on the knowledge, advice, or actions of other landlords. Rents for the small-scale professional were determined by assessing what other landlords were charging in the immediate neighborhood. Landlords typically acquired this information by looking at newspaper ads for available rentals in the neighborhood or asking landlords of neighboring properties what they were charging. One owner stated: "I try to get market value rent for equivalent units in the area. I look at the newspaper, interview fellow realtors. This is modified by personal interviews with tenants. I know market value is $350. Older couple—no children—go down on the price: less wear and tear. Cut to $325. Families with kids more wear and tear, I might charge more" (ibid., 170). Another owner commented: "I check with several buildings, find out what they are getting and I try to get equalization. . . . I have my resident people go or I know a few landlords; they tell me what they are getting, what their rent increase was. So I find out from other buildings" (ibid.).

On a more formal basis, local, statewide, and national landlord organizations promulgate policies suggesting how much rent should be charged. The local apartment owners' association, for example, frequently offers advice on rent levels and increases. A landlord who is new to a market can turn to the association to get an idea of "what the market will bear" in a particular neighborhood. The local apartment owners' association serves to bring the large- and small-scale professional landlords together to discuss and coordinate pricing policies. The small-scale landlord thereby begins to learn the "rules" for profit maximization. One interviewee stated:

> There is rent control in the market, there is an area rent base. We discuss this at the rental association meetings; this serves to keep costs down and exchange ideas. You become a professional through these meetings. [The] average owner has five to ten units. Management companies are always there to get small property owners for their business. Irregardless of your costs the market determines rents. If the area has a $300 rent base and you charge $350 you are going to die. [ibid.]

And according to a director of an apartment owners' association, "We advise our members to look at neighboring rentals, see what they get and go by the quality of the apartment. Look at the age of the building. Nine times out of ten I can help them with what rent to charge'' (ibid., 171).

A large-scale owner, active in the apartment owners' association, reported:

> I get calls from dozens of people asking me what they think rent should be. _____ [one of the apartment owners' association directors] will make recommendations in terms of how much rent to charge. You call them all. You look at the apartment owner association newsletter. _____ [the apartment owner association director] is your best source for rent increases. No better entity to figure out rents, but try to hold out for good tenants even if it means keeping some units vacant. [ibid.]

Large-scale professional landlords are less dependent on informal networks and associations in determining rents. Typically, they set rents according to a systematic consideration of regional housing needs and costs, believing that if they set rents simply as a function of what nearby landlords are charging, they would be underpriced. Rent, according to a number of large-scale landlords, is best determined by comparing the internal and external amenities of a unit to similar units throughout the region. According to a landlord who owns over 900 units:

> I am not concerned with what the other guy in the neighborhood is renting his unit for, because it might be underpriced. I am only interested in what kind of property we have. What is the general condition of the area for determining rent—not just the rent next door. I don't look around me. I look at the location and stability of the area in commanding rents. Is the building near the Y.M.C.A., commuter train, shopping area or a park? [ibid., 173]

On the other hand, some large-scale professional landlords *did* consult the actions of other landlords in setting rents. For example:

> I take the general area and compare it to what other landlords are charging. Take a mile circle, compare my buildings. I call Joe, I call Morocco, I ask them what they are charging for a three room or a two room. I then average out my rents to what everyone else is [charging]. It is called being competitive. I don't want to charge a rent that is higher than these guys [are charging]. It just wouldn't make sense. This is always my first consideration. [ibid., 172]

As we have suggested, the aim of the large-scale professional landlord is not necessarily to earn a market rate of return in comparison with similar rental housing; rather, the standard is other investments of comparable risk. One way to assure such a return is to set an initial rent on the basis of such considerations, and then adjust rents annually by a predetermined amount necessary to maintain the worth of the investment.

Management companies afford another cross-cutting set of relations that are significant in determining rent levels and increases. For a fee of 6 to 10 percent of the total gross rents, management companies will operate an apartment on a day-to-day basis. Their duties normally include rent collection, maintenance, selecting and evicting tenants, representing owners in small claims court, and consulting with the owner on rent increases.

If management companies control a large portion of the rental stock, their role in determining rents can be crucial. Since these companies have closer contact with daily operations than the owners, company opinions concerning increases are often decisive. The companies are thus in a position to affect uniform rent changes that, in turn, affect numerous owners, this constituting a major force for reducing competition. Management companies have a large stake in increasing rents, since their fees are directly tied to gross revenues.

A number of studies have found that rents are higher when properties are operated by management companies rather than by individual owners (Krohn and Fleming 1972; Manzer and Krohn 1973; Dreier, Gilderbloom, and Appelbaum 1980; Gray 1979; Ipcar 1974). A study of Isla Vista, California (Dreier, Gilderbloom, and Appelbaum 1980) found that only five management companies controlled three-quarters of all apartment buildings of ten units or more. In another study of the same rental market, Gray (1979) estimated that managed units charged an annual average of $168 more than nonmanaged units. Large management firms were sued in Boston for "routinely setting rents in collusion rather than competing with each other in the market" (Dreier, Gilderbloom, and Appelbaum 1980:169). In East Lansing, Michigan, Ipcar (1974:11) reported that the price of rental units was 6 to 14 percent higher when they were owned by large-scale landlords or managed professionally.

Much additional research needs to be done in this area before firm conclusions can be drawn. Unfortunately, much of the evidence is based on a few studies, and often fails to take other factors into account (such as differences in quality or service) that may be associated with professional management. Nonetheless, we believe that noncompetitive price setting by professional management, particularly in markets that are dominated by a small number of large-scale professional landlords, permits a far greater degree of rent coordination than is ordinarily believed to exist. Such coordination is especially likely where vacancies are low, although, as we shall see in the "evidence section" of this chapter, substantial coordination may occur with moderate vacancy levels as well.

VACANCY RATES AND THE DETERMINATION
OF RENT

Housing economists generally assume that landlords will reduce rents when long-term vacancies exist in order to fill their units, and will raise rents when vacancies are scarce, because they can afford to do so without fear of losing tenants (see, for example, Beyer 1966; Olsen 1973). This assumption is questioned by a number of empirical studies (Dreier et al. 1980; Vitaliano 1983; Rydell 1977), including our own research (reported later in this chapter).

Some studies have also found that reducing rents in order to fill vacant units is not necessarily the most rational long-term economic behavior for a landlord (Kelley 1975; Lowry 1981a; McGuire 1981; Feagin 1983:150; Downs 1983: 35).

More than a half-century ago, Monroe (1931) argued that reducing rents on vacant units to attract tenants would induce current tenants to demand similar reductions. As a result, total rental income could actually be reduced, even though all units were rented. According to Monroe (28),

> anyone who is familiar with districts where apartment houses or office buildings have been "overbuilt" knows that the managers of these properties often maintain rentals surprisingly steady in the face of continued vacancies. Is this simply because there are not enough tenants to go round? Rarely. There are usually a considerable number who would be glad to come in from inferior quarters, if the price were low enough. The reason is more likely to be that the managers realize the impossibility of getting more tenants except at rentals which would, if granted to all, lower their total returns.

Conversely, when vacancy rents are low, landlords will not necessarily act immediately to increase rents above the existing market rate. Blank and Winnick (1953) suggest that a landlord, initially confronting low vacancies, is likely to be satisfied with the rise in income resulting from the increase in occupancy, especially to the extent that knowledge of market demand may be lacking. However, Blank and Winnick (189) also argue that once "uncertainty" is reduced in the market and the vacancy rate has reached a low enough level, landlords will respond by raising rents.

In a more recent article, Kelley (1975), writing for the Institute of Real Estate Management (IREM), told landlords that they were making a mistake if they maintained a zero vacancy rate. Kelley argued that landlords, in this case, would be underpricing their units and should, instead, raise rents, even if the vacancy rate went above 5 percent. Drawing on first-hand experience, Kelley showed the results of raising rents 7 percent across the board on a 490-unit garden apartment complex. Despite the fact that the vacancy rate went from zero to 6 percent, the total revenue *increased* by $320. A few months later, the thirty vacant units were rented out, increasing the total rent collected by $9,000 a month over the original total. The process of raising rents would be repeated until profit maximization occurred, which is measured by maintaining a steady vacancy rate.

This kind of strategy, however, is limited to large owners who can afford to have units vacant. We believe that, depending on the number of units owned, professional landlords will respond in different ways to vacancies. For small-scale professional landlords, units are either rented or vacant (Blank and Winnick 1953:199; McGuire 1981); even one or two vacancies can cut significantly into total revenues. For such owners, *any* rent reduction to fill vacancies will improve the total picture. McGuire (34) points out that, as a result, small landlords are more likely to use a strategy of "turnover minimization." Since small landlords cannot easily test the market to find the highest possible rent, they opt to minimize turnover by keeping rents low, "since it is better to get less rent from a stable tenant than to have a [temporary] vacancy at higher rents" (35). As a result, a housing market that is highly fragmented, with small, individual owners predominating, is likely to maintain low to zero vacancy by below-market rents. Conversely, a housing market that is characterized by large-scale sophisticated owners is likely to exhibit higher rents, coupled with high vacancy rates, so that an optimum investment return can be realized. Large owners are thus less responsive to changes in relative supply and vacancy than are smaller owners.[2]

In the previously mentioned study of landlords in Orange, New Jersey, Gilderbloom (1985c) found that the desire to attract "good tenants" frequently resulted in maintaining vacancies while suitable tenants were sought. Most large-scale professional landlords, in particular, felt that rents had to be high enough to discourage low-income persons from renting, out of fear that low-income tenants would frighten away well-to-do tenants. According to one owner, "I hold off units from renting until I get the right class of people. If you can't find good tenants don't rent it out. One obnoxious family and the rest of the tenants will run. Don't rent to someone on welfare; that doesn't help the community" (ibid., 166). Another owner elaborated: "I won't take welfare or children in my rentals. In other areas I limit the children. Yes, I will empty out a welfare building of 66 units. I'd rather be 75 percent full without welfare than 100 percent with welfare" (ibid.).

Landlords may allow vacancy rates to rise far above the 5 percent level, conventionally regarded as the dividing line between "loose" and "tight" housing markets, and still not lower rents due to such concerns. One landlord, with a 25 percent vacancy rate for his 125 units, expressed concern that if rents were lowered, "derelict and welfare families" would move in, frightening existing tenants and ultimately making the building desirable only to the very poor. He also noted that poor tenants could not afford annual rent increases, especially large ones. The strategy of maintaining high vacancy rates was seen as preferable to lowering rents and thereby reducing vacancy rates. According to this landlord, if the units came to be inhabited by "derelicts," the only way to make a profit would be to "burn down the building and collect insurance" (see also Gray 1979). Another large-scale professional landlord argued that an owner's return is limited when the apartment is inhabited by the poor: low incomes mean low rent levels. In this situation, he suggested that an owner "vacate the building, do a rehab job and bring in a higher class of tenants. . . . When you lower the economics of an area you can't raise rents" (Gilderbloom 1985c:166).

A number of large-scale landlords echoed the belief that extremely low vacancy levels indicated underpriced units that could, potentially, bring in substantially more rent. The optimum vacancy rate for a large building, it was argued, was not zero, but ranged from 3 up to 10 percent: "To run a good show you have to have a 5 to 10 percent vacancy rate. You must learn to stimulate other people to come in. If you have a 100 percent occupancy, your rents are too low. If you have a 3 room apartment at $150, rent it out for $165. If that doesn't work try $158. Market place tells you whether the rent is correct based on buyer behavior" (ibid., 167).

One landlord claimed that he "maintained" a 6 percent vacancy rate in his units in order to operate the building as efficiently as possible. Another landlord claimed that the strategy of maintaining vacancy rates was recommended by both the "Residential Apartment Managers and [the] Institute of Real Estate Management." Another large-scale professional landlord reported that if the rent were set too high and "move outs" occurred, he would lower rents, but never to a point where all the units were rented out.

Unlike large-scale professional landlords, small-scale owners often were not in an economic position to "maintain" a vacancy rate, as some large-scale landlords do. Most of the small-scale owners we interviewed, like amateur owners, sought to maintain a 100 percent occupancy rate. As one such apartment owner remarked, "I am opposed to vacancies psychologically." Another landlord noted, in more detail: "We have to have 100 percent occupancy rate in order to make it. We can't go over $300 a month without creating a vacancy rate. Other big units can have a vacancy. More units you have the less the expenses are"(ibid.).

As indicated above, small-scale professional landlords appear to set rents largely on the basis of implicit and explicit cues from the landlord community. As one of the landlords suggested, "We get ideas about what to charge from other landlords." While the goal is to reduce the vacancy rate to zero, landlords in this group calculated vacancies as part of their business costs. This practice provides a small cushion against income lost from vacancies and reduces the pressure to lower a unit's rent immediately, whenever it becomes vacant. Small-scale professional landlords often expressed confidence that vacant units would eventually be leased, since the asking price was comparable to that for similar units in the neighborhood.

Should the landlord perceive that a unit is "above market," the rent would be reduced accordingly, to "market levels." Small-scale professional landlords will rarely reduce rents below market to attract tenants. Such reductions could have a negative effect on the building's resale value, since this is normally determined in large part by the total rent revenue. Only one small-scale professional landlord argued that if a "good tenant" could not be found, he would keep the unit vacant.

Landlords may induce vacancies in order to gain federal and local tax advantages. Moreover, landlords with incomes in high tax brackets might purposely create vacancies in order to reduce their federal tax liability. On the local level, a landlord who is planning to appeal his or her tax assessment might purposely keep vacated units off the market, so that the rent roll is lessened and the case for an appeal is improved. For purposes of reselling rental units, by which a large proportion of a landlord's profits is usually made, owners might prefer to keep rent levels as high as possible, to show the "true value" of the apartment, as opposed to lowering rents to fill vacancies. This strategy is also applied for insurance purposes; for example, in case of fire, the owner(s) can claim a higher loss. In fact, some argue that the most efficient way for a landlord to optimize total rent rolls is to maintain a vacancy rate in the 5 percent area.

Amateur Landlords

RENTAL HOUSING AS A SHORT-TERM INVESTMENT

Amateur landlords, in contrast with professionals, tend to give greater weight to a variety of social and personal considerations in making rental decisions. Rather than strive only for the highest net return, amateurs often seek steady, long-term income. They generally maintain their units well, setting rents that are often below market (see, especially, Krohn, Fleming, and Manzer 1977, and Stegman 1972).

Of course, one factor that contributes to lower rents is lower costs. Amateurs often hold their properties for a long time, resulting in relatively low mortgage payments (or no payments at all, if the mortgage is paid). Also, maintenance costs are often lower for amateurs, since the owners either take care of maintenance and repairs or insist that the tenants do so.

LANDLORD–TENANT RELATIONS

Another factor contributing to the lower rents charged by amateurs, in comparison with professionals, is the former's face-to-face contacts with tenants. Desire for a high return is held partly in check by concerns for the tenants' welfare, a concern bred of face-to-face contact, friendship, and long-term acquaintance. Thus the amateur landlord often prefers to rent to family, friends, and long-term tenants at levels well below the market. Often, these landlords are not members of the local apartment owners' association, and may not think of themselves as a landlord in the popular sense.

Amateur landlords, in sum, typically show a very different orientation toward tenants than do professionals. For example, a tenant's income appears to play a minor role in the determination of rent, as rental levels are shaped by the needs of both parties. Dealing with a tenant—who might be a member of the family, a close friend, or someone who has been living in the same unit for a number of years—the amateur landlord frequently shows empathy and acts on personal considerations in adjusting rent levels. As one owner stated, "It's not even a business investment. I do all the repairs. I rent only to members of my family. The rent is based on what they can afford, no sound business acumen. In one of my apartments my mother lives for free" (Gilderbloom 1985c:165).

Making returns comparable to those from other kinds of investments is not usually a concern for these landlords. One such landlord remarked: "We don't want any return on investment. We just don't want to sell it because that is where we were born and raised. My parents built the house as a matter of fact, just after I was born and we all grew up there. It's right next door to my uncle, cousins and what not. Right across the road is where my grandparents live" (ibid.). In return for low or reduced rent, amateur landlords reported, their tenants might reciprocate by "keeping the place up" or "taking care of things."

FORMAL AND INFORMAL NETWORKS AND THE SETTING OF RENTS

Networks do not appear to play a major role in determining rents among amateur landlords. Amateurs generally avoid management companies, ordinarily do not belong to the local or statewide apartment owners' groups, and therefore lack the contacts to approach other landlords to find out what they are charging. As a typical practice, the amateur landlord consults immediate family members to decide what kind of rent is reasonable, given their operating costs and the needs of the tenant.

VACANCY RATES AND DETERMINATION OF RENT

Amateur landlords treated vacancies in two ways. If a tenant was needed so that the landlord could pay his or her mortgage, rents were held below market levels so the unit(s) could be rented immediately. Under such circumstances, vacancy rates were a fairly important force in maintaining low rent levels. On the other hand, if the mortgage was very low or had been paid off entirely, landlords could afford to be more selective in their choice of tenant—a fact that was particularly important if the landlord resided in the same building as the tenants. In certain cases, however, even amateur landlords would hold units off the market until a "suitable" tenant could be found by word-of-mouth advertising among friends.

DETERMINANTS OF RENT: AN INTERCITY ANALYSIS

In this section, we assess the impact of various determinants of rent through an examination of relatively autonomous housing markets. Given the impediments to "frictionless" market operation (identified in Chapter 3), along with the scarcity of empirical studies on the subject, an investigation of this kind seems warranted. The hope is to shed additional light on the factors that might affect rent in different cities.

In the present analysis, we examine all U.S. urbanized areas that could be considered relatively self-contained housing markets, free from the effects of adjacent market areas. To do this, we include all urbanized areas in the United States (excluding only Hawaii and Alaska) that meet these two criteria: the area (1) contains only one central city of 50,000 population or more and (2) is at least 20 miles from the nearest central city of 50,000 or more. The U.S. Bureau of the Census provides maps of each state, showing the location of each area and permitting us to distinguish those cities suitable for inclusion in this study. A large portion of the data base came from Appelbaum et al. (1976), although the original data set was extended to include additional variables and places, and was updated to 1980.

According to the 1980 Census, 140 such urbanized areas exist. The data are aggregated measures for the entire urbanized area, since we are interested in studying the impact of *inter*city sources of variation in rents. As we saw in Chapter 3, most analyses of the determinants of rents have focused almost exclusively on *intra*city sources of variation in demand for rental housing, focusing on such attributes as locational advantages, house characteristics, and environment. Our approach attempts to measure such variables at an aggregate level across different housing markets, along with several measures of supply and market structure. We are especially interested in the latter, and particularly in the degree of "professionalization" of the rental housing industry, which —for reasons indicated earlier in this chapter—we believe to be a highly neglected source of intercity variation in rents.

Determinants of Rent

The variables selected for the study were based on the models described in Chapter 3, subject to constraints on available data for the cities selected. Under the assumptions of a purely competitive marketplace, a principal determinant of rent should be the relative supply of rental housing, *ceteris paribus*. Accordingly, three variables were chosen to measure supply:

1. *Rental vacancy rate,* equal to number of year-round vacant units, available for rent, expressed as percentage of total rental inventory. The average vacancy rate for the 140 cities was 8 percent, with a standard deviation of 2 percent. Many economists argue that the vacancy rate is the best single measure of housing scarcity. When the vacancy rate is low, rents are expected to be high; conversely, areas with high vacancy should have lower rents.

2. *New construction,* measured as percentage of rental housing built between 1975 and 1980. Many theorists hold that because new construction reduces

scarcity, housing markets with large increases in new rental housing experience lower rent levels, in comparison with their slower-growth counterparts. On the other hand, it is often the case that rents in newly constructed buildings tend to be higher than rents in the existing inventory. The average percentage increase in new rental units over the period 1975–80 in our study was 17 percent, with a standard deviation of 8 percent.

3. *Proportion of total housing stock that is rental.* There are two conflicting hypotheses about the effect of this measure on rents. On the one hand, it is argued that housing markets with a large proportion of rentals provide tenants with a wide range of choices, leading to a more competitive market and, hence, lower rents. Conversely, cities with a low percentage of rentals would provide fewer options for tenants and correspondingly higher rents. Work by Anderson and Crocker (1971; see also Beyer 1966:134) has shown that as the proportion of rental housing units in a market increases, rents will fall. On the other hand, it can also be argued that in cities with high percentages of rental units, more income-property trading occurs, making investment in apartments more attractive for the professional landlord. This line of reasoning would lead one to expect higher rent levels in cities with a high proportion of rental housing. The percentage of housing units available as rentals averaged 36 percent in our cities, with a standard deviation of 6 percent.

We noted in Chapter 3 that most analyses of housing markets have focused on demand factors, with a near-complete exclusion of supply and institutional factors. The following aggregate variables were chosen to redress this inadequacy:

1. *Urbanized population,* shown in previous studies to be a good index of demand for housing and, hence, positively correlated with rent levels (Appelbaum 1978:29–37; Dreier, Gilderbloom, and Appelbaum 1980; U.S. Bureau of the Census 1973a; Hoch 1972). Analysts argue that larger places offer more amenities or advantages (sporting events, museums, restaurants, etc.) than smaller places; this results in a greater demand for the former and, consequently, higher rents. The average population of the cities studied was 261,200, with a standard deviation of 315,600.

2. *Decennial population growth rate (1970–80),* an index of growth-induced demand for housing. Research has found that rapidly growing cities tend to have higher rents because of an inability of construction to meet the higher demand for housing (Appelbaum 1978:37; Dreier, Gilderbloom, and Appelbaum 1980; Stegman and Sumka 1976; King and Mieszcowski 1973). New residents also tend to pay more for housing because of "information lag" (Stegman and Sumka 1976; King and Mieszcowski 1973). To protect themselves financially, landlords sometimes require more

rent, in the form of security or last-month deposits, from newcomers who do not have established credit or employment in the area. As a result, urban areas undergoing a large population increase will often be associated with high rent increases. Existing residents, through their network of friends, have a better chance of finding the "best buy"; no such grapevine exists for newcomers in the housing market (Stegman and Sumka 1976; King and Mieszcowski 1973). Our cities grew an average of 21 percent between 1970 and 1980, with a standard deviation of 24 percent.

3. *Regional differences* can also affect demand and, therefore, rents. It has been found that rents are generally lower in the South than in other regions in the United States, even when other factors are controlled (U.S. Bureau of the Census 1972; Appelbaum 1978). Whether this condition would hold today, in light of the economic boom in Sunbelt cities, is open to question. Forty-four percent of the urban areas in our study are in the South.

4. *Percentage of nonwhites* can have a significant impact on demand and, therefore, the cost of housing (Ridker and Henning 1967; Anderson and Crocker 1971; Susser 1982). It is unclear, however, which direction this impact takes. For example, Anderson and Crocker (1971) found that the percentage of nonwhites had either a negative or positive impact on housing price, depending on which city they examined. Ridker and Henning's (1967) analysis of Census tract data in St. Louis found that the price of single-family housing rises in nonwhite tracts. Stegman and Sumka's (1976) analysis of nonmetropolitan housing markets in North Carolina found a small positive relationship between race and rent. As a result, two alternative hypotheses have emerged to explain these contradictory results. One of them argues that because of discrimination by whites, nonwhites pay higher rents for equivalent housing. The other argument counters that when nonwhites live in an area, the housing demand falls because of racial fear among whites (Muth 1969:107–8). Although we include a measure for this variable, we make no prediction concerning its impact. Seventeen percent of the population in our study were classified as nonwhite, with a standard deviation of 14 percent.

5. *Quality of rental stock,* another common index of demand, is measured by two variables: percentage of units lacking plumbing[3] and proportion of units built before 1940. Studies have found that these two variables are significant determinants of housing prices (Cubbin 1970; Wilkinson 1971; Kain and Quigley 1970; Anderson and Crocker 1971; Stegman and Sumka 1976). Units that are either old or lack some plumbing tend to have a lower value. Lowry (1960) argues that demand for these units falls because of technological obsolescence, style obsolescence, and deterioration. Accordingly, one might predict that markets with a large proportion of rental units that are old or lacking in plumbing facilities would have lower rent levels, although it is possible that this effect could be offset because of rents that are bid up in the

fewer remaining higher-quality units. Consequently, we would predict either a negative relationship between these measures of poor housing quality and rents, or no relationship. In our cities, approximately 2.3 percent (standard deviation 1.2 percent) of the units lacked adequate plumbing, while 22 percent (standard deviation 14 percent) were built before 1940.

6. *Median family income* is a strong measure of demand for rental housing. In a perfectly competitive housing market, median income should not affect rents, once other differences in demand and supply are controlled. However, to the extent that competition is imperfect, landlords will be able to charge "what the market will bear" and, hence, high-income areas will pay high rents for similar-quality housing. Ball (1973) has therefore argued that an adequately specified model of housing price determinants must include income as an independent variable when a cross-section of cities is examined.[4] Anderson and Crocker (1971) have found income to be significantly related to the determination of house prices in their studies of Washington, St. Louis, and Kansas City (see also Whitte 1975). Vaughan (1972) and Harvey (1973) argue that rent for low-income tenants is tied more to income than to the quality of the housing unit. Stegman and Sumka (1976), using regression analysis to test Vaughan's argument, find only a small overall relationship between income and rents. They report that rent will only increase 1 percent if income increases 10 percent. The median income in the cities studied averaged $19,500, with a standard deviation of $2,200.

7. *Median home cost* is a possible index of the demand for rental housing, since high costs of homeownership can force households to rent rather than buy. Whereas in the 1950s two-thirds of all families could afford to purchase a home, in the late 1970s the ratio had dropped below one-quarter (Frieden and Solomon 1977). The percentage of first-time home buyers fell from 36 percent in 1977 to 14 percent in 1981 (Christian and Parliment 1982). In California, the State Department of Housing and Community Development estimated in 1979 that 90 percent of the state's renters could not afford to purchase a median-price home (California Housing Task Force 1979; California Department of Housing and Community Development 1977). The decision to buy usually occurs when the cost of renting is roughly the same as monthly payments on a house, after adjusting for the tax advantages of homeownership. Thus the price of homes could create a top limit on rents. This "ceiling," however, rose steeply during the past fifteen years as the cost of homes climbed. Rents appear to vary directly with the cost of homes, leading some to conclude that soaring home prices were largely responsible for rapidly rising rents during the late 1970s and early 1980s. The median home price is $47,600 among the cities studied, while the standard deviation is $13,500.

8. *Climate* is a neglected yet potentially significant determinant of demand for housing. Boyer and Savageau (1981:1–2) argue that "most people prefer (or say they prefer) mild, sunny climates. . . . Biometeorologists— scientists who study the connection between weather and health—generally agree that an average temperature of 65 degrees Fahrenheit, with 65 percent humidity, is ideal for work, play and general well-being." Boyer and Savageau (1981: 4) have ranked urbanized areas according to their climates. Beginning with a maximum base of 1,000 points, they deducted points according to "negative indicators": very hot and very cold months, seasonal temperature variations, heating and cooling days, freezing days, zero-degree days, and 90 degree days. As a result of this system, places like Green Bay, Wisconsin (score: 425), are ranked near the bottom, while California coastal communities, like Santa Barbara (score: 861), are rated at the top. Climate rankings should play a role in determining rent levels for two reasons (Hoch 1972). First—other things being equal—demand for places like Santa Barbara (with a climate described as "paradise") is bound to be greater than for Green Bay ("hot and humid summers, bitter cold winters"). Second, given that the cost of gas, electricity, heat, and air conditioning can be considerably higher in places like Green Bay, a majority of renters in the former area will have less money to spend on rent after utilities are paid for. Conversely, tenants have more money to spend on rents in urban places that have a mild climate. The average climate score in the studied cities was 542, and the standard deviation was 103.

9. *Professionalization of the rental housing industry* is a potentially significant barrier to the competitive operation of rental markets, as we argued in Chapter 3. The dominance of professional landlords in a community may help to drive average rents up. To recapitulate the argument, there are two kinds of landlords in most housing markets: large-scale professionals and small-scale amateurs (see Lawson 1980; Krohn, Fleming, and Manzer 1977; Stegman 1972; Gilderbloom 1985c). Research suggests that the rent-setting behavior of these two groups differs significantly, reflecting the distinctive economic situations and social concerns of each. Stegman (29) argues that "sophistication and permanence of operations increases with size of holdings." Professional landlords pursue the highest net profit in economically rational terms, being primarily interested in short-term returns that are based in large part on the tax-sheltering aspects of real estate investment. Generally, their rate of return must be high, since alternative investments always beckon. This pushes rents up, both through speculative pressures and the need to maintain a competitively profitable cash flow. The scale of such ownership places them in a strategic position to administer rents in a community. In contrast, the amateur landlord tends to give great weight to a variety of social and personal considerations, and—rather than striving for the highest net return—often seeks only

steady, long-term income from rents. Amateur operators generally maintain their units well and set rents that often are below market (Krohn, Fleming, and Manzer 1977; Gilderbloom 1985c). Also, they are under less pressure to raise rents frequently, because their long-term property holdings result in low monthly mortgage payments and because their alternative investment horizons are limited.

We have two measures of this variable: the percentage of a city's rental housing stock that is comprised of ten or more rental units at a single address, and the percentage comprised of fifty or more units. In the cities in our study, the former percentage has increased from 18 percent in 1970 to 22 percent in 1980; the latter has increased from 5 percent to 13 percent. "Mom and pop" apartment units are being demolished and replaced by large, professionally managed, multi-unit complexes.

Results of the Analysis[5]

To examine these relationships, we performed an ordinary least-squares regression analysis across the 140 communities that satisfied our two criteria, estimating 1980 median rent as a function of various combinations of the preceding set of variables. We utilize this approach because we are interested at the present time in comparing the effects of differing conditions *across* housing markets, rather than analyzing the determinants of rents *within* housing markets. We recognize, of course, that our conclusions are limited to inferences concerning the former, rather than the latter. It should be emphasized that no attempt was made to specify a full casual model of the determinants of intercity rent. Rather, the main focus was on the impact of a few variables measuring supply, market structure, and income, taking informal account of other relevant factors in the literature. The method thus isolates certain factors of anticipated importance and estimates their apparent influence.[6] The models satisfy the requisite assumptions for ordinary least-squares multiple regression analysis.[7]

The results of the regression analysis are presented in Table 5.1. Two alternative models are examined, differing only on the measure of professionalization employed: equation 1 uses the percentage of ten or more rental units at a single address, and equation 2 uses the percentage of fifty or more units. Additionally, Table 5.1 adjusts rent for the number of rooms—a control for quality of the unit (equations 3 and 4). We shall first discuss the determinants of rent, then rent adjusted for quality of the unit.

The variables in the equations account for 77 percent and 75 percent of the variation in rent, respectively. In equation 1, seven of the predictor variables are statistically significant (at the 10 percent probability level, or better); in equation 2, eleven are significant. To evaluate the importance of the independent variables, standardized regression coefficients (betas) are examined,

TABLE 5.1
FACTORS AFFECTING 1980 INTERCITY RENT DIFFERENTIALS AND THE
IMPACT OF LANDLORD AND TENANT SOCIAL CHARACTERISTICS

Variables	1980 MEDIAN MONTHLY RENT		1980 MEDIAN ROOM RENT	
	Equation 1	Equation 2	Equation 3	Equation 4
Median house cost ('80)	.29‡	.34‡	.29‡	.36‡
	[.0009]	[.0002]	[.0003]	[.0003]
Vacancy rate ('80)	.06	.10*	.05	.10
	[.845]	[1.407]	[.2090]	[.4235]
Region in U.S. (South)	−.10	−.12†	−.03	−.06
	[−6.569]	[−8.48]	[−.524]	[−1.3184]
% units lacking	.07	.13†	.15†	.23‡
plumbing ('80)	[1.841]	[3.711]	[1.304]	[2.0605]
Climate score	.15‡	.12†	.13†	.09
	[.05]	[.040]	[.014]	[.0096]
% housing rental ('80)	.05	.14‡	.07	.19‡
	[.2470]	[.77]	[.1198]	[.3309]
Urban population ('80)	−.05	−.01	−.06	−.004
	[−.000005]	[−.000001]	[−.000001]	[−.0000001]
% rentals created	.03	.05	.03	.04
(1975–80)	[.148]	[.20]	[.0387]	[.0582]
% population growth	.12*	.12*	.06	.06
(1970–80)	[.1723]	[.1697]	[.0286]	[.0280]
% non-white ('80)	−.12*	−.12†	−.16†	−.16†
	[−.2926]	[−.296]	[−.1168]	[−.1174]
Professionalization	.24‡	—	.31‡	—
(10 or more rentals	[1.129]	—	[.4490]	—
at each address, '80)				
Professionalization	—	.12†	—	.16‡
(50 or more rentals,	—	[.1965]	—	[.0838]
at each address, '80)				
Median income ('80)	.38‡	.45‡	.28‡	.37‡
	[.00595]	[.0070]	[.0013]	[.0017]
% rentals built before 1940	−.18†	−.21‡	−.21†	−.25‡
	[−.4293]	[−.5190]	[−.1549]	[−.1890]
R Square	.77	.75	.71	.69
F	31.695	29.023	23.134	20.67
N	140	140	136	136

*≤ .10
†≤ .05
‡≤ .01

Note: standardized regression coefficients are presented first; unstandardized regression coefficients are in brackets.

permitting the researcher to make direct comparisons of the relative importance of each variable (Pindyck and Rubinfeld 1976:71).[8]

Looking first at equation 1, we find a number of indicators of demand that are significant in predicting rent: home price, climate, proportion of units built before 1940 (a measure of housing-stock age and, hence, quality), and median income. All are significant at the 5 percent level or better, while population growth and percentage of nonwhites are significant at the 10 percent level.

As predicted, the cost of homeownership has a strong, positive impact on rents, suggesting that homeownership acts as a lid on how much landlords can get for rents in a particular area. The variable that measures climatic mildness is also positively correlated with median rents, as predicted. Urban areas with a large proportion of older housing stock have lower rent levels, suggesting that lower quality has an aggregate depressing effect on rents.

Median income is the strongest predictor of rents, suggesting that in many housing markets landlords are able to charge what the market will bear, even after differences in demand and quality are taken into account. Income, apparently, has a stronger effect in urban areas of 50,000 or more than in smaller, nonmetropolitan urban places. Stegman and Sumka (1976:151), for example, found in their study of small nonmetropolitan cities that income had only a small impact on rents. They found that a 10 percent increase in income leads to only a 1 percent increase in rents. In a study of intercity rent variations for large cities in New York state, Vitaliano (1983) calculated that a 10 percent increase in income would result in a 9 percent increase in rents. Our results lie between the two, indicating that a 10 percent increase in incomes would produce a 6 percent increase in rents.

Percentage increase in population weakly but positively impacts rents, supporting the hypothesis that in rapidly growing urban areas, newcomers pay higher rents (Stegman and Sumka 1976:159), because they tend to be ignorant of local market conditions and because they often lack jobs and credit, thereby constituting a risk. This result shows why "growth" is supported by developers and landlords (see Logan and Molotch 1986). A slight negative relationship was found between the proportion of nonwhites and rent levels, supporting Shlay's (1983) finding that white residents devalue residential areas that have a high percentage of nonwhites.

Looking next at indicators of supply, we find that rents are not lower in places with favorable supply conditions. On the contrary, all three variables that measure supply—vacancy rate, new construction, and proportion of housing stock rental—were found to be either nonsignificant or had signs that were in a weak positive direction.

Vacancy rate is positively, but not significantly, associated with rents. This result lends support to our reasoning in Chapter 3. On the one hand, it suggests that the institutional structure of landlording may indeed serve to restrain competition, so that the absence of scarcity, by itself, is not sufficient to drive rents downward. It may also be true, however, that for some owners, a low or zero vacancy rate may not be an economically optimal situation, and that some level of vacancy may be maintained as a rational business strategy. This would, of course, weaken the relationship between vacancy and rents.

The absence of a relationship between new construction and rents is supportive of our hypothesis that housing markets do not behave competitively, for the reasons previously outlined. These findings are in sharp contrast to conventional economic thinking, which argues that urban areas, undergoing significant increases in new rental housing construction, will experience lower rent levels because of the increase in vacancy. Our results show this not to be the case. We also note that there is no significant zero-order correlation between construction and vacancy, suggesting that the construction of new housing stock generally responds to market demand and has little appreciable effect on supply.

Our earlier work used the proportion of housing stock that is rental as a proxy measure of the degree of market professionalization, on the grounds that markets with a high percentage of rentals are likely to be characterized by a great deal of economic activity and therefore prove attractive to large real estate investors (Appelbaum and Gilderbloom 1983; Gilderbloom 1985d, Table 2).[9] Although we acknowledged that this is an imperfect indicator, we found a positive association with rents in both 1970 and 1980. In our present equations, we have a more direct measure of professionalization, the inclusion of which apparently eliminates the significance of our earlier variable.[10]

Finally, we turn to our measures of the professionalization of the local rental housing industry. Two indicators are used (the percentage of ten-plus units at a single location and the percentage of fifty-plus units), since we lack a clear understanding of the relationship between scale of ownership and professionalization. Comparing equations 1 and 2, we see that regardless of which measure is employed, there is a strong and statistically significant relationship between professionalization and rents. Rents are clearly higher in markets characterized by large-scale rental units. This finding supports our belief that the institutional structure of housing markets is a major (if neglected) factor in the determination of rents.[11] Rent is not simply the result of economic forces in unconstrained housing markets; rather, it is (at least in part) a social result. The results lend credence to the earlier work of Cronin (1983), who found that intraurban rent differentials were correlated with the number of rental units in a neighborhood controlled by a single landlord.

Equation 2 displays the same model, except for the variable that measures landlord professionalization. The results show that the relationship between professionalization and rents is strong in both instances, although the effect is twice as large when professionalization is operationalized as ten-plus (rather than fifty-plus) units. Additionally, in equation 2 the proportion of housing stock rental is now significant, along with an additional measure of housing

TABLE 5.2
FACTORS AFFECTING 1970 INTERCITY RENT DIFFERENTIALS AND THE
IMPACT OF LANDLORD AND TENANT SOCIAL CHARACTERISTICS

	1970 MEDIAN MONTHLY RENT		1970 MEDIAN ROOM RENT	
Variables	Equation 5	Equation 6	Equation 7	Equation 8
Median house cost ('70)	.12*	.14†	.22†	.27‡
	[.00067]	[.00080]	[.00037]	[.00044]
Vacancy rate ('70)	.06	.07	.02	.04
	[.36829]	[.48695]	[.03476]	[.08780]
Region in U.S. (South)	−.25‡	−.29‡	−.21†	−.28‡
	[−8.6173]	[−9.90300]	[−2.14823]	[.08780]
% units lacking	.01	−.004	.01	.01
plumbing ('70)	[.02961]	[−.02019]	[.02039]	[.00436]
Climate score	.02	.03	−.02	−.01
	[.0035]	[.0048]	[−.00115]	[−.00023]
% housing rental ('70)	.02	.05	−.05	.01
	[.05558]	[.1424]	[−.04142]	[.00556]
Urban population ('70)	−.04	−.02	.07	−.05
	[−.000003]	[−1.66486]	[−.00000]	[−.00000]
% rentals created	.13*	.24‡	.03	.23†
(1965–70)	[.26085]	[.50023]	[.017367]	[−.035230]
% population growth	.18‡	.15†	.11*	.06
(1960–70)	[.08103]	[.06881]	[.01500]	[.00890]
% non-white ('70)	.07*	.07	.03	.02
	[.01354]	[.01216]	[.00179]	[.001301]
Professionalization	.22†	—	.45‡	—
(10 or more rentals	[.43070]	—	[.25715]	—
at each address, '70)				
Professionalization	—	.06†	—	.18†
(50 or more rentals,	—	[.34]	—	[.288850]
at each address, '70)				
Median income 1970	.46‡	.49‡	.22*	.28†
	[.00725]	[.00771]	[.00102]	[.00130]
% rentals built				
before 1940	−.12†	−.10*	−.15*	−.12
	[−.11418]	[−.10073]	[−.04366]	[−.03523]
R Square	.88	.87	.78	.70
F	55.59881	49.86564	26.2362	20.94747
N	112	112	110	110

*≤ .10
†≤ .05
‡≤ .01

Note: standardized regression coefficients are presented first; unstandardized regression coefficients are in brackets.

quality (the percentage of units lacking some plumbing) and regional location. Rents are now found to be higher in places with a high proportion of rentals, with a higher percentage of units lacking plumbing, and outside the South. All other variables remain roughly the same as in equation 1 in terms of sign and overall impact.

Equation 2 isolates the effects of a high degree of professionalized rental housing markets, since it controls for the domination of extremely large apartment complexes. We may conjecture that in such highly professionalized markets, competition is further reduced, thereby producing the following results. First, a large percentage of housing stock as rental units permits considerable market activity, thereby helping to drive up rents. Second, a larger proportion of substandard rental housing does not reduce rents, but drives them up, perhaps because in highly professionalized markets tenants in the remaining higher-quality units have little choice but to pay higher rents.[12]

Equations 3 and 4 recalculate the dependent variable (median monthly rent) to room rent. This allows an additional control for the quality of the unit. This change in the specification of the dependent variable does not substantially alter the results found in equations 1 and 2. In other equations (not shown), various combinations of median home price, climate mildness, and the professional landlord index were removed from the model. In all cases, the key measures of supply, vacancy rate, and new construction remain unrelated to rent.

A replication of this analysis with 1970 data, presented in Table 5.2, found that one definition of professionalization, percentage of rental housing consisting of 50-plus units at one address, was not significant in 1970. This suggests that the importance of professionalization has grown over the past decade, as the percentage of large apartment complexes has increased from 5 to 13 percent.

SUMMARY

Rent is conventionally understood to be a function of supply and demand. This argument has usually been tested by using variables that measure the attributes and qualities of particular rental units on an intracity level. The results show that a substantial proportion of the variance in rent can be explained by examining a rental unit's attributes. The relative importance of *supply* on rents has yet to be fully examined.

In an attempt to shed light on this issue, we examined 140 relatively self-contained urban housing markets in the United States to study the relationship between supply factors, income, landlord professionalization, and rent. The observed relationship between supply factors and rent provides little support for the conventional viewpoint. Vacancy rates, percentage housing-stock rental, and new construction are found not to be significantly related to rents when examined in a model that includes measures of professionalization. Income was found to have the strongest impact on rents, followed by average home price. More importantly, in our view, landlord professionalization was found to be positively associated with rents. Population growth rate, region, climate mildness, percentage nonwhite, and rental housing quality were also found to be significant in various versions of the model. About three-quarters of the variance in rent were explained by the models.

Although we found no statistically significant relationship between vacancy rate and rent, it is clear that at some level of supply, relative to demand, rental housing markets could be expected to behave according to the model of pure competition. At what level of vacancy does this occur? As we saw in Chapter 3, a 5 percent vacancy rate is conventionally believed to be the point where competition is restored. In our earlier work (Appelbaum and Gilderbloom 1986), we argued that the critical point may be closer to 9 percent.[13]

The case of Texas is instructive, since the collapse of its oil-based economy has caused high unemployment and outmigration, resulting in vacancy rates of 10 to 20 percent in metropolitan areas. In Dallas, where vacancy rates ranged from 9 to 14 percent during the period 1983–86, monthly rents increased by some 11 percent over the same period (from $400 to $443) (Drummond 1986:1). In Houston, vacancy rates have been considerably higher, ranging from 16 to 19 percent; rents have declined by some 17 percent (from $375 to $313) (ibid.). Barton Smith,[14] director of the Center for Public Policy at the University of Houston, predicts that once the vacancy rate falls below 10 percent, profitability will be restored and rents will again begin to rise.

In both these cases, 10 percent appears to be the point at which competition again occurs—a level consistent with our earlier findings (see Appelbaum and Gilderbloom 1986). We strongly suspect that while low vacancy rates are always associated with higher rents, high vacancy rates are not necessarily associated with lowered rents.

We believe that this analysis strongly supports our earlier contention that rental housing markets do not operate competitively, particularly where ownership is highly professionalized and vacancy rates are below a critical level, which in some places may be as high as 10 percent. Our variable for measuring professionalization probably serves as a rough indicator of owner-ship concentration.

We argued in Chapter 3 that as concentration increases, so does cooperative price setting by and among landlords. This is one reason why tenants' income plays such a large role in determining rents: landlords are partially able to set rents according to the ability of tenants to pay. This would be reinforced in markets where the high costs of homeownership trap many households as long-term renters, who would otherwise become homeowners.

Stated somewhat differently: in noncompetitive housing markets, wage gains among workers may be offset by increases in the cost of rental housing. Contrary to the findings of the President's Commission on Housing, we believe that simply raising incomes and building additional housing will not solve the problems of affordability.

6
Local Supply Restraints and Housing Costs

In the previous chapter we sought to demonstrate that the institutional structure of rental housing is an important, though neglected, determinant of rents. In the present chapter we turn to an argument that has hardly suffered from neglect: high housing prices are primarily due to excessive local interferences in the production of rental housing. As we shall see, this argument is widely shared, by economists, policymakers, and even by tenant activists. We believe it is wrong. We will first present the case against regulation, examining it in light of existing studies, then offer our own study of a highly regulated California housing market.

THE OVERREGULATION HYPOTHESIS

California is, arguably, the most restrictive state in the nation with respect to statewide and local housing regulations. At the same time, California has some of the highest housing prices in the country. These two factors have led many researchers to conclude that the former is responsible for the latter, and that California is simply an extreme example of the adverse housing prices that result from excessive governmental regulation. The most vocal proponent of this view is Bernard Frieden, whose influential book *The Environmental Protection Hustle* (1979a) blames environmental restrictions and growth controls for California's housing troubles.

Johnson (1982), in his introduction to a Pacific Institute collection of articles that argue that growth controls, land-use planning, and even zoning are the principal sources of housing inflation, summarizes this viewpoint when he notes (9) that

> normally, this increased demand [for housing in California] would stimulate the production of housing, and price increases would be modest. . . . However, the supply of housing in California has been regulated in such a way as to prevent that increase in the last decade. Instead of a supply response, there has largely been a response in prices—higher prices. Growth control measures such as restrictive zoning, water and sewer moratoria, building codes, rent controls, and condominium conversion controls have all had the effect of reducing the available land and housing over what they might have been without those policies. The ultimate result has been an increase in housing prices.

Johnson contends that "the unintended consequences in the regulation of the housing market are such that today, throughout California 90 percent of the renters cannot afford to buy median-priced homes" (5).

This position has been echoed in many quarters. The Urban Land Institute, for example, while acknowledging the importance of extralocal factors, concludes that "it has become evident that growing public restrictions on development, coupled with the decreasing financial resources of many communities, have greatly exacerbated the problem of rising housing costs" (ULI 1980). President Reagan's Commission on Housing, while acknowledging that nonlocal factors (such as federal deficit spending) are in part responsible for housing inflation, holds state and local governments responsible for having excessively regulated the housing industry. The President's Commission singles out "construction standards, environmental restrictions, Davis-Bacon wage requirements, the Federal Flood Insurance Program, municipal rent control and condominium/cooperative conversion laws, and local land-use policies" as major causes of the housing crisis (President's Commission on Housing 1981:ii). The remedy calls for encouraging a

> stable economic environment for homebuilding by reducing restrictions on the industry and terminating excessive regulation of land development and housing production. The free market would then be able to provide housing at lower prices and thereby make housing more widely available. These measures will enable the market to meet future housing demand. [3–4]

This argument has strong bipartisan credentials. It first was made by President Carter's Task Force on Housing Costs (1979), and by other federal studies as well (see, for example, U.S. Comptroller General 1979; U.S. HUD 1979), and it underlies the Reagan administration's housing program, which calls for deregulation, urban enterprise zones, and dismantling all governmental controls over the private sector.

We term this argument the *overregulation hypothesis* to convey the sense that regulations are considered to be unnecessary or excessive, usually with regard to some unspecified standard.[1] To better understand the concept of overregulation, it is useful to classify governmental regulation of land and housing into two broad categories (Elliot 1981), according to whether such regulations primarily affect the quantity (for example, downzonings, growth ceilings, construction quotas) or the quality of new housing (for example, landscaping requirements, ecosystem preservation, architectural aesthetics). While the two types of restrictions can be closely related in practice, they may differ in the way they exert price effects. Restrictions that lower allowable densities or establish urban development limits may induce a scarcity of land for housing, and hence, by decreasing potential supply, indirectly cause inflation (see Ohls et al. 1974; Stull 1974; Black and Dunau 1981).

On the other hand, other requirements (solar stub-ins, open space, impact reports) directly push up developers' costs—which may then be passed on to consumers (Seidel 1978). These costs have been estimated to add as much as 30 percent to housing prices (National Association of Home Builders 1982:5; California Construction Industry Research Board 1975), although many studies place the figure considerably lower, with estimates ranging from 2 to 8 percent, and most falling under 5 percent (see, for example, Franklin and Muller 1977; Stull 1974; Orange County Cost of Housing Committee 1975; Tagge 1976; and Bickert, Browne, and Coddington 1976).

A final source of price inflation, derived from the other two, is that developers who somehow manage to bear the accumulated costs of gaining market access may find themselves in a *quasi-monopolistic position* and, hence, able to exact price increments not otherwise possible (Dowall 1980a:119).

The full statement of the overregulation hypothesis, insofar as it bears on housing prices and rents, can be set down as follows:

1. For certain urban areas, policies of constraint cumulate to limit the aggregate growth of housing. That is, the scale of effects transcends the effects associated with the traditional exclusive suburb (for which growth control in the form of large-lot zoning has always been present). What is new is that outcomes are determined for entire housing market areas. Frieden (1979a:139) asserts, for example, that in such large metropolitan areas as San Francisco the effect of growth controls has been to block a "very large" amount of housing—"large enough to make a difference in the price and availability of housing in the region."

2. These market effects are prevalent in parts of the country where market interference has been most intrusive. For example, California's price parity with the rest of the country ended in 1974, resulting in a rapidly growing home-price differential. This differential is attributed in large part to environmental regulations, although other factors (for example, the price of money) are occasionally recognized as part of the problem. In other words,

taken together, all regulations are treated, under the overregulation hypothesis, as having a single effect on housing prices and rents: to raise them.
3. As a corollary, it is argued that while these detrimental price effects fall on all consuming groups, low-income people are especially hard hit: they cannot afford to purchase homes, and they confront a rapidly diminishing rental housing stock that is characterized by escalating rents. Furthermore, given the spillover from the single-family housing market to the rental market, price effects on the former will carry over to the latter, even if rental units are not similarly regulated: would-be owners are driven to compete with other renters for the available stock of rental units.
4. In some instances, increased housing costs mean that workers can no longer be attracted to the local labor force; existing industries fail and new ones cannot be attracted. Local wealth is no longer generated, unemployment goes up, retail trade diminishes, and other service business is destabilized. Thus higher housing costs inevitably loop back to stifle economic growth (Kimball and Shulman 1980).

In sum, proponents of the overregulation hypothesis argue that environmental constraints have lowered the quality of housing, imposing harsh economic tradeoffs upon those of modest means who remain in the affected areas. These policies, they argue, should be abolished or at least balanced against the costs they induce.

PRICE EFFECTS OF REGULATION: SOME GENERAL CONSIDERATIONS

According to Frieden (1979b:24–25), San Francisco's "1977 [home sales] price level was one and one-half times the national average, with most of the difference probably resulting from the combined effects of growth restrictions, environmental politics, lawsuits, construction delays, and project revisions." Similarly Gruen and Gruen (1977) attribute 20 to 30 percent of San Jose's price inflation during the decade 1967–76 to that city's growth-management policies, in a study that assumed *all* price increases for land were the direct result of such policies, irrespective of general inflation and other market factors (Katz and Rosen 1980:26). Frieden (1982:28) attributes 38 percent of the increase in new-home costs in Orange County during the period 1972–78 to large lot sizes, development fees, and land restrictions in general.

Even anti-growth attitudes have been found to raise prices. In a study of 1976 sales in fifty Bay Area communities, Gabriel and Wolch (1980:13) found that sales prices were 8 percent higher (some $4,200) in cities where a majority of city council representatives were antidevelopment, once characteristics of the housing stock and other indices of regulation were statistically controlled. As stated by the Urban Land Institute: "It has become evident that state and local regulations are responsible in part for the dramatic increases in housing costs that have occurred in recent years" (Priest 1980).

How compelling is the evidence that regulation is responsible for rising housing costs? Before we review earlier studies, it is useful to recall that regulations are not the only influences on local housing supply, and that supply itself is only half of the equation. These caveats may seem obvious, but most studies ignore larger market factors that influence local supply and demand. It is clear, for example, that the state of the national economy powerfully influences housing construction; one study, for example, found that 71 percent of national housing starts are predicted simply by the growth of constant-dollar GNP (Weintraub 1982:89–90).

Regional demand shifts are likewise important. In a study that controlled for a number of supply and demand variables, Stutz and Kartman (1982:232) found that per capita income, along with solar radiation and seasonal temperature differences (the latter two variables are surrogates for regional demand shifts), explained almost two-thirds of the variance in housing prices. It is not surprising, therefore, to find that prices in California have risen much more rapidly than the national average during the past decade. What *is* surprising is the numerous studies that attribute all such inflation exclusively to local restrictions.

Furthermore, new housing construction typically accounts for only a small percentage of the total housing stock, and restrictions on construction are likely to have only a marginal effect on overall price levels: "Production of new housing in most cities amounts to no more than 3 percent of the existing stock and thus a 50 percent cut in this *flow* supply would amount to a cut of only 1.5 percent in *stock* supply in the first year" (Markusen 1979:153). Markusen attributes price increases in Canada during the period 1972–75 primarily to significantly increased demand from rising real incomes, falling real mortgage rates, rising rate of inflation, and the introduction of high-ratio mortgages. After analyzing a number of models, he concludes that "large, unanticipated changes in new supply may not have significant effects on asset price" (163).

The findings reported in Chapter 5—that rents are unrelated to supply—support Markusen's conclusion. In that discussion we offered another interpretation of these results: Due to the institutional structure of the rental housing industry, cooperative pricing practices among landlords may strongly mute the supposed relationship between supply and price. The preceding section, where we examined in some detail the social organization of landlording, provides additional support for this reasoning.

Primary Effects of Regulation

REDUCTION IN HOUSING SUPPLY
Moratoria, permit-allocation systems, urban limit lines, and density restrictions all serve to restrict the supply of housing. A large number of studies have examined the relationship between such supply restrictions and price.

Katz and Rosen (1980), in a study of sixty-four Bay Area cities, treated price as a function of such characteristics as income, property tax rates, commuting time to San Francisco, population, age, presence of a moratorium or growth-management plan, and the sum of development fees. They found that building moratoria and other growth-management plans increased 1979 housing prices by 18 to 28 percent (fees were not significant in their equation). Their study fails to model demand adequately however, since there are no variables to tap recent population growth or other demand pressures that might have simultaneously bid up the price for housing and led to growth controls in certain communities.

Additionally, four of their five regression equations had multiple R-squares of 0.99 or higher, strongly suggesting significant problems of multicollinearity among their independent variables. Gabriel and Wolch (1980), in a study of 1976 sales in fifty Bay Area communities, regressed price on structural characteristics of housing units, neighborhood attributes, measures of public finance, vacancy, accessibility to employment, and several indicators of restrictiveness (large lot zoning, development fees, city council attitudes toward growth). They found that "after controlling for traditional determinants of house prices, community land-use controls account for approximately 14 percent of the price of a typical Bay Area home" (14). However, their equation fails to specify differences in demand, which very likely account for a major part of the price differentials they observe.

In a study of ninety-seven Bay Area cities during the period 1977–79, Dowall and Landis (1982) regressed price on indices of land availability, density, development fees, changes in housing supply, vacancy rates, employment access, income, tax rates, and house size. They found that tax rates and supply variables were not significant in linear versions of their model. When the logarithmic form of the variables was used, however, they found that a 10 percent reduction in land resulted in a small price increase ($450), while a 10 percent increase in density reduced sales price by about $1,000 (81–82). They concluded that "after accounting for inflation, the price effects of such controls are far less than anticipated" (83). According to their econometric estimates of new housing prices, "the combined effect of increasing development densities by one unit per acre, reducing development fees by 50 percent, and doubling supplies of vacant land—all drastic steps—would be to lower the sales price of a new home by $6000. This estimate amounts to roughly 6 percent of the average price of a new Bay Area home in 1979" (88).

In a study of 559 sales in Florida, Nicholas (1981) looked at the price effects of regulation, along with various size/amenity characteristics. He found that while the latter were significant in explaining price, the regulation variable was significant only at the 0.1 probability level. The price increment attributed to regulation was estimated at approximately $4,700, which amounted to 4 to 8 percent of the sales price of a single-family home, depending on the number of bedrooms, bathrooms, and other characteristics (392–93). Since Nicholas elsewhere finds that Florida developers estimate the direct cost of regulation at approximately $550 per unit, he concludes that roughly 12 percent of the price differential between regulated and nonregulated units ($550/4,700) can be attributed to the direct regulatory costs experienced by the builder; the remainder result from increased scarcity (393).

DIRECT REGULATORY COSTS

Government regulation can add directly to housing cost in a variety of ways. Large subdivisions may carry requirements for environmental impact studies, whose cost the developer must bear, and additional fees may be levied for many other purposes. Local authorities may require environmental mitigations, site improvements, and other dedication requirements: extra open space, various facilities and amenities, and the basic infrastructure. Enhanced building codes may be adopted. According to Dowall (1980a:117), "developers are willing to provide costly amenities in order to obtain development approval," particularly where permit point systems reward the provision of amentities.

While many such impositions have long been accepted as part of the legitimate responsibility of localities to provide for the general health, safety, and welfare, developers increasingly criticize what they regard as "unnecessary" or "excessive" regulation that exceeds the historic levels. Obviously, the criteria for such a determination are in part historical and subjective, although Dowall (1980a:117–18) suggests that the distinction is whether the services serve a general public benefit or whether they benefit the project itself.

Particularly since the passage of tax-reduction measures such as California's Proposition 13, development costs have increasingly shifted from the tax-paying public to projects themselves, through capital-budgeting programs, fees and development charges, and dedication and subdivision requirements. In California, such fees rose by 35 percent (in constant dollars) between 1976 and 1979 as a direct result of Proposition 13 (Dowall and Landis 1982:7).

Estimates of the net costs of such regulation are necessarily imprecise. We have previously noted, for example, that Florida developers calculate such costs at about $550 per unit, or less than 1 percent of total cost (Nicholas 1981:393). Costs of environmental review are generally negligible when distributed over the multi-unit projects for which they may be required (Frieden 1982:26). One study estimates average per unit environmental review costs at only $242 in California and $546 in Florida, with roughly one-third of the cost attributed to delays and the remainder to preparation, review, and litigation (James and Muller 1977). Dowall and Landis' (1982) study of ninety-seven Bay Area cities during the period 1977–79 (previously reviewed) concludes that development fees are generally minor, adding dollar for dollar to total costs. Frieden (1982:25) obtains somewhat higher estimates for "typical" 1,500 square foot homes in various parts of California in 1979: $4,400 in Orange County, $4,033 in subdivisions on the rapidly growing periphery of the Bay Area,

$2,520 in Middle Bay Area suburban rings, and $1,290 in inner-core Bay Area cities. Frieden, however, does not distinguish between necessary and unnecessary fees, attributing all costs to regulation.

Gabriel, Katz, and Wolch (1979) estimated total development fees on a standard three-bedroom house at $1,907 throughout the Bay Area in 1979; such fees included charges for school impact, sewer and water connections or facilities, capital improvements, parks, storm drainage, construction taxes, and subdivision map filings. The Association of Bay Area Governments (ABAG 1980) derived a figure of $2,800 for 1980. Between 1979 and 1981, median total development fees in the Bay Area rose 32 percent for single-family and 28 percent for multifamily housing; the median total for growth-impact fees rose 26 percent. These increases are in line with the rate of inflation over the period, during which the CPI increased by about 27 percent (ABAG 1982). In all areas, development fees were found to be "only a small percentage of total building costs" (ABAG 1982:6). Furthermore, areas with higher fees (the fastest-growing areas) were found to have the lower-priced units, with the higher fees having no deterrent effect on growth (6). The component of development fees that could be attributed to environmentally mandated requirements was minimal: only 10 to 21 percent of total planning fees, and 0.1 to 2 percent of total development fees (4).

In sum, the costs of "excessive" requirements are generally found to be minimal, however that term is defined. In an earlier study for the Kaiser Commission, according to Dowall (1980a:117), "Burns and Mittelbach (1968) estimated that excessive subdivision and zoning requirements added 2 to 4 percent to the price of new housing." Similarly, Seidel (1978) reports that in New Jersey, "unnecessary" or "excessive" site improvement costs (defined as those an "experienced developer" would consider excessive) add only 2.3 percent to sales price. Such evidence notwithstanding, a survey of the 26,000 members of the National Association of Home Builders found that 72 percent of respondents reported at least 5 percent of final selling price was due to "unnecessary" aspects of regulation (Seidel 1978).

Finally, in a now-classic study of the effect of constraints on single-family home costs in SMSA's (Standard Metropolitan Statistical Areas) in 1966–67, Muth and Wetzler (1976:57) conclude that "the findings suggest that the quantitative effect of constraints on the costs of one-family houses is small. Local building codes probably add no more than 2 percent."

Secondary Effects of Regulation

REORIENTING CONSTRUCTION TO
LUXURY MARKETS

Frieden (1979b, 1982:26–27), Dowall (1980a:120), and Schwartz et al. (1979) argue that growth-control measures result in a market reorientation toward higher-income purchasers, with the resulting production of higher-quality (and more expensive) units. As a result, highly regulated communities become more desirable, more exclusive, and more costly (Rosen and Katz 1981:332). The reasoning is to the extent that growth-management systems raise builders' costs while creating scarcities, builders have every incentive to raise their prices. This is reinforced by growth-management programs such as those of Petaluma, California, which reward higher-quality units by means of a point system. According to this reasoning, builders raise prices because *their* costs rise *and* because they are able to do so without suffering a significant drop in demand.

The ability of builders to realize greater profits by building more expensive units depends on two factors: the elasticity of demand for housing in the growth-controlled market area and competitiveness among builders. In general, the ability of builders to shift costs forward, onto consumers, rather than absorb such costs themselves, is greater where demand is inelastic and market control is large.

One study, which examines a shift toward more expensive units, was conducted in Petaluma by Schwartz et al. (1979), who found that homes increased from 1,600 square feet before controls to 1,900 square feet after. They attribute this to "both the incentive provided under the evaluation system under which allocations were awarded and to the economic response of builders who were faced with fixed quotas. . . . The builder, when faced with a fixed building quota, will try to obtain the maximum profit from each unit, which requires building the largest possible salable house" (55).

They conclude (54) that Petaluma's growth-control efforts have resulted in price inflation from 13 to 25 percent vis-à-vis neighboring (uncontrolled) Santa Rosa, depending on the characteristics of the unit. Most of that inflation they attribute to the shift to larger homes, which they believe is due to the incentives of Petaluma's point system. After controlling for changes in home size, they found that the direct price effects were only 7 to 8 percent.

The study by Schwartz et al. has a number of flaws, however, that render their conclusion suspect. Most significant among these is that they never take into account demand shifts over time that might have bid up both the size and price of homes in Petaluma, and might have resulted in that city's growth-control measures. Petaluma, which is some 50 miles north of San Francisco, has fallen year by year within the range of upper middle-class commuting. In the 1960s, commuters to San Francisco seldom traveled beyond Novato, some 30 miles north of the city. At that time, home prices in Novato were almost twice those of homes in Petaluma—a difference that has all but vanished as commuting has extended to the latter area. According to Schwartz et al. (1979:4), during the period 1970–75 median income rose by almost 20 percent (current dollars) in Petaluma. Over the same period in Santa Rosa, which is another 17 miles north of Petaluma, median income rose by only 5 percent.

In other words, the increased size of homes following growth management in Petaluma may simply be a continuing market response to growing income and demand, and have little to do with growth management. Some evidence for this conclusion is provided even in Schwartz et al. (1979), inasmuch as they found that prices in neighboring Rohnert Park increased as much as in Petaluma, despite the fact that Rohnert Park, at the time under study did not have growth controls. While the authors attribute this to the "interdependence" of the two housing markets, it would seem that unless housing demand in Rohnert Park were highly inelastic, its price inflation would not be as great as Petaluma's—unless both were subject to identical market forces (such as increased demand from well-to-do commuters).

Schwartz et al. (1979) have been criticized on a number of other grounds —most notably, their assumption that housing demand is highly inelastic in Petaluma, which would explain why demand wasn't shifted to neighboring Rohnert Park as soon as Petaluma prices started to rise. Other problems with their modeling include a failure to take into account changes in property taxes, public service expenditures, and transportation costs. In sum, one cannot conclude from this study that quality or price changes in Petaluma are due primarily to growth-control programs.

DELAYS IN OBTAINING PERMITS

Increased regulation means longer, more complex, and more uncertain procedures for processing building permits. Such delays raise prices in several ways: by creating temporary shortages; by increasing landholding and other overhead costs; by raising construction costs during inflationary periods; by increasing exposure to rising interest rates; by increasing the opportunity costs of tying up capital; by impeding market response to the volatile changes in demand that characterize the housing industry; and by creating uncertainty for builders, who raise the price of remaining units to compensate (see, for example, Frieden 1979b:24; Frieden 1982:30; Dowall and Landis 1982:118).

The California Association of Realtors estimates that a typical housing development required 2.5 years to build in 1980, and the California Construction Industry Research Board claims that this adds 14 to 21 percent to sales prices (both reported in Frieden 1982:25). There is no hard evidence for either claim, however. Dowall and Landis (1982:n. 24), reporting the results of a national survey, say that in 1970, 97 percent of all developers reported receiving approval in less than one year, but this figure had declined to 42 percent by 1975. They qualify this finding by noting that "the blame for such delay rests as much with builders who prepare improper submissions, as with overzealous reviewers" (72). Dowall and Landis (n. 27) cite another study that found that in 1975, delays attributed to the California Environmental Quality

Act, which mandates environmental review for large developments, added 4 to 7 percent to the selling price of new units. We have seen, however, that other studies estimate the costs due to environmental review as significantly lower.

REDUCED COMPETITION AMONG PRODUCERS
OF HOUSING

Growth-control ordinances, it is argued, help to reduce competition among builders and developers. While under permit-allocation systems there may be strong initial competition for permits, once permits are granted there is less competition, and so builders are in a position to charge higher prices: "Any developer who manages to survive the regulatory reviews will have a virtual monopoly . . . and will be able to market his homes at an exceptionally high return" (Frieden 1979b:24; see also Frieden 1982:29). Regulations thus "act as barriers to market entry—reducing competition in the housing market" (Dowall 1980a:115). Developers who understand the regulations and have good relations with local planners are advantaged. This would appear to favor (1) large firms, which are better able to sustain the higher front-end costs associated with preparing and shepherding proposals through review processes (119–20), and (2) local firms, which have better knowledge of the local bureaucracies.

Unfortunately, none of these conclusions has been subjected to empirical examination to date: there is no evidence that growth-controlled market areas are less competitive or are characterized by large or local builders. Until some evidence is available, these conclusions must remain conjectural.

Pervasiveness of Controls throughout a Market Area

As we have noted, the price effects of regulations depend on two interrelated factors: the perceived uniqueness of the community and the pervasiveness of controls throughout the market region. In other words, to the extent that there are substitutes for higher-cost housing in adjacent areas, consumers will shift to those areas, bidding prices down in the controlled community: costs will be shifted backward to the seller, rather than forward to the consumer (Nicholas 1981:386). As Rosen and Katz (1981:20) observe, "the degree to which the increase in costs will be reflected in higher new housing prices depends on the elasticity of demand, [which in turn depends] on the amount of substitutable developable sites available in the surrounding municipalities and elsewhere in the region."

The more pervasive the controls and the stronger the demand, the more inflationary the impact (Rosen and Katz 1981:332). In a test of this hypothesis, Elliott (1981) selected 100 California cities, half of which he characterized as having strong growth controls and the other half as having weak controls. The surrounding counties were similarly characterized, and price changes during the period 1969–76 were studied in a regression analysis. Elliot found that where controls were purely local, inflation was no different between controlled and uncontrolled communities, since demand could be met in neighboring places at the original price. On the other hand, where both city and county construction was heavily regulated, regulations accounted for an average 22 percent price increase over the period. Furthermore, prices increased significantly faster in such places.

Elliot further distinguished between rate-controlled and quality-controlled places—the former limiting the amount of construction and the latter exacting such amenities as greater open-space requirements, planned urban developments, easement requirements, and even social cost/benefit analyses. These two approaches, in turn, give rise to two sorts of inflation: "demand pull" and "cost push." Elliot (115), who tested this hypothesis in a substudy of the San Francisco region, found that "in the extensively regulated San Francisco Bay Area, the 1969–76 housing price increase was 35 percent higher in rate-controlled communities and 20 percent higher in quality-controlled communities than in no-control communities."

It is not clear how one should interpret these findings, however, since Elliot's data source, Security Pacific Bank's monthly *California Construction Trends,* reports only the value of building permits, and not the value of land. While such permits may be a useful indicator of "cost push" inflation, they are not a measure of "demand pull" inflation, which is reflected in the sales price of land.[2]

A related test of the effects of pervasiveness is provided by places whose controls consist of urban limit lines that restrict development to a specific portion of the metropolitan area. In theory, urban limit lines should depress prices of undevelopable parcels outside the lines while increasing prices of developable parcels within the limits (Dowall 1980a:115–17; Dowall and Landis 1982:6–7). In one study, Gleeson (1979) examined Brooklyn Park, Minnesota, which restricted urban services to part of the city. It was found that the average value of developable land was greater than that of undevelopable land, although the difference was much greater for farm parcels than for vacant urban lots. A regression model was then created that included variables for whether or not a parcel was developable (for example, within the urban limit), as well as for access, size, topographical constraints on development, and availability of urban services. Gleeson (360) found that "with all other factors accounted for, the value of *farmland* in the developable portion is 135 percent more than that of farmland in the undevelopable portion"—but the same was not true for urban parcels: "segmenting has had no positive effect on the estimated market value per acre of vacant urban parcels, taking other factors into account."

In sum, then, there are strong theoretical reasons to expect that the impact of local regulations depends on their pervasiveness, but the empirical evidence is limited to a few studies.

EFFECTS OF REGULATION IN SANTA BARBARA: A CASE STUDY

In order to estimate the effects of local government regulations on housing markets, one of the present authors (Appelbaum 1986c) examined a California housing market that is widely perceived as having enacted extremely stringent growth-control measures in recent years.[3] In this section, we report the results of that study.

To study comparable growth-controlled and uncontrolled communities, we looked at two subregions in the same California county, Santa Barbara. These subregions included the city of Santa Barbara, in the south, and the cities of Santa Maria and Lompoc in the north. Since the urbanized areas of the two subregions are distant from one another (some 50 or more miles), each subregion was treated as a relatively self-contained housing market, although some transfer of effects was deemed possible. Since growth controls were pervasive throughout one of the two subregions, the resulting impacts on housing were likely to be maximized rather than diffused to neighboring, uncontrolled municipalities (see Elliot 1981).

We employed time-series analysis to examine market effects over a 44-quarter period (see Box and Jenkins 1976; Box and Tiao 1965, 1975; McCleary and Hay 1980; Granger and Newbold 1977; Jenkins 1979). Examining changes over time within a single housing market permitted more accurate model specification than cross-sectional analysis, while the parallel analysis of the noncontrolled subregion permitted comparative conclusions as well. Since controls were adopted about a third of the way through the study period, it was hoped that relatively long-term as well as immediate effects could be observed.[4]

This approach enabled us to statistically control for influences other than growth controls that might be expected to exert a major impact on the Santa Barbara housing market. Demand was controlled with a variable that measured consumer expenditures on major shoppers' goods, on the assumption that this was an index of overall purchasing power. Nonlocal influences included mortgage interest rates, alternative investment opportunities, and regional housing market trends that extended far beyond the study area. Purely local effects, attributed in the present model to demand characteristics and local regulation, were then isolated by the time-series analysis.

The Santa Barbara metropolitan area, of some 150,500 persons, lies approximately 100 miles northwest of Los Angeles; it occupies a narrow strip of land that is bordered by the Santa Ynez mountain range to the north and the Pacific Ocean to the south. The area, locally referred to as the South Coast because of its south-facing orientation, is comprised of two cities: Santa Barbara, population 74,400, and Carpinteria, population 10,800. It also comprises the largest unincorporated urbanized area in California.

Population growth on the South Coast was rapid during the 1950s and 1960s, averaging approximately 3.5 percent annually during the former decade and 6.5 percent during the latter. Most of this growth was in the unincorporated areas outside the city, particularly in Goleta Valley to the west. The average annual growth in the unincorporated areas averaged around 8 and 12 percent for the two decades, respectively. At the same time, the city of Santa Barbara grew at just under 3 percent annually during the 1950s, under 2 percent during the 1960s, and under 1 percent during the early 1970s, as "buildout" of available land was achieved (Appelbaum et al. 1976:5).

In response to rapid growth, the city of Santa Barbara adopted an interim downzoning measure, cutting apartment densities roughly in half during the third quarter of 1973, and subsequently enacted a permanent downzoning measure during the second quarter of 1975. Water moratoria, enacted throughout much of the remaining South Coast at about the same time, halted residential development throughout the remainder of the subregion. With only one exception, the entire subregion has had some form of growth control (downzoning or water moratoria) since early 1973.[5]

The ensuing decade saw very little housing development in the subregion —but a massive escalation in home prices and rents. In 1972, a typical single-family home in the city of Santa Barbara sold for $37,000. Eight years later, that figure had increased fourfold, to $150,000 (Appelbaum 1980). Median rents increased from $135 to $317 during the intercensal period (U.S. Bureau of the Census 1972, 1983a). In the eyes of opponents of growth controls, the region's limitation measures were directly responsible. Yet only one systematic study had been done to test this hypothesis (Mercer and Morgan 1982).

Santa Maria and Lompoc, on the other hand, two cities in the northern part of the county (locally termed the North County), had courted (and been the recipients of) considerable growth over the period of the study. Lompoc and Santa Maria are about a 60- to 90-minute commute from the city of Santa Barbara. Both northern cities, and the North County generally, are perceived as extremely pro-development. It was therefore believed possible to determine if growth-control measures on the South Coast had transferred development to the north.

Because we were interested in looking at marketwide effects, we also examined Santa Barbara County as a whole, to determine if effects in one subregion offset those in another, thereby nullifying the effects for the entire housing market.[6] The principal findings can be summarized as follows.[7]

In terms of single-family housing starts, the growth-control measures did not have a significant effect in the city of Santa Barbara. Only Southern California construction trends predicted city starts. These results suggest that the city's own ordinance, which was directed against apartments, did not have a "chilling effect" on single-family housing construction. Rather, single-family home builders, who were unable to build elsewhere on the South Coast, may have sought an outlet in the city. There was also evidence that an increase in single-family home building in the North County was associated with the adoption of growth-control measures on the South Coast—although other factors, notably regional trends and Treasury Bill rates (a measure of alternative investment opportunities), were of far greater influence. For the county as a whole, there was no net impact from the growth-control measures. Only Southern California single-family housing starts significantly predicted countywide production.

For multifamily housing starts,[8] neither the city's downzoning nor any other variable significantly predicted multifamily starts in the model. Nor did there appear to be a significant increase in apartment construction in the North County following the adoption of growth controls in the South, although construction levels varied considerably, with almost no building being done at either end of the study period. Southern California construction trends, on the other hand, were significant in predicting North County starts. For the county as a whole, the two growth-control measures appeared to have opposite and canceling effects, although the result may have been a statistical artifact.[9]

For single-family permit value, the growth-control measures revealed no significant effect in the city of Santa Barbara. While average permit values (a reflection of construction cost) were associated with both demand factors and Southern California permit value trends, the restrictions associated with the growth-control measures did not appear to have bid up prices significantly, a result attributed to the minimal effect of controls on single-family starts in the city, which, relative to total stock, were not likely to have an appreciable impact on overall housing supply. The same was found to be true for "North County" and for the county as a whole. In the former, only Southern California permit values proved significant, while in the latter, both Southern California values and home mortgage interest rates were significant. In all three instances, single-family construction costs mirrored Southern California trends, were inversely responsive to the cost of credit, and had little to do with local growth controls.

For multifamily per unit permit value, growth control had no significant effect in the city of Santa Barbara. Only demand factors and mortgage interest rates were found to be significantly and directly related to permit values. Thus the city's downzoning did not appear to have significantly restricted apartment construction in the city or resulted in higher per unit permit values, once other factors were controlled.[10] For the county as a whole, only demand factors were significant in predicting per unit multifamily permit prices; growth control did not appear to have had a countywide effect.

Rents in detached units in the city of Santa Barbara were strongly and positively responsive to mortgage interest rates, negatively responsive to alternative investment opportunities, and positively (though weakly) associated with Southern California home starts. A similar pattern was observed in the North County, although the relationships were considerably attenuated. For the county as a whole, the same pattern was observed, except that rents were positively associated with demand factors. In neither subregion, nor in the county as a whole, were rents affected by local growth controls, once the other variables were taken into account.

Finally, multifamily rents in the city of Santa Barbara were found to be a function of mortgage interest rates, demand factors, and Southern California multifamily housing starts. None of the variables in the model significantly predicted rents in the North County, while interest rates and Southern California starts were significant for the county as a whole. Again, it appeared that local growth controls did not influence rents, once the other variables were taken into account.

CONCLUSIONS

We conclude that growth controls, by themselves, were of negligible importance in determining local housing starts, costs, or rents. We believe this finding is largely due to the extreme nationwide volatility in housing starts and costs, both of which are the result of high inflation and interest rates. Under such conditions, we believe that local restrictions are likely to be swamped by nonlocal influences. This is especially true when new, nonregulated construction represents only a small fraction of the housing stock. As for governmental influences, we argue that national policies in the areas of credit and taxation are far more decisive in influencing local housing production and prices than are purely local restraints.

THE
FUTURE
OF
NATIONAL
HOUSING
POLICY

Part III

7
Rent Control and the Tenants' Movement

During the late 1970s and early 1980s, rent control established itself as the principal strategy advocated by organized tenants to reduce rent levels in U.S. cities (Atlas 1982; Atlas and Dreier 1980; Harvey 1981; O'Connor 1981; Lowe and Blumberg 1981; Heskin 1983; Gilderbloom 1981b). The past few years have witnessed the creation of hundreds of locally based tenants' unions; statewide organizations in California, Michigan, Massachusetts, New Jersey, Texas, and Illinois; and a National Tenants' organization (see Dreier, Gilderbloom, and Appelbaum 1980; Dreier and Atlas 1980).[1] Over 200 municipalities and counties in the United States currently have some form of rent regulation, including 110 municipalities in New Jersey, 66 in New York state (Marcuse 1986:Appendix G), and places in Massachusetts, Virginia, Maryland, Alaska, Connecticut, and California. About one-quarter of all rental units in California are rent controlled (Baar 1986:47), as is an estimated 10 percent of the nation's housing stock (Baar 1983:725).[2]

The attempt to organize tenants around the issue of rent control has been successful in communities with high rent levels and high home prices. As we saw in Chapter 2, rent increases outstripped tenants' wage gains by a factor of two during the 1970s. In 1970, one-third of all renters paid more than a quarter of their income into rent; by 1983 this figure had risen to over one-half. Tenants in many middle-class communities organized for rent control because they found themselves unable to afford homeownership, and became alarmed at the

127

rate of increases. Many tenants came to regard landlords as an oppositional and exploitative group, an attitude that fueled the growing tenant organizations. Capek (1985:219) declares that a successful tenants' movement must develop the power to redefine the roles of landlord and tenant, framing the issues of "fairness" and "democracy" from their own vantage point. In so doing, tenant leaders were able to draw on a deep-seated historical antipathy to landlording. As one commentator has noted (Lawson n.d.:9), "Leaving aside the owner of the sweatshop, the landlord has a worse reputation in American urban mythology than the employer."

An examination of rent control as an effort to redistribute wealth between landlords and tenants demonstrates the kinds of gains renters can hope to achieve through concerted action. It also demonstrates the structural barriers to challenging existing property relations. What kind of power do tenants really have to change existing rent levels? In what ways can tenants organize politically to offset the superior formal and informal networks among landlords (discussed in Chapter 5)? Can tenants hope to impact rents effectively, in the face of powerful market forces and potentially strong institutionalized networks among landlords? It is well known that tenants have historically been a disorganized and largely ineffective force in influencing the conditions under which they live (Heskin 1981a; Marcuse 1981b; Dreier and Atlas 1980). What happens when renters become organized?

WIDE VARIETY OF RENT CONTROL LAWS

Although rent regulation has been the principal objective of the tenants' movement in numerous cities and counties across the United States, there is a wide divergence of opinions of what actually constitutes rent control. Rent control laws are intended to provide protection against extreme increases, unjust evictions, and poor maintenance. Broadly speaking, it is possible to categorize rent control measures into three classes: restrictive, moderate, and strong.

Restrictive Rent Control

Prior to the sixties, most rent control programs in the United States were restrictive; that is, they set ceilings on rents without guaranteeing that landlords could maintain a given level of return on their investment (postwar New York City is the classic example).[3] Such restrictive rent controls, most studies claim, contributed to disinvestment in rental housing—a decline in construction, maintenance, and overall rental property value (see, for example, Friedman and Stigler 1946; Hayek 1972; de Jouvenel 1948; Paish 1950; Rydenfelt 1949; Samuelson 1967; Willis 1950; Seldon 1972; Pennance 1972; Keating 1976).

Moderate Rent Control

Attempts to avoid these problems resulted in the introduction of moderate rent controls. Most of the cities that have enacted rent regulation since the 1970s have chosen moderate rent controls. Moderate rent controls are diverse in scope, but have in common the intent of balancing the interests of landlord and tenant. This is achieved by attempting to guarantee a "fair and reasonable return" to landlords while eliminating the possibility of "excessive" rent increases ("rent gouging"). Fair-return formulas vary from locale to locale. Hoboken, New Jersey, for example, has defined "fair" as 6 percent above the maximum local passbook savings-account interest rate. Los Angeles in 1985 determined that a 4 percent annual rate of rent increase was equitable to both landlords and tenants, in light of the rate of inflation at that time; prior to that, maximum rent increases were pegged at 7 percent.

The formula governing annual rent adjustments may be established in the original ordinance, or may be periodically determined by local authority. Thus, rather than holding levels relatively constant, moderate rent controls attempt to regulate the increase on a year-to-year basis. The rents charged under these rules are supposed to represent a "competitive" housing market. According to a New Jersey Supreme Court ruling concerning rent control,

> where inflated rents are the result of a housing shortage, "value" refers to the worth of the property in the context of a hypothetical market in which the supply of available rental housing is just adequate to meet the needs of the various categories of persons actively desiring to rent apartments in the municipality. [Baar and Keating 1981:41]

To meet this criterion of guaranteeing a fair return, most moderate rent control ordinances exempt new construction, either on the initial setting of rents or for a specified period; require adequate maintenance as a condition for rent increases; guarantee annual increases sufficient to cover increases in operating costs; and provide for "passing through" major capital costs (generally on an amortized basis). If the allowable rent fails to provide for a reasonable return on investment, or is inadequate to cover costs of major capital improvements, the landlord may apply for a "hardship increase." On the other hand, should maintenance or services decline or code violations arise, the rent control board can either reduce the amount of rent collected or prohibit future increases until the problems are corrected.

Additionally, moderate rent control ordinances are often coupled with "vacancy decontrol"—the provision that a unit is exempted from rent control when it becomes vacant. Under vacancy decontrol, the rent on a vacated unit may increase considerably faster than that of controlled units, as a study of rental housing in Los Angeles found. Clark, Heskin, and Manuel (1980:6, 34) report that rents on "decontrolled" units increased two or three times as fast as the rate of controlled ones.

Tenants rarely make up a majority of rent control boards, since members are typically appointed by the city government, which takes care to ensure a balance between landlord, homeowner, and tenant interests (Mollenkopf and Pynoos 1973; Baar and Keating 1981). The typical New Jersey rent control board consists of five members: two tenants, two landlords, and one homeowner. Baar and Keating (1981:60) found in their study of forty-six rent controlled cities in New Jersey that twenty-seven of the sixty-five board members whom they surveyed, or 42 percent, identified themselves as either a "landlord or realtor;" no board members identified themselves as a "tenant organizer." In an early case study of Boston, Mollenkopf and Pynoos (1973) found that real estate interests dominated both the rent control board and its administration.

In New Jersey, where approximately 110 cities have moderate rent control, the average annual cost of administration is estimated to be less than $3 per unit (Baar 1983). Most rent controlled New Jersey municipalities employ only a part-time secretary and legal counsel, with the rent control board working on a volunteer basis (Gilderbloom and Keating 1982). Funds for administering New Jersey's rent control laws typically come out of the municipality's general budget. Rent control boards that do not have adequate funding and professional staff tend to act more favorably to landlord interests (Gilderbloom and Keating 1982).

In general, cities that have enacted moderate rent control allow rents to increase in line with increases in the Consumer Price Index (CPI) for all items. Data collected by Gilderbloom (1984) examine allowable rent increases in eighty-nine rent controlled New Jersey cities between 1975 and 1976. These increases, shown in Table 7.1, were compared to the rent component of the CPI for all nonrent controlled cities surveyed annually by the Bureau of Labor Statistics. The data show that a majority of rent controlled cities allowed about the same increases as nonrent controlled places. Only 35 percent of the rent controlled cities had allowable increases that were below the national CPI rent index. This figure, however, is almost identical to the proportion of nonrent controlled cities surveyed by the Bureau of Labor Statistics that were below the national CPI rent index. Furthermore, all but two of the rent controlled cities were only one or two percentage points below the national CPI rent index. New Jersey cities that were found to be well below the national index have also had their rent control laws ruled unconstitutional, as confiscatory (Baar and Keating 1981; Atlas 1981).

The nonrestrictive nature of moderate rent control laws can also be demonstrated in terms of landlord requests for "hardship appeals"—for additional rent increases, above the allowable ceilings to permit "a fair and reasonable return on investment." In a survey of forty-six rent controlled cities in New Jersey, Baar and Keating (1981) found that the median number of requests for "hardship increases" from landlords per thousand rental units was only one-half of 1 percent of all rent controlled units (ibid.). Furthermore, the

TABLE 7.1

RENT INCREASES FOR RENT CONTROLLED VERSUS NONREGULATED
CITIES, 1975-76

Amount Rent Increase	Rent Controlled Cities in New Jersey*	Nonrent Controlled Cities†
Less than 5%	35% (31)	33% (8)
Between 5 and 6%	22% (20)	21% (5)
More than 6%	43% (38)	46% (11)
Total	100% (89)	100% (24)

*Data unavailable for 12 New Jersey rent controlled cities because (1) a number of cities didn't respond to the questionnaire, (2) some of the cities don't have a set formula, (3) certain cities adjust rents on a case-by-case basis, and cities compute their own cost of living index.
†CPI rent-component figures show increases for 27 cities surveyed by U.S. Bureau of Census on an annual basis. Three cities—Boston, Washington, D.C., and New York—were not included in totals because they were rent controlled. The percentage rents increased between 1975 and 1976 was 4.85% in Boston, 5.75% in New York, and 6.2% in Washington. The average residential rent increase in the U.S. between 1975 and 1976 was 5.4%.
Source: Gilderbloom (1976); U.S. Bureau of the Census (1981b:467).

median yearly number of appeals was only three or four. Of the 616 requests sampled in the forty-six cities, over 70 percent of the appeals were given full or partial approval by the rent control board. Because a landlord has the money to hire expert lawyers and accountants, a rent control board can usually be persuaded to support a landlord's request for a hardship appeal, in spite of tenant protests (Gilderbloom and Keating 1982).

Strong Rent Control

A third form of rent regulation—strong rent control—arose because, in overheated rental housing markets, moderate controls came to be perceived as simply stabilizing rents, rather than mitigating rent burdens that were felt to be excessive. Strong rent controls have been enacted in three California cities: Berkeley, Santa Monica, and West Hollywood. These ordinances typically call for rent increases that are substantially lower than the CPI; do not permit vacated units to be even temporarily decontrolled; and provide for well-funded administration.[4] Rent control boards are made up of elected members who, reflecting their overwhelmingly tenant constituencies, frequently give preference to tenant needs over landlord interests. Finally, strong rent controls grew out of (and contributed to) broad-based tenant movements that focused on acquiring overall municipal power.

The restriction of rent increases, from one-third to one-half of the CPI, is intended to keep adjustments in line with increases in a landlord's actual costs.

So-called net operating income (NOI) formulas peg rent increases to increases in landlord costs, net of capital costs, on the grounds that the latter consist of fixed mortgage payments that do not fluctuate from year to year. On the average, one-third to one-half of landlords' costs are unaffected by inflation (Santa Monica Rent Control Board 1979; Gilderbloom 1978:14; Jacob 1977:2; Los Angeles RSD 1985b; Sternlieb 1974:33, 1975:4).

Sternlieb (1974:33) examined the operating expenses of 3,893 nonrent controlled units in the greater Boston area, where total operating costs, including mortgage payments, rose 6.85 percent between 1971 and 1973; at the same time, the CPI for all items rose 12.9 percent. These findings are replicated in another study by Sternlieb (1975:4) of rent controlled apartments in Fort Lee, New Jersey. In this study, Sternlieb examined the operating expenses of 2,769 apartment units between 1972 and 1974. Total operating expenses, including mortgage payments, increased 10.9 percent over the two-year period, compared to a 23.3 percent rise in the CPI.

Using figures supplied by the Institute of Real Estate Management, the Santa Monica Rent Control Board (1979) estimated that landlords' costs in 1978 went up 4.7 percent, in contrast to the 10.5 percent increase in the CPI for that year. In Los Angeles, operating and maintenance expenses in rent controlled units increased 36 percent between 1977 and 1983, while the CPI increased 64 percent over the same period (Los Angeles RSD 1985b: Exhibit 3-12 and p. 75). This is particularly true in California, where, under Proposition 13, annual property tax increases are limited to 2 percent until the property is sold. Moderate rent control, by pegging increases to the full CPI, can therefore result in increased income over time; strong rent controls seek, instead, to maintain the same level of profitability.

IMPACT OF RENT CONTROL ON RENTAL HOUSING MARKETS

Conventional economic theory holds that rent regulation will have adverse effects on local housing markets. By interfering with the landlords' profits, it is argued, rent control will discourage new construction, cause undermaintenance, and eventually produce a deteriorated housing stock. It is further argued that unprofitable apartments will increasingly be abandoned or converted to condominiums. Because of the presumed decline in new construction, undermaintenance, and abandonment, the rent controlled community's tax base will suffer. In the long run, tenants would appear to be the most hurt by rent control, because of the decline in the quantity and quality of rental housing.

This set of beliefs is pervasive among economists. One survey of economists, for example, found that only 2 percent disagreed with the following statement: "A ceiling on rents reduces the quantity and quality of housing available" (Kearl et al. 1979). One economist (Fisch 1983:18) has gone so far as to declare that rent control "can be the same as a nuclear blast in very slow motion." Professional real estate organizations on the federal, state, and local levels have been both eager and successful in disseminating this knowledge to the media, as well as their membership. Gilderbloom (1983:137–38) has shown how major media organizations, including the *Wall Street Journal*, *Los Angeles Times*, and *Forbes Magazine*, have editorialized against all forms of rent control, referring to them as a "disaster" and "unworkable."

For example, an editorial in the *Los Angeles Times* (1985b:6) is illustrative of the bias the mass media have against any form of rent control:

> Whenever price controls have been tried in peacetime, they have proved a resounding failure. So we don't have them anymore, except in one area: residential rents. . . . From a societal point of view rent control is a mistake, with harmful consequences. It inevitably results in the deterioration of a city's housing. Maintenance of existing places suffers, and builders and landlords shy away from constructing new housing because their return on investment will be artificially depressed.

An editorial in the *San Francisco Chronicle* (1985) expresses the same belief:

> Rigid rent control is exactly the wrong way to go about stimulating more housing in this state. Controls strangle the market. They discourage builders from risking their money on construction. And they discourage landlords from investing in the upkeep of their buildings. In the long run, controls do renters a disservice.

And the *Oakland Tribune* (1985) sounds this dire alarm:

> Although New York best showcases the urban decay produced by controls that force landlords to neglect, abandon, or even destroy their units, plenty of other communities have suffered a similar fate. . . . Rent control is eating away at America's cities like a swarm of termites.

The President's Commission on Housing (1983; see also Downs 1983) has called for federal legislation to ban local rent controls, which the Commission characterizes as "so dangerous and addicting a narcotic that it cannot be withdrawn cold turkey" (1983:xxviii). The widely held belief that rent controls, in any form, spell disaster for a city reflects the power of the real estate industry to influence the media, politicians, and academicians through the expenditure of millions of dollars on lobbyists, advertising in print and electronic media, film documentaries, and sponsorship of supportive research (see, for example, Schoonmaker 1987; Dreier 1979). Politicians at the state and local level receive generous campaign contributions for supporting and sponsoring anti–rent control legislation. For the most part, tenant groups lack the money to combat these efforts effectively.

The arguments against rent control are not supported by most independent

studies, nor are they an accurate reflection of the controls in the 200 cities that
have enacted regulation. Any debate on the pros and cons of rent control must
take into account the wide diversity of laws regulating rent. Yet much of the
debate continues to invoke New York City's original restrictive rent control law
as typical of all rent control. The President's Commission on Housing
(1982:xxviii), for example, erroneously asserts:

> While the blame for all urban ills can hardly be placed at the feet of rent
> control, New York City stands as the horrible example of the long-term results
> of rent control. It has by far the largest proportion of deficient housing units of
> any large city. . . . Little is built or rehabilitated without government subsidy.
> . . . Abandonment has swept bare large sections of the city.

This view of rent control is held by Republicans as well as Democrats. For
example, California's liberal Democratic Senator Alan Cranston (1986) has
stated that "there is no evidence that rent control benefits the poor. Quite the
contrary, it helps a small, privileged group of longtime residents, largely
middle-class, while driving up rents." And Wisconsin Democratic Senator
William Proxmire (1978) concludes: "Fix rents by law. What could be
simpler? The only trouble with that solution . . . is that it does not work."

There is little research that systematically examines the differences between
restrictive, moderate, and strong rent controls in cities across the United States
(Marcuse 1981a). This chapter will attempt to fill that gap by a comprehensive
review of studies by economists, political scientists, planners, and sociologists.
Such a review suggests that neither moderate nor strong forms of control have
caused a decline in either the quality or supply of the rental stock.[5] Although
such findings do not, of course, prove that rent controls are without deleterious
effect, they provide no warrant for drawing the conventional conclusions. In
fact, the very lack of restrictiveness that characterizes moderate rent control
may also account for its failure to provide across-the-board, general rent relief
for tenants. While moderate rent controls serve to limit extreme or erratic rent
increases, they often (intentionally) have little effect on tenants, whose
landlords are merely earning a fair and reasonable return on their investment.

Construction of Multifamily Housing

Short-term moderate rent controls have had no impact on the rate of rental
housing construction. Gilderbloom's (1983) multiple regression analysis
showed no statistically significant differences in the rate of multifamily housing
construction between twenty-six rent controlled and thirty-seven nonrent
controlled New Jersey cities in the mid-1970s, after statistically controlling for
median rent, city type, population, tax rate, employment increase, per capita
income, percent black, percent tenant, and pre–rent control construction. In
fact, when Gilderbloom compared construction figures for the two categories
of cities, he found a greater overall decline between the periods 1970–72 and

1975–77 for nonrent controlled cities: 82 percent, compared with only 26 percent for rent controlled communities. (Most communities experienced declines, because of larger regional and national construction trends.)[6]

Appelbaum (1984:16–17), conducting a time-series analysis that allowed for other influences to be controlled, found that even strong rent control in Santa Monica was unrelated to increases or decreases in multifamily housing construction. The only variable that approached significance in his regression equation was a regional control for multifamily starts throughout Southern California.

Vitaliano (1983:27–31) examined eleven rent controlled cities and compared them to twenty-three nonrent controlled cities in the state of New York.[7] He found, through cross-sectional regression analysis, that rent control did not cause a decline in the number of rental units available between 1960 and 1970. In fact, Vitaliano found a slight positive correlation between rent control and increases in rental construction. As another measure of the available supply of rental housing, he used rental vacancy rate as a dependent variable in his regression model. The results show that rent control is not related to the vacancy rate.

The most exhaustive study to date of rent control in a single housing market, by the Los Angeles Rent Stabilization Division [RSD] (1985a), concluded that the low vacancy levels in rent controlled Los Angeles are "more attributable to broad market forces than rent stabilization." The study found, in fact, that new construction declined more in adjacent nonrent controlled cities than in Los Angeles during the period 1978–82 (1, 2). Any effect of rent control on new construction, the study concludes, "has declined over time to the point where it undetectable." Other recent studies, although not as rigorous methodologically, have produced similar findings, including studies of New Jersey (Gruen and Gruen 1977), Alaska (Sorenson 1983), Massachusetts (Achtenberg 1975), and Los Angeles (Clark, Heskin, and Manuel 1980; see also Los Angeles Community Development Department 1979).

Builders continue to build in rent controlled communities because the laws generally allow for an exemption on all new construction, which allows builders to set initial rent levels. The guarantee of a fair and reasonable rate of return provides additional assurance for builders who fear that controls might eventually be extended to their initially exempted units. Most builders are reluctant to leave communities with which they are familiar. Understanding demographic trends, business plans and government projects; familiarity with building codes; knowledgeable and dependable employees who live in the area; and intimate understanding of the planning and project-review bureaucracies are critical to a builder's success. All these factors may help overcome a builder's initial distaste for rent control.

Underlying the issue of new multifamily construction is the rarely challenged assumption that building new rental housing is the key to lower rent levels

(Johnson 1982). Yet, as we saw in Chapter 5, even this fundamental assumption is questionable (see also Vitaliano 1983; Appelbaum and Gilderbloom 1983, 1986).

Maintenance and Capital Improvements

Numerous studies have shown that maintenance expenditures are unaffected by moderate rent control. Sternlieb (1975), for example, found that expenditures on maintenance increased by 21 percent over a two-year period in eleven rent controlled buildings in Fort Lee, New Jersey (see also Lett 1976). He also found such increases to be approximately the same between rent controlled and nonrent controlled buildings in the greater Boston area: 20 percent vs. 21 percent over the two-year period 1971–73 (Sternlieb 1974).

Vitaliano (1983:30) reports that the rate of dilapidation over a ten-year period in New York state is not significantly higher in eleven rent controlled cities than in 23 nonrent controlled cities.

A study by Achtenberg (1975), examining permits issued for additions, alterations, and repairs in Massachusetts rent controlled cities found that permits for upgrading rental units are increasing.

Another study, by Eckert (1977), examining audited income and operating statements in Brookline, Massachusetts, found that the percentage of the rent dollar going into maintenance had not declined since the enactment of rent control six years earlier. Similar findings were made by the Apartment and Office Building Association (1977) report on rent control in Montgomery County, Maryland. In 1972, according to the data, 4.8 percent of the rent dollar went into maintenance and repairs; by 1974 the distribution of the rent dollar into this category had increased to 6.4 percent. The percentage of the rent dollar going into painting and decorating remained the same. A recent study in New York City (Marcuse 1986:Section VI) concludes that rent control has not affected maintenance in that city.

Recent research in California by Wolfe (1983:31–33), involving interviews with 103 landlords in three rent controlled cities (Berkeley, Oakland, and Hayward) and one nonrent controlled city (Fremont), reports that rent control does not impact maintenance expenditures. Wolfe's conclusions are based on operating expense data of landlords and on interviews with them. The data show that in the three rent controlled cities, 8 percent of the revenues goes to maintenance, while in the nonrent controlled city an average of only 6 percent of the rents collected went into maintenance.

Clark, Heskin, and Manuel (1980) provide data showing an increase in permits for alterations, additions, and repairs following the adoption of Los Angeles' moderate rent control ordinance.[8] The most recent Los Angeles study (Los Angeles RSD 1985a:3–4) found that between 1977 and 1984 (the period of rent control), the percentage of surveyed tenants reporting maintenance problems increased from 12.5 percent to 15.6 percent—a far lower rate of increase than in the adjacent nonrent controlled comparision cities (where the increase was from 4.8 percent to 15.9 percent).

On the basis of these data, it seems reasonable to conclude that nonrestrictive rent control has not caused a reduction in the amount of money going into maintenance; in some instances, in fact, maintenance has actually increased. The reason for this, according to rent control board members and analysts interviewed by Eckert (1977) in New Jersey, Massachusetts, and Florida, is that most laws allow landlords to pass the full costs of repairs and improvements on to the tenant.[9] Moreover, Eckert found that almost all ordinances in New Jersey and Massachusetts require landlords to retain the same level of services and maintenance that existed before the enactment of controls. If maintenance declines, tenants can file a complaint with the rent control board.[10] According to Shirley Green, former rent control director of Newark, New Jersey, if a landlord wants to increase his or her rent in excess of the maximum allowable, the property must be free of code violations (Gilderbloom 1978).[11] Eckert (1977:324) concludes that these positive and negative inducements cause maintenance to remain stable.

Abandonments and Demolitions

There is no evidence that rent control, whether moderate or restrictive, leads to abandonment. In 1978 the U.S. General Accounting Office conducted a major study of abandonment by mailing a questionnaire to the chief executive officer of 201 of the largest cities in the United States. Of the 149 who responded, 113 declared that abandonment was a problem in their cities; at the time only six of these cities had rent control. Of the eight cities in which abandonment was a "major problem," only one (New York) had rent regulation. Of the eighteen cities in which abandonment was declared a "substantial problem," only two (Jersey City and Trenton) had rent control.

Marcuse (1981a:5–6), using Annual Housing Survey data, listed the Survey's twenty sample cities with the highest rates of abandonment and found that only four of them had rent control. Marcuse then used the Annual Housing Survey Data and a 1978 General Accounting Office Study (U.S. Comptroller General 1978) to determine whether cities with rent control had problems of abandonment. Of the 101 cities in his sample, Marcuse (1981a) could identify only eight cities with moderate to major problems of abandonment. In his study of New York rent regulation, Marcuse (1981a) finds that the levels of abandonment tend to be highest in neighborhoods with the fewest units subject to the city's rent stabilization ordinance, while levels of abandonment tend to be lowest in neighborhoods with a high proportion of regulated apartment units. In a more recent study (1986:Section VI), Marcuse again found that rent control in New York City is unrelated to abandonment. These findings reinforce the earlier work of Roistacher (1972:281), which found very little difference in rates of abandonment between the regulated and unregulated low-income housing stock in New York City.

In an exhaustive critique and review of the determinants of housing abandonment in New York City, Bartlet and Lawson (1982:60–61) concluded:

> The presumed relationship between rent regulations and abandonment is, in the main, a symbolic one, developed in the fray of landlord opposition to continued controls. The evidence is strikingly clear on one point—removal of regulations is not likely to affect the levels of abandonment, and instituting controls is unlikely to produce abandonment to any significant extent. . . . Rent regulations are likely to be largely irrelevant to landlord income in decaying neighborhoods—because rapid turnover among the poor has raised legal rent to levels higher than the market can bear. Limited incomes among poor people are thus the prime cause of abandonment since they discourage mortgage lending, encourage milking rather than maintenance, etc. They often leave a landlord in a situation where the only hope in getting his or her investment out of a building is through fire insurance ("the Bronx equivalent of conversion"), unless the neighborhood is on the edge of a gentrification movement.

Nor do demolitions appear to be a likely consequence of rent control. Gilderbloom's (1983) study of rent and nonrent controlled New Jersey communities found, for example, no statistically significant relationship between demolitions and rent control, once other variables were included in the model. In fact, in simply comparing the numbers of demolitions between 1970–72 and 1975–77 for the two categories of communities, Gilderbloom found a decrease of 13 percent for rent controlled places and an increase of 25 percent for nonrent controlled communities.

Valuation of Rental Housing and the City's Tax Base

Since we have shown that moderate rent control does not adversely affect construction, maintenance, capital improvements, or in general the quality or quantity of the housing stock, it should come as no surprise that the valuation of rental property (and hence a city's tax revenues from this source) is not depressed. Increases in value for rent controlled units have been reported for Cambridge, Massachusetts (Massachusetts Department of Corporations and Taxation 1974); Fort Lee, New Jersey (Gilderbloom 1981a); Los Angeles (Los Angeles RSD 1985a; Clark, Heskin, and Manuel 1980:105); and Brookline, Massachusetts (Revenue and Rent Study Committee 1974).

Clark, Heskin, and Manuel (1980:105) found that market value for apartment buildings of ten or fewer units in Los Angeles continued to increase at a rate similar to the rates during the nonrent controlled period, while the market valuation of large buildings of ten units or more had declined slightly.

This decline, however, is attributed to "changing investor sentiment and/or increasing interest rates," which negatively affected both rent controlled and nonrent controlled cities during 1979 and 1980. A report by the Massachusetts Department of Corporations and Taxation found that rent control had no systematic effect on property valuation. Similarly, a study by Brookline's Revenue and Rent Control Study Committee reported that the gross rent multiplier had remained about the same since the enactment of rent control (Eckert 1977).

Eckert's (1977) study of Brookline found that rent control had not caused the burden of taxes to shift from landlords to homeowners. In fact, it found that gross rent multipliers in rent controlled buildings were no different from those before the commencement of rent control. Later, Appelbaum (1984:14) found that rent control was not a significant factor in the total valuation of newly constructed apartments in Santa Monica, although he notes that there appears to be a tendency (not statistically significant) to build less costly and/or smaller-scale construction after the city adopted rent controls.

The study by the California Department of Housing and Community Development of rent control in New Jersey (Gilderbloom 1978:28) found virtually identical increases, about 25 percent, in assessed value for the three years preceding and following the enactment of rent control—increases that were identical with those in nonrent controlled communities over the same periods. Similarly, Gilderbloom's (1983:31) multiple regression analysis found that rent control made no difference in the tax base of New Jersey cities. Gilderbloom concluded that in rent controlled cities, the percentage of taxes paid by the rental housing sector had remained unchanged since the enactment of rent controls five years previously.[12]

IMPACT OF CONTROLS ON RENT AND AFFORDABILITY

Moderate Rent Control

The success or failure of rent control in providing across-the-board relief to tenants depends on the *kind* of control enacted. Moderate control, at least in New Jersey, has not resulted in lower rents relative to nonrent controlled cities. Gilderbloom (1986a) recently examined the mean rents in 1970 and 1980 for the twenty-six rent controlled and thirty-seven nonrent controlled cities in his original study (Gilderbloom 1978, 1983). (The results are summarized in Table 7.2.) The average percentage rent increase between 1970 to 1980 was almost identical for the rent controlled and nonrent controlled cities (105 vs. 106 percent). Gilderbloom, after breaking cities down into three categories —suburban, urban-suburban, and urban[13]—found no difference between rent controlled suburbs and nonrent controlled suburban municipalities. Rent

TABLE 7.2
MEAN RENT INCREASES, 1970–80

Locations	RENTS ($)		INCREASES	
	1970	1980	Percent	Dollars
Rent controlled cities (26)	136	279	105	143
Urban (10)	113	219	94	106
Urban-suburban (8)	143	333	133	190
Suburban (8)	159	300	89	141
Nonrent controlled cities (37)	122	251	106	129
Urban (8)	97	207	113	110
Urban-suburban (12)	119	243	104	124
Suburban (17)	147	278	89	131

Source: U.S. Bureau of the Census (1970, 1980).

controlled urban-suburban cities had higher-percentage rent increases (132 percent) than comparable nonrent controlled places (104 percent). Only urban rent controlled cities had lower percentage rent increases than their nonrent controlled (113 vs. 94 percent) counterparts. Mean rents for 1980 were actually higher in all three categories (urban, urban-suburban, suburban) of rent controlled cities than the nonrent controlled cities.

Gilderbloom (1986a) confirmed these results through a multiple regression analysis, which predicted rents as a function of city population, 1970 median rent, income, percentage housing rental, population increase, and the presence or absence of rent control (the results are summarized in Table 7.3). In column 1 we see that 1980 monthly rents averaged $25 higher in rent controlled cities, although the effect is not statistically significant (only 1970 rents and income were significant in the equation). In column 2 a similar effect is found with regard to the amount of rent increase between 1970 and 1980: such increases averaged $24 higher in rent controlled places (although, again, the difference is not statistically significant).[14]

Similar results were found by Heffley and Santerre (1985) in their study of New Jersey rent controls. They examined 101 rent controlled cities and found that the average price per room was 8 percent higher in rent controlled cities. No statistically significant difference was found between rent controlled and nonrent controlled cities in overall median contract rent. Studies on the impact of controls on rent levels in other parts of the country have drawn similar conclusions. Mollenkopf and Pynoos (1973:71), in their study of Cambridge, Massachusetts, claimed that not only had rent control failed to reduce rents, it had also resulted in "some cases [in] increasing rates of returns to landlords." Daugherbaugh (1975:2) found that Alaska's rent control programs in Anchor-

TABLE 7.3
IMPACT OF RENT CONTROL ON MONTHLY RENTS

Variable	1980 Rent	Rent Increase, 1970–80
Rent control	25.317	24.143
	14.624	15.371
1980 city population	−0.00027	−0.00024
	0.00023	0.00024
1970 median rent	0.810*	−0.193
	0.317	0.321
1980 median income	0.00320*	0.00330†
	0.00140	0.00143
Percent housing rental, 1980	−0.3200	−0.3086
	0.3790	0.4299
Population increase, 1970–80	0.00065	0.00073
	0.0009	0.00093
Constant term	93.635	92.373
Adjusted R-square	0.52	0.17
Degrees of freedom	6/55	6/53
F ratio	11.95	3.13

Note: Figures are unstandardized regression coefficients, with standard errors immediately below.
*significant at $p \leq .05$
†significant at $p \leq .01$

age and Fairbanks were ineffective in holding down rents because of the structure and administration of the law.

These data suggest that, at a minimum, the impact of moderate rent control has been to eliminate rent gouging, thereby keeping average rents in line with nonrent controlled jurisdictions. However, such rent controls have likely had minimal impact on reducing landlords' (or increasing tenants') incomes. At the same time, it seems likely that rent controls were initially adopted in housing markets that were experiencing the greatest rent pressures.[15] Where this is true, to the extent that rent controls resulted in levels comparable with less inflationary markets, they produced some rent relief relative to increases that might have occurred in the absence of controls altogether.

Strong Rent Control Laws

There is, on the other hand, evidence that strong rent control ordinances, adopted by Berkeley, Santa Monica, and West Hollywood, have resulted in substantial income redistribution between landlords and tenants. In a study of Santa Monica, for example, Shulman (1980) estimates that under rent controls, rents increased from $281 to $320 in 1980—a rise of 14 percent. If no controls had existed during that period, he estimates that rents would have risen to an average of $446 a month—an increase of almost 59 percent in two years. Shulman (13) calculates that, as a result of rent control, the rent lost to landlords and the income gained by tenants amounts to roughly $108 million over a 24-month period.

The vacancy decontrol characteristic of moderate rent control results in significantly higher average rents than those that occur under strong controls (which lack the decontrol provisions). A study by Gilderbloom and Keating (1982) found that in Springfield, New Jersey, rents in decontrolled apartments increased an average of 56 percent, from a low of 21 to a high of 89 percent. A similar finding was noted in San Francisco, where rents in decontrolled units went up an average 30 percent per year over a two-year period (Hartman 1984:241).

Clark and Heskin (1982) report that rent levels for decontrolled units were substantially higher than for controlled units in all six rent controlled districts in Los Angeles. Depending on the part of the city, rents in decontrolled apartments ranged from 22 to 39 percent higher than controlled units, with an overall average of 29 percent higher in noncontrolled units.[16] They also report that, given the vacancy decontrol provision in the law, minorities appeared to get the greatest amount of protection from rent controls because their mobility rate was lower than whites' (112).

Rydell (1981) estimated that if Los Angeles had maintained the 7 percent annual maximum increase that existed under rent control in 1980, rents in decontrolled units would rise an average of 16.7 percent. He also estimated, however, that if allowable increases were limited to 5.6 percent, rents in decontrolled units would rise an average of 18.6 percent. The Los Angeles RSD study (1985b:IV–V) found that under the city's vacancy decontrol provision, a significant portion of the average monthly rent savings[17] resulted from an income transfer from tenants who moved frequently to those who did not, since the provision resulted in landlords' "marking up" vacated units to compensate for below-market rents on occupied units. Contrary to the widely held belief that rent control is primarily a middle-class subsidy (see, for example, Devine 1986), the principal beneficiaries of rent control are the least mobile tenants, which includes low-income families, senior citizens, and single-person households.[18]

In simulations of several California housing markets, Appelbaum (1986a) compared the effects of strong and moderate rent controls. Using Berkeley, West Hollywood, and Santa Monica as case studies, Appelbaum compared a ten-year forecast of rents and affordability under their strong control laws with the probable results under moderate laws that would have permitted vacated

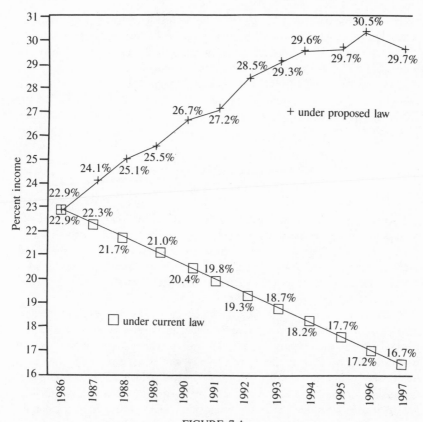

FIGURE 7.1
SANTA MONICA: PERCENT INCOME SPENT ON RENTS UNDER
CURRENT LAW AND UNDER PROPOSED LAW

units to be temporarily decontrolled.[19] The results for Santa Monica are illustrative of all three cities, and are summarized in Figure 7.1.[20]

Under Santa Monica's law (the strongest in the country), the proportion of income going into rents will decline from an average of 23 percent to just under 17 percent. Under a vacancy decontrol provision, on the other hand, average rents would rise to about 30 percent of tenants' incomes as landlords take advantage of tenant turnover to raise vacated units to market levels.[21] Under this simulation, average decontrolled rents in 1997 would reach about $1,125, in comparison with $630 under the present ordinance. In 1986 there were 15,400 "unaffordable"[22] rental units in Santa Monica—some 48 percent of the city's approximately 32,000 rental units. Under its current law, this number is projected to decline to 9,400 by 1997. Under moderate rent control with a vacancy decontrol provision, on the other hand, the number of unaffordable units would increase to 17,000. Over the entire ten-year period, landlords would realize an additional $1.1 billion in rents under the moderate ordinance.

Strong rent control laws, in other words, would produce a substantial redistribution of wealth from landlords to tenants, in comparison with moderate ordinances. Similar results were obtained for Berkeley and West Hollywood.[23] It is worth noting, moreover, that despite Berkeley's strong rent control measures, two-thirds of the city's landlords reported that "ownership is profitable."[24]

THE POLITICAL RAMIFICATIONS OF RENT CONTROL

Santa Monica provides an interesting case study of the kinds of political and economic gains tenants can win by organizing themselves as a collective force. Until 1978, Santa Monica, like most American cities, was run by a loosely knit coalition of real estate, development, and commercial interests—what Molotch (1976) terms the "local growth machine." Political analysts could safely label the town as conservative (Capek 1985).

In the latter part of the 1970s, rents began to rise steeply, and tenants responded by putting rent control on the ballot in 1978. The measure lost by a narrow margin, in a poorly funded and badly organized campaign in which landlords argued that Proposition 13—the statewide, tax-cutting measure being voted upon in the same election—would produce substantial property tax savings for landlords, which would be passed along to tenants in the form of lowered rents. When the passage of Proposition 13 was followed by substantial rent *increases,* rent control was again put on the ballot. This time tenants, who comprise 70 percent of Santa Monica's population, voted for adoption. Soon after, a slate of pro-rent control candidates was elected to its rent control board and city council. The central concern of the victorious candidates was to defend the rent control law from landlords' court challenges.

Santa Monica tenants won not only rent control but a political program that promised them tangible benefits in the form of a progressive platform that included—besides rent control—cooperative housing, limitations on commercial expansion, inclusionary zoning programs,[25] assistance to farmers' markets and food cooperatives, support for neighborhood anti-crime efforts, and controls on toxic wastes. The city also attempted to democratize city hall by funding numerous neighborhood organizations, appointing citizens' task forces and commissions, and making extensive use of public hearings. For the first time, city hall considered the needs of tenants, along with the traditional constituencies of homeowners, developers, and business and commercial interests.

It was this program, according to Santa Monica Renters' Rights (SMRR) coordinator Derek Shearer, that inspired tenants to vote. According to Shearer,

I think it [the program] shows that the vote for Reagan was not a conservative vote. It was a vote against inflation and wishy-washy, middle of the road, Carter-type Democrats. When Democrats and local activists ran on a progressive program very clearly spelled out, there was a lot of support for it. [Cockburn and Ridgeway 1981]

Tenants have also been instrumental in electing progressive candidates in other parts of the country. In March of 1981, the voters of Vermont's largest city, Burlington, replaced a five-term conservative Democrat as mayor with a self-proclaimed socialist, Bernard Sanders. Sanders focused on the basic issues confronting Burlington's heavy blue-collar population: high rents, unchecked development, property taxes, and neighborhood preservation. His victory was largely attributed to his pro-tenant stand, which attracted a coalition of tenants, senior citizens, municipal unions, and liberal homeowners. During the election, Sanders appealed for their votes by proclaiming:

We have a city that is trying to help a developer build $200,000 luxury waterfront condominiums with pools and health clubs and boutiques and all sorts of upper middle class junk blocks away from an area where people are literally not eating in order to pay their rent and fuel bills. . . . The issue here is that people have been exploited, thrown out of houses. In Burlington a tenant has no rights at all. Hundreds of people have been forced to move from apartments in Burlington because of rent increases. It's about time tenants have legal protection. [McKee 1981:8]

Similar appeals to the "tenant vote" have been successful in electing David Sullivan to the Cambridge city council and Peter Shapiro to the powerful position of Essex County executive in New Jersey (Krinsky 1981:10; Atlas and Dreier 1981:8). Shapiro was nominated the Democratic candidate for governor of New Jersey for 1985, but lost to popular incumbent Republican Thomas Keene.

The 1984 election of Boston Mayor Ray Flynn was due, in part, to his strong pro-tenant identification (70 percent of Boston households are renters). Peter Dreier, a sociologist whose academic and political work with tenant organizing and legislation was well known in the Boston area, was one of Flynn's chief campaign coordinators, and currently serves as director of housing for the powerful Boston Redevelopment Authority. Taking advantage of Boston's economic boom and highly inflationary housing market, Flynn has implemented rent controls, restrictions on condominium conversions, and provided strong support for low- and moderate-income residential development. Working in conjunction with nonprofit agencies, the city is seeking to refurbish a sizable number of vacant or deteriorated rental units, while preventing HUD from selling properties in receivership. Boston has also implemented linkage[26] and inclusionary zoning programs to provide additional affordable housing (see Boston 1986).

Tenants have also played a role in reforming archaic landlord-tenant laws, particularly in New Jersey, which has the most progressive law in the United States. Through the efforts of the New Jersey Tenants' Organization (NJTO), which claims 60,000 dues-paying members, over 100 cities have rent control (Atlas and Dreier 1981:34). According to Atlas (1981:227), "without strong political organizations no useful reforms will be passed." In Detroit, the United Community Housing Coalition (UCHC) began in 1975—from a church basement, staffed by a Vista volunteer, and with a $20,000 budget. Today, UCHC has fifteen full-time staff members and a budget of $300,000 (Rosentraub and Warren 1986). In Vermont, a statewide tenant organization has been started with the founding of a tenant resource center. In Orange, New Jersey, the city funds a "tenant advocate" so that tenant interests can be protected. The advocate works to improve existing rent control law and represent tenants at rent control board meetings.

The New Jersey Tenants' Organization (NJTO) has been successful, in part, because it has fought pragmatically for moderate legislation it thought could be won. Under NJTO prodding, the New Jersey legislature has passed "truth in renting" laws, requiring landlords to disclose their identities to tenants, as well as the identities of their superintendents and mortgage holders. The state has also passed NJTO-sponsored legislation, requiring that tenants be made aware of their rights under state law (Atlas 1981:228). NJTO was also successful in securing passage of a state law that prevents eviction except for "just cause" (failure to pay rent, disorderly conduct, or instigating property damage). Just-cause laws protect tenants against politically motivated evictions and thus protect (and presumably encourage) the growth of political organizations such as NJTO itself. Victories in passing pro-tenant legislation have contributed to the growth of NJTO. Many of the new laws have been copied by other tenant groups and adopted in other states.

The issue of rent control has led to the building of broad-based tenant coalitions in several states (Lawson 1984; Capek 1985). Such coalitions consist of seniors, blue-collar workers and minorities; and women frequently play prominent leadership roles in them (Jacob 1979, Leight et al. 1980; Kirschman 1980). During the past ten years, women have been elected president of the statewide tenant associations in New Jersey and California. Coalitions often unite middle- and working-class renters with unemployed tenants in a common cause, overcoming traditional divisions between these groups.

Debate over whether a city should adopt rent control frequently divides tenants on the fundamental issue of human versus property rights (Atlas and Dreier 1981). When people affirm the need for rent control, either through referendum or their elected officials, they are often stating that landlords' private property rights are not absolute, that the needs of landlords must be balanced with the needs of the tenant (Atlas and Dreier 1983). The traditional "sanctity" of private property rights falls under public scrutiny (Harvey 1979) as tenant leaders assert the right to limit landlords' profits, in accordance with a putative right to affordable shelter.

Even where tenants agree that some kind of rent control is needed, there is frequently disagreement over the degree of restrictiveness (Hartman 1979; Renters Alliance 1980; Kirschman 1980). The argument centers on whether fairness to landlords can be balanced with fairness to tenants—although the issue may be skirted in hopes of avoiding legal challenges or in the interest of political pragmatism (for example, in view of what the voters and courts will likely accept). According to Heskin (1981c), this can create sharp divisions among renters:

> Another activist said the division in the tenant movement (and society) manifested itself in what was called a "racist" City of Los Angeles rent control law. The law limits general rent increases helping white population gain control over the problem of rapidly rising rents, but it allows the pass through of the cost of repairs that are necessitated by housing code violations. The law does not relieve the affordability problem for minority tenants, who are now threatened with increasing rents if they demand even the minimum conditions of habitability required by law.

With the enactment of rent control, the parameters of the discussion are further changed. According to Atlas and Dreier (1980:11),

> in these areas where people have fought for rent control, it is always attacked as anti-free enterprise and anti-business. After victory the debate shifts to what level of profit the landlord deserves: for example, six years ago most New Jersey tenants believed landlords could charge as much as they wanted, just like any business (That's the way it has been, that's the way it is). Now many believe that a landlord's need for profit must be balanced against the tenant's needs for an affordable and decent place to live. These are important changes in people's consciousness.

The success of tenants' ability to pass legislation on their behalf depends partly on their degree of identification as tenants. Heskin (1981c:1) defines "tenant consciousness" in terms of these characteristics: (1) viewing oneself as belonging to a group (tenants) that shares similar problems, (2) a shared understanding of the causes of one's housing-related problems, and (3) a collective political purpose that responds effectively to those problems. Heskin (1981c, 1983) further argues that tenant consciousness develops through political action on housing issues. In his survey of renters in Santa Monica and Los Angeles, Heskin (1983:88) found that approximately one-quarter of the tenants in both cities agreed that the marketplace, by itself, could not solve the housing problem and that direct government intervention was therefore necessary. Naturally, such an understanding (which Heskin held to be indicative of high tenant consciousness) was stronger among tenant leaders than among ordinary renters.

Of the many actions tenants could take, rent control generates the greatest mass involvement with the smallest personal risk. Rent strikes or "squatting," for example, expose the participant to the dangers of arrest, loss of possessions, legal costs, fines, and perhaps imprisonment. On the other hand, campaigns to lower interest rates or increase housing subsidies are "too remote in their targets, too long term in their potential results, too indirect and diffuse in their impact and at least in the United States today, too little" (Marcuse 1981b:86). Rent control, in contrast, promises to have a direct and immediate economic impact with little personal risk.

When tenants organize for better housing conditions, they learn that simply protesting is not enough to meet their needs. They find that they must involve themselves directly in the electoral system if they wish to see long-term change (Hayden 1979–80; Booth 1981). A valuable lesson results: Ordinary people, working collectively, can affect significant change in terms of gaining greater control over the conditions of their lives. According to Atlas and Dreier (1983), winning one reform can spark demands for even more fundamental changes.

THE FUTURE OF THE TENANTS' MOVEMENT[27]

Analysis of the tenants' movement in the United States shows that moderate economic and political gains have been made. It should be kept in mind, however, that the American tenants' movement is relatively new. In 1969 there was very little tenant activity in the United States; only a few cities had rent control or tenant unions. Today, the tenants' movement is a potent political force in many cities and several states. As we have seen in the case of Santa Monica, the fight for decent and affordable housing can help to build bridges between various disenfranchised groups and bind them into an organized body, demanding even greater economic and political change in other spheres of life.

In the effort to enact rent control, larger issues are brought to public debate. Important political and economic questions are raised concerning the production and distribution of housing. As we have noted, a fundamental question concerns the balancing of equities between human and property rights. The debate over rent control, therefore, makes an important political impact. It has taught tenants that if housing conditions are to improve, they must get involved in the political system. They must vote for referenda and elect candidates who will serve their interests. Tenants' traditional political apathy is overcome by an issue that directly affects them.

We believe that, in most cities, rent control has had more a political than economic impact. In purely economic terms, most rent control ordinances serve primarily to avert very large rent increases, possibly bringing highly inflationary housing markets more into line with other places. Rent control has also provided protection against arbitrary evictions, incentives for maintaining units, and predictable rent increases. From the tenant's perspective, these are tangible improvements.

Rent control has *not*, however, brought average rents down to affordable levels. Recognizing this problem—and playing on the willingness of many tenants to accept government intervention in the marketplace—tenant groups are pushing harder for more stringent rent restrictions.

The continued success of rent control as a significant component of local housing policy seems cloudy. The benefits are often small, relative to the problem, while the efforts required to enact and maintain rent control are enormous. Some tenant organizers have come to question the efficacy of rent control as the chief objective of the tenants' movement, with many pushing innovative housing programs in addition to rent control. Large-scale cooperative housing programs for low- and moderate-income persons have become major organizing themes for some tenant groups (Gilderbloom 1982:212–60; Lawson 1984). Tenant leaders who continue to advocate rent control as the chief strategy appear to be waging an increasingly defensive campaign simply to keep it alive where it already exists, rather than extending it to other places. Real estate groups have launched a well-financed attack on rent control lobbying and have passed legislation that undermines the effectiveness of rent control laws.

On the other hand, rent control might continue to be a part of tenants' housing policy if the federal government continues to cut back on low- and moderate-income housing programs, and if the 1986 Tax Reform Act further reduces profit margins, forcing rents up another 20 percent (see Chapter 4). Additionally, constitutional challenges to rent control were dealt a setback when the Supreme Court upheld the constitutionality of Berkeley's strong ordinance. If housing conditions continue to worsen, as we anticipate, and if the federal government reduces its already limited programs, tenants will have to look to local solutions. Rent control agitation could rejuvenate itself, although the debate will certainly continue over whether it represents symbolic or redistributional politics (Edelman 1967).

8
European Housing in the Postwar Period: Some Lessons for U.S. Policy

President Reagan's Commission on Housing (1982:xvii) assures us that "Americans today are the best-housed people in history." Unfortunately, this is not the case. Many West European nations have gone considerably further in assuring the availability of high-quality, affordable housing to all segments of their populations, particularly low-income households. As we saw in Chapter 4, the United States has relied almost entirely on the private marketplace to satisfy its housing needs, limiting the public sector to subsidies and other supports to the building and rental industries. Publicly owned and managed housing has been restricted to a small percentage of the very poorest families. In many European countries, however, housing has come to be regarded virtually as a right of citizenship, and intensive public interventions have sought to assure widespread availability and affordability.

In this chapter we examine in some detail the strengths and weaknesses of one of Europe's principal success stories—the Swedish welfare state. On most indices, Swedish citizens are better housed than their American counterparts, and for this reason a comparison with Sweden is instructive. The ways in which that nation solved its post–World War II housing crisis provide important lessons for U.S. housing policy. First, however, it will be useful to make some

This chapter is partially adapted from Appelbaum (1985b and 1986d). Material from the latter article appears courtesy of Rachel G. Bratt, Chester Hartman, and Ann Meyerson, editors of *Critical Perspectives on Housing*, Temple University Press.

general observations concerning other West European nations, in order to provide a context in which to evaluate Swedish housing programs.

Our brief survey will demonstrate that many West European capitalist nations have routinely adopted programs that in the United States would be considered unthinkably radical. In particular, we shall note a widespread commitment to public-sector solutions that is thus far absent from American housing policy. We shall also note some common failings of these approaches —shortcomings that are also present in the Swedish example, and that we hope to avoid in the National Comprehensive Housing Program we offer in Chapter 9.

HOUSING IN THE CAPITALIST ECONOMY: SOME WEST EUROPEAN APPROACHES

The overall level of housing investment in the United States is generally lower than in Western Europe. In 1976, for example, investment in housing as a proportion of total fixed capital investment was 18 percent higher among the seventeen nations of Western Europe than in the United States; only Austria, Norway, West Germany, and the United Kingdom had lower levels in that year (adapted from Wynn 1984:4). Partly as a result of this, Western Europe had, on average, achieved slightly higher ratios of dwelling units to population: 356 per thousand persons, in comparison with 333 in the United States. In some countries, the ratios were considerably higher—for example, in France (399 per thousand), Denmark (397), Belgium (395), Sweden (394), Switzerland (390), Austria (388), and West Germany (383) (ibid.).[1]

These levels of investment were achieved through a mixture of public and private initiative that varied considerably across nations and time, although in most cases the public commitment was considerably higher in Europe than in the United States. It is useful to bear in mind that most European countries emerged from the Second World War with acute housing shortages, resulting from the cessation of housing construction during the war and the destruction of significant portions of the housing stock. It is estimated that as much as one-fifth of housing in many countries was rendered uninhabitable during the war (Wynn 1984:1). The war also left a legacy of strict, nationally mandated rent controls throughout Europe. While in some cases rent regulation had preceded the war, wartime controls, which typically took the form of rent freezes, were virtually universal.[2]

Public commitment to housing in Western Europe typically took several forms:

- Support for publicly or cooperatively owned low-cost rental housing
- Subsidies to lower the cost of existing public and private rental housing,

including support for new construction and rehabilitation (for example, through interest subsidies), and housing allowances for tenants
A willingness to protect tenants from high rents and eviction

We shall consider each of these public initiatives as we look at housing programs in France, West Germany, Great Britain, Denmark, and Italy. Swedish programs will be considered in detail in the second part of this chapter.

Social Housing Forms: Public and Cooperative Housing

During the 1960s and early 1970s a sizable proportion of the housing stock in many West European countries was constructed outside the private sector. For example, public authorities and publicly controlled cooperative associations accounted for over a third of the housing built in Belgium, Denmark, France, the Netherlands, Britain, and West Germany during the period 1960–75 (Wynn 1984:3). In the United Kingdom and the Netherlands almost half of all new construction during the period consisted of nonprofit housing. By 1970, such nonmarket forms accounted for a sizable portion of the total construction in Denmark (29 percent), France (33 percent), West Germany (21 percent), and the United Kingdom (54 percent) (6–7).

These figures mask considerable differences in approach, however. Britain, for example, was strongly committed to the construction of "council" (that is, public) housing, which accounted for almost half of all construction in 1970. In Denmark, France, and West Germany, on the other hand, subsidized housing was generally undertaken by cooperative associations with substantial public support. In both cases, however, this housing was removed from the marketplace: public housing was rented at affordable rates through local housing authorities, while cooperative housing constituted a hybrid form of tenant-ownership in which equity controls precluded resale speculation. While rates of nonmarket housing construction were especially high in the decade or so following the war, by the late 1970s levels in most places had declined considerably. By 1979, for example, private-sector housing construction in West Germany had reached 91 percent of total housing construction; in France, 52 percent (in 1981); and in England, 57 percent (1981) (Wynn 1984:6–7).

FRANCE
Throughout the 1970s the HLM low-rent sector was the major source of inexpensive housing for low-income groups in France, accounting for more than one-fifth of all rental housing construction. HLM construction was frequently undertaken by large state companies or joint public-private firms, with low-cost financing available through state loans or grants. By the 1970s, however, the private sector had effectively replaced the government as the dominant force in housing, as mandated in the 1977 Housing Act, which called for a return to the marketplace (Pearsall 1984:9).

WEST GERMANY

Germany had suffered considerably more destruction than France during the war; one-third of its housing stock was damaged or destroyed; and its postwar population was swollen by East German refugees. Although 43 percent of all units built between 1949 and 1978 had substantial governmental participation and were therefore subject to social controls,[3] very little public housing was built during this period (less than 5 percent of the housing stock) (Kennedy 1984:57). The high point of social housing construction was reached during the immediate postwar period, accounting for some 69 percent of all new construction in 1950–52. It declined thereafter as private rental construction boomed, dropping below 50 percent of new construction in 1960 and below 30 percent a decade later (it presently stands at roughly 25 percent) (Marcuse 1982:93). Housing in West Germany is again officially regarded as the province of the private marketplace.

UNITED KINGDOM

Under the postwar Labour government (1946–51), the majority of building was done by local housing council authorities. This continued a tradition dating to the end of the First World War, when the British government had determined that the marketplace could not provide adequate affordable housing and, therefore, that a heavily subsidized, municipally run public housing sector would be necessary. By 1958, however, the private sector had overtaken the public, exceeding the latter in every subsequent year, although to a lesser degree under Labour governments. Despite wide partisan differences in commitment to public housing, the percentage of British housing under public ownership increased steadily during much of the postwar period, eventually reaching almost one-third of all housing. At the same time, private rental housing declined from 30 percent to 15 percent over the period 1961 to 1980 (Smith 1984:77, 93).

By the late 1970s, public housing began to come under serious attack from the Conservatives. Inflation, economic recession, and the rising cost of social welfare undermined support for expensive housing programs. Conservatives alleged that many public housing projects were ugly, poorly designed and constructed, unsafe, and bureaucratically mismanaged. An increasingly middle-class population turned its back on the council housing programs that had been a mainstay of British housing for over sixty years. During the mid-1970s, for the first time, the British government began to exert controls over local housing programs, significantly limiting new construction.

Since 1979, housing has borne the brunt of the Conservative government's retrenchments, absorbing half of all budget cuts (Schifferes 1986:522). Housing expenditure has been cut by almost half, and with it public housing starts (Smith 1984:107).[4] Housing, once a chief expenditure in the British welfare state, has become one of the smallest (Schifferes 1986:522). The Thatcher government, like the Reagan administration (see Chapter 4), has initiated a program of selling off the public housing stock to its tenants at discounts of 35 to 50 percent (Smith 1984:108).

There is no question about the preference for owner occupancy in Britain, or that council conversions are welcomed by those who can afford to buy such units (113). This provides ownership opportunities for middle-class public housing tenants, but it seriously curtails the number of low-cost housing units in Britain. Between November 1980 and March 1982, 9 percent of public housing tenants had applied to purchase their units, and 2 percent of the stock had been sold by the latter date. For the first time in this century, public housing in Britain has declined in both absolute and relative terms (Doling 1983:477).[5]

DENMARK

The Danes have long pursued a cooperative approach to housing, with the first nonprofit cooperatives appearing in the 1860s. Fully half of all housing units were constructed by nonprofit and cooperative associations during the immediate postwar period. This ratio had dropped to around 30 percent during the 1970s (Wynn 1984:6–7), and is currently under 20 percent (Haywood 1984:199). Co-op tenants typically pay a nominal portion of the cost of their unit (about 3 percent) as a down payment, which is refunded (adjusted for inflation) when they move out. Financing is through a mixture of federal, local, and private funds, with subsidies reducing initial rents by as much as 40 percent below market levels (200–201).

Given the virtual absence of public housing in Denmark today, the government's role is largely financial: grants, low-cost loans, and other construction subsidies. After the high cost of this approach was criticized during the 1950s, support was curtailed and a sharp decline in the number of newly built cooperative units ensued. During the 1950s, "nonprofits" averaged 36 percent of the 22,000 housing units completed each year (and reached as many as half), but by 1960 they comprised only 21 percent of 28,000 units—an absolute decline from 8,000 to 6,000 cooperative units annually (Haywood 1984:186).

Construction increased during the 1960s, but rising costs and interest rates adversely affected affordability. Increasingly expensive subsidies to the nonprofit sector were further cut back in 1972, and housing starts, compared to the first half of the decade, dropped by almost one-third. By the early 1980s, overall construction levels were even lower than they had been in 1975, with 17 percent of all units in nonprofit cooperatives, 24 percent in private rentals, and the remaining 59 percent in single-family homes—the tenure preference of the large majority of Danes (accounting for four of every five new housing starts). There is virtually no public housing construction at the present time (Haywood 1984:187, 195).

Denmark stresses industrialized housing construction, and standardized modular design coordination was mandated by federal law as early as 1961. During the 1970s, the large majority of high-rises were prefabricated, permitting the tripling of construction during the period 1965–75. However, the design features in the large housing projects often reflect a strong social concern for easing the burden of domestic labor, and many services are collectively organized (including restaurants, laundries, cleaning services, and day care) (Haywood 1984:192, 184–85).

ITALY

State-subsidized public housing was built for specific crisis situations as a part of postwar reconstruction. Public housing was financed through government grants to agencies set up for that purpose, principal among which was INA Casa, created in 1949 to provide public housing. During the 1950s, which were a period of substantial economic growth and heavy investment in housing construction, accompanied by massive urbanization, approximately 82 percent of housing investment was through the private sector, with 19 percent from the public sector; and the latter declined to only 6 percent by 1978. Public housing construction dropped from 25 percent of all starts in 1951 to only 6 percent by the mid-1960s (Padovani 1984:257–58, 262, 265).

The first postwar center-left government took office in the early 1960s, and in 1962 the Public Housing Areas Act enabled localities to acquire land for public housing through expropriation, although little was actually done (Padovani 1984:269). During the early '60s, construction was stagnant, and much public housing was even sold off. The Housing Reform Act of 1971 was the first serious Italian attempt at a national housing policy. Little was done to improve the housing situation, but these measures created a legislative framework for the future. The 1978 Ten-Years Plan set norms for the construction and financing of public housing, and established a Committee of Housing, within the Ministry of Public Works, to develop technical standards and promote experimental programs and research.

Subsidies and Other Forms of Housing Support

As in the United States, the principal form of housing assistance throughout Western Europe has consisted of a variety of subsidies and supports, intended to buttress the private marketplace while redressing some of its inequities. These measures have generally been for the building of structures (for example, interest subsidies for new construction) and income supports to tenants (for example, housing allowances). This mixed approach, combining market and social objectives, has extended even to publicly owned and nonprofit coopera- tive housing. As we have seen, such "social" housing was generally built by private development companies with publicly subsidized private financing. As Marcuse notes (in connection with German housing policies), the chief objective has been "to permit maximum scope and support to the private housing industry (property owners, builders, suppliers, finance, management), with government regulation and subsidy limited to supporting that industry except for those situations in which other overriding priorities exist" (1982:88).

The principal variation has been the degree to which "overriding priorities" have been allowed to intrude on market objectives. A universal consequence of this approach has been an extreme susceptibility of public supports to inflationary pressures. As interest rates, construction costs, sales prices, and rents have risen, the high cost of underwriting the private marketplace has undermined the political viability of government programs in many countries.

FRANCE

During the 1950s France came to rely heavily on the public sector for financing and initiative, a reliance that was facilitated by the country's traditionally strong state control over its banking industry. Financing for the HLM low-rent sector, for example, came from state loans and grants, with terms as favorable as 2 percent interest (on sixty-five-year loans) to cover 95 percent of construction costs (Pearsall 1984:17).

The state has provided funding for housing assistance to renters, as well as support for homeownership. State aid to the private sector *(secteur aide),* for example, was a major means of promoting homeownership for the middle class, by providing loans for up to 70 percent of approved construction costs at fixed interest rates. The *secteur aide* accounted for roughly one-third of all construction in 1953 and for over half in 1963, before declining to one-third by 1973. In addition to these public subsidies, since 1953 all firms of ten or more people in France contribute approximately 1 percent of their wages, which may go into a housing construction fund or be used directly for construction. By 1975, this "One Percent Fund" exceeded the state's budgetary allocations for housing (Pearsall 1984:17–18).

Despite considerable urban population increase during the 1960s, persistent shortages, and the growth of immigrant slums, the role of the state in French housing was reduced. Less favorable loan terms were made available to the *secteur aide,* for example, with a higher percentage of construction cost to be met by the purchaser. Regulation of banks was reduced to encourage greater private mortgage lending. During the 1970s, however, housing shortage and quality problems had been significantly ameliorated (Pearsall 1984:28–29), and the emphasis turned from new construction to rehabilitation supported by state funds.

As noted above, the 1977 Housing Act called for the state to play a secondary role in housing provision, trusting rather to the private marketplace. Rents and interest rates were to be increased to market levels, with state expenditures correspondingly reduced. Subsidized state loans were extended from cooperatives to all developers, and low-cost homeownership loans were introduced for lower-income households. Despite the election of a socialist government in 1981, little has changed in French housing policy. Although the highly privatizing 1977 Housing Act was formally abandoned, its reforms remain in effect, although the socialists spent more money on housing than their predecessors (Pearsall 1984:39, 46).

WEST GERMANY

Although major public involvement was required for postwar reconstruction, the German government did not want to be a visible provider of low-cost housing. As an interim solution, the state channeled significant subsidies through nongovernmental nonprofit institutions; in the long run, it was expected that economic recovery would restore the marketplace to its central position. This, in fact, began to be achieved in the late 1950s, as the German economy became healthy and the housing need therefore less critical. Privatization continued until the Social Democratic victory in 1969, which marked the beginning of somewhat increased subsidies, primarily in the form of housing allowances (Marcuse 1982:69).

The immediate postwar period saw emergency reconstruction with heavy public involvement, with the private sector subordinated to public interests. The 1950 Housing Construction Act provided for direct governmental loans and grants, at reduced interest, to specified housing developers (mainly nonprofits); rents in such social housing were set by law, with subsidies provided to make the rents economically feasible to the developers. During this period roughly two-thirds of all construction was social; *all* was for low-and moderate-income people (Marcuse 1982:93).

As economic recovery proceeded, however, governmental controls were gradually relaxed, and emergency measures were formally dismantled in 1960. The following decade witnessed the large-scale reprivatization of German housing, which was to be reintegrated into the private economy. Various acts removed price restrictions on land purchases and based social housing rents on costs rather than statute. Housing allowances were initiated when rent controls were lifted in 1963, and were substantially expanded in 1965. Financing shifted from public loans and grants to interest-rate subsidies, as private capital played a growing role in the provision of housing. During this period, the proportion of workers who owned their homes increased dramatically, from 19 percent in 1957 to 44 percent in 1978 (Marcuse 1982:65).

Tax benefits to homeowners (generally upper-income) likewise increased substantially over this period. Public low- or no-interest loans and grants dropped from 43 percent of all new housing capital in 1952 to 29 percent in 1959, 9 percent in 1963, and 3 percent in 1978 (Marcuse 1982:97). Between 1950 and 1974, over a half-million units were built annually—the so-called German housing miracle. Notwithstanding the fact that much of this construction was subsidized with very low or no-interest government loans, tax rebates, and housing allowances, the government had no ownership in social housing.

The German social housing stock remained primarily privately owned (Kennedy 1984:56–57, 69).

As a result of the growing privatization of housing, affordability deteriorated during the late 1960s. Recession, rising interest rates, inflation, and the militancy of the 1960s all contributed to a rethinking of housing policy. The 1969 election of the Social Democrats led to a partial reversal of the trend toward privatization, resulting (among other policies) in increased allowances to compensate for rising public housing rents. During the 1970s, however, social housing construction declined markedly, as funding was redirected into private rehabilitation. Furthermore, the amount that was paid for social housing varied greatly by class, with much social housing occupied by middle-class tenants (Kennedy 1984:66). By the 1980s, the retreat into the private marketplace was complete, and tenant militancy was again rising because of high costs and low vacancies—as indexed by a squatters' movement that had spread throughout some seventy cities in Germany (Marcuse 1982:100–101).

GREAT BRITAIN

The postwar Labour government strongly encouraged local authorities to build council housing, and sufficient subsidies were provided to make it available to all sectors of society. In addition to subsidizing public housing, legislation sought to contain sprawl through the construction of New Towns, and permitted local authorities to zone for green belts. The Conservatives, who governed from 1951 to 1964, eased building restrictions, and between 1954 and 1964 the annual output of private homes increased from 88,000 to 210,000 (Smith 1984:84). In general, the Conservatives encouraged market activity, reducing support for council housing and New Towns construction. These policies had the predictable consequence of eroding the progress that had occurred after the war.

When the Labour government returned to power in 1964, a renewed commitment was made to public housing. The 1967 Housing Subsidies Act provided large interest subsidies for council housing, and the Land Commission Act (1967) provided for public purchase of land, to be sold or leased to private bodies. Many slums were cleared and replaced by high-rise construction; indeed, high-rises accounted for half of all council housing during the 1960s. This created all the problems conventionally associated with such construction, and toward the end of the decade Labour began to reemphasize detached homes and rehabilitation, with legislation providing for rehabilitation grants and tax relief for home mortgage interest payments. Homeownership steadily increased between 1961 and 1980, from around 42 percent to 55 percent (Smith 1984:90, 96–97, 93).

The Conservatives returned to power briefly in 1970 and promptly reduced subsidies to council housing, forcing the tenants to pay a "fair rent." This legislation was repealed with Labour's return, four years later, and subsidies were again increased. The 1976 Community Land Act provided for land banking and comprehensive local housing plans (Smith 1984:99, 103). The economic stagnation of the late 1970s thwarted Labour's plans to municipalize much of the private rental sector, and local authority renovation fell by two-thirds between 1973 and 1975 (Schifferes 1986:522–23).

As we have noted, the return of the Conservatives in 1979, and the triumph of Thatcherism, spelled substantial cutbacks in Britain's traditional commitment to housing. Under the Thatcher government, public rent subsidies have been significantly reduced, with the result that rents increased 250 percent between 1978–79 and 1984–85, especially in inner cities (Schifferes 1986:525). This loss of rent subsidy contributed to the declining attractiveness of council housing, as it was intended to do.

On the other hand, even under the Conservatives housing rights have increased. There is consensus in Britain that everyone is entitled to a decent, affordable home, although Labour favors council housing and eviction protections while Conservatives want public housing tenants to purchase their units. In 1972 the Conservative government introduced, as an entitlement program, financial assistance for low-income households in both public and private rentals. This was updated in the 1982–83 Housing Benefit System, which provides that all people in need of rent supplements are entitled to receive them. At present, roughly two-thirds of council tenants and one-third of private tenants receive such benefits, although cutbacks have occurred in recent years. Furthermore, the Homeless Persons Act, enacted in 1977, guaranteed the right to housing for all families and elderly people who were homeless. A half-million persons have received assistance under this legislation, mainly in public housing, where homeless persons now constitute one-fifth of all rentals (Schifferes 1986:526, 527).

DENMARK

In 1946 the Building Subsidy Act provided low-cost government grants for all forms of housing. During the late 1940s and 1950s, some 90 percent of all housing was built with government subsidies. During the 1950s, however, the high cost of public involvement was questioned, and in 1954 low-interest loans were replaced by loans tied to market rates. In 1958 the government withdrew entirely from the direct mortgage market; as interest rates, land prices, and construction costs rose steeply, even nonprofit associations could not produce housing that was affordable to lower-income households. As interest rates and land costs continued to inflate, the gap between rents in older and newer properties increased (Haywood 1984:184, 186, 187). By the 1970s, in the face of mounting costs, subsidies were cut back in the nonprofit sector, as total housing starts dropped sharply. In 1974 an agreement between the six major political parties called for replacing housing subsidies with greater market regulation. During the same period, legislation called for regional and local planning as a requirement for subdivisions and other development.

At the present time, Danish housing is financed through conventional mortgages at market interest rates. Homeowners can deduct interest payments, maintenance costs (typically, 1 percent of assessed value), and local property taxes, but must report the imputed rental income of their homes according to a formula set by law. Capital gains on the sale of homes are not subject to taxation. Since standard tax rates exceed 50 percent, homeowning is the most profitable form of housing tenure in Denmark. Private rental housing is no longer profitable, and little is being built. Total housing construction in Denmark is considerably below postwar highs and is insufficient to meet demand, which exceeds supply by almost two-thirds (Haywood 1984:198, 215). Squatters are appearing in Denmark, as well as Germany.

ITALY

Although the housing situation has improved considerably during the postwar period,[6] all places and classes have not benefited equally. For example, overcrowding is so severe that as many as one-quarter of all families would have to be relocated to eliminate it altogether. Almost half of the metropolitan housing stock is in need of some repairs; one-quarter is in serious disrepair (Padovani 1984:248).

High rates of housing construction occurred during the 1950s, with strong government support for private enterprise; indeed, housing investment at times reached 6 to 7 percent of GNP. During the same period, public housing declined from 25 percent of total housing investment in 1951 to only 6 percent in the early 1960s, at the same time, construction stagnated and much public housing was sold off. Rents increased sharply as a consequence, contributing to the increase in homeownership. The emphasis on new construction resulted in neglect and subsequent deterioration of the existing housing stock. As a result, the latter part of the 1960s and first half of the 1970s witnessed a reduced emphasis on new construction, with greater attention on rehabilitation, redevelopment, and planning in general. The 1967 Town Planning Reform Act shifted some infrastructure costs from localities to developers while calling for greater planning—a policy that was strengthened ten years later in the Land Regulation Act, which partially exempted public and low-cost housing (Padovani 1984:263, 265, 274).

Regulation of the Rental Housing Market

European governments, whatever their political orientation, have been far more willing to regulate rents and conditions of tenancy than has been the case in the United States. Controls for private rental housing have routinely been a matter of national policy in many European nations, while in the United States they are generally regarded as purely local.[7]

Controls have historically been the principal method of dealing with high rents. Throughout Western Europe, wartime freezes were extended after the conflict ended, but rent controls were eased everywhere at the end of the 1950s. By the early 1960s, the remaining rent freezes—often limited to older units—were producing disinvestment in the frozen sector and major inequities in rents between old and new property. From the 1960s onward, many governments moved from control to regulation, allowing rents to rise with costs; and by the 1970s, much of the European housing stock was free of controls altogether, in fact if not in law. Everywhere that rent control was enacted, security-of-tenure protections were adopted to prevent large-scale evictions (Harloe 1985:363, 365).

Although rent control has declined in recent years, this is not true of tenant protections—although there is reportedly widespread noncompliance, since it is typically up to the tenant (rather than the public) to take action (Harloe 1985:370). The economically weakest tenants often have little choice but to accept what landlords offer, are most easily exploited, and are least protected by the law. As Harloe concludes, "The relationship between landlord and tenant in practice is socially constructed rather than legally determined" (380).

FRANCE

Rent controls were first introduced in France in 1914. Severe pressures on rents in the immediate postwar period led to the 1948 Rent Act, incorporating some 6 million units into the "fixed rent sector" *(secteur taxe)*. The postwar subsidized stock, and the Parisian stock generally, were controlled; units elsewhere were freed. Technically, this act provided for vacancy decontrol and a gradual increase in market rents—provisions that, though not consistently implemented, have led to an overall decrease in the number of controlled units (Pearsall 1984:12). The 1982 Rent Act attempts to combine tenant protections with greater flexibility in rent setting. Rent contracts, negotiated between landlord and tenant organizations, assure rents based on costs, and tenants who cannot afford the negotiated rents receive housing allowances (43). Security-of-tenure protections in France are generally for the term of the lease only in private, unsubsidized rental housing—somewhat less protection than in other West European countries (Harloe 1985:366).[8]

WEST GERMANY

As noted above, West Germany has rent controls in social housing, and private developers receive subsidized loans in exchange for fifteen years of governmental controls and allocations. The postwar freeze was seriously weakened during the 1960s reprivatization, when rent controls and tenant protections were replaced by vacancy decontrol-recontrol.[9] Controlled rents were to be tied to increases in costs rather than set by statute (Harloe 1985:363). The adoption of vacancy decontrol brought a weakening of security protections as well. The election of the Social Democrats in 1969 resulted in the extension of rent stabilization to private housing, and further eviction protections in 1971

(Marcuse 1982:90). Increased housing allowances compensated for increased rents in public housing. At the present time, tenants have continuing security, except when a contract clause is violated or the unit is required by the landlord or his or her family. Tenants in rented rooms, students, holiday sublets, and "special tenements" are not covered by security protections (the latter includes duplexes where the landlord lives) (Harloe 1985:367).

GREAT BRITAIN

Rent control was introduced in Britain in 1915 as a wartime measure. Vacancy decontrol was enacted in 1925, but eased for small houses in 1933 and 1938 as harmful to the poorest families. Rent controls were continued and strengthened throughout the period immediately following the Second World War. They were again eased in 1954 by allowing rent increases to cover costs of repairs. The 1957 Rent Act marked the decline of rent controls, through the blanket decontrol of expensive properties and decontrol on vacancy of low-income units. By the mid-1960s, such decontrols were leading to evictions and otherwise harming tenants, as was documented in the 1965 Holland Report (Smith 1984:91).

The 1965 Rent Act was the response: it called for a recontrol under "fair rents," based on prevailing rent levels and conditions (rather than, for example, tenants' ability to pay). Under this legislation, rents are reset every three years based on what they would be in a 'freely functioning market" (Harloe 1985:363). This general easing of rent controls has significantly hurt the poorest. The transition from control to regulation was resisted in many places, and rising rents are creating pressures for renewed controls. Even where controls exist they are often evaded (Harloe 1985:114, 365). Tenure protections exist when there is no resident landlord. In theory, protected tenants have lifetime security of tenure, although there are numerous grounds for eviction. There is no consistent national model code governing rental agreements.

DENMARK

Rents were frozen in 1939 and security of tenure was given to all tenants. Rent controls were extended in 1951 to property built after 1939. In 1955, controls were eased somewhat; certain rent increases were allowed in subsidized units, while property built without government subsidy was freed from controls altogether. In 1974 controls on private rentals were restricted to localities of 20,000 or more people, a policy that remains in force. Presently, one-third of all units are decontrolled; rents in the remainder are tied to costs and property values (Harloe 1984:363). A distinction is made between lifetime security for controlled tenants and contract-length security for others. Legislation in 1975 extended security protections from tenants in controlled units to all tenants (not just those in controlled units). There are, presently, very limited grounds for eviction.

ITALY

Italy's rental housing stock is under a national system of rent controls. The 1978 Fair Rent Act extended postwar controls, establishing four-year tenancies that are renewable at the landlord's discretion. Rents are pegged to a percentage of dwelling units' value, and increases are linked to the cost of living index (Padovani 1984:276).

Conclusions

Although there are exceptions, West European postwar housing policies share common features, such as the following:

* Wartime rent freezes were continued into the postwar period, until the most acute shortages had been addressed. Subsequently, rent controls were eased, either through vacancy decontrols or pegging rent increases to the cost of living index, or some combination of both. In some cases, rent controls were eliminated altogether. The viability of rent regulation depended in large part on the philosophy of the ruling governmental party or coalition.
* During the crisis period following the war, extensive public involvement in reconstruction was common. Continuing commitment thereafter varied from country to country. In some instances, public housing construction was initially seen as the mainstay of a viable housing program; elsewhere, public housing was secondary in importance to cooperatives and heavily subsidized (and restricted) private rental housing. An early emphasis on new housing construction typically gave way to the rehabilitation of existing structures. Again, commitment to one of the several modes of housing tenure depended, in part, on partisan considerations.
* By the late 1970s there was a return to more market-oriented housing policies, including renewed emphasis on single-family home construction.

At this point it will be useful to examine in some detail the West European country that arguably has gone furthest toward solving its housing problems. Although Sweden offers an innovative approach to the provision of housing, its programs, as we shall see, suffer from an ambivalent attitude to the marketplace. Nevertheless, we hope to derive some insights that will prove useful when we develop a National Comprehensive Housing Program for the United States in Chapter 9.

SWEDISH HOUSING IN THE POSTWAR PERIOD

In 1965 Sweden embarked on a ten-year program to bring affordable housing within reach of its entire population. The United States made a similar public commitment three years later.

The rates of anticipated new construction were unprecedented in both countries, approaching 10–13 units per thousand people and foretelling a one-third increase in the respective housing stocks over a ten-year period. The United States, lacking any real means to implement its goals, fell 4.5 million units short of the projected 26 million units, or almost one-sixth. Of its 6 million targeted subsidized units, only 2.7 million were built—a shortfall of 55 percent (Stone 1980b). Sweden, by contrast, surpassed its ten-year target, achieving construction rates 20 to 25 percent higher than previous levels (Nesslein 1982:241). With housing regarded as a public right rather than as a commodity, it appeared by the mid-seventies that Sweden had achieved its goal of providing adequate and affordable shelter for its entire population (Headey 1978; Appelbaum 1985b, 1986d).

The remainder of this chapter, which examines Swedish housing policy during the postwar period, looks at the extent to which Social Democratic housing goals have been met, and some reasons for the initial successes—and current failures—of Swedish housing programs. We are particularly interested in Swedish efforts to "steer" housing production toward nonmarket alternatives, by means of quasi-market mechanisms that permitted housing investors a considerable degree of choice. This hybrid approach created a number of problems that the Swedes are trying to resolve, and from which we can learn.

Introduction

In 1965, amid much fanfare, Sweden initiated its ten-year program to bring affordable housing within reach of its 8 million people. By 1975, more than 1 million units had been constructed, greatly overreaching original targets, with average annual increases of 20 to 25 percent over previous construction rates (Nesslein 1982:241). With housing defined as a public right, construction was directed toward the public-owned and cooperative sectors. In 1970, for example, 43 percent of all construction was undertaken by nonprofit municipal housing companies, with an additional 16 percent done by cooperatives. Owner-occupied homes accounted for 28 percent of the total, with private rental housing amounting to only 13 percent. A complex system of subsidies and housing allowances assured that no person need spend more than 20 percent of his or her income on housing. By the mid-seventies, it appeared that supply had been brought into balance with demand and that Sweden had achieved its goal of providing adequate and affordable shelter to its population.

In the following pages we will examine both the means and the extent to which the "Swedish miracle" was achieved. Sweden's approach is of particular interest in that national policy sought to stimulate nonmarket alternatives alongside traditional (albeit highly regulated) ones. It was the expectation of Swedish policymakers that such alternatives would, over time, prove more attractive than owner-occupied homes and private rentals. These alternative housing forms were to be achieved by inducements or "steering mechanisms" that redirected private investment toward nonprofit forms of tenure. As we shall see, these methods included interest subsidies, land-use planning, and controls on prices and rents—all within the context of a vastly expanded public commitment to the housing sector.

Yet the Swedish zeal for a "middle way" has not been without its problems. In attempting to socialize housing within a market economy, Sweden was able to achieve a great many of its objectives; yet there have always been difficulties not far beneath the surface. In particular, the economic and ideological appeal of homeownership remained strong as the Swedish population has become increasingly middle class. As a result, some of the gains achieved over the past two decades now appear to be threatened.

The "Third Stream": Nonmarket Alternatives to Private Homes and Rentals

Sweden's current housing policy originated immediately after World War II, when the ruling Social Democratic Party began to think of housing in terms of what subsequently has been referred to as the "socialist market."[10] By the end of World War II, partly as a consequence of rapid urbanization, the people of Sweden were among the most poorly housed in Europe, particularly in the rapidly growing metropolitan areas of Gothenburg, Malmo, and Stockholm. Thirty-eight percent of the 2.1 million dwellings were owner-occupied, with most of the rest involving various forms of tenancy, mainly private rentals (35 percent) or rentals based on employer-employee relationships (10 percent). Only 2 percent were rentals in public housing, and 5 percent cooperatives (Lundqvist 1981:1). It was in this context that the Social Democrats sought to encourage the provision of nonmarket housing while, at the same time, "re-educating" the public to the virtues of more communal tenure forms, in contrast to the privatizing tendencies of the conventional suburban home. In power almost continuously since 1932 (the exception was the six-year period 1976–82), they have had an unparalleled opportunity to do so.

In 1945 the Royal Commission on Housing and Redevelopment, which had been in existence since 1933, issued its report, calling for a comprehensive national housing policy. Under the Commission's program, all risks were to be socialized; speculation would be eliminated. The program became the guide-post for three decades of Swedish housing policy, and its objectives are summarized by Headey (1978:74)[11] as follows:

1. To eliminate the housing shortage by means of a Fifteen-Year Programme (1946–60). The output of new housing was to be stabilized at a level that would be sufficient to meet the increase in the number of households and also meet the need for improving housing standards and urban redevelopment.

2. To raise space standards by increasing the production of dwellings containing at least two or three rooms and a kitchen. The use of one-room flats as family housing was condemned.
3. To raise equipment standards in new housing and to improve older dwellings. Standards for rural housing were to be brought up to the same level as for urban housing.
4. To keep down rent levels, partly through government action, so that spacious, modern, family dwellings would be within reach of average wage earners. It was considered that an average industrial worker should pay no more than 20 percent of his wage for a fully modern flat consisting of two rooms and kitchen.
5. To encourage public financing of housebuilding.
6. To invigorate local authorities in their housing activities.
7. To discourage speculative building by offering favorable loan terms to individuals, housing associations and local authorities.

Before we examine in some detail exactly how these objectives were to be achieved, it may be useful to comment on the political context of Swedish housing policy.[12] The "organizing of Swedish society" (Headey 1978:60) into politically active interest groups was largely completed during the decade following World War II. These groups, which can be classified as supporting either the Social Democrats on the one hand or the "bourgeois parties" (as they are called in Sweden) on the other, play a central role in Swedish politics. On controversial issues they are represented on the Royal Commissions, which generate national policy as well as build consensus. Interest groups are thus frequently and formally consulted and, in exchange, play important roles in eventual policy implementation.

In the housing sphere, groups that generally support the Social Democrats' programs include the construction, trade, and white-collar unions; the League of Municipalities; the large cooperative associations; the National Association of Swedish Public Housing Enterprises (SABO); and the National Tenants' Union. The "pro-bourgeois" interest groups include university graduates and higher civil servants' unions; farmers' organizations; employers' and industrialists' federations; private builders; landlord and homeowner associations; and the banks. The very success of the Social Democrats' housing program has served to build the strength and membership of those groups that supported it. Public opinion, at least until very recently, has also strongly favored the Social Democrats' approach. Before they became relatively affluent, most Swedes supported programs that promised cheaper public and cooperative housing, housing allowances, and other forms of subsidy (Headey 1978:64).

The stage was set for the present approach during the beginning of World War II, when housing construction all but ceased. In the face of rapid urbanization, public demand soon outstripped supply in the larger cities. In response to the perceived failure of the private market, the Social Democratic government became heavily involved in housing production, subsidizing over 90 percent of wartime construction during the period 1942–45. Building targets were met each year (Headey 1978:72). The increased state intervention clearly favored nonprofit builders and working-class consumers at the expense of developers, private investors, landlords, and potential homeowners. It was made possible partly because of the national consensus generated by the war, but also because of the Social Democrats' decisive electoral victory of 1941, when they obtained a clear majority for the first time since winning power in 1932. When the war ended, the Social Democrats could therefore point to past successes, relying on the administrative legacy of greatly enhanced wartime planning. It is against this backdrop that the vision of the 1945 Royal Commission must be assessed.

The Social Democrats by no means had free rein to promote a thoroughgoing socialist housing program. During most of the forty-four-year period (1932–76), they were forced into coalition governments (legislative majorities were held only from 1941 to 1951 and from 1967 to 1973). As Headey (1978:59) summarizes the Social Democrats' position, "Retention of power hinges on 5 percent of voters and seats, so that public opinion and the parties and interest groups which represent centrist opinion have to be carefully cultivated. Compromise is a political necessity not just a national characteristic." Yet, at the same time, the importance of almost half a century of Social Democratic governance should not be underestimated: the party became strong and disciplined, both nationally and locally (where it held power as well), while administrators and bureaucrats could become reasonably confident that the government's housing programs were relatively permanent.

Cooperative Housing in Sweden

The cooperative movement was Sweden's first major alternative to private rental housing, with its origin preceding the Social Democratic government by about two decades.[13] The principal cooperative organization, the National Association of Tenants' Savings and Building Societies (HSB), was founded in 1923–24 on the initiative of the National Tenants' Association, at a time when wages were falling and rents rising.[14] HSB developed a two-tier structure: a regional savings society, which also provided technical assistance, and local tenant-owner associations, which the national organization aggressively sought to create. By offering depositors who eventually purchased co-op units preferential interest rates, HSB was able to raise substantial amounts of capital to greatly increase the amount of cooperative construction under its sponsorship. The Association was (and is) run democratically, with elected boards in the local projects. HSB thus combined building and savings, cooperative ownership and mutual assistance. It grew rapidly during the thirties, becoming a nationwide movement. As its capital base grew, HSB was able to acquire suppliers' firms and manufacturing facilities, and engage in bulk purchases. At the present time, HSB estimates its membership at almost 350,000.[15]

A second cooperative association, Svenska Riksbyggen, was founded in the 1940s, when 40 percent of the members of the building trades were out of work. Riksbyggen's membership base was in the trade unions, and it intended to revitalize the home construction industry by building public housing units as well as cooperatives. Smaller than HSB, it presently manages some 180,000 dwelling units. Together, HSB and Riksbyggen account for two-thirds of all cooperatives and approximately one out of every ten dwelling units in Sweden (Lundevall 1976:38).

The cooperative movement in Sweden was highly self-conscious about its goals, seeking no less than the transformation of housing tenure in the country. It sought to provide quality housing at prices working people could easily afford, removing housing from the inflationary effects of the marketplace. The cooperative form of tenure, a hybrid between tenancy and private ownership, was appealing in that it promised security while presumably discouraging "privatization." Until 1969, controls prevented units from being resold at market prices, thereby guaranteeing price stability as well. It was anticipated that once cooperatives had acquired a significant segment of the market, private rents would be forced down in competition.

Public Utility Housing

While cooperatives were a part of the socialist vision of housing as a "social right, rather than a private good,"[16] the cooperative movement came to occupy the conservative position within the Social Democratic approach to housing. The more radical position, favored by the socialists, was to deny private ownership altogether, in the form of a greatly expanded "public utility housing" sector. Under this approach, private landlords would eventually be displaced by public forms of ownership. This was to be achieved through the large-scale construction of flats by nonprofit municipal housing companies, financed by the central government and facilitated by significantly enhanced local empowerment.

The Housing Provision and Building Acts of 1947 allocated to the municipalities responsibility for solving the housing shortage, along with the right to decide how all land within municipal boundaries was to be used (Svensson 1976:5–13). This "planning monopoly" made possible extensive land banking, long-range planning, and the construction of public housing units on municipally owned land. Municipalities were given the rights of expropriation and first refusal on land, and later (in 1973) they were given the right to expropriate existing rental housing that failed to comply with building standards (Jussil 1975:176–77).[17] The national government viewed its role as providing enabling legislation and financing; the localities had the responsibility for planning and construction.

By 1980 there were some 250 municipal housing corporations throughout Sweden, which had produced two-thirds of all rental construction during the previous decade. One-quarter of all dwelling units were owned by these companies, which amounted to half of all rentals. Within the cities, close to three-quarters of all new housing construction were built on municipally owned lands. Tenancy in public housing extended well into the middle class; indeed, an objective of the massive public housing construction during the period 1965–74 was to "de-class" this form of tenure. As with the cooperative movement, the long-term strategy underlying public housing was to increase the market share to the point where public housing became price-leading. Since such units were provided on a nonprofit basis, this in turn would make housing generally available at lower prices (Lundqvist 1981:1).

Thus Swedish postwar housing policy, particularly during the period 1965–74, sought, through heavy governmental subsidy and strong local planning, to "steer" new construction away from the private sector and toward the public rentals and quasi-private cooperative ownership preferred by the Social Democrats (Jussil 1975). By 1980, 20 percent of all housing units were owned by municipal housing companies, and 15 percent were in cooperatives. At the same time, the share of private rentals had declined to only 20 percent of the market, with owner-occupied homes making up the balance (about 40 percent) (SI 1980:2–3).

Table 8.1 summarizes recent trends for the multifamily housing stock.[18] Almost two-thirds of all units built in 1945 were private rentals, while approximately one-fourth were in cooperatives and one out of eleven in public enterprises. Cooperative housing construction peaked in 1960 at 38 percent, and subsequently has fluctuated around postwar levels. Private enterprise

TABLE 8.1

MULTIFAMILY HOUSING IN SWEDEN: NEWLY COMPLETED UNITS AND
EXISTING STOCK BY OWNERSHIP TYPE, 1945–79

	NEWLY COMPLETED UNITS						EXISTING STOCK				
Ownership Type	1945	1960	1965	1970	1975	1979	1945	1960	1965	1970	1979
Private enterprises	65%	21%	20%	19%	12%	12%	80%	55%	49%	41%	38%
Housing cooperatives	26	38	27	22	20	27	11	22	24	24	24
Municipal and public utility enterprises	9	41	53	59	68	61	9	23	27	34	38
Total	100	100	100	100	100	100	100	100	100	100	100

Source: Svenska Riksbyggen (1980:4,6).

construction had declined to only 12 percent by 1979, while public enterprise construction increased to 68 percent in 1975 (it declined somewhat thereafter). As a consequence, the multifamily housing stock went from 80 percent private rentals in 1945 to 38 percent in 1975. Cooperatives at that time accounted for almost a fourth of the multifamily housing stock.

The "Swedish Miracle"

The accomplishments of the Social Democrats in achieving their housing objectives during the period 1965–74 were, by any standards, substantial. By allocating an annual average of 6.7 percent of GNP to housing,[19] a total of 1,005,600 units was constructed (Headey 1978:48). The ten-year program witnessed six significant accomplishments:

1. *Large-scale construction of housing of a quality unimaginable two decades earlier.* In 1945, only 21 percent of all dwelling units in Sweden had a bath or shower, 36 percent had an inside toilet, and 46 percent had central heating. These figures had improved only marginally by 1955. By 1974, however, fully 93 percent of all households had central heating, shower or bath, inside toilet, refrigerator, stove, and similar amenities (Headey 1978:50–51). Slum areas have been eliminated, although one study estimates that "some 8000 people have no decent home" (Wiktorin 1982:248).[20] Historically, Swedish housing has been small and crowded, by American standards, but this situation had also improved considerably by the seventies, with a shift in construction to larger two- and three-bedroom units.

Most significantly, working-class people enjoyed these amenities to the same extent as those in the middle class. In 1974, for example, 97 percent of salary earners lived in "modern" dwellings with a full range of amenities; the figure for wage earners was 92 percent (Headey 1978:51–52). In fact, one of the principal achievements of Swedish housing policy was to provide all Swedes the housing opportunities available in most countries only to the middle class. Headey (50, 52–53) has summarized this accomplishment:

> In most countries—as in Sweden in the past—lower income groups are constrained to live as tenants of either private landlords or public authorities in relatively poor, run-down neighborhoods. In modern Sweden, by contrast, working class people, like middle class people, have an effective choice of living in cooperative as well as tenant housing and also of being owner-occupiers. . . . The significance of this extension of opportunity should not be minimized. In most countries working class people are not able to choose whether to live in town, close to work and entertainment, or to join the green wave living in simulated countryside. The Swedish worker is relatively fortunate in being able to house his family according to preference rather than according to the tyranny of what economists, accustomed to analyzing "free" rather than socialized markets, term "effective demand."

There is some evidence that the lowest-income people are not as well housed as middle- and working-class Swedes. Immigrants, for example, are more likely to live in overcrowded conditions: a study in 1976 found that one-quarter of Finnish workers and almost one-half of immigrants from southern Europe were living two or more to a room (excluding kitchens and living rooms). The same study concludes, however, that "people with unsatisfactory housing conditions . . . [are] very marginal in proportion to the whole population," tending to be low income and low status, but otherwise heterogeneous in terms of ethnicity, household size, and social status (Wiktorin 1982:248–50).

2. *Creation of planned suburban communities.* For ideological as well as economic reasons, a great deal of housing construction consisted of large apartment complexes, particularly in the major metropolitan suburbs. In the Stockholm area, for example, close to four out of every five persons lived in apartments by 1970 (Daun 1979:1), while nationwide the figure is currently almost half.

Suburban housing, particularly public housing projects built during the late fifties and early sixties, were often characterized by the alienating, high-rise, functionalist architecture often associated with Swedish public housing. Yet much recent construction has been in row houses and small flats, in well-planned suburban communities built around service and commercial centers, and integrated with highly efficient mass transit systems. The visitor to the Swedish suburbs is struck by their "new towns" atmosphere: cluster development, large amounts of open space, children's play areas, centrally located shops, and a range of amenities seldom found in their U.S. counterparts.[21]

3. *Elimination of private landlords as a significant force in the determination of rents.* When the postwar system of rent controls was lifted in Sweden in 1975[22] with the decontrolling of 350,000 private rental units in the large urban areas (Nesslein 1982:237), the groundwork had already been laid for the "socialist market" in rent setting. A series of national laws, beginning with the Rent Act of 1968, established key safeguards for tenants, including mandatory collective bargaining between tenants' and landlords' organizations. Every year, representatives of the large nonprofit municipal housing companies negotiate rent levels with representatives of the National Tenants' Association. By law, public-sector rents then serve as guidelines for rents in the private sector. Rents are determined on the basis of "utilization value" only—equal rent for dwellings of equal quality.

Under rent control, rents reflected initial production expenses (with adjustments for rising costs), but "utilization value" rent setting is designed to ensure that newer, more costly units in a locality are not priced above older units of comparable quality (Nesslein 1982:237). Under this "fair-rent structure," neither location nor capital costs are supposed to influence rents; only the size of a unit, its amenities, and its overall maintenance are to be considered. This has resulted in a system that "leads to rent agreements that are independent of the property owner's actual costs" (Ronmark 1981:11). In practice, this means that the large public and private rental companies must practice "rent pooling," whereby rents in their newer, high-cost units are subsidized by rents in older, lower-cost ones.[23]

Because of "fair-rent" provisions in Swedish housing laws, tenants are protected against large increases, a major source of involuntary displacement. Tenants enjoy other protections as well, particularly safeguards against arbitrary eviction. Swedish law also protects against eviction through "luxury renewal"—the upgrading of property so that it becomes too expensive for its present tenants. It is, in fact, very difficult for landlords to evict tenants who pay their rent on time.

Disputes over lease conditions and violations, as well as rent levels, are handled by local rent tribunals and, on appeal, by the National Housing Court. Landlords who fail to maintain their units adequately are subject to stringent controls. Under the 1973 Housing Renewal Act, local rent tribunals can force landlords to bring their units up to acceptable standards. The 1977 Housing Management Act empowers the rent tribunals to temporarily suspend landlords from management duties until necessary repairs have been made. In extreme cases, the right of landlords to mortgage their property can be suspended for up to five years (Lundqvist 1981:26).

4. Creation of a system of housing allowances that reaches almost 40 percent of all households (Nesslein 1982:236), that stipulates that no household need pay an excessive percentage of its income on housing. Allowances are based on income, number of children, age, and housing expenditure. They extend to households in all three forms of tenure, reaching 26 percent of homeowners, 33 percent of cooperative owner-tenants, and 42 percent of tenants in public and private rental housing (Lundqvist 1981:20).[24] Support levels were at one time pegged at one-fifth of household income, although the inflation of recent years has made such a goal increasingly remote. As recently as 1974, families with children spent an estimated 16 percent of their income on rents, but there is evidence that the figure for all households may now be considerably higher, possibly approaching 25 percent.[25] For all households receiving allowances, approximately one-third of housing expenditures are covered (20). For a typical working-class family paying roughly one-quarter of its income for rent (approximately $200 per month), allowances would cover 54 percent of rent payments (SI 1980:3). Unlike the United States' Section 8 program, housing supports extend well into the middle class, so that recipients are not stigmatized.

5. *Municipal land-banking of almost all developable land in the major urban areas*. Public lands are used as sites for the construction of public nonprofit housing units, or are leased to developers, or are sold outright under stringent controls, with the consequence that three-quarters of all construction in the municipalities (excluding urban renewal) has been on municipal holdings (Heimburger 1976:31). Furthermore, under the so-called "land condition," state loan subsidies for the construction of rental units are made only for projects built on land obtained from municipalities (Svensson 1976:31–32). Since, as we will see, such subsidies are sizable, this gives the localities further leverage over speculation and land use generally.

Swedish municipalities, along with responsibility for assuring adequate housing, have been granted extremely strong land-use planning powers in order to do so. National legislation empowers localities to set construction, design, and equipment standards for all housing, regulating its type, location, and timing (Nesslein 1982:238). Under the "planning monopoly," all development must reflect annual and "rolling" five-year municipal plans. As previously noted, localities have rights of expropriation and first refusal (Svensson 1976:14–32; Jussil 1975:176), with compensation laws designed to discourage speculation. They are also in a position to get land-procurement and leasehold loans on highly favorable terms (Jussil 1975; SI 1980:3).

6. *Elimination of shelter poverty*. In Sweden, where the average blue-collar worker earns $12,000 a year, an unsubsidized four-bedroom unit rents for about $245 a month (all utilities included). A comparable cooperative costs $40 less (estimated from Lundqvist 1981: Tables 5 and 6; SR 1980:8). According to Headey (1978:86):

> There is now a housing surplus rather than a shortage and almost everybody lives in a good quality dwelling in a pleasant neighborhood. The government could reasonably claim that it had achieved its stated aim that "The whole population should be provided with sound, spacious, well planned and appropriately equipped dwellings of good quality at reasonable costs."

Nonetheless, new problems have emerged, and housing controversies are as fierce as ever. Before we examine some of these difficulties, however, let us look at the mechanisms by which the Swedish government has "steered" housing investment in the direction dictated by the "socialist market."

Steering Mechanisms

The Swedish government has used two principal means to achieve its housing objectives: legislation empowering localities to solve their own housing problems, and the financial mechanisms necessary to do so. We have mentioned some of the former: the planning monopoly and land condition, rights of preemption and expropriation, and strong powers of code enforcement that, at the same time, prevent luxury renewal. There are also provisions in the tax code to discourage speculation. Since 1968, the capital gains tax has been strengthened, with a rate of 75 percent for short-term gains, net of a small deductible (see Svensson 1976:28–29). The chief financial mechanisms have included housing allowances, loans to municipalities for land banking, and a system of interest subsidies designed to promote more public forms of ownership. Interest subsidies are the main "steering mechanisms" by which the Swedish government is able to direct the marketplace toward socially desired objectives.

The financing of construction is based on large government subsidies to private borrowers (see Lundqvist 1981:17). Seventy percent of the total cost of land and development is financed through long-term (forty-year) private "primary loans" at slightly less than market rates.[26] A variable part of the remaining 30 percent is financed by state housing loans, according to the type of tenure. Thus nonprofit municipal public housing corporations receive the entire 30 percent in state loans; cooperatives receive 29 percent; owner-occupied houses, 25 percent; and private rentals, 22 percent. This, in effect, means that no monies need be advanced for the construction of public housing, while cooperatives require only 1 percent of the total cost, detached homes 5 percent, and private rentals 8 percent.

This investment hierarchy is reinforced by a parallel system of "preferred" loan subsidies. New housing in Sweden has a guaranteed mortgage interest rate on the entire loan, set initially at extremely low levels, with government subsidies covering all interest payments in excess of the guaranteed rate. For cooperatives and rental units, the guaranteed rate in 1981 was 3 percent for the first year of the loan, rising at 0.25 percent per year thereafter until it reached the market rate. For owner-occupied homes, the initial rate was 5.5 percent, rising considerably more steeply—at 0.5 percent per year. Together, these financial mechanisms have worked well to discourage the production of single-family homes, vis-à-vis other forms of tenure,[27] and to encourage the production of public rentals instead of private ones.

Originally, the "steering effects" of interest subsidies were to be secured by a tax system that neutralized any economic bias in favor of single-family housing. Homeowners in Sweden were allowed to deduct the unsubsidized portion of interest paid on mortgage loans from taxable income, as if it were a business expense, but such an expense was to be set against the hypothetical income that would result from actually renting the property out—income that was taxed at 2 percent (Headey 1978:86–87).[28] When nonsubsidized interest rates were also at 2 percent, taxes more or less offset the interest deductions (Headey 1978:87; Lundqvist 1981:21), and homeowners received no tax benefit by virtue of their tenure. As we will see, this is no longer the case.

Some Recent Problems

By the mid-seventies, Sweden had pronounced its housing problems essentially solved. With completion of the "1 million" program, supply had, in theory, been brought into balance with demand. The minimum standard of two bedrooms for a four-person family was widely achieved. Speculation had largely disappeared because of a balanced market, the removal of most developable urban land from the marketplace, and the replacement of market rental pricing by a system of rent negotiations. The termination of the postwar system of rent controls, as unnecessary in a "balanced market," was a direct result of these achievements.

The past five years, however, have revealed fundamental problems.[29] Increasingly, affluent Swedes have demanded (and received) detached suburban homes, despite more than forty years of socialist "education" promoting the virtues of public housing and cooperatives. Whereas surveys in the fifties indicated that only 30 to 40 percent of the population preferred to live in detached homes, the figure is now 80 to 90 percent (Daun 1979:2, 6). Today, 72 percent of all newly constructed units are single-family homes, a dramatic reversal from ten years ago (see Table 8.2). Only one-fifth of all units are in public rentals. Vacancy rates in high-rises, especially in suburban areas, rose in the early seventies, although in some areas shortages are again being felt.[30] In some projects, middle-class Swedish tenants have been replaced by immigrant workers, who now comprise one-eighth of the total population. Segregation is regarded as a potentially serious problem.

Re-Commodification of Swedish Housing?

The highly successful cooperative sector has come increasingly to resemble ordinary homeownership. Co-op members now have virtually total control over the use and resale of their units. This control was greatly reinforced with the removal of resale price controls on cooperative units in 1969. Prior to that time, Swedish law conferred control over equity appreciation to the directing

TABLE 8.2
HOUSING PRODUCTION IN SWEDEN, BY TYPE OF HOUSING (1970–79)

Housing Type	1970	1975	1979
Single family (1–2 units)	32%	63%	72%
Multifamily (3+ units)	68	37	28

Source: Svenska Riksbyggen (1980:5).

boards of the major cooperative organizations, which generally limited price increases to the initial down payment, augmented for any improvements plus compensation for inflation. In 1969, however, HSB dropped its resale price controls. A variety of reasons were given: the black market for co-op units in the face of housing shortages, the difficulty of enforcement, the unfair advantage conferred on owners of private homes.[31]

The political climate was harsh criticism of the Social Democratic housing programs on the part of the nonsocialist media and other parties, reinforced by housing shortages in the major urban areas (Headey 1978:83–86). The Social Democrats received their lowest vote since 1932 in the municipal elections of 1966 (42.2 percent). Decontrol of rents and co-op units was part of the restructuring of the new government's housing policies.

Presently, co-op members are free to sell their shares on the open market. There are pressures to make legal what already exists in fact: private ownership of cooperative units, or the condominium form of ownership.[32] As a result of these developments, there are also strong pressures to convert rental units to cooperatives, especially in Stockholm, where a housing shortage is again being felt. Such conversions are still a marginal problem in Sweden, but where they occur they are highly profitable, because (as in this country) the combined value of co-op units greatly exceeds the value of the building as a rental and because, under Swedish financing, cooperatives qualify for favorable terms for government rehabilitation loans.[33] Conversions, which tend to be favored by private landlords and tenants who benefit by acquiring their units, are strongly opposed by the National Tenants' Association and the National Association of Swedish Public Housing Enterprises (SABO), which view conversion as a retreat from the "socialist market" and a threat to their political power base.[34] They fear that the most desirable rental housing will be sold off, lost to the inflationary market stream. Because of "rent pooling," rents in all the remaining apartments could go up, if the converted units are the older, less costly ones (Lundqvist 1981:28). The central cities, where much of the desirable rental housing is located, would then become gentrified, with resulting displacement and economic segregation. Tenants in the remaining rental housing would bear the stigma that attaches to public housing in the United States.

The major cooperative associations have taken somewhat differing positions on the conversion issue. Although HSB stands to benefit from the management contracts it would gain, it has close historical ties with the National Tenants' Association and therefore has shown no interest in converting public housing to cooperatives. Riksbyggen, closely affiliated with organized labor, favors conversions, but under new cooperative forms that would end speculation. Under its Spring 1981 housing rights program, for example, vacated units would be resold to the association, which would then sell it to another member. This would be equivalent to reestablishing equity controls on cooperative shares. Another Riksbyggen program (the "Stockholm Model") envisions cooperative tenant-management association boards in public housing, which would subcontract managerial responsibility from the companies (which would be represented on the boards). This would produce a quasi-conversion that realizes the goal of cooperative management while leaving the unit legally in the public domain.

The nonsocialist governing coalition of 1976–82 favored a return to market allocations in housing. A 1981 Governmental Committee, for example, charged with responsibility for developing legal options for condominium ownership, recommended "making possible a quite considerable change from tenancy to cooperatives," involving the conversion of as much as 40 percent of public rentals (cited in Lundqvist 1981:28). Needless to say, this would represent a dramatic reversal of close to four decades of Swedish housing policy. With the return of the socialists to power in September 1982, however, there has been a return to the original ideals of the cooperative movement, in the form of resale restrictions such as those envisioned in Riksbyggen's housing rights program. It is highly unlikely that the Social Democrats will permit significant amounts of cooperative conversion so long as they remain in power.

The reasons for recent trends away from the ideals of the "socialist market" are many and widely debated. They have partly to do with the very success of the Social Democrats in producing an affluent middle-class society that views homeownership with increasing favor. In the rental sector, the reasons reflect dissatisfaction with bureaucracy and inflexibility in public housing management, where enormous municipal companies are seen as unresponsive to the needs of tenants. The once-radical tenants' movement is now an organization of some 600,000 members that functions primarily to negotiate rental agreements for tens of thousands of units.

Some "Qualitative" Issues

The difficulties are widely acknowledged, and some tentative moves have been taken to confront what was once referred to as the "qualitative" issues of Swedish housing (Headey 1978:93). Foremost among these are changes in the management of public rental units that would give tenants a considerably greater role (Lundqvist 1981:29–35). These changes range from slightly expanded managerial responsibility to co-determination, or joint tenant-management decision making. Experiments with the latter have begun in public housing corporations outside of Stockholm (Nackahem) and Gothenburg (Alebyggen), where tenant committees help determine the budget for maintenance and are able to rebate savings to residents.

A somewhat more far-reaching approach, "selective tenancy," was begun by the National Association of Swedish Public Housing Enterprises (SABO) in

May 1981. Under this concept, the large, citywide corporations set up minicompanies in each housing complex, and tenants have access to the full budgeting process. Tenants are then able to choose how to spend the money allocated to their complex—for example, setting higher or lower standards of service (with corresponding increases or decreases in rents). A major purpose of these programs is to promote the ideal of economic democracy among tenants, decentralizing at least one aspect—management—of tenant-landlord relations.[35] At present, the programs are limited in scope, voluntary for the housing companies, and—according to Swedish leaders—have not yet sparked the imagination of most tenants.

Other "qualitative" issues include equipping dwellings with services to benefit families in which both parents work, and adapting dwellings to the special requirements of singles, divorcees, and old people living alone (Headey 1978:94).[36] Finally, a large part of recent Swedish research on housing has focused on energy efficiency. This is vital, because of Sweden's long and harsh winter climate and because of the cost of imported energy.

Preferences for Private Ownership

The principal problem, as viewed by the Social Democrats, remains the move toward private ownership. This is attributed to several factors. There is, unquestionably, an increased preference for owner-occupied housing, particularly in the suburbs. Although the demand for apartments remains strong in the large cities, the high-rise public housing flats in the suburbs often combine the geographic and social isolation of suburban living with all the disadvantages of small apartments. The costs of apartment living are also high, relative to other forms of tenure. Because of the Swedish system of "rent pooling," rents on older units (with lower financing costs) are the same as rents on new units of comparable quality; as we have seen, the former subsidize the latter. Given the relative newness of the Swedish public housing stock, the high costs of recent construction have served to raise average costs—although the costs of the newest units have been somewhat lower. It will be some time before rent-averaging brings overall costs down (Kemeny 1978:318).

These disadvantages of rental housing are reinforced by tax laws that increasingly work to the advantage of homeowners. Of the three forms of housing, owner occupancy is in theory the most expensive, once maintenance, heating, and utilities are taken into account. One study, for example, estimated that in 1978 an average homeowner spent $255 per month, compared with $245 for tenant rentals and $205 for cooperatives. When the homeowner's tax deductions were taken into account, however, the cost of homeowning dropped to $195, the least expensive of the three forms. The study concluded that an "average homeowner could get almost one-fourth of his total housing expenditure covered by the increase in disposable income caused by the right to deduct his deficits on housing from his taxable income" (Lundqvist 1981:15,

TABLE 8.3

GOVERNMENTAL SUBSIDIES TO EXISTING HOUSING STOCK IN
SWEDEN, 1975–78

Form of Subsidy	MILLIONS OF DOLLARS*				PERCENT			
	1975	1976	1977	1978	1975	1976	1977	1978
Housing allowances	720	900	960	1,060	44.5	44.1	38.7	36.8
Mortgage interest subsidies	360	440	560	620	22.2	21.6	22.6	21.5
Tax deductions for owner-occupants	540	700	960	1,200	33.3	34.3	38.7	41.7
Total	1,620	2,040	2,480	2,880	100.0	100.0	100.0	100.0

*Estimated at 5 Swedish kroner to the dollar.
Source: Lundqvist (1981:Table 7).

22). As Swedes have become increasingly affluent, even the middle class confronts high marginal tax brackets. Homeowners' interest deductions are thus extremely attractive.

With the recent rise in housing costs and interest rates, homeowners' tax deductions have become the most rapidly growing form of government housing expenditure. In 1975, tax deductions for owner-occupants amounted to 33 percent of all governmental subsidies for the existing housing stock; by 1978 the figure had grown to 42 percent (Table 8.3). One recent estimate has found expenditures on tax deductions to be as high as 53 percent of the current housing total (IUT 1982:1–2). During the three-year period, tax expenditures relative to homeownership grew more than twice as fast as those on housing allowances and interest subsidies combined—122 percent versus 55 percent. This has placed a severe strain on Swedish fiscal resources.

The nonsocialist government had encouraged these trends, but the new socialist coalition remains committed to the old vision of "equal cost for equal quality," regardless of tenure. Sverker Gustavsson, director of the National Swedish Institute for Building Research, in June 1981 outlined to me a three-part program the Social Democrats have sought to implement since their return to power in 1982. First, a systematic, across-the-board attempt to eliminate what crowding remains, thereby addressing one of the chief failures of public housing during the sixties. Second, greater tenant participation in management, building on the tentative experiments presently under way. Third, a restructuring of the subsidy program, with the goal that no household pay more than one-fifth of its income on housing.

How the Social Democrats can afford such a program is another matter. It is highly unlikely that the costly but popular tax breaks for homeownership can be altogether abolished. On the other hand, the Social Democratic victory, though small, was decisive: the party received 45.6 percent of the popular vote and 166 seats (out of 349) in parliament, compared with 45.1 percent and 163 seats for the three other principal parties combined.[37] The new government is confronted with an international economic recession, enormous public expenditures (two-thirds of GNP), and large budget deficits. The Swedish economy, like that of most other Western nations, has been stagnant, with declining investment and output. Rising import costs have led to sizable balance of payments deficits, with the resulting need to borrow abroad at high interest rates. Unemployment is close to 4 percent—high by Swedish standards. It is within this context that the Social Democrats undertake the difficult task of resolving Sweden's housing problems.

Conclusions

Harloe (1985:380) concludes his survey of landlord-tenant relations in Western Europe and the United States with this observation:

> Put simply, the problem is that the free market has, historically, been unable to provide housing to socially acceptable standards at a cost which is affordable by low-income households. Limited recognition of this fact provided the basis for the development of housing policy and subsidies in each of the six countries—principally by the institution of state-subsidized rental housing provided by local authorities or other non-profit bodies. But . . . these provisions have never covered more than a proportion of all households who require them.

Harloe notes that there has been a steadily declining subsidy to private landlords, who in many cases have become the leasors of last resort for the poorest (381). And, as we saw for the United States in Chapter 4, private landlords have been tightly squeezed in recent years. In Western Europe as in the United States, many tenants cannot afford to pay at the rates necessary to make private rental housing viable economically.

In the following chapter, we shall argue that one possible solution to these problems is to bypass the marketplace altogether to secure affordable housing for those who are willing to forgo the speculative returns associated with private ownership. The programs reviewed thus far have sought to balance social housing objectives with a fundamental commitment to private enterprise. This has resulted in great financial costs and has failed to adequately serve those who are most needy. We believe that a strong commitment to a "third stream" of nonmarket housing, financed through a system of direct government grants to nonprofit builders and developers, can avoid the pitfalls of the hybrid approaches reviewed in this chapter.

9
Some Proposals for U.S. Housing Policy

In this chapter we examine the potential role of the federal government in directly promoting programs aimed at low- and moderate-income households. Drawing heavily on the work of a national task force on housing policy, we offer an approach that rethinks the ways in which housing is produced, allocated, and consumed in the United States. This rethinking takes as a point of departure the goal established by the National Housing Act of 1949, "a decent home and a suitable living environment for every American family." In our proposed program, this commitment would be expanded into a legal declaration that every American household has the right to housing that is decent, safe, sanitary, affordable, compatible with resident needs, and under democratic residential control. Adequate and affordable housing would thereby become a universal national entitlement: all citizens would have the right to adequate housing at an affordable price.

Such housing would be secure with respect to tenure, permit locational choice, and respect the special problems of women, minorities, and the disabled. Attainment of such housing would become a national goal of the highest order, to which substantial public resources would be devoted. To achieve this goal, the program would assert that local, state, and federal

This chapter is based on a National Comprehensive Housing Program by a national task force on housing policy working under auspices of The Institute for Policy Studies' Alternative Program for America Project (see Appelbaum et al. 1986).

governments have a responsibility to use their powers to meet the housing needs of all segments of the community.

Throughout this book we have sought to demonstrate that the market economy has failed to provide adequate housing to those who need it most, in both of its two principal "streams": private ownership and rentals. The program would therefore establish that alternative forms of housing allocation and tenure must be implemented for a significant portion of the housing stock. We term this portion the "third stream" of community-based housing. It would exist alongside the two principal streams, to serve the needs of the growing numbers of households that are ill served by the marketplace.

By "community-based housing" we simply mean housing that is nonprofit and is produced and operated according to the principles of the national housing goal. There are many examples of such housing, of which the most familiar are public housing and cooperative housing with resale price controls. Other examples include university student and faculty housing, military housing, and housing owned by a nonprofit or governmental entity. The principal difference among these forms of housing is the degree of title to the unit. In cooperative housing, residents are considered to be tenant-owners, while in other forms they are regarded solely as tenants. Tenant-owners are permitted some investment stake in their unit while tenants are not. Other differences may have to do with tenants' rights (for example, modifying one's unit, or subletting), management style, and security of tenure. Under the proposed program, however, tenants in *all* community-based housing forms would be guaranteed the rights associated with ownership, as well as full protection against eviction, involuntary displacement, and other threats to tenure.

In exchange for these rights, tenants in community-based housing would forgo the right to resell their housing at a speculative profit. In community-based housing, the role of profit would be eliminated over time and the principle of community control would be substituted. This would apply not only to the production, financing, ownership, and sale of housing, but to decision making in housing in general. These guarantees need not entail centralization of housing programs in a federal bureaucracy, for the federal government's role would be limited to setting standards and minimal requirements, providing financing, and assuring enforcement. Administration would be local.

Community-based housing would be created through a series of mechanisms that

- Produce significant amounts of new and substantially rehabilitated housing for community-based ownership
- Promote the transfer of privately owned rental housing to the community-based sector while encouraging the voluntary conversion of private homes

to social ownership by fostering opportunities for homeownership without speculation
* Mandate the conservation, upgrading, and enhancement of existing public and subsidized units
* Assure residential security in the remaining private rental housing

Each of these mechanisms would be embodied in a separate act (reviewed below, following the discussion of short-term measures). Localities would be required to develop and implement plans for the creation of affordable, community-based housing by utilizing a combination of strategies, taking into account specific local needs and market conditions. Federal funds would be provided for a variety of programs that could be designed at the local level to accomplish these objectives, consistent with federal standards and specified national housing goals. The program would also call for a variety of tax and financing measures to enhance the growth of the community-based housing sector.

Although much of the program would not be attainable in the immediate future, many "starting points" could be implemented today. Indeed, some components are based on initiatives and experiments already carried out in Sweden, as well as in other parts of Europe and America, albeit in a limited way. Building upon these examples, the program would be responsive to current conditions, as well as supportive of broader changes. We therefore begin with some short-term measures that might constitute an interim or bridge to the more radical, long-term components. These proposals are designed to alleviate some of the difficulties confronted by tenants and other low- and moderate-income households, although they do not address the root causes. They are moderate measures that are consistent with past approaches to the housing problem.

SHORT-TERM PROPOSALS

Tax Measures

Although parts of the Internal Revenue Code ostensibly encourage productive investment in housing, in fact, as we have seen, they promote speculation, resulting in higher prices and overconsumption of housing. The present tax system contributes materially to inflation in rents and prices, while costing the Treasury billions of dollars annually in revenues lost to income tax deductions and other loopholes.

The goal of any progressive tax reform is to promote community housing goals, end speculation, and redirect resources into productive investment in the nonprofit sector. A secondary objective is to make the tax system *more* progressive, through eliminating measures that redistribute wealth upward. Finally, to the extent that tax reform generates increased public revenues, such revenues could finance the long-term community housing programs proposed below. These reform measures will not by themselves generate sufficient revenues to fund the entire housing program, but they have the potential of recapturing tens of billions of dollars lost to tax loopholes.

The homeowner deduction for mortgage interest and property taxes cost the U.S. Treasury an estimated $70 billion in 1986. Allowing homeowners to deduct mortgage interest and property taxes is extremely costly, and contributes to overconsumption and inflation in housing. Furthermore, homeowner deductions almost entirely benefit upper-income owners, because homeownership is, in part, a function of income and because most homeowners who itemize deductions fall into the highest tax brackets. Only one-quarter of all households claim the homeowner deduction, while 60 percent of all benefits accrue to the top 10 percent of the income distribution.

On the other hand, it is clear that the homeowner tax deduction enjoys considerable popularity, and is widely (though in our view incorrectly) perceived as of benefit to homeowners. In the short term, therefore, several measures would extend the benefits of this deduction to all homeowners, reduce its contribution to inflation and housing overconsumption, and generate additional tax revenues by reducing the level of tax expenditure.

As a first step, the homeowner deduction on second homes (such as vacation homes) could be eliminated. In the somewhat longer term, however, the homeowner deduction could be replaced with a tax credit and cap. This would make it available to the large majority of homeowners who do not itemize deductions, since tax credits are claimed directly on the 1040 form. The credit would be set equivalent to the tax bracket of middle-income homeowners —around 25 percent, prior to the 1986 Tax Reform Act. That is, 25 percent of interest and property tax payments could be used to offset other tax liabilities, regardless of the taxpayer's bracket. A cap would be set on the amount of credit that could be claimed, based on median home prices, interest rates, and property taxes in the local housing market. Such an interim limitation would not generate large amounts of revenue since, at the same time, it will extend tax benefits to a much larger number of households than presently claim them. It would, however, reduce housing demand at the top end and thus have a dampening effect on inflation.

A second set of tax reform measures would address the problem of depreciation allowances for rental property. While the costs of maintaining rental property are rightfully capitalized as ordinary business expenses, fully depreciating the property's value over fifteen to eighteen years (or, under accelerated depreciation, writing off 46 percent in the first five years) provides a windfall to the owners of rental property, is costly to the U.S. Treasury, and encourages the rapid turnover of rental property as its short-term benefits as a tax shelter are exhausted. Depreciation thus encourages rental housing to be regarded as another short-term component in an investment portfolio, to be bought and sold according to the conditions of the capital markets. This is perhaps one reason why there has been a trend toward greater professionalization of rental housing ownership in recent years.

While the 1986 Tax Reform Act will partially address this problem by extending the depreciation period and reducing acceleration (see Chapter 4), we feel the Act does not go far enough and therefore propose the following measures. As a first step, all accelerated depreciation for rental housing should be eliminated. As an interim measure, ordinary (straight-line) depreciation could be extended to thirty years and be made contingent on certified code compliance and evidence of adequate maintenance. In the long run, all rental housing depreciation allowances on the original-cost basis could be eliminated, although provisions would also be made for depreciating capital improvements or deducting the cost of a replacement reserve. While there will undoubtedly be some reduction in private rental construction, the federal savings resulting from such measures could fund offsetting community-based housing construction. Elimination of the depreciation allowance would remove a major incentive for speculative and inflationary trading in the existing private rental housing stock.

A third set of reform measures concerns capital gains and antispeculation taxation. It makes little economic sense to give preferred treatment to capital gains realized from the sale of land or housing. Capital gains taxation, like the depreciation allowance, is intended to encourage productive investment by reducing the tax liability on profits that are earned as a result of such investment. In the case of housing, however, it is difficult to argue that profits from sales result from such productive investment, in the ordinary sense of the word. Rather, profits in most cases result from inflation alone, particularly in the value of land.

In the long run, therefore, capital gains preference for income from the sale of rental housing could be replaced by a windfall profits tax on all sales.[1] As an interim measure, local antispeculation or deed transfer taxes could be encouraged. Such taxes, which have been adopted by some localities, have rates that are inversely graduated, according to length of holding. For example, the gain on property held less than one year might be taxed at 95 percent, with the rate declining by 5 percent per year through the tenth year and by 2 percent per year thereafter, eventually leveling off at 10 percent for property held longer than thirty years. Such a tax would likely be politically popular, particularly if sales or profits below a minimal amount were exempted. Such a tax would also have the advantage of raising revenues while discouraging speculation; this, in turn, would help cool overheated housing markets, thereby stabilizing neighborhoods threatened by rapid inflation.

Finally, a number of measures are directed at local tax reform. The present property tax is regressive, since low-income households pay a higher percentage of their incomes for housing than higher-income households, and assessment practices have been shown to exacerbate the inequities. This is particularly true where property values have inflated much more rapidly than incomes in recent years. (It should be recalled that rental property owners pay these taxes out of rents.) The wave of anti-tax measures, beginning with California's Proposition 13, is a response to these inequities; but the benefits of such measures have gone largely to the wealthy.

The property tax could be made more progressive by charging higher rates for more highly valued property. Such a reform might apply to all residential real estate, including residentially zoned vacant lots. A minimum full-tax exemption, tied to local conditions, could provide "circuit breaker" relief to low-income homeowners and low-income residents of private rental housing (in this case, rents would have to be controlled to assure that the tax savings were passed through to tenants). A portion of the local property tax could be earmarked for community housing programs. In similar fashion, a luxury housing tax could assess higher rates on certain classes of luxury housing.[2]

Financing Affordable Housing

A number of programs could generate various forms of subsidy *within* the private credit economy. To the extent that costs are borne by private credit institutions, they involve no significant public costs. They are intended to "steer" private credit toward community housing objectives. For example, an extension of the concept implicit in the Community Reinvestment Act could include not only geographical responsibility, but an obligation to meet the housing needs of low- and moderate-income, as well as minority, households by expanding and upgrading the housing supply. Differential taxes could be levied on private credit institutions, with rate differences rewarding preferred types of lending. Revenues raised by such taxes can be used as direct grants to the nonprofit housing sector. Loan set-aside provisions could require lenders to invest specified amounts (for example, 5–10 percent of assets) for designated community housing objectives.

Differential reserve requirements are another means of steering credit allocation. In this approach, special reserve requirements would be established for mortgage loans, with larger reserves for higher-cost mortgages. Low-cost mortgages could be exempted altogether, and lenders given a reserve credit for such loans as well. The mortgage reserve balances could then be invested in low-cost housing. To the extent that lenders meet housing targets, the differentials would be reduced or eliminated.

Finally, a certain percentage of loans would be made at below-market rates for community housing purposes. This would result in an internal transfer (cross-subsidy) among borrowers, whereby recipients of low-interest loans would be subsidized by other borrowers. This approach is similar to inclusion-ary zoning, whereby developers are required to price a targeted percentage of units for low- or moderate-income occupants.

Given the increasing role of insurance companies, pension funds, and other nonbanking institutions as sources of housing credit, care must be taken that such measures, if adopted, are not punitive toward traditional lending institutions. Any legislation that creates such measures should apply them equally to all sources of credit, and carefully monitor the results to ensure that the private credit economy is not destabilized.

Building on Existing Government Programs

There are a number of federal programs that could be modified to provide community housing. In any federal project where private developers receive funding (such as Urban Development Action Grants), a federal requirement could be established whereby some community housing must be provided as part of the project. For example, urban redevelopment programs often offer the potential for public acquisition of land, as well as public control over its development, and thus could facilitate construction for community ownership.

Tax-exempt bond financing could be replaced with direct federal financing through Community Development Block Grant and Urban Development Action Grant programs. Despite their limitations, these two programs constitute existing mechanisms whereby direct disbursements are made from the federal Treasury to localities for public purposes.

Finally, turnkey-type programs, including the few public housing projects under construction, can continue to provide units, so long as projects are subject to appropriate design and construction standards.

A LONG-TERM PROGRAM

To repeat, our intention is to provide housing that meets the needs of low- and moderate-income households not served by the present system. To achieve this end, we offer a number of long-term measures that can serve as a guide for future action. These measures are intended to secure and enhance the rights of use ordinarily associated with private ownership: security of tenure, privacy, the right to modify one's living environment. Only the right to profit in housing would be unavailable to households that choose this alternative. Because community-based housing eliminates profits from production, financing, and ownership, its cost will include only operating and maintenance expenses. Nonetheless, subsidies will be provided where necessary to assure that rent payments reflect true ability to pay. Under this program, housing is operated only for resident and community benefit.

The community-based housing stock will increase, both as a result of production programs and from conversion of market housing to various forms of nonprofit or public ownership. At the same time, existing housing that is subject to some form of similar ownership or control—such as public housing, limited-equity cooperatives, and some assisted housing—must be safeguarded against demolition or sale to private ownership. The program will arrest these processes, maintaining and enhancing the existing stock.

It is important to recognize that low- and moderate-income housing, in whatever form it takes, can be designed in such a way as to create a community feeling and inhibit crime. Newman (1980) has demonstrated that multifamily housing that fulfills certain minimal design requirements can be as livable as the conventional home. Newman calls for low-rise units with a clear demarcation between private, semi-private, and public space, affording optimum surveillance of all exterior communal space. Where appropriate, child-care and playground facilities can be incorporated in the design, which in any case should complement prevailing community standards. Part of the opposition to public housing stems from its often drab, jail-like atmosphere. There is no good reason, however, why such housing cannot incorporate a "human feel" of uniqueness and individuality that makes residents and neighbors proud (as numerous examples of high-quality public housing attest). As we argued in Chapter 2, housing is a symbol of self that confers status within society.

Cooperatives with resale restrictions offer a useful example of attractive multifamily community-based housing (Lauber and Hinojosa 1984:18), since they provide many of the guarantees ordinarily associated with home ownership (Franklin 1981:393–94). These guarantees include protection against rising capital costs, equity accrual, tax advantages such as interest deduction, eviction protection, reduced maintenance costs, lowered turnover, and —perhaps most importantly—a community sense of "we-ness." As a result upkeep is typically superior to ordinary rentals, while the incidence of crime is typically lower. As we saw in Chapter 8, several west European countries have strongly encouraged the construction of such cooperatives, as central components of their housing programs.

Cooperatives are operated through a nonprofit corporation which holds a single mortgage on the property.[3] The corporation is democratically run, with an elected board of directors. Under typical arrangements, each new owner purchases a share for a minimal down payment. Monthly payments include each owner's share of the common mortgage, plus a fee for maintenance and operating expenses. When an owner wishes to move, she or he sells the share back to the cooperative, which resells it to a new owner. Since the whole process takes place within the cooperative corporation, no new financing or real estate fees are involved.

The cooperative is termed "limited equity" because appreciation in the value of each member's share is limited by common agreement to a low level.[4] Cooperative members cannot sell their shares for what the market will bear. In this way, the sale price of units quickly falls below the market price for comparable housing. While a typical home or condominium is sold and refinanced at ever-inflating prices many times over its life span, a limited-equity cooperative is never sold. The original mortgage is retained until it is fully paid off, at which time the monthly payments of the owners decrease to the amount necessary to operate and maintain the units.

The principal difference between cooperative and private ownership is that, within cooperatives, owners may change many times without the cooperative itself ever changing owners. Owners share the full rights and privileges of private ownership, including the tax benefits, which are not available to tenants in rental housing.

Figure 9.1 compares the monthly cost over a twenty-year period of a rental

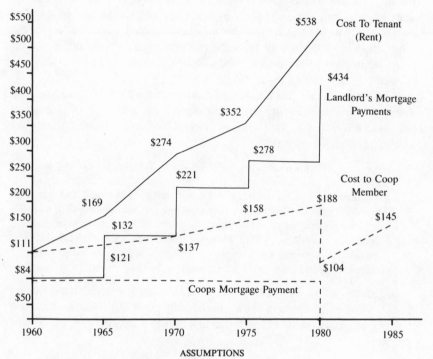

ASSUMPTIONS

Total construction cost: $174,193.00
12 unit building built in 1960 (3 bedroom apartments)

Rental Property Mortgages			Coop Mortgage		
1960	6.25%	$139,354	1960	6.25%	$139,354
1965	6.5%	$212,515			
1970	9.5%	$285,677			
1975	9.5%	$358,838			
1980	13.5%	$432,000			

FIGURE 9.1
COMPARISON OF COST BETWEEN LIMITED EQUITY COOP AND
RENTAL PROPERTY

Source: Glennon and Appelbaum (1980:13).

unit and an identical limited equity cooperative in Santa Barbara, California (Glennon and Appelbaum 1980; in Gilderbloom *et al*. 1980:242). It assumes that both units are constructed in 1960, and are financed with conventional twenty-year fixed-interest mortgages at 6.25 percent. Thereafter, the rental unit is sold every five years at prevailing rates of interest and appreciation, while the co-op unit is never sold. Monthly mortgage payments on both units are initially $84; rents are $111. By 1980 the apartment unit has been sold four times, resulting in monthly mortgage payments of $434 and rents of $538. The co-op unit, on the other hand, still has its original mortgage, so that rents have had to increase only to $188 to cover rising maintenance costs (assumed to increase with inflation). After twenty years the co-op mortgage is paid off, and rents actually drop to $104. By now the differential in rent between these two identical units is dramatic—$538 versus $104.

New York City has had considerable experience with low-income housing cooperatives. According to one recent study, the overall level of resident satisfaction is extremely high. Lawson (1984:92) offers the following summary of his survey of co-op tenants:

> Tenants were almost unanimous that this housing is better and cheaper than rental housing, that it has saved many of them from displacement, and has given them a sense of control that they had not previously known. They scored well, collectively, on other basic indicators of effective management also, with low vacancy rates, turnover rates that are considerably below average, and good marks on services provided. Moreover, the tenants stated overwhelmingly that they preferred living in a coop to having a landlord. The coops must therefore, in general, be acknowledged as good for their tenants.

In another study done in Houston, Gilderbloom, Rosentraub, and Bullard (1987) found that 54 percent of their sample of persons qualifying for Section 8 housing assistance would be interested in a limited equity cooperative housing program.

Producing and Financing Community-based Housing

With the example of limited equity cooperatives in mind, we turn to the first of several components of our proposed program, the "National Housing Production and Finance Act," which sets national production and rehabilitation goals for community-based housing. Under this act, production would be directed increasingly toward nonprofit developers. Finance would become the responsibility of the federal government, rather than private credit institutions, through a system of direct capital grants. Ownership would reside in the residents, public agencies, or community organizations. In all instances, management would be structured to promote resident involvement and encourage resident control over the use of space.

In populous and growing locales, new construction of community-based housing would be a first priority under this act. In areas that are not growing, or are declining in population, acquisition (and rehabilitation) of deteriorating rental housing stock might prove suitable for publicly owned housing, community-owned housing, or limited-equity cooperatives.

Community-based housing units are the *only* units to be constructed, rehabilitated, or financed under this act, which calls for a redirection of all federal financial assistance to the nonprofit sector. All such units would be targeted toward low- and moderate-income households. The act's production and rehabilitation goals would take into account the quality of the existing housing stock, preservation and upgrading of existing community-based housing units, goals for converting private rental units to the nonmarket sector, and shortages confronted by specific population groups (see Angotti and Dale 1981). Needs assessments would be conducted by localities as part of their federally mandated housing plans (see below), taking into account their fair-share housing needs. Production and rehabilitation goals would be reassessed and revised every four years, on the basis of performance.

In the short run, it is anticipated that construction will be by private, for-profit builders; in the long run, the objective of this act is construction by the "third stream" of nonprofit developers and public agencies, whose principal concern is providing decent, affordable housing, rather than profit-maximizing. This would be accomplished by offering technical assistance and additional funding to such groups.

All federal financing for housing construction and rehabilitation would be limited to either the community-based housing sector or to privately owned units that are converting to that sector. Financing would consist exclusively of direct grants. Only in this fashion can costs be controlled and the production of affordable housing disentangled from private credit markets, whose economic cycles and volatile interest rates were shown in Chapters 4 and 6 to add appreciably to costs.

While we believe that the most cost-effective method for producing subsidized housing is through the use of direct grants for both equity and debt capital, we recognize that the federal government can raise the money for such grants through two methods: taxation and borrowing. In terms of the principles and objectives of this program, there is a distinct tradeoff between these two approaches. Taxation, provided it is progressive, is the more equitable of the two. Debt financing, in contrast, adds the burden of interest expenses to capital costs, a profit that typically is realized by wealthy investors. Over time, furthermore, debt service becomes an enormous component of ongoing costs, resulting in political pressure to reduce new allocations. Such pressures could jeopardize the housing program in the long run. On the other hand, borrowing has the immediate advantage of reducing current costs, thereby permitting a greater extension of limited resources in the short run. Given the urgent need for additional housing, borrowing may provide the best way to produce the most units in the shortest time.

The preferred financing method would depend on such considerations as interest rates, expected inflation, and the rate at which future costs are discounted to their present value; the valuation of present need over future costs; the long-term economic danger of contributing to a mounting national debt; and the political difficulties inherent in debt financing. The balance between the two methods would necessarily reflect economic and political considerations at the time annual allocations are made through the ordinary federal budgetary process. To the extent that borrowing is used, however, we offer two guidelines: first, the borrowing and repayment plan should be as progressive as possible; and second, firm commitments should be sought for the level of actual housing production in future years. Regardless of how the federal government might raise its revenues for the proposed housing programs, localities and other agencies would realize their revenues for such programs through direct federal grants.

We believe that any impediments to direct federal financing of housing are largely ideological and political, rather than economic. Military housing is a prime example of such an approach. In communities where the private housing stock is inadequate, the armed services have built over 400,000 units of family housing for their personnel. Construction, maintenance, and modernization have largely been implemented by direct allocations from congressional appropriations to the Defense Department budget. Other examples include FmHA's Section 514/516 program, which has been successful in producing low-cost rural housing, and, more recently, HODAG and Rental Rehabilitation grants. (These direct grant programs are of course not restricted to community-based housing and therefore, in our view, serve to subsidize the inefficiencies of the marketplace.)

A portion of federal capital funding should go toward public site acquisition, through land banking or other means to acquire sites for housing under this program. While the exact portion devoted to such purposes must be determined in accordance with local plans, the objective would be to reduce future costs of public development by acquiring suitable land as it becomes available.

Costs of operating community-based housing will be considerably lower than in the private sector, since they reflect only operation and maintenance. Direct federal financing of construction would remove the substantial capital cost component ordinarily included in rental charges, while community or resident ownership would eliminate ordinary landlords' profits. Despite the lower costs, however, many households will still have incomes too low to cover monthly operating and maintenance costs, and so each project would receive a commitment of universal operating subsidies. These subsidies would also be available to privately owned rental units in communities that have adopted adequate local housing plans. The operating subsidies would greatly enhance affordability while increasing the attractiveness of community-based housing.

As noted, operating subsidies are necessary initially, because, given the present income distribution, a gap will frequently remain between ability to pay and rents, even in the community-based housing sector. As we have seen in Chapter 4, ability to pay is a function of disposable household income *after* outlays on such nonshelter necessities as food, health care, clothing, and so forth. This, of course, varies with income, household size, and other characteristics. These operating subsidies will, however, be only approximately one-half of current Section 8 subsidies, reflecting the lower rents.

Unlike Section 8, which requires recipients to pay 30 percent of their income, regardless of how low the income or how large the household (and therefore its nonhousing expenses), the proposed operating subsidy levels will not reduce family income needed for other necessities. As a first step toward replacement of the arbitrary 30 percent formula with a formula tied to an ability-to-pay criterion, the 30 percent ratio would be applied to *adjusted* annual income on rents, the adjustment consisting of a $1,200 deduction for each household member, plus child-care and extraordinary medical expenses (Table 9.1). Under this new formula, a four-person family with an annual total income of $20,000 and no child-care or unusual medical expenses would pay $380 in monthly rent (23 percent of total income), with any difference between rent and actual housing cost covered by the operating subsidy; another four-person family, earning $10,000 annually, would pay $130 per month, or 16 percent (Stone 1983:111). Over time, the formula could be adjusted to account for nonshelter expenses as estimated by the Bureau of Labor Statistics—an approach that would be more accurate and equitable, though more complex to administer.

If a program were enacted that initially provided 200,000 newly constructed units and 400,000 substantially rehabilitated units per year, the first-year cost would be $20 billion—assuming new-construction costs of $60,000 per unit and rehabilitation costs of roughly one-third that amount. Additionally, operating subsidies will reach a total of 6.5 million units, at a total cost of $13 billion—assuming an average per unit subsidy of $2,000 per year (or $167 per month). The total cost of the production program, with operating subsidies, would therefore be $33 billion per year.

Converting Existing Market Housing to the Community Sector

Conversions from private to community-based housing would be encouraged under a "National Housing Conversion Act," the second major component of our program. Such conversions may occur because an owner wishes to sell; is forced to sell because s/he faces mortgage or property tax foreclosure, or costly

TABLE 9.1
SUBSIDIZED RENTS UNDER PROPOSED FORMULA*

Gross Annual Income	Amount Proposed Rent	% Available Income
$1,000	$4	5.0
2,000	8	5.0
3,000	13	5.0
4,000	17	5.0
5,000	21	5.0
6,000	30	6.0
7,000	55	9.4
8,000	80	12.0
9,000	105	14.0
10,000	130	15.6
11,000	155	16.9
12,000	180	18.0
13,000	205	18.9
14,000	230	19.7
15,000	255	20.4
16,000	280	21.0
17,000	305	21.5
18,000	330	22.0
19,000	355	22.4
20,000	380	22.8

*Rent = 30% net income (gross income less $1,200 deduction per person). Assumes minimum rent of 5% of gross income.
Source: Stone (1983: Tables 4.1 and 4.2, pp. 111–112). Table appears by courtesy of Michael Stone, and Chester Hartman (ed.), America's Housing Crisis: What Is to Be Done? (Boston: Routledge and Kegan Paul).

code enforcement; or finds him/herself in receivership. HUD-held units constitute yet another source. In any case, there must be a nonprofit owner who is technically and financially capable of acquiring the property; rehabilitating it, if necessary, while avoiding displacement; renting it at an affordable price; and administering operating subsidies.

Under the provisions of this act, the federal government would provide financial and technical assistance to localities, which in turn would set local targets for rental housing conversion to the community-based sector. In addition to administering the funds and providing technical assistance to groups that undertake conversions, localities would be responsible for establishing legal mechanisms to facilitate such conversions.[5] The purchase price for conversions would necessarily be determined by market value. If the proposed program were adopted in full, then, under conditions of adequate supply and in the absence of tax sheltering and speculation, market value could be expected to reflect the value of the unit as a place of residence more closely, taking into account such factors as location, condition, space, and amenities, while excluding the effects of tax sheltering and speculation. In the absence of such conditions, however, paying full market price may in some places be costly, as well as supportive of a speculative pricing system. For this reason, localities would have to set maximum purchase prices for different types of units.

In addition to these measures, provision could be made for a permanent offer of purchase, at a reasonable price, of any low- or moderate-income rental property in which the mortgage has been paid in full and to which the owner holds clear title. The local government, using federal funds, would be the principal purchasing agency and would subsequently either transfer such housing to an appropriate community-based owner or administer it through the local housing authority. The purpose of such a provision is to facilitate property transfers in which the owner, for whatever reason, wishes to divest him/herself of property at a fair price. Such a provision would be well publicized, would be especially attractive to owners who support the concept of community-based housing, and would expedite quick transfer by providing what is essentially a standing offer to buy.

Low- and moderate-income rental property that is being foreclosed by the bank or tax collector could also provide an important source of housing conversions. Notice of impending foreclosure proceedings could be provided to the appropriate local housing agency. In foreclosures where the market value of the property exceeds the back taxes or debt, the locality could offer to purchase the properties from their owners for an amount not to exceed that value, thereby acquiring the property for the community-based sector. Such an offer would be subject to the maximum price limitations for conversions, as indicated above. Back taxes would be paid upon purchase. In most instances, the loans would also be paid in full, although the nonprofit owner might in some cases wish to assume the loan (for example, when the interest rate is extremely low) to reduce short-term costs. (Long-term costs are minimized by paying all debts upon acquisition.) Where debts exceed the market value, the property could be allowed to go through regular foreclosure proceedings. Under the provisions of this act, the local government or a community-based nonprofit entity would have first option to purchase the property from the bank or tax collector, for the amount of the remaining debt or less.

Properties that are in substandard condition must be brought up to code. Owners who could not afford to do so could choose to sell the property to a community-based owner, at a price that could not exceed the market value. Alternatively, direct capital grants could be made available to the owner to bring the property up to adequate health and safety standards, provided the owner agreed to sell the property to a community-based owner after a specified time. The buy-out price could be determined by negotiation between the locality and the owner, and would reflect the current value of the unit, excluding the amount of the improvement grant. This would enable the owners to derive benefit from their property for a specified period, while securing future community-based housing at below-market prices.

Although we are primarily concerned with rental housing, the single-family housing stock constitutes another resource for community-based housing that should not be overlooked. In particular, housing that is in foreclosure can be readily and inexpensively converted to the community-based housing stock, at the same time protecting homeowners against foreclosure and eviction. Such a program will be of particular benefit to elderly homeowners who find themselves in mortgage or tax arrears. For example, homeowners could have the option of deeding their house to a community-based entity, in exchange for lifetime security of tenure at an affordable monthly cost. This option would be especially attractive for homeowners who face mortgage or property tax foreclosure. This form of protected ownership, which lies between private and community-based ownership, would safeguard the continued residence of the owner while "banking" the unit for future inclusion in the community-based sector. A related program could provide home improvement grants in exchange for deeding the property to a nonprofit entity after a specified time. This program would operate in a fashion similar to the rehabilitation grant program for rental property.

Initially, we propose the annual conversion of 160,000 rental units at a per unit cost estimated at $35,000, and an equal number of homes at $50,000 each. Additionally, 81,000 HUD-held units would be acquired at an estimated cost of $1.2 billion. The total annual cost of all conversion programs is thus estimated at $14.8 billion.

Upgrading and Protecting "Assisted" Housing Stock

"Assisted" housing, such as public housing, is in danger of being demolished, sold, or otherwise transferred from the nonprofit or governmental sector. Such housing is an important resource that embodies many of the characteristics we call for in our community-based sector. Accordingly, a third component of our proposed program, a "National Home Protection and Improvement Act," would address these problems, while providing for the upgrading of such units. Under the provisions of this act, for example, when the removal of assisted housing residents might be required for some public purpose, adequate relocation benefits and compensation would have to be provided (with one-to-one replacement of lost residential units). Grievance procedures would be mandated to ensure tenants due process and the right of appeal. Stringent removal protections could be enacted, including prohibitions against conversion to private ownership or demolition (unless some clear public purpose were served). To assure adequate maintenance of the assisted housing stock, the act could mandate code enforcement while providing adequate federal funding for capital expenditures, maintenance, modernization, and ordinary operations. A program that might reach approximately 500,000 units (about 10 percent of all socially owned units) would cost an estimated $5 billion initially, at an average cost of $10,000 per unit.

A related problem is that assisted units are sometimes lost to low- and moderate-income households, because they are occupied by households that no longer meet the income-qualifying standard or because government housing assistance payments fall, in absolute terms or relative to the cost of living. The act would assure continued affordability of existing assisted units by reserving them exclusively for qualifying households and by using the universal operating subsidy program to assure that no such household spends more than it can afford.

A final problem concerns poor management in assisted housing projects. One of the principal attractions of single-family homeownership is the control it affords over the use of space. Private rental housing, by contrast, typically affords residents little control over common areas and, often, immediate living space. Furthermore, since tenants are often subject to arbitrary eviction, either directly or through rent increases, they may not experience strong personal identification with their place of residence. "Pride of ownership" is absent in most rental situations. Other provisions of the program are intended to provide residents in the community-based housing sector with all the benefits and securities of homeownership, excluding the right to resell at a profit. In this act we seek to maximize democratic resident control over housing in the community-based sector (including existing assisted housing), moving toward eventual management control on the part of residents. The act, accordingly, would mandate resident participation in all significant aspects of management in the community-based housing sector, while providing training and technical assistance as needed.

Assuring Residential Security in Private Rental Housing

Privately owned rental housing should be regulated to protect tenants from inadequate maintenance, arbitrary evictions, and unreasonable rent increases. A fourth and final component of our proposed program, a "National Private Tenant Protection Act," would seek these objectives by a mixture of binding regulation and voluntary compliance. First, it would prohibit certain classes of evictions, including those for luxury rehabilitation, demolition, or condominium conversion (unless prior one-to-one replacement and relocation benefits are provided), as well as eviction for any temporary inability to pay rent that results from involuntary loss of income.

Second, it would tie federal housing grants, block grants, and other funding to demonstrated local compliance with the objectives of this housing program. Localities would be placed under an obligation to provide adequate and affordable housing for their present and projected population, and required to demonstrate such compliance (subject to local conditions) to be eligible for federal funds connected with housing or urban development.

Finally, the act would establish a series of model ordinances whose adoption would automatically meet federal requirements. These ordinances would include (but not be limited to) such tenant protections as rent control, condominium conversion and demolition controls, just-cause eviction, warranty of habitability, resale controls, and receivership.

Some measures would be universally mandated while others would be local-option measures that would become mandatory only when it was determined that a local housing emergency exists. Such a determination would be based on vacancy and unemployment rates, inflation in rents, and other local conditions, which would be specified as part of the local housing program. Specific measures would include:

* *Antidiscrimination.* All localities would be required to ensure maximum freedom of choice in the selection of housing. Moreover, they would be required to legislate against arbitrary discrimination against any person in the sale or lease of residential property. "Arbitrary discrimination," in this context, would include (but not be limited to) discrimination based on race, national origin, religion, sex, age, source of income, physical disability, marital status, sexual preference, family size, or presence of children.
* *Warranty of habitability.* All localities would require landlords to provide housing that complies with minimum standards of health, safety, and livability. Over time, these standards would be upgraded to achieve adequate levels of residential amenity with regard to energy efficiency, space utilization, security, and resident services such as child care.
* *Eviction controls.* All localities would be obligated to protect tenants from arbitrary eviction, aside from such "just causes" as nonpayment of rent, willful destruction of property, or gross violation of community standards. In these cases, tenants who are being evicted would be afforded due-process guarantees. When a local housing emergency is determined to exist, evictions for luxury rehabilitation, demolition, or condominium conversion would also be prohibited, except where a compelling public purpose is served (see below). In any case, adequate relocation assistance would be provided. Other exceptions would be based on local needs and conditions, subject to federal approval. Additionally, during a local housing emergency, tenants could not be evicted because of any temporary inability to pay rent that resulted from an involuntary loss of income.
* *Rent control.* Local regulation of rents would be required whenever it is determined that a local housing emergency exists. Local rent control ordinances would meet minimal federal standards, including (a) allowable rent adjustments, limited to reasonable operating cost increases, and (b) retention of controls for all units subject to the ordinance, regardless of changes in tenancy, until the emergency conditions that triggered the ordinance are determined to be over.

- *Conversion controls*. Regulation of conversions to condominiums or nonresidential use would also be triggered by a local housing emergency. Acceptable local ordinances would have to contain a blanket prohibition against conversions, with two exceptions: conversions to community-based forms of ownership and conversions approved by three-quarters of the residents, which also provide for prior one-for-one replacement with equivalent housing. In both cases, adequate notice, relocation benefits, and other safeguards would be required for displaced tenants.
- *Demolition*. Where a local housing emergency is determined to exist, localities would prohibit all demolition of rental housing, except as required for a compelling public purpose, with prior one-for-one replacement of equivalent units and adequate tenant notice and relocation benefits. Arson for profit, which, as we saw in Chapter 2, results in significant housing losses in some communities, would be combated by strict enforcement of anti-arson laws, as well as by local legislation requiring that all insurance payments be reinvested in the damaged housing. In extreme cases, unsafe housing would be acquired by local government through eminent domain.

Total first-year program costs, summarized in Table 9.2, are estimated at approximately $55 billion. While this would appear to be a large sum, it is less than the annual tax expenditure on homeowners' deductions, and less than one-fifth the proposed 1987 military budget. The question of housing finance ultimately depends on national spending priorities. There *is* no shortage of capital for housing or any other public objective. There is, however, a shortage of *affordable* capital, which results from three sources: (1) misallocation of resources to nonproductive uses, principal among which (in our view) is the military budget; (2) reliance on private credit markets for funding; and (3) wasteful speculation rather than productive investment.

Although we have addressed only the latter two problems, it should be clear that no adequate housing program is possible without the redirection of a significant portion of military spending. There is no magic formula by which the necessary new funds can be generated, short of a major reduction in military spending. Although some funds can be generated by eliminating inequities in the tax system, an adequate housing program requires a shift in national priorities and commitments.

Program Implementation: Federally Mandated Local Housing Programs

Most of the program measures discussed in previous sections are implemented at the local level, but the role of government at the federal level would be twofold: to establish guidelines and minimal requirements to assure that the housing needs of low- and moderate-income people, would be met; and to

TABLE 9.2

NATIONAL COMPREHENSIVE HOUSING PROGRAM, FIRST-YEAR COSTS

Implementation	Cost/Unit (Thousands)	No. Units (Thousands)	Total Cost (Billions)
New construction for social owenership*	$60	200	$12.0
Rehabilitation for social ownership†	$20	400	$8.0
Operating subsidies for social housing‡	$2	6,500	$13.0
Conversion of private rental units§	$35	160	$5.6
Conversion of homeowner units‖	$50	160	$8.0
Conversion of HUD-held units#	—	81	$1.2
Modernization of existing social units**	$10	500	$5.0
Administration††	—	—	$2.0
Total	—	—	$54.8

Source: Appelbaum et al. (1986).
*Based on 1984 construction costs, adding land and subtracting finance costs, since financing will be through direct grants. See Hartman and Stone (1986).
†Rehabilitation only (acquisition costs are included under conversion element); per unit cost is based on various rehabilitation projects.
‡Operating expenses only (debt service included under conversion element). Derived from 1983 operating cost data, adjusted to 1985, and applying Stone's affordability scale (see Hartman and Stone 1986).
§Assumes full payment of negotiated price in year purchased (see Hartman and Stone 1986:500–501).
‖Assumes full payment at time of acquisition for mortgage balance and negotiated equity.
#Based upon Achtenberg (1985).
**Existing assisted stock only; assumes that most units need modest, not major, rehabilitation.
††Conservative estimate.

provide the necessary financial and technical resources. In other words, administration of the various elements of the program is to be as decentralized as possible. This would, simultaneously, avoid federal bureaucratization and maximize resident participation and control.[6]

Local compliance with the various acts of the housing program would be a threshhold requirement for receiving federal funds. Yet the acts would operate through existing state and local planning or housing departments, utilizing the police powers through which state and local governments are able to regulate the private sector. As a consequence, each locality would exercise a great deal of control over the housing plan's design and implementation, although the plan's parameters would be established and monitored federally. The principal provisions of this act would establish or require

- A state and local duty to evaluate, plan for, and adopt a program that responds to the needs of all households, including a regional fair share of low-income and minority families.
- Federal funds for housing, highway and sewer construction, economic development (including small businesses), Urban Development Action Grants (UDAG), Community Development Block Grants (CDBG), and other federal programs that directly and indirectly impact housing would be restricted to states and localities that are meeting their housing responsibilities.
- Local governments to adopt complying local housing plans, utilizing all their powers and resources to carry out the programs in those plans.
- States to adopt statutes that designate an existing housing or planning agency with primary enforcement responsibilities for ensuring that localities comply with the act.
- HUD as the secondary enforcement body, with authority to certify the adequacy of state statutes and state compliance, and with additional authority to block or delay grants from federal agencies to noncomplying states.

Each locality's housing plan would be required to make adequate provision for the existing and projected needs of all economic and racial segments of the community, and would provide for adequate sites for new construction. The act would further require that each local government not only assess its own needs and adopt broad goals and policies consistent with those needs, but include in its housing formula an action plan for meeting those needs. The local housing plan would provide for the production and rehabilitation of community-based housing, conversion from private to community-based ownership, and the regulation of private rental housing.

CONCLUSION:
HOUSING AS AN ENTITLEMENT

As a growing portion of our national housing stock is acquired, produced, financed, and owned by the community-based sector, and as increasingly adequate public resources are channeled for these purposes, adequate and affordable housing will become a universal national entitlement. Accordingly, in the long run this program will guarantee every resident the rights provided by all the legislative acts, such as the following.

Affordability

The basic, nonspeculative nature of community-based housing, with operation and resale for profit prohibited, will significantly reduce housing costs and enhance affordability over time. Additionally, since housing in the community-based sector will eventually be debt free (with new construction and rehabilitation funded through direct grants and the mortgage debt on converted properties retired), capital costs will be permanently eliminated from ongoing shelter expenses. Occupancy costs will be further reduced through progressive property tax reform and increased reliance on nonprofit management, making community-based housing affordable for the vast majority of residents.

Universal operating subsidies, provided on an entitlement basis, will further assist residents who are unable to meet even the basic cost of housing in the community-based sector. With rents increasingly geared to ability to pay, and taking into account the variability in household income and nonshelter expenditure levels for different types of families, housing affordability will be permanently guaranteed for residents. An equivalent level of affordability and subsidies will be guaranteed for tenants and owner-occupants whose units are in transition to community-based ownership. Tenants who remain in the private sector will also find their housing considerably more affordable, as rent control and other components of the program that reduce opportunities for speculative profit are implemented.

Over time, housing operating subsidies will become increasingly resident-based (as distinguished from project-based)to maximize freedom of choice for residents within the community-based sector. This approach, of course, can only be accomplished within a strictly regulated housing market that includes a substantial nonmarket component, to avoid inflationary effects. Ultimately, housing subsidies might be replaced by a negative income tax, which would enable low-income people to meet their shelter and other needs adequately.

Habitability

As the community-based housing sector expands, the quality of the housing stock and the physical standard of habitability to which residents are entitled will be upgraded. For housing that is owned by (or in transition to ownership by) nonprofit entities, direct grants will assure an adequate level of capital repairs while operating subsidies facilitate ongoing project viability. Unlike the present market-oriented system, where resources are invested in housing upkeep and renovation only when it is profitable for an owner or lender to do so, community-based ownership, financing, and production will guarantee both the incentive and the resources for continuing residential improvement.

Over time, with adequate capital and operating resources, new housing that is produced for the community-based sector and housing that is converted to such ownership will be upgraded to achieve higher levels of residential amenity. This includes improved physical features, such as unit layout, apartment configuration, and site and building design, especially in response to the needs of special constituencies (such as the handicapped and single women with children). It also encompasses operating amenities, such as increased energy efficiency and security, as well as social amenities, such as day care and other services that are logically residential based.

Additionally, voluntary upgrading by residents with enhanced security of tenure and control of their housing will continuously improve the quality of the community-based housing stock. Tenants in housing that remains within the private sector will also achieve significant improvements in the quality of their living environments, as higher standards of residential amenity are adopted over time.

Security of Tenure

Under the proposed system of community-based ownership, production, and financing, security of tenure (the right to continued occupancy of a housing unit of choice) will be achieved as an aspect of residential entitlement. All community-based housing residents, including tenants and owner-occupants whose units are deeded or optioned to the community-based sector, will be guaranteed lifetime tenure, except where removal of the housing unit is required for a compelling social purpose, or removal of the occupant is necessitated by significant and repeated violations of community standards. With occupancy charges based on true ability to pay and management policies subject to resident control, instances of nonpayment, destruction of property, and other traditional causes of eviction in our market-oriented housing system will be minimized.

Additionally, increasing regulation of conditions, use conversion, demolition, and eviction for other than "just cause" will protect tenants who remain in the private sector from forced displacement, while rent control and other measures will enhance security by promoting greater affordability. The creation of new ownership and tenure options, *not* based on the protection of property values, will encourage greater acceptance of neighborhood change and inclusionary housing patterns, providing a new basis for community security. As the discriminatory uses of housing in our profit-oriented economy are eliminated, with affirmative efforts to expand housing mobility and to revitalize minority communities, the right of residential security will encompass a locational aspect: the right to remain in place or to move to an alternative neighborhood of choice.

Control

The right of residents to control their living situations will be progressively achieved under the proposed program. Low- and moderate-income homeowners' ability to maintain control over their housing in the face of burdensome mortgage debt, property tax, and repair obligations will be enhanced through programs that offer increased affordability and security of tenure, without opportunity for speculation. Increased protection of tenants' rights in the private sector, through collective bargaining as well as limitations on landlords' authority to dictate rents, occupancy terms, tenure, and living conditions, will free residents (to some extent) from the arbitrary control exercised by others over their living situations. At the same time, our program for the regulated conversion of the private rental housing stock will significantly expand opportunities for direct ownership and control by resident associations, tenant cooperatives, and individual owner-occupants on an affordable, nonspeculative basis.

Ultimately, the control afforded to community-based housing residents as a matter of entitlement will be significantly greater than that experienced by many homeowners today. Positive features of conventional homeownership, such as the ability to modify and adapt one's living space to changing needs, will be retained and enhanced as residents achieve permanent affordability and security of tenure. And since resident and community benefit is the sole purpose of housing production and ownership through the community-based sector, residents and neighbors will be entitled and motivated to participate in housing design, development, and management decisions. As more and more of the community-based housing stock is developed and managed by resident-controlled nonprofit entities, opportunities for building and operating housing in a way that is truly responsive to resident needs will be significantly enhanced.

Finally, the removal of opportunities for speculation in housing will enhance community control by increasing neighborhood stability. Enhanced resident and neighborhood control of housing also implies an obligation for increased collective responsibility—that is, for mediation and settlement of residents' disputes and grievances. It also requires that control be exercised responsibly within the framework of basic democratic and nonexclusionary principles, and not be misused to deny housing access or opportunity. As the concept of residential entitlement is realized, the corresponding notion of residential responsibility will also be achieved.

CONCLUSIONS

Part IV

10
The Institutional
Structure of Rental
Housing Markets

Most social problems have given rise to a plurality of conflicting explanations within and among disciplines. Anthropology, political science, sociology, history, and economics have all made their contributions to our understanding of various features of the social world. Within these disciplines, opposing viewpoints have often done battle against one another, fueling research and, occasionally, the growth of knowledge.

No such debate has been generated on the subject of rental housing. Contemporary perspectives and analyses on rental housing have been generally sterile, dominated by conventional economic theory. Examples readily come to mind. When the popular news show *Nightline* examined the impact of the 1986 Tax Reform Act on rental housing, the entire discussion was devoted to the views and needs of investment brokers, bankers, builders, and professional landlords. The perspective of the debate was informed by a single viewpoint —that of conventional economic theory. The viewpoints of tenant leaders and progressive social scientists were never sought out. In a similar instance, when NBC ran a fifteen-minute news segment on soaring rents during the 1984 Democratic convention, the show was devoted to the views of James Rouse, one of the country's largest and most visible commercial and residential developers. The empty chair on the podium next to him could well have been filled by a person expressing a progressive viewpoint concerning rental housing. It is not that the views expressed were necessarily incorrect; it is only that they were never acknowledged as partial perspectives that might benefit from a dialogue with some well-thought-out alternatives.

The development of an alternative perspective on rental housing cannot occur within economics alone: the challenge can only come from outside. Fine-tuned hedonic equations have made important contributions, but if our understanding of rental housing markets is to grow, we must go beyond this limited domain. We believe that the next important contribution to understanding rental housing will be the integration of political and social aspects into our understanding of supply and demand. Sociology is well suited for this task, as a few sociologists have already argued.

Historically, one of sociology's central concerns has been with the problems of the disadvantaged—minorities, disabled, women, elderly, poor, or working people. Cutting across all these categories are tenants, yet very few sociological studies have been conducted that make renters a central focus of concern. This is surprising since by any measure renters have historically been viewed as second class citizens who have never achieved the "American dream of homeownership."

One advantage of the sociological perspective is its willingness to adopt an interdisciplinary approach to the study of social issues. While concerned with macro-level structural processes, it acknowledges that institutions are shaped by individual actors—at the same time that institutions constrain individual action. It is such a sociological perspective that we have attempted to bring to the institutional analysis of rental housing markets. We have combined structural analysis with an effort to understand the social relationships that constitute the world of landlords and tenants.

The potential for a significant sociological contribution to the study of rental housing has yet to be fully realized. This is unfortunate, for sociology has historically played a pivotal role in providing analysis and even direction on a variety of critical issues, including civil rights, sexism, poverty, and inequality in its various forms. Sociology loses its importance and vitality when it ignores the important social problems of the day. A review of sociology journals and conventional textbooks amplifies this point. Too often, the gatekeepers of sociological knowledge appear to believe that market behavior is the proper province of economists, or that the role of the state is best analyzed by political scientists. In the case of housing, sociology has forfeited an important opportunity to look at a major social problem, affecting millions of Americans, by turning the issue over to other disciplines.

Sociology should be on the cutting edge, probing and investigating the most important social problems of the day. As Collins (1986:1336) recently commented,

> there is a rather widespread feeling that sociology in recent years has been in a depression. There are many complaints from many directions: that the field

has grown repetitive, stagnant, fragmented; that it has lost its public impact or even its impulse to public action; that it lacks excitement; that it no longer gets good students or has good ideas.

Collins (1986:1354) concludes that "there must be new ideas, new results, new models and visions of the world," and he calls for a "sociological economics":

> Economics is in crisis on both theoretical and empirical fronts, and its idealized mathematical models are going to be challenged, especially from our discipline. This will provide some of the fireworks of the near future. [1352–53]

Freeman and Rossi (1984:571) have similarly called for a redirection of sociology, to a more closely applied concern with the major political and social issues of the day. They fear that if this is not done, sociology will lose its relevance, not to mention its funding base:

> We have been faulted by many in influential positions for the lack of relevance of our work to the solutions of contemporary social and political problems. This criticism has been used to undermine governmental and foundation support for sociological research and training. An increased commitment among sociologists to work on solutions to contemporary social problems and critical policy issues would help to counter such criticism and advance our discipline in the queue for extra-academic support.

Cummings (1986:193), in a provocative and bold critique of the status of contemporary urban and applied sociology, argues that the legacy of urban sociology has been conservative for the most part:

> Social scientists, including sociologists, can no longer afford to view themselves as detached, objective observers of social phenomena. Nor should sociology, in the face of mounting pressures to serve the interests of the business classes, abandon its allegiance with those groups and classes most severely impacted by the problems of industrial society. . . . A social science capable of enhancing the human condition is a vision worthy of preservation.

In the present political climate, sociology appears to have lost its purpose and direction. Indeed, the sociological imagination has been lost.

We began this book by discussing the work of R.E. Pahl, who argued that urban sociology in particular is badly in need of rejuvenation. To reestablish its relevance, he argues that research should focus on the unequal distribution of scarce resources between cities. According to Pahl, one worthwhile avenue of investigation would be constraints on the equitable allocation of affordable housing. For Pahl, the focus of the urban sociologist's analysis should be the city's "urban managers" (landlords, banks, and local government) who control the provision of housing, as well as the consumers of housing (tenants).

In this spirit, we have throughout this book attempted to develop a sociological understanding of the dynamics of rent.

Our view is at fundamental odds with the contemporary conventional economic perspective in at least three basic regards: we believe that a severe rental housing crisis exists; we argue that this crisis is best understood by analyzing the ways in which rental housing markets are institutionally structured by political and social forces; and we conclude that the prescription for a cure lies not in the supposedly "free" market but in the creation of nonmarket housing alternatives.

Our broadest goal, then, is to develop a plausible alternative perspective for better understanding rental housing, giving rise to a genuine debate that bridges economics, sociology, and public policy.

There Is a Rental Housing Crisis

We strongly disagree with the Reagan administration's contention that no rental housing crisis exists. In Chapter 2 we found that the proportion of income going into rent has steadily risen in recent years, so that today one-half of the nation's renters must pay rents that are considered unaffordable even by lax governmental standards, which we believe significantly understate the problem. Between 1970 and 1983, the rent to income ratio increased from one-fourth to almost one-third for the average U.S. renter. Today, one-fifth of all renters pay at least one-half of their income into rent. Black, Hispanic, disabled, and female-headed households currently bear the brunt of these rapidly rising rents, although many other groups are adversely affected as well. High rents contribute to overcrowding, disruption of social networks, family stress, and even social unrest. One key indicator of the extent of the current crisis is homeless persons, whom we believe number between 1 and 2 million. And these conditions are expected to get worse in the near future, as economic conditions and the 1986 Tax Reform Act combine to pressure landlords to further raise rents by as much as one-quarter over present levels.

The Reagan administration has failed to acknowledge this growing crisis, which it views as a personal, rather than social, problem. Instead, as we indicated in Chapter 4, it has sought to reduce the federal government's already limited role in providing decent, affordable housing, calling for dramatic cutbacks in all existing low-income housing programs. The administration believes that the private market, rather than the government, is best suited to supplying housing for all economic groups. This belief is grounded in conventional economic theory, which views all pricing—including rent setting—as best understood as the result of supply and demand interactions in unconstrained markets. This view is shared by the popular press, lawmakers, real estate interests, and even tenant groups. It leads to policy prescriptions for deregulation of supposedly overregulated markets and a free-market response to shortages of supply.

As pervasive and convincing as this view appears to be, we believe it is wrong: it neglects significant factors that are essential to an adequate understanding of rental housing markets.

Rental Housing Markets Are Institutionally Structured

We disagree with the traditional view on both theoretical and empirical grounds. We argue that the conventional explanation only partially addresses the dynamics of rent. While we are not denying that rents are partly a function of conventional supply and demand factors, we believe that rents are also a function of nonmarket forces that serve as institutional constraints. These forces, we have argued, are best understood sociologically.

Our work calls for a rethinking of rental housing from a sociological perspective. Although we cannot presently parcel out the institutional factors in terms of their precise effect, we hope to add to the limited body of knowledge about rental housing markets, demonstrating in the process how sociologists might make a contribution to this field. While the case for proving a causal link between rent and social-political factors still needs a significant amount of work, we hope that this book demonstrates that such an investigation will prove fruitful.

Until now, most of the research on rent has been carried out by economists focusing on *intra*city rent variation. This research has focused almost exclusively on demand-side variables that measure the qualities and attributes of particular rental units, and shows that a substantial proportion of the variance in intracity rents can be explained in terms of such measures. The impact of supply variables on a unit's rent or the city's overall rent level has not been studied in great detail. For various reasons, having to do both with economic theory and problems of measurement, researchers have preferred a more microeconomic approach to understanding why rents remain stable, rise, or fall.

The few studies of *inter*city rent differentials are unsatisfactory because of their research designs, city samples, control variables, and often primitive analytic techniques. Despite these drawbacks, we have found the studies to be significant because they find the relationship between supply and rent to be either nonexistent or to take the opposite direction from that which most economists would predict. We have attempted to improve upon these studies, in Chapter 5, by examining a large number of geographically self-contained urban areas, using regression analysis to control for various supply and demand factors. We have combined our statistical analysis with qualitative research on landlords, particularly the considerations faced by different classes of landlords when they set rents. We hope that the combination of these two methods has shed new light on the institutional features that impact market operation.

How, then, are rents determined? Figure 10.1 presents a schematic model of

1.0 National Level
  1.1 Federal Government
     Federal Reserve System
     Legislative and Executive Branches
     Judiciary
  1.2 National Housing Industry Organizations
     National Multi-Housing Council
     National Association of Home Builders
     National Association of Realtors
     National Leased Housing Association
     Coalition for Low-and Moderate-Income Housing
     Council for Rural Housing Development
     National Association of Housing Redevelopment Officials
     Public Housing Agency Director's Association
     Institute for Real Estate Management
  1.3 Low-Income Housing Advocacy Organizations
     National Low-Income Housing Coalition
     National Coalition for the Homeless
     National Tenants' Union
     National Tenants' Organization
     National Rural Housing Association
     ACORN
  1.4 Major Corporations (National, Multinational)
2.0 State Level
     Statewide Housing Councils
     Statewide Apartment Owners' Associations
     Statewide Tenants' Organizations
3.0 Local Level
  3.1 Local Government
     Municipal and County Councils
     Redevelopment Agencies
     Planning Bodies
  3.2 Housing Industry Organizations
     Housing Councils
     Apartment Owners' Associations
     Property Management Companies
  3.3 Tenants' Organizations
  3.4 Individual Landlords
     Professional Landlords
     Amateur Landlords

FIGURE 10.1
PRINCIPAL ACTORS IN DETERMINATION OF RENT

the principal institutional actors we believe play a key role in shaping the supply and cost of rental housing. Together, these actors constitute the structural framework within which—according to conventional economic thinking—the supposedly "frictionless" negotiations between individual land-lords and tenants occur. We reject the atomistic model that underlies much of conventional thinking regarding housing market dynamics and policy. The factors that affect rent are, instead, conceptualized in our analysis as a complex of overlapping institutional forces, some internal to local housing markets, but often—and often significantly—external to any particular locality.

The model in Figure 10.1 is not intended to provide an exhaustive analysis of the determinants of rent. Rather, it is a highly simplified first effort to identify the key actors and institutions that we have identified in our own research as impeding the operation of the frictionless marketplace. As with all such models, something is gained by this approach—and something is lost. What is gained is an economy of analysis that permits the identification (and therefore isolation) of key elements in the rent-setting process, which in turn can direct our attention to fruitful avenues for research (assuming the model is correct). What is lost is a sense of the complexity and nuance of the entire system within which the rent-setting process occurs. (If we have omitted any key elements of this process from our model, our conclusions may prove deficient in unknown ways.)

Figure 10.1 makes two sorts of assumptions that should be noted at this point. First, the model abstracts from world economic conditions that clearly play a significant role in determining rents. For example, the cost of mortgage finance is in part a function of national monetary policy, which in turn partly reflects concern over international credit and exchange rates. To take a second example, the demand for rental housing is partly a function of tenants' incomes, which in many localities are severely impacted by an international economic restructuring that has resulted in the loss of formerly high-paying industrial jobs to Third World countries, and their replacement by low-wage service work. Or—to offer a final example—fluctuations in the worldwide supply and cost of energy impact the cost of utilities (often a part of rent), the amount of income tenants have to pay for housing, and even tenants' income—as the heavily oil-dependent economies of Louisiana, Texas, and Alaska show. (We have ignored world-level actors in the interests of simplicity for our analysis; but a complete understanding would need to take this into account.)

Second, the model conceptualizes rent as determined by actors rather than abstract forces. For example, the demand for rental housing as an item of consumption is conventionally treated as a function of such factors as the relative cost of homeownership, the city or neighborhood's amenities, and locational considerations in general. We choose, rather, to focus on actors because our concern is with the institutional framework within which individual choice occurs. Insofar as such forces enter our model, they do so as considerations in decisions taken by individuals within such an institutional framework.

Having offered these caveats, let us summarize our argument within the framework offered by Figure 10.1. At the national level, the four principal categories of actors we shall consider are the federal government itself, national associations concerned with rental housing, national organizations that advocate low-income housing interests, and major corporations. Let us take up each of these in turn.

The federal government, arguably, exerts the most important influence on rent. It exercises its influence both directly and indirectly, through a variety of agencies and processes. Construction loan and mortgage interest rates—which our research has suggested was the most important factor during the 1970s —are strongly influenced by federal monetary policy, which controls both the supply of money and the discount rate. In this sense, the Federal Reserve Board (the Fed) exerts enormous influence over rents, even though it is not conventionally regarded as an institutional actor in the field of housing, and is invisible to most tenants and landlords. Significantly, the Fed has little concern with the production or cost of rental housing; its concerns, instead, lie in stimulating economic growth while dampening inflation. As a result, especially during potentially inflationary times, the Fed's tight credit policies can have a highly adverse effect on the housing market by raising the cost of borrowing and, consequently, pushing up the capital costs of rental housing.

Both the legislative and executive branches of government influence local rents through the legislative process. First, the Internal Revenue Code has a major influence on investment patterns. In the field of housing, we have seen how depreciation schedules, capital gains preferences, deductions for mortgage interest, and the sheltering provisions of the tax code all significantly shape investor behavior. This, in turn, influences not only the supply of rental housing, but its rate of turnover and, thereby, speculative pressures on sales prices (and hence rents). It also affects the willingness of professional landlord-investors to forgo cash-flow rental income in favor of tax preferences of various sorts. We have argued that rents are lower than they might otherwise be in the absence of such preferences, and that the 1986 Tax Reform, which significantly reduces many tax advantages, will likely have extremely adverse impacts in this regard.

Second, federal spending patterns are a chief determinant of local growth and hence demand for housing. Defense contracts are particularly important in this regard, at least for the localities that receive them.

Third, social welfare spending plays a role by providing income supports such as housing allowances and other welfare benefits. While these are minor in amount and impact, their intended effect is to buttress the private marketplace by stimulating demand and thereby allowing for higher rent levels.

Finally, the judicial branch, at its various levels, has also played a role by ruling against discriminatory rental practices and by sustaining certain types of local rent control ordinances. In order to avoid successful court challenges on the grounds of being confiscatory, rent control laws have been written to assure a "fair and reasonable" return to landlords. This has taken many forms, but it has not always worked to the benefit of tenants, whose income often fails to grow sufficiently to support a rate of return that the courts would determine is reasonable. For this reason, moderate rent controls often fail to reduce the proportion of income spent on rents (as we noted in Chapter 7). Strong rent control ordinances, while more effective, are continually under attack.

Also operating at the national level are associations concerned with housing, which play an important role in the determination of rents. First (as we noted in Chapter 5), housing industry organizations such as the National Multi-Housing Council, the National Association of Home Builders, the National Association of Realtors, and the Institute for Real Estate Management lobby in Washington for legislation favorable to their interests, including tax treatment and (unsuccessfully, to date) legislation restricting or outlawing local rent control. Such organizations are well funded and often maintain well-appointed offices with extensive research staffs to bolster their arguments before congressional committees. Second, they often advise state and local members on matters ranging from public policy to rent setting. Local building councils, realty groups, and property managers may draw on the resources of their national organizations in their efforts to influence housing policy.

Other Washington-based lobbying organizations include the National Leased Housing Association, which lobbies on behalf of private development interests, and particularly for leased Section 8 housing; the Coalition for Low and Moderate Income Housing, which represents housing syndicators; the Council for Rural Housing Development, which represents rural housing developers; the National Association of Housing Redevelopment Officials; and the Public Housing Agency Directors' Association.

Finally, large national and multinational corporations also have an effect on rents. The decision to open, expand, or close a branch office or factory can be a key determinant of local growth, wealth, and hence demand for rental housing. As we have shown in Chapter 5, for example, a community's overall income level is a key predictor of rent levels.

One also finds organizations at the state level that represent the interests of the housing industry as well as tenants. Many states have Apartment Owners' Associations and Housing Councils, for example. Like their national counterparts, these statewide organizations perform a twofold function. First, they provide technical services and advice to local organizations and are major sources of funding in campaigns to defeat local rent controls. Second, they lobby at the state level on behalf of their member organizations, including legislation that would restrict or eliminate local rent control. In some states (New Jersey, Massachusetts, and California in particular) there are statewide tenants' associations and, occasionally, other low-income housing lobbyists who represent special groups (for example, farmworkers, mobile-home owners, or low-income tenants). As might be expected, in recent years such organizations have fought hard against budgetary cutbacks and legislation inimical to low-income households. Relative to their housing industry counterparts, however, they conduct their efforts with meager financial resources.

On the other side, low-income housing organizations include the National Low Income Housing Coalition, representing a broad range of housing interests; the National Coalition for the Homeless; the National Tenants' Union, advocating on behalf of tenants in general; the National Tenants' Organization, representing public housing tenants; ACORN, representing squatters; and the National Rural Housing Coalition. These groups, although severely underfunded relative to their housing industry counterparts, have provided an effective and respected voice for low-income housing interests. The National Low Income Housing Coalition, in particular, has lobbied, with partial success, against the severe budgetary cutbacks proposed by the Reagan administration and in favor of legislation favorable to low-income renters. For example, the Coalition has helped avert the complete elimination of federal low-income housing assistance, prevented proposed rent increases in federally subsidized housing, and obtained provisions in the 1986 Tax Reform Act that will encourage investment in low-income housing.

At the local level, we have identified four broad categories of actors who exert influence in determining rents. These include local-government officials, housing industry organizations, tenant groups, and, of course, landlords.

Local government includes municipal and county councils, redevelopment agencies, and planning bodies—all of which play an important role in determining zoning, land-use planning, and patterns of urban growth. On the one hand, restrictive policies can add to the cost of housing by creating artificial supply imbalances and by adding directly to production costs. We reviewed this "overregulation hypothesis" in some detail in Chapter 6, where we argued that, at least in recent years, the costs of growth controls have added far less to the cost of housing than is conventionally believed. We found no evidence in support of the overregulation hypothesis. New construction in most localities represents but a small fraction of the total housing stock and therefore is not likely to significantly impact prices, particularly in the short run. Moreover, local construction responds in large part to regional and national economic forces, rather than purely local ones.

The construction industry has suffered greatly during the past fifteen years under the impact of inflation, high credit costs, and economic stagnation. Under such conditions, nonlocal factors are likely to swamp local ones in determining construction, prices, and rents. At the other extreme, aggressive pro-growth policies may take the form of redevelopment and other low-cost housing clearance programs, which can drive up the cost of housing for the affected groups.

In general, though with notable exceptions local governments are dominated by homeowners' and real estate groups, and are therefore not especially sympathetic to the interests of tenants. Their stance may range from mere indifference to active opposition to proposals for low-cost housing projects or rent control. Planning is typically designed to enhance the value of real estate and stimulate local growth. Equity concerns for tenants seldom make the local political agenda.

Local housing industry organizations, as we argue in Chapter 5, play a key role in determining rents. The principal organizations are the housing councils and apartment owners' associations, which comprise the formal networks through which landlords share experiences and evaluate common rent-setting policies, and local boards of realtors, which represent housing industry interests. Under conditions of relative scarcity—which, as we indicated in Chapter 5, we believe occurs under vacancy rates as high as 9 percent —landlords are able to raise rents by common amounts without losing tenants to competitors. Association newsletters may recommend guidelines for rent increases, or increases may be discussed at meetings. During the past decade, landlord organizations have also led campaigns against local rent control, fights in which they frequently depend on technical and financial resources from their parent statewide organizations.

Property management companies provide another tie that permits rent coordination. Their ability to exact uniform rent increases for the properties they manage constitutes a significant abridgment of competition, since they typically manage properties for otherwise competing landlords. Because the management firms typically receive a percentage of the rents, it is in their economic interest to raise rent levels as much as possible.

In general, housing industry organizations wield considerable political power at the local level. They contribute heavily to preferred candidates and campaigns, and are therefore well represented on municipal councils. Their power to elect or decide upon local government officials is unmatched. This domination of the local political process often promotes unbridled urban growth, which helps to drive up property values and eliminate low-cost housing through redevelopment projects. It can also produce land-use policies that restrict the amount of low-income housing that can be produced.

Tenant groups are the third principal actor at the local level—where they exert influence. We noted in Chapter 8 that, in many European countries, tenant associations have a legal role in rent negotiations, particularly in public-sector housing. This is not the case in the United States, where organized tenants have thus far been limited to enacting, preserving, and strengthening local rent control. Except in a few places (such as Santa Monica), organized tenants have been unable to secure political power, beyond control over elected rent control boards. In most cases, however, these boards are appointed, and tenants who campaign as tenants have had little success winning seats on municipal councils. We indicated in Chapter 7 that the

American tenants' movement is weak and fragmented—and far weaker, politically and financially, than the housing industry organizations.

The principal key actors at the local level are the landlords. Again in Chapter 5, we distinguished between two broad categories of landlords who play different roles in determining rents. These categories—conceptualized as pure types for clarification only—we have denoted as professionals and amateurs. Professional landlords own large numbers of rental units, which they regard as investments. They are therefore unlikely to be involved in the details of property management, leaving them to special companies or other professional managers. Nor are they necessarily concerned with realizing profits primarily through cash flow. Rather, they often regard rental housing as only one option in a wide range of investment opportunities, representing various degrees of risk and return. When returns on a housing investment are not adequate, the investment is transferred to an alternative. Since investment considerations are in large part shaped by the Internal Revenue Code, professional landlords have tended (until now) to "turn properties over" every four to six years, thereby contributing to speculative price increases and higher rents.

Professional landlords tend to be highly rational actors of the traditional economic model: they carefully weigh their options, collect relevant data in determining rents (including surveys of comparable units), and act to maximize their income. They often follow sophisticated marketing approaches to maximize short-term profitability—approaches that fail to take into account their tenants' welfare. Since they own large numbers of properties, professional landlords are the source of the ownership concentration we noted in Chapter 5. Highly concentrated rental housing markets can be thought of as oligopolies, since a handful of landlords, acting in formal or informal concert, can have a decisive voice in determining the overall rent structure. In cities dominated by a network of professionals, rents are likely to reflect cooperative price setting, rather than competitive practices.

Amateur landlords are "mom and pop" entrepreneurs whose primary concern is deriving long-term income (often supplementary to other sources) from rents. They are more likely to set rents on the basis of personal criteria, rather than the highest return. Like tenants, their knowledge of prevailing rents tends to be impressionistic rather than informed by a detailed analysis of market conditions. Unlike professional landlords, who may tolerate or even encourage rental vacancy as a means of maintaining desired levels, amateur landlords are constrained by their small number of units to strive for full occupancy at all times. This means that they are more likely to accept the rents that the market initially offers, rather than "hold out" for tenants who can pay a premium. For these reasons, vacancy rates and rents tend to be lower in markets dominated by amateur landlords, while the opposite will be true in markets dominated by professionals.

Our investigations have led us to conclude that certain key assumptions, necessary for a market to operate competitively, are seldom met in rental housing markets. Landlords are often able to exert, however imperfectly, various forms of control. These controls stem from the concentrated ownership that characterizes the few housing markets in which ownership patterns have been studied. Concentration, we believe, permits market dominance by a small number of actors. This dominance is abetted by formal and informal networks that operate on the national, state, and local levels. Explicit and implicit norms within these networks encourage landlords to behave in a cooperative rather than a competitive manner. Rents, as a result, become in part socially defined and constructed as by-products of these interactive processes. How widespread these networks are cannot be determined at present, but their extent should be investigated.

In our examination of the assumptions of pure competition in Chapter 3, we sought to show that the relationship between landlords and tenants is generally asymmetrical, because tenants' mobility is limited by a variety of social, psychological, and economic factors. Tenants—especially low-income tenants —tend to be "trapped in space." We believe they are much more likely to be forced to play by the rules of competition than are landlords—an unequal contest that works to the detriment of the former. One consequence is that supply is frequently less a factor in determining rents than conventional economic theory would predict, particularly in tight housing markets or markets dominated by a small number of large-scale, professional landlords. We found in Chapter 5, for example, that neither new construction nor vacancy rate predicts median rents in U.S. housing markets, once key indicators of demand, housing quality, and market professionalization are controlled. Income, on the other hand, remains strongly associated with rent. This, we believe, is indicative of landlords' ability to charge "what the market will bear," rather than a rent that more closely reflects actual costs, as would be the case (in the long run) under purely competitive conditions.

We therefore conclude that while local factors might help explain why rents vary *across* cities, they do not address the behavior of rents across *all* cities, particularly the drastic increases that began in the early 1970s. These causes must be sought in federal tax and monetary policy: generous tax shelters for residential real estate, extremely high interest rates throughout much of the period, and a tight credit policy to combat inflation.

Can the Rental Housing Crisis Be Solved?

In addressing this question we examined several answers. In Chapter 4, we looked at the current federal approach, which has been largely oriented toward private market activity. Even public housing relies on private construction and financing, while rent supplements are explicitly intended to support demand in the private rental market. Limited as these federal approaches are, the Reagan administration has managed to achieve significant cutbacks in funding. There is no national housing policy in the United States, except to encourage private market activity and construction. Such encouragment is best achieved, according to the Presidential Commission on Housing, by ending local regulations of all sorts—growth controls, environmental requirements, "excessive" building code requirements, and rent control. In the official view, the role of government should be limited to encouraging and occasionally subsidizing private-sector efforts.

Tenant organizations, not surprisingly, reject this prescription and the analysis that underlies it. We believe their skepticism to be justified, in light of our findings concerning the failure of new construction to produce lower rent levels. We saw in Chapter 7 that tenant groups have attacked the problem where they most deeply feel it: rising rents. Whether rent control addresses the causes or merely the symptoms of the housing crisis is a moot point to most renters, who experience that crisis first and foremost in their pocketbooks.

Historically, tenants have been unorganized and, consequently, ineffective in influencing rent levels. This was true until the 1970s, when, sparked by sharp increases in rents, tenants across the country organized for rent control. At the present time, over 200 cities, from Boston to San Francisco, have adopted some form of rent restriction. The overall impact of these laws, however, depends on the kind of laws enacted, the efficacy of their administration, and rent inflation within the housing market. In general, we find both the positive and negative economic effects of moderate rent control (its most widespread form) to be limited. The principal value of rent control appears, instead, to be political. Tenant movements on behalf of rent control have sought to educate renters about the nature of the housing market, thereby contributing to their own growth. This movement, in turn, has been able to press for a variety of housing-related demands while creating a climate in which the conventional approaches to housing can be more effectively questioned.

We do not believe that a demand for rent control, by itself, will solve the housing crisis. What is needed is a broad-stroke, fresh approach to housing —creation, for the first time, of a national housing policy. To identify the contours of such a policy, we looked in Chapter 8 at several West European housing programs to determine the approaches that have either worked or failed. We then looked at Sweden, which has been relatively successful in solving its housing problems. It has done so by transforming a substantial portion of its private rental housing stock into cooperative and public forms of ownership. Although the Swedish approach is not without problems, there are lessons to be learned from both its successes and failures.

We concluded our analysis by offering, in Chapter 9, some proposals for a

Comprehensive National Housing Program, designed to create a nonmarket "third stream" of housing, alongside private ownership and rentals, to serve those who have been (or will be) marginalized by the profit-oriented housing delivery system. The concept behind this program is community-based housing of high quality, affordable, secure with regard to tenancy, and controlled by residents. Such housing could take many forms, from limited-equity cooperatives to public housing units. It would be financed by direct government grants, and developed and administered by localities under an affirmative obligation to do so.

Such a program would be costly, but it is far from unfeasible. Furthermore, it might attract a broad base of support—from tenants, who would see in it a viable alternative to the high costs and uncertainty of renting; from builders, many of whom have suffered from the highly cyclical nature of the rental housing construction industry; and from employers, who correctly perceive that forever-rising rents often translate into higher wage costs. Ultimately, the success of such a program will depend on the growing strength of its primary constituent—tenants. Given today's conservative climate, the immediate adoption seems unlikely. However, should the rental housing crisis continue to worsen, a tenant movement may arise that is willing to press for, and capable of achieving, such a national program.

Notes | References | Indexes

NOTES

FOREWORD

1. Robert E. Park and Ernest W. Burgess, *Introduction to the Science of Society* (Chicago: University of Chicago Press, 1924), p. 507.
2. Scott Greer, *The Emerging City* (New York: Free Press, 1962), p. 8.
3. Michael Micklin and Harvey Choldin, eds., *Sociological Human Ecology: Contemporary Issues and Applications* (Boulder, Colo.: Westview Press, 1984).
4. John Kasarda, "The Implications of Contemporary Redistribution Trends for National Urban Policy," *Social Science Quarterly* 61 (December 1980): 373–400.
5. Brian J. L. Berry and John Kasarda, *Contemporary Human Ecology* (New York: Macmillan, 1977), p. 402.
6. See Mark Gottdiener, *The Social Production of Urban Space* (Austin: University of Texas Press, 1985); Susan S. Fainstein et al., *Restructuring the City* (New York: Longman, 1983).
7. Joe R. Feagin, *The Urban Real Estate Game* (Englewood Cliffs, N.J.: Prentice-Hall, 1983).

CHAPTER 1

1. Feagin (1986a:531) further asserts that "some mainstream ecologists are the gatekeepers who keep much space-oriented (neo-Weberian and neo-Marxist) urban analysis out of major sociology journals."
2. For further discussion see Starr and Esping-Anderson (1979); Tabb and Sawers (1978).

CHAPTER 2

1. Lowry's "constant quality rent index" adjusts rents for changes in the quality of the unit.
2. There are fifteen conditions that, in various combinations, can cause a unit to be defined as "needing rehabilitation" by the Congressional Budget Office. For an enumeration of these conditions see President's Commission on Housing (1981:16).
3. Until the Reagan administration revised the standard, HUD had classified as "unaffordable" any rental unit that cost more than 25 percent of household income. The Reagan administration has raised the standard to 30 percent. Problems with any fixed index are considered later in this chapter (see "shelter poverty").
4. Myers and Baillargeon (1985:66) provide a convincing case for using rent/

225

income ratios as the most appropriate measure of housing deprivation. While they focus on the problem of rental housing in Texas, their work reviewing indicators of housing deprivation deserves serious attention for its comprehensiveness and insight.

5. For a more detailed discussion of Hispanic and black housing needs, see Gilderbloom (1985a, 1985b); Bullard (1984); for a detailed discussion of elderly and disabled housing needs, see Gilderbloom, Rosentraub, and Bullard (1987).

6. This is how the *Los Angeles Times* (1980) described an overcrowded unit:

The room costs $260 a month and is barely longer and wider than two beds placed end to end. At one time, because of the housing shortage in Los Angeles, eight people—four adults and four children; two unrelated families—called it home. Tables, chairs and beds are crammed so tightly together that there is almost no space for walking or playing. Possessions—blankets, clothes, toys for the children, a T.V., portable stereo—are piled high on every surface, and spill over onto more tables and chairs that line the tiny bathroom. A single unshaded light bulb bounces harsh shadows off the green, gold and purple wallpaper that was someone's whim. It was so crowded when eight people called the room home that one man slept in his car every night, while his wife slept with relatives. The crowding eased a bit last month when the man who slept in his car moved out, taking his wife with him. Now there are only six people crammed into that one-room apartment. They would like a larger place they say. But this was the best they could afford when they were forced out of their much larger $160 a month apartment because the building was being demolished. . . . The housing buck in Los Angeles stops with low-income families like these. They are the people who are being squeezed against the wall, sometimes literally. . . . Their plight cannot be seen from the freeways or even from most city streets.

7. See, for example, the bibliography and many of the articles in Erickson and Wilhelm (1986); see also U.S. House of Representatives (1984, 1985).

8. Freeman and Hall (1986) make a similar national estimate, but since theirs is based on a survey of street and shelter people in a single city (New York), it is of questionable validity (see Malone 1986:24). Rossi's study (1986) of Chicago is the most sophisticated effort to extrapolate to a citywide figure from a scientific sampling of homeless persons. Unfortunately, Rossi's projection (1400 in the fall and 500 in the winter) of unsheltered homeless is based on a miniscule sample of street persons throughout the city (23 in the fall and 30 in the winter), and is therefore of dubious validity. For a further critique see Appelbaum (1986b).

9. One of the present authors (Appelbaum) testified on the accuracy of the HUD Report before two congressional hearings (U.S. House of Representatives 1984, 1985). By examining HUD's raw-data protocols, it was determined that HUD obtained its estimates mainly from central cities, then divided those estimates by the population totals of the entire metropolitan areas. The resulting percent homeless was then projected to a national homeless figure. This method had the effect of excluding most homeless not found in central cities from HUD's projections. In Boston, for example, HUD derived its estimate largely from a single study that found 2,800 homeless persons in parts of the city. HUD then used this number as if it applied to the greater metropolitan area, which includes virtually the entire urbanized Eastern seaboard —some 3.7 million people in 41 cities, 5 counties, and 2 states (Massachusetts and New Hampshire). HUD completely ignored the homeless outside of Boston, even though the city itself contains only 15 percent of the metropolitan area population. HUD made the same error in most of the cities it surveyed. Because of this (and other

disclosures), officials at the Federal Emergency Management Agency, which administers much of the federal funding for the homeless, now regard HUD's figures as "discredited" and do not cite them in official reports (Kondratas 1986:148).

10. Passage of the Mental Retardation Facilities and Community Mental Health Centers Construction Act in 1963 initiated a process to house the mentally ill in community centers and Halfway Houses, rather than state hospitals. Unfortunately, although the hospital population declined from 505,000 in 1963 to 125,000 by 1981, the expected local facilities have not developed apace (HUD 1984:25). While as many as two-thirds of the deinstitutionalized have been cared for by their families (Lamb 1986:269), many who otherwise might be in state hospitals are now on the streets.

11. To afford the median-price Los Angeles home ($114,871), one needs an income of $43,884 a year, whereas the median household income is only $28,800—a gap of almost $15,000 *(Los Angeles Times* 1985a:20). Not included in these calculations is the estimated $23,000 for the down payment on the average-price house.

12. For additional research on this topic see also Belcher 1970; Berger 1960; Dreier 1982b; Michelson 1966, 1977; Morris, Crull, and Winter 1976; Perrin 1977; Rakoff 1977; and Williams 1971.

CHAPTER 3

1. We shall consider the effects of supply in the next section of this chapter.

2. As of this time, interest rates are no longer lower than inflation or appreciation, and the 1986 Tax Reform Act will remove many of the benefits of tax sheltering. If rental housing was an "endangered species" in 1979 (U.S. Comptroller General 1979:xx), it is far more so today.

3. Prior to the 1981 Tax Act, the IRS offered guidelines (rather than fixed terms) for depreciation, with 40 years being the preferred term for new apartments. While the Accelerated Cost Recovery System (ACRS) of the 1981 Tax Act reduced this period to 15 years and provided a fixed schedule for accelerated depreciation, it also lowered the top tax bracket from 70 to 50 percent, somewhat reducing the attractiveness of all tax shelters to wealthy investors.

4. In fact, as we have seen, rent increases outstripped the CPI increase during the period 1970–83 (the former increased 192 percent, the latter 157 percent). Thus, for landlords who neither sold nor refinanced their property, rent increases were (on average) more than sufficient to cover increases in operating and maintenance costs. Assuming constant financing costs (given the preponderance of long-term, fixed-payment mortgages), only operating and maintenance costs actually increase with the rate of inflation. Such costs are typically 40–50 percent of total costs, at least in buildings that have not recently been purchased and refinanced (Sternlieb 1974, 1975; Santa Monica Rent Control Board 1979; Los Angeles RSD 1985b: Exhibit 3-12). This implies that *total* landlord costs—barring refinancing—increase at only 50–60 percent of the rate of inflation (Gilderbloom and Jacob 1981:35–40; Los Angeles RSD 1985b). To reconcile the fact that rent increases outstripped operating and maintenance costs with the conclusion that overall profitability, based on rent alone, has declined sharply over the past two decades, it is necessary to assume that the finance component has risen sharply. This in fact has occurred, as we have seen: inflation, rising interest rates, high

rates of speculative turnover, and the resulting refinancing have all served to drive up total landlord costs, to the point where net rental income alone is insufficient to maintain profitability.

5. The model takes into account such factors as rents, operating costs, interest rates, market value, leveraging, and tax benefits resulting from depreciation.

6. Although mortgage interest rates had dropped below 10 percent by early 1986 in many housing markets, the rate of inflation was negligible, resulting in a fairly high (7–9 percent) *real* rate of interest.

7. A Real Estate Research Council report, "Housing Opportunities in Apartments," concluded that "during 1978–84, total returns from apartments (income and unrealized appreciation) averaged 17.4 percent," with apartments generally outperforming other forms of real estate during the period 1980–85 *(Housing and Development Reporter* 1986).

8. Even casual inspection of these data from Blank and Winnick's rent and vacancy table, with adjusted per capital income added, shows that rents vary according to fluctuations in per capita income.

9. Author's interview with Department of Planning staff, Thousand Oaks, California.

10. This topic will be discussed more fully in Chapter 7.

11. While in this section we focus on artificial constraints on the supply of housing, we have previously noted how discriminatory practices, aimed at families with children, minorities, and low-income persons in general, place limitations on the *demand* for rental housing as well.

12. An alternative strategy, based on the demand side of the equation, would be to reduce demand for rental housing by devaluing new or existing units in order to lower rents. This could be achieved by producing smaller houses with fewer amenities, on the one hand, or greatly easing building codes on the other. Both strategies are currently being pursued.

CHAPTER 4

1. For more detailed analyses, see Stone (1980a, 1983); Rybeck (1982); Hartman (1975, 1983); Downs (1983); Sternlieb and Hughes (1981); U.S. Comptroller General (1979); and President's Commission on Housing (1982). The best historical overview of federal housing policy can be found in Rodgers (1984).

There are a number of secondary sources of the increase in housing costs that we have not discussed in this book. These include property taxes, which are highly regressive, and utility costs, which have risen steeply in recent years. And demographic changes, while not causing the housing crisis, reinforce it by creating greater demand. Past fertility patterns (the 1950s "baby boom" children are now reaching the age of initial household formation) and new preferences for household size (single-parent and second-family households) have combined to greatly increase the numbers of households seeking shelter. An estimated 16.8 million household formations are forecast for the present decade (Bureau of the Census 1979:P-25, no. 805).

These long-term demographic changes are compounded by shorter-range geographic shifts, both within metropolitan areas and across regions. The most significant changes at present involve the declining industrial areas of the Northeast and Midwest and the corresponding rise in the South (mainly Florida and Texas) and West (mainly California and Arizona). Between 1973 and 1980, for example, Michigan lost 17 percent of its manufacturing base while California gained 21 percent and Texas gained 32 percent (Harper's 1985:37). These shifts have contributed to acutely depressed housing economies in the declining industrial regions and to frequently inflated housing costs in the high-growth areas.

2. Not all residential mortgage debt is used for housing, since some refinancing is used for general consumer borrowing. This is likely to increase in the future, since the 1986 Tax Reform Act disallows tax deductions for consumer interest expenditures while retaining the deduction for mortgage interest.

3. The long-term impact of the rise in monthly interest costs can be substantial. By way of illustration, a $40,000 loan at 6 percent over a 30-year period entails total interest payments of $46,000; if that same loan were 7 percent, the total cost would be $9,000 more. If the interest rate were 10 percent, the loan cost would total $126,360—more than triple the original loan itself. At an interest rate of 15 percent, the total cost would be $182,160.

4. Variable interest rate mortgages directly track either the Federal Home Loan Bank Board rate or Treasury Bill rates, since they are typically set a fixed amount above these indices.

5. The annual *number* of sales increased by 81 percent during 1972–75, declined by a quarter during the two years following the 1974–75 recession, and resumed its upward climb during the remainder of the period, reaching prerecession levels by 1980.

6. These results must be taken as provisional, since they are subject to a number of conceptual and methodological shortcomings. First, deflating by the general rate of housing inflation will tend to underestimate the impact of speculation, since the deflator itself includes the effect of speculation: not only does it include rapid-turnover properties, but insofar as the price increase of rapid-turnover properties has a "halo" effect on slower-selling properties, the general deflator will include the effects of speculation. Second, all sales of income properties are not listed through the Multiple Listing Service, which tends to feature smaller complexes (under ten units). Insofar as such properties differ in price increase from all rental properties, an unknown bias may be introduced into the results. Third, Appelbaum and Glasser did not statistically control for changes over time in the size and quality of units sold. Insofar as such changes differ between rapid-turnover and nonrapid-turnover properties, an unknown bias was introduced into their results—although there is no reason to expect such systematic differences to exist. Fourth, they did not attempt to control for the effect of capital improvements on price changes, although again there is no reason to believe that the amount of such improvements differs between the two classes of property.

7. The average rapid-turnover property had sold twice within 466 days; the average slow-turnover property had sold twice within 1,455 days.

8. HUD's Experimental Housing Allowance Program (EHAP) began in 1970, involving 30,000 low-income households at 12 locations, at a total cost of $160 million. The results are summarized in USGAO (1986); see also the partial bibliography in Hartman (1986:369).

9. While the EHAP study did not find evidence of measurable rent inflation, this was likely due to the small size of the experimental programs relative to the total housing markets involved. For example, in Green Bay and South Bend, countywide rent spending increased only 1.2 percent as a result of the experimental program.

10. These are the provisions in effect as of the Tax Reform Act's adoption. It is expected that many of the Act's provisions will be modified as their full effects are known and powerful interest groups seek to reshape tax policy as a consequence.

11. The previous depreciation schedules dated to the 1981 Economic Recovery Tax Act's "accelerated cost recovery system."

12. The Act partially exempted owners earning under $100,000 per year, who were permitted to deduct up to $20,000 if they "actively participated" in management—an exclusion that was phased out as income grew to $150,000.

13. Fuhrman Nettles, vice president of Robert A. Stanger and Company, a New Jersey investment advisory firm (quoted in Furlong 1986:16).

CHAPTER 5

1. This division neglects the substantial differences among professional landlords, based on the size of their holdings. For example, some researchers (Stegman 1972; see also Krohn, Fleming and Manzer 1977) divide "professional landlord" into two distinct groups, based on number of units owned: small/medium-size investors (5 to 100 units) and large investors (more than 100 units).

2. A different interpretation of "vacancy rate," on the other hand, has been made by Lowry (1981a), who argues that the current national low in vacancy rates is an indication that "rents are bargains" (1981a:5). Lowry reasons that if rents were truly high, renters would be consuming less space and the vacancy rate would be greater. Thus, according to Lowry, vacancy rate is an ambiguous factor in trying to determine whether rents are reasonable. According to this reasoning, vacancy rate is not a sign of a housing emergency, but an indication that rental units are underpriced.

3. This variable is defined in the census as the percentage of units that lack one or more of the following characteristics: "hot and cold piped water inside the structure, as well as a flush toilet and a bathtub or shower inside the structure for the exclusive use of the occupants of the unit" (U.S. Bureau of the Census 1973b).

4. One of the problems with much empirical work examining the determinants of rent on the demand side is that the coefficients are highly unstable from city to city. Ball (1973) feels that if measures of supply and income were controlled, the demand coefficients would become more reliable and uniform.

5. Data for this analysis came primarily from the Census of Population (U.S. Bureau of the Census 1973a, 1983a), County and City Data Book (U.S. Bureau of the Census 1973b, 1983b), and Places Rated Almanac (Boyer and Savageau 1981).

6. While previous analyses based on this approach have met with acceptance (see Appelbaum and Gilderbloom 1983 and 1986; Gilderbloom 1986a; Gilderbloom and Appelbaum 1987; Vitaliano 1983a, 1983b; Heffley and Santerre 1985), we believe that a fully adequate approach would take into account intracity variation in rents over time, as a function of new construction, and such other local and nonlocal characteristics as regional construction trends, interest rates, and demographic conditions. Such a research project would be prohibitively expensive, however.

7. In particular, based on an examination of zero-order coefficients, there was no evidence of multicollinearity problems (see Nie et al. 1975:340–42). None of the simple correlations between the independent variables in the equation are higher than

.54; if any were higher than .70 there would be a danger of multicollinearity. An additional procedure is to run alternative equations, observing the consistency among the estimators, since regression coefficients can be extremely sensitive to model specification (Vitaliano 1983a:20). Inconsistent estimators are another indicator of possible multicollinearity. This procedure indicated that the variables of substantive interest were generally consistent in terms of sign and strength, regardless of the specification of the equation.

8. The standardized regression coefficient measures the number of standard deviation changes in the dependent variable associated with a change of one standard deviation in the independent variable.

9. To repeat our earlier reasoning, urban housing markets with a small proportion of rental housing may not be as attractive for large, profit-oriented investors since property turnover tends to be lower, affording less opportunity for speculation. Professional landlords would therefore appear to be attracted to urbanized areas where a large proportion of the housing stock is rental.

10. The two measures of professionalization are moderately correlated ($r = .35$).

11. It is possible that the large, more professionalized landlords tend to rent to higher-income tenants whereas smaller landlords rent to lower-income tenants. If this were true, one could expect that cities dominated by professional landlords would have higher-income renters, larger and better-quality rental units, and hence higher rents. We believe we have accounted for this possibility in controlling for median family income.

12. We have no hypotheses concerning the relationship between region and professionalization at this time.

13. The regression analysis for low-, medium-, and high-vacancy cities in our earlier work (Appelbaum and Gilderbloom 1986) was rerun, using the additional variables in the present analysis—in particular, our current measure of professionalization. In our earlier analysis, rents were found to increase with income in all except high-vacancy (over 9 percent) cities, leading us to conclude that competition is restored at that level. In the present analysis, however, rents were found to increase with income even in high-vacancy cities.

14. Interview with John I. Gilderbloom, Nov. 11, 1986. The best empirical work examining the market dynamics of the Houston housing market can be found in the work of Barton Smith (1986). Smith predicts that rents could increase, given current changes in tax law, two and a half times in Houston between 1986 and 1992. Consequently, rents could increase by an average of $470 in the next six years. According to Gilderbloom (1985:149), more than half of Houston's renters are paying more than 25 percent of their income into rental housing. Another study by Gilderbloom, Rosentraub, and Bullard (1987) found that 46 percent of low- and moderate-income households pay more than 25 percent of their incomes into housing. One third of those low-income persons paying excessive housing costs are living in overcrowded housing. Neither Houston, with its small drop in rent, nor any other American city is immune to a national housing crisis.

CHAPTER 6

1. The precise meaning of the concept is unspecified because the standards defining

"necessity" are inevitably subjective: some might find environmental protection acceptable; others would draw the line at minimal health and safety standards; while a few reject outright all land-use controls and even zoning (see, for example, Karlin 1982).

2. Elliot acknowledged this difficulty in a personal communication with Richard Appelbaum in 1983, but stated that the Security Pacific data were the only available data and that, furthermore, "permit valuation tends to be highly correlated with price, with considerably more variation."

3. See, for example, Mercer and Morgan (1982).

4. This approach does not attempt to fully model complex longitudinal processes. Rather, it seeks to "de-trend" the data in such a fashion that the only remaining influences are the independent variables of interest to the researcher. Typically, these include policy interventions. All other variables are treated as confounding influences, and their impact is statistically removed. This removal is accomplished by examining several possible models intended to capture the relationships over time between elements in the series. Diagnostic statistics, measuring the degree of autocorrelation in the series, permit the researcher to determine which model best de-trends the series. The family of models utilized is termed ARIMA, for the three diagnostic models employed: autoregressive, integrative, and moving average. In autoregressive models, earlier influences are assumed to decay exponentially with time; in integrated models, the series is assumed to trend with time, the effects of which are eliminated by subtracting earlier influences from later ones (a process termed *differencing*); and in moving-average models, earlier influences are assumed to have a finite persistence, affecting only adjacent time observations. Time series analysis also permits seasonal and cyclical patterns to be removed, by utilizing the same three models. The choice of model is determined by inspection of the residuals from the regression equation; the adequacy of the ARIMA model is judged by its ability to produce randomly distributed ("white noise") residuals. The result is a highly parsimonious modeling whereby uninteresting variables (from the standpoint of policymaking) are treated as stochastic influences in a de-trended time series, so that those few variables of direct policy relevance may then be related to one another and their influence estimated. For greater detail see Appelbaum (1986c).

5. That exception is the city of Carpinteria, population 11,000, some 15 miles to the east.

6. We had hoped to look at the entire South and North Coast subregions separately, but unfortunately the primary data source, Security Pacific Bank's *California Construction Trends*, could not be disaggregated in that fashion.

7. For more detailed analysis and results see Appelbaum (1986c).

8. The city's apartment density "down-zoning" at first appeared to reduce construction significantly, but this result was found to be largely a statistical artifact: one of the city's largest apartment construction projects had occurred immediately prior to the adoption of growth controls, thereby elevating the level of the pre-control construction series artificially. When this project was excluded from the analysis, no statistically significant effect was observed.

9. This result was attributed to multicollinearity between the two growth-control measures: when only a single measure was employed, growth control was no longer significant, and only the regional control predicted multifamily housing starts.

10. No conclusions could be drawn for the North County, since a lack of apartment construction in nine quarters precluded time-series analysis.

CHAPTER 7

1. For additional information on the tenants' movement see Gilderbloom and Capek (1988); Gilderbloom (1981b); Lawson (1983; 1986); Hartman, Keating, and LeGates (1981); Heskin (1983).

2. Several factors are important in understanding why the tenants' movement flourished in some places but not others. Previous social movements were important; for example, many rent controlled cities had experienced significant anti-war organizing in the sixties (San Francisco, Boston, New York, Los Angeles, and Washington, D.C., in particular). The availability of financial and technical resources have also played a critical role. Rent control campaigns have often been dependent on private philanthropy as well as governmental funding of staff and support services. Both VISTA volunteers and Legal Services workers have also played critical roles (see Capek 1985; Dreier 1982b; see also Zald and McCarthy 1979).

3. In fact, even New York City rent control permitted landlords to appeal their rent levels on the grounds of hardship, and after 1947 exempted new construction as well. Marcuse (1986:Section IV) argues that the lack of repairs in New York City rent controlled units was due in large measure to the city's extremely tight rental market.

4. The cost of administering a strong rent control ordinance can be as high as $72 a unit (Baar 1983:763), due in part to the high legal costs of defending such ordinances against frequent court challenges by landlords and by apartment owner associations.

5. The few studies with contrary findings are subject to a wide variety of methodological flaws that render their conclusions doubtful. These flaws include (1) data provided by landlords (who have a vested stake in the outcome), which are not subject to independent verification; (2) small sample sizes for surveys, with no adequate control for bias in nonresponse; (3) failure to compare rent controlled and nonrent controlled places; (4) failure to control statistically for other influences whose effects may be confounded with rent control; (5) falsification of results or conclusions; and (6) failure to make distinctions about the kind of rent control enacted. (For a detailed critique of this research see Gilderbloom 1981a; Achtenberg 1975.)

An adequate study of the effects of rent control must (1) compare rent controlled communities with a comparable set of nonrent controlled ones and (2) consider the effects of other influences as reflected in apartment construction, maintenance, and valuation. Gilderbloom's (1983) research attempts to satisfy these two requirements which compared 26 rent controlled New Jersey cities with 37 nonrent controlled cities in that state. He looked at all cities with over 13,000 people, and a minimum 15 percent of the housing stock in rental units. Only cities that had enacted rent control during the period September 1972 through April 1973 were considered. In analyzing the effects of rent control on construction, demolitions, and tax base in rent controlled communities, Gilderbloom compared rates for the two years prior to rent control (1970–72) with rates for the period 1975–77. (The period immediately following rent control, 1973 to 1974, was eliminated because of possible "pipeline" effects.) Utilizing multiple regression analysis, Gilderbloom statistically controlled for such confounding influences as population, urban growth, tax rate, median rent, percentage of housing units available for rent, type of city (urban, urban-suburban, suburban), and construction activity and demolitions prior to rent control. The results of this study, along with other studies, are summarized in the following pages.

6. There was indeed a decline in investment in rental housing during the study period, but it was not due to rent control. The U.S. Comptroller General (1979:24–25), for example, reported that it was no longer profitable to build rental housing, except luxury apartments. As a consequence, over 60 percent of new multifamily housing starts were subsidized in the late 1970s and early 1980s. The recent wave of condominium conversions, which afflicts rent controlled and nonrent controlled communities alike, is also due to the greater profitability of privately owned residences.

7. Vitaliano excluded New York City from his study. The importance of Vitaliano's analysis is that these eleven rent controlled cities had yet to be systematically examined, prior to his research. Almost all of the studies (roughly twenty) that we have read concerning rent control in the state of New York look only at New York City.

8. While Rydell's (1981:37–38) study of rent control in Los Angeles concluded that the percentage of gross rents spent on maintenance and services declined with rent control, his figures show that such declines were limited entirely to painting (3.3 percent to 3.0 percent over three years), groundskeeping (2.1 percent to 1.5 percent), and management costs (8.9 percent to 5.4 percent). On the other hand, increases were observed for repairs (4.8 percent to 5.4 percent), general services (0.9 percent to 1.2 percent), and utilities (8.6 percent to 10.9 percent).

9. According to Eckert (1977:324), "One positive and successful Board policy for encouraging maintenance involves a provision for special limited hearings for landlords who wish to make major repairs, capital improvements or renovations. . . . These hearings result in the landlord's receiving a guarantee from the Rent Board as to the amount of additional rent he can charge once the capital improvements are made."

10. Eckert argues (1977:324): "Tenants proving negligence in maintenance can expect a rent reduction until the problem is corrected, and in some cases the Board might initiate a full building hearing if tenants' complaints seem particularly widespread in a particular building. It is probable that in this atmosphere landlords simply are not able to cut maintenance or capital improvements significantly without the Board taking action to stop this reduction in services."

11. Sylvia Aranow, rent control chairperson for Fort Lee, noted that it was often difficult to get landlords to fix code violations before rent control was enacted (Gilderbloom 1978): "Before rent controls, landlords could easily overlook bad conditions if there was a violation in existence just by ignoring it. Finally, the building inspector would get fed up with it and haul him into court, and the judge would fine him $15. Big deal, it didn't correct the violations. It was easier to pay that than to go out and pay $1,000 to correct what really was the problem to begin with—lack of maintenance."

12. Even though rent control does not depress the value of rental property (and hence property tax revenues) in comparison with nonrent controlled places, it does not follow that rent control has no effect on values and tax revenues. Clearly, to the extent that rent control keeps rents lower than they otherwise would be, gross rent multipliers, property values, and hence property taxes are lower than they would be in the absence of controls in the same markets.

13. The definition takes into account population density and geographic location relative to other cities (see New Jersey Department of the Treasury 1970–77).

14. Gilderbloom is currently re-estimating these equations with a variable that takes into account the strength of the rent control law. Preliminary analysis suggests a weak inverse relationship between the strength of rent control and rents.

15. We do not have direct evidence for this, but such a conclusion is supported by the fact that rents are marginally (if not significantly) higher in places that have enacted rent controls.

16. We have calculated these percentages based on the data collected by Clark and Heskin (1982:113).

17. Monthly savings were estimated between $7 and $18, depending on the definition of market rent (the standard of comparison) that was used.

18. Devine's (1986) study of Berkeley and Santa Monica is typical in that limited research is used to draw sweeping conclusions concerning the presumed beneficiaries of rent control. For example, he demonstrates that Santa Monica is largely middle class, concluding that primarily such people are protected by rent control—without looking at the actual composition of protected tenants (as was done in the Los Angeles RSD study [1985a and 1985b]). Although Berkeley's average income is much lower, Devine attributes this to the presence of students, who he apparently believes are only temporarily poor and therefore not deserving of rent control protections. In fact, an earlier survey of Berkeley tenants found that while only 17 percent were students, 47 percent of all tenants paid more than 30 percent of their income on rents (one measure of "shelter poverty" [Baar and LeGates 1984; data reanalyzed in Appelbaum 1986a]).

19. The simulations were intended to shed light on the possible impacts of a California state assembly bill, which would have required all rent control ordinances to decontrol vacant units (units would be recontrolled once reoccupied). Additionally, the measure would have exempted single-family homes from rent control altogether. The vacancy decontrol provision was directed primarily at Berkeley and Santa Monica (the two principal California cities with full controls) and to a lesser degree at West Hollywood (which permitted decontrol, subject to a 10 percent maximum increase every two years). It was also intended to prevent major cities like Los Angeles and San Francisco from adding full control provisions to their ordinances at some future time. The measure eventually died in committee.

20. The following assumptions were employed in the Santa Monica analysis: (1) tenants' household income increases 6 percent annually; (2) CPI increases 4.5 percent annually (three-quarters as fast as income); (3) under current control formulas, rents increase two-thirds of the CPI annually (about 3 percent), with no provisions for decontrol; and (4) rents under the decontrol simulation increase 8.5 percent annually. This last figure reflects the historic relationship between increases in market rents and tenants' income in Southern California (the former increases an average of 113 percent faster annually than the latter), augmented slightly to permit current below-market Santa Monica rents to catch up to prevailing rents in the West Los Angeles area.

21. Or possibly slightly above market levels. See our discussion of vacancy decontrol and the Los Angeles RSD (1985) study elsewhere in this chapter.

22. The present federal standard of affordability is used; for example, less than 30 percent of household income is spent on rent.

23. In Berkeley, average rents were projected to drop from 24 percent of income to

16 percent under the current law, and to rise to 30 percent under vacancy decontrol. Some 5,400 additional rental units would be lost to affordability (out of 24,000 total units), with a cumulative income transfer to landlords of $729 million. In West Hollywood, whose ordinance permits vacancy decontrol (subject to a 10 percent biannual cap), the percentage of income spent on rents would decline from 23 percent to 22 percent under the current ordinance, and rise to 30 percent under decontrol. Units that would be lost to affordability would number 1,800 (out of 17,000 total units), with a cumulative income transfer to landlords of $290 million.

24. These figures must be compared to 89 percent in unregulated Fremont and 91 percent in Hayward, where a moderate rent control ordinance is in effect (see Wolfe 1983).

25. Inclusionary zoning requires subdivision or multi-unit rental developers to offer a fixed percentage of their units at prices or rents that are affordable to designated lower-income groups.

26. Linkage programs require downtown developers of office buildings to pay a fee, based on the size of the development, to mitigate the cost of housing that will be necessary for the additional workers.

27. For an excellent (if critical) analysis of the political significance of the tenants' movement see Marcuse (1981b).

CHAPTER 8

1. On the other hand, housing units are on the average considerably larger in the United States, which in 1976 averaged 120 square meters of floorspace, in comparison with 91 square meters in Western Europe (adapted from Wynn 1984:4).

2. Rent controls were adopted in many U.S. cities during the war as well, although as a local initiative rather than national policy. The best-known example is, of course, New York City (see Chapter 7).

3. The social housing program, enacted in 1950, provided for subsidized loans to private developers, who in exchange agreed to rent controls, specified tenants' rights, and public allocations for fifteen years (Kennedy 1984:57).

4. Between 1979 and 1981 council housing construction declined by 56 percent, while private starts dropped only 4 percent (Smith 1984:109).

5. In 1978, 32 percent of Britain's housing stock was in public housing; in 1981 the figure was 31 percent (Doling 1983:477).

6. For example, in 1951 Italy had 0.8 rooms per person; the figure is presently 1.5.

7. The exception is in publicly assisted private rental.

8. The small number of controlled tenancies also provide lifetime security of tenure (Harloe 1985:366).

9. Under this system, units are removed from rent control as they become vacant, and are recontrolled when reoccupied.

10. In Headey's (1978:44) terms, " 'socialist' because it was intended to operate in accordance with governmentally imposed policy objectives and priorities, 'market' because competition among builders providing different types of housing (multi-family apartment blocks, single family houses, etc.) for different types of owner and tenant was not wholly abolished.''

11. Headey bases his summary on Greve (1971:63).

12. The following discussion is based on Headey (1978:57–97).

13. Another alternative—what is termed *self-help construction* in the United States (in Sweden it is called *small house building*)—originated during the same period. It involves do-it-yourself construction on a cooperative and nonprofit basis, under the direction of a public agency (Smahusavdelningen), which arranges for everything except labor. Some 12,000 units were provided in the Stockholm area during the period 1927–76, targeted at working-class households (Witt-Stromer 1977). Another form is the "collective" house, dating to 1935 and the architectural school of Sven Markelius. Collective houses were large apartments with common kitchens and public space. This form, once seen as a major solution to the housing problem, has never grown to more than a small number of units (Vestbro 1979).

14. Lundevall (1976:3–4) notes that wages fell 30 percent during the period 1920–23, while rents rose 20 percent. HSB was not the first cooperative association in Sweden, but its influence in creating a national cooperative movement was decisive.

15. Members pay annual dues to the local organization, and in some cases are required to deposit funds with the savings association as well. In exchange, they receive a place in the queue for units and the right to "co-determination" in the affairs of the local and national organizations, on the one-person-one-vote principle. Membership is open to anyone who chooses to join. See HSB (1975) for a detailed discussion of HSB's history and operations, with numerous photographs and co-op designs. For a more general collection of articles on the Swedish co-op movement, see HPP (1976).

16. Phrase of Sverker Gustavsson, director of the National Swedish Institute for Building Research, in personal interview, June 1981.

17. Compensation is at market value, although since 1972, in certain cases of rapid land inflation, it corresponds to market value ten years prior to the taking, under the theory that the increased value is due to community-initiated improvements and amenities (Heimburger 1976:28–29).

18. Single-family housing tends overwhelmingly to be privately owned, although there has been a slight trend toward cooperative and public ownership in this sector as well. In 1976, for example, 94 percent of single-family homes were classified as privately owned, 5 percent as publicly owned, and 1 percent in cooperatives. By 1979 the figures were 87, 8, and 5 percent respectively (HPP 1980:13).

19. Investment levels reached a high of 7.4 percent of GNP in 1966–70, and have averaged 6.8 percent since the early fifties. The United States has invested approximately 4.6 percent (Headey 1978:179; Nesslein 1982:239).

20. This study goes on to note that slum "tendencies" still remain: "In almost every municipality there exist at least a few badly maintained houses, more or less exclusively occupied by alcoholics, criminals and other social outcasts." Such houses are not geographically concentrated, however (Wiktorin 1982:248).

21. For a comparison of Swedish and American suburbs see Popenoe (1977).

22. Rent and price controls were enacted in 1942, but rent controls were phased out in smaller towns and urban areas throughout the postwar period. Rent control remained in effect in the major urban areas until 1975, however.

23. This is because the age of the unit is not supposed to be a factor in determining rents, apart from differences in quality that might be associated with age. Thus a new unit with high capital expenses must, under law, charge the same rent as an old unit with

238 | Notes to Chapter 8

low expenses, providing both are of equal quality. There is, of course, some divergence in practice from this ideal model of rent setting, although rents are far less variable in Sweden (when quality is controlled) than in most other countries. One study found, in a random sample of 83 public housing companies, that two-thirds charged within 8 percent of the median rent for all units. The same study found, however, that the age of units continues to play a significant role in determining rents (see Turner 1981).

24. For families with children, the percentage reached by allowances is quite high. Seventy-eight percent of renters with three or more children, for example, receive allowances (Lundqvist 1981:20).

25. Headey (1978:57) estimated 15.6 percent in 1974, prior to the general price inflation of recent years. The International Union of Tenants reports that Swedish tenants in 1982 paid 27 percent of their income on average—although it is not clear whether this figure takes into account government housing allowances (IUT 1982:1–2). The cooperative society, Riksbyggen, provides a similar estimate, noting that poorer families pay higher percentages than wealthier ones. These estimates, however, are based on assumptions about "typical" expenditures rather than actual surveys. The role of housing allowances is unclear in this case as well (SR 1980:9).

26. First mortgages are provided by the Urban Mortgage Bank (established 1909) and second mortgages by the Sweden Housing Loan Bank (established 1929). These are specially chartered commercial banks, with guaranteed funds provided by the state; their loans are thus risk free (Headey 1978:66).

27. Lundqvist (1981:18) demonstrates that recent (1980–81) changes in the subsidy system have increased the bias in favor of tenancy and cooperatives.

28. The imputed rent is a percentage of the house's assessed value, determined on a five-year assessment cycle. This system should be contrasted with that in the United States, under which interest and property taxes can also be deducted from income, while there is no requirement to offset imputed rental value against such expenses.

29. For a study that attributes all Swedish housing successes to postwar affluence, and all the problems to "serious resource misallocation" and "housing market disequilibrium" resulting from excessive governmental intervention, see Nesslein (1982). This study suffers, however, from a highly selective interpretation of secondary materials.

30. There were 26,628 vacant units in January 1974, of which almost four-fifths were in public housing (Headey 1978:90). In September 1974 the vacancy rate throughout metropolitan Stockholm was 7.2 percent; metropolitan Gothenburg, 10 percent; and metropolitan Malmo, 7.8 percent (Nesslein 1982:241). Since that time, however, the surpluses have declined and vacancy rates are considerably lower (Stockholm, for example, was estimated to have a vacancy rate of only 1.6 percent in 1978). See Nesslein (1982:242).

31. Interviews in June 1981 with Rolf Trodin, director of Planning, HSB, and Olle Lindstrom, deputy managing director, Riksbyggen. According to Lindstrom, his studies found that 95 percent of all Riksbyggen sales in the early seventies followed prices recommended by the Co-op Board. He thus viewed the relaxation of controls as having little effect on prices in most cases, at least where the market was relatively "balanced" between supply and demand.

32. Presently, one cannot legally own a flat in an apartment building in Sweden.

33. Partly because of this latter reason, however, and partly for administrative

reasons, co-op conversions in Sweden involve the attempt to sell a majority of units to current occupants.

34. The National Tenants' Association has criticized conversions as part of the "wild speculation in housing" (Kjellberg and Burns 1981).

35. The key aspect, of course, remains rent setting, which is achieved through a highly bureaucratized system of tenant-management negotiations that closely resemble organized labor's wage negotiations. While the average tenant has a voice in this process, it is very small.

36. Facilities for the handicapped have long been a part of Swedish housing policy (see Beckman 1976).

37. This meant that the Social Democrats could govern without forming a coalition with the Swedish Communist Party, which kept 20 seats (with 5.6 percent of the vote). The remaining 3.7 percent of the popular vote went to a small "Christian" party and the new Green Party, neither of which received the 4 percent necessary to gain a seat in parliament. See Leijonhufvud (1982).

CHAPTER 9

1. There are several caveats, however:
- An overly steep windfall profits tax could eliminate virtually all incentive to buy and sell rental housing. Therefore, the tax would have to be restricted to an appropriate range, to ensure market allocation.
- Such a tax might have the effect of reducing the incentive to construct rental housing. To mitigate this effect, the tax could exempt the first sale of any building by its developer, in which case profit would be taxed at the ordinary rate.
- Similar considerations should apply to substantial rehabilitations and other capital improvements. Such productive investment should be encouraged, and the resulting increase in value therefore should be taxed at ordinary rates.

2. The principal features of such a tax might include a
- Progressive tax on the landlord's rental income from luxury units—units, that is, that rent for more than a specified amount, determined by local tenants' median income
- Progressive deed-transfer tax on luxury rental units—units that sell for more than a specified amount, based on local market characteristics
- Progressive deed-transfer tax on luxury homes.

3. The following discussion is adapted from SCIP (1980), as reproduced in Gilderbloom (1981b:240–41).

4. For example, California law limits appreciation to 10 percent annually of the original down payment, plus approved improvements.

5. For example, legal mechanisms could be developed to
- Grant the right of "first purchase" to tenants' organizations, community groups, government entities, and other legally defined community-based owners
- Determine the maximum buyout price that uses public funds, to discourage excessively costly purchases (for example, luxury and speculatively priced units)
- Determine the proportion of tenants required for first-option purchases, while protecting tenants who choose not to buy into the conversion

- Require permanent community-based ownership, once transfer is completed (for example, no housing is sold from the nonprofit stock, unless some important public purpose is served)
- Establish procedures for speedy tax-title searches, to enable localities to obtain control of housing that is in tax arrears
- Define the community-based ownership forms that will qualify for funding under the provisions of this act.

6. We estimate first-year federal administration costs at approximately $2 billion (see Table 9.2).

REFERENCES

ABAG [Association of Bay Area Governments]. 1980. "Development Fees in the San Francisco Bay Area." Berkeley: ABAG.

———. 1982. "Development Fees in the San Francisco Bay Area." Berkeley: ABAG.

Achtenberg, Emily P. 1975. "Critique of the Rental Housing Association Rent Control Study: An Analysis of the Realities of Rent Control in the Greater Boston Area." Boston: Urban Planning Aid.

———. 1976. "Evaluation of Rent Control as a Housing Policy." In Bureau of National Affairs Housing and Development Reporter and the Institute for Professional and Executive Development (eds.), *Seminar on Rent Controls*. Washington, D.C.: Bureau of National Affairs Housing and Development Reporter (pp. 1–45).

———. 1985. "Subsidized Housing At Risk: The Social Costs of Private Ownership." Paper presented at conference, Housing Policy in the Eighties: Choices and Outcomes. Institute for Policy Studies and Virginia Polytechnic Institute and State University, Alexandria, Virginia, May 17–18.

——— and Peter Marcuse. 1983. "Towards the Decommodification of Housing: A Political Analysis and Progressive Program." In Chester Hartman (ed.), *America's Housing Crisis: What Is to Be Done?* Boston: Routledge and Kegan Paul.

Agnew, J. W. 1978. "Market Relations and Locational Conflict in Cross-National Perspective." In Kevin Cox (ed.), *Urbanization and Conflict in Market Societies*. New York: Methuen (pp. 128–143).

Alford, R., and Roger O. Friedland. 1975. "Political Participation and Public Policy." *Annual Review of Sociology* 1.

Alford, R., and H. Scoble. 1968. "Sources of Local Political Involvement." *American Political Science Review* 62:1192–1205.

Alonso, William. 1964. *Location and Land Use: Toward a General Theory of Land Rent*. Cambridge, Mass.: Harvard University Press.

Anderson, Robert J., and Thomas D. Crocker. 1971. "Air Pollution and Residential Property Values." *Urban Studies* 8:3.

Angotti, Thomas. 1977. "The Housing Question." *Monthly Review* 29:5.

Angotti, Thomas R., and Bruce Dale. 1981. "Urban Renewal without Removal." In John I. Gilderbloom (ed.), *Rent Control: A Source Book*. San Francisco: Foundation for National Progress.

Angrist, Shirley S. 1974. *Dimensions of Well-Being in Public Housing Families*. Pittsburgh: Carnegie-Mellon University.

Apartment and Office Building Association. 1977. "Fact Sheet—Deterioration and Abandonment." In National Association of Realtors (eds.), "Rent Control Report." Chicago: National Association of Realtors (pp. 130–140).

Apgar, William C., and Arthur A. Doud (n.d.). *Tax Reform and National Housing Policy*. Philadelphia: Arthur Doud Associates.

241

Apgar, William C., H. James Brown, Arthur A. Doud, and George A. Schink. 1985. "Assessment of the Likely Impacts of the President's Tax Proposals on Rental Housing Markets." Cambridge, Mass.: Joint Center for Housing Studies of MIT and Harvard University.

Appelbaum, Richard P. 1978. *Size, Growth, and U.S. Cities.* New York: Praeger.

──────. 1981. *Home for Whom? Housing on the South Coast.* Santa Barbara: South Coast Information Project.

──────. 1981. "The Housing Crisis in Santa Barbara: Some Preliminary Findings." In Richard P. Appelbaum, *Home for Whom? Housing on the South Coast.* Santa Barbara: South Coast Information Project.

──────. 1982. "Concentration of Ownership in Isla Vista." Santa Barbara: University of California, Department of Sociology. Unpublished manuscript (Xerox).

──────. 1984. "The Effects of Rent Control on the Santa Monica Rental Housing Market." Paper presented at Lincoln Land Institute Colloquium on Rent Control. Cambridge, Mass.

──────. 1985a. *Regulation and the Santa Barbara Housing Market.* Berkeley, California Policy Seminar.

──────. 1985b. "Swedish Housing in the Postwar Period." *Urban Affairs Quarterly* 21: 2:221–244.

──────. 1986a. "An Analysis of Rental Housing in Los Angeles, Santa Monica, Berkeley, and West Hollywood under Current Rent Control and A.B. 483." Santa Barbara: University of California Department of Sociology.

──────. 1986b. "Problems in the Estimation of Homelessness." Paper presented to George Washington University Conference on Homelessness.

──────. 1986c. *Regulation and the Santa Barbara Housing Market.* Berkeley: California Policy Seminar.

──────. 1986d. "Swedish Housing in the Postwar Period: Some Lessons for American Housing Policy." In Rachel G. Bratt, Chester Hartman, and Ann Meyerson (eds.), *Critical Perspectives on Housing.* Philadelphia: Temple University Press.

──────, Jennifer Bigelow, Henry Kramer, Harvey Molotch, and Paul Relis. 1976. *The Effects of Urban Growth: A Population Impact Analysis.* New York: Praeger.

Appelbaum, Richard P., et al. 1986. *National Comprehensive Housing Program.* Washington, D.C.: Institute for Policy Studies.

Appelbaum, Richard P., and John I. Gilderbloom. 1983. "Housing Supply and Regulation: A Study of the Rental Housing Market." *Journal of Applied Behavioral Science* 19:1:1–19.

──────. 1986. "Supply Side Economics and Rents: Are Rental Housing Markets Truly Competitive?" In Rachel G. Bratt, Chester Hartman, and Ann Meyerson (eds.), *Critical Perspectives on Housing.* Philadelphia: Temple University Press.

Appelbaum, Richard P., and T. Glasser. 1982. *Concentration of Ownership in Isla Vista, California.* Santa Barbara: USCB Housing Office.

Apps, P. 1971. "An Approach to Modeling Residential Demand." Paper given at CES Seminar on House Prices. December.

Ashford, D., and G. Salmonsen. 1978. "Property Rights versus Personal Rights, and the Impact of Housing Opportunities for Children." *Fair Housing Forum* 1:4:36–37.

Atlas, John. 1979. "Mortgage Money: Must We Pay Higher Prices for It?" *New York Times,* Mar. 18, p. 24.

————. 1981. "Writing a Strong, but Legal Rent Control Law." In J. Gilderbloom (ed.), *Rent Control: A Source Book*. Santa Barbara: Foundation for National Progress, Housing Information Center (pp. 121–126).

————. 1982. *National Tenants' Union Platform: Rent Control Plank Draft*. East Orange, N.J.: National Tenants' Union.

———— and Peter Dreier. 1980. "Legislative Strategy: Fighting for Rent Control." *Shelterforce* 5:4.

————. 1981. "Making Tenant's Vote Count in New Jersey." *Social Policy* (May/June).

————. 1983. "Mobilize or Compromise? The Tenants' Movement and American Politics." In Chester Hartman (ed.), *America's Housing Crisis: What Is to Be Done?* Boston: Routledge and Kegan Paul (pp. 151–185).

Baar, Kenneth. 1983. "Guidelines for Drafting Rent Control Laws: Lessons of a Decade." *Rutgers Law Review* 35:4:721–885.

————. 1986. "Facts and Fallacies in the Rental Housing Market." *Western City* (Sept.):47–86.

———— and Dennis Keating. 1975. "The Last Stand of Economic Substantive Due Process—The Housing Emergency Requirements for Rent Control." *Urban Lawyer* 7:3:490.

————. 1981. "Fair Return Standards and Hardship Appeal Procedures: A Guide for New Jersey Rent Leveling Boards." Berkeley: National Housing Law Project.

Baar, Kenneth, and Richard LeGates. 1984. "Rental Housing under the Berkeley Rent Stabilization Ordinance: A Survey of Tenants and Landlords." Berkeley: Rent Stabilization Board.

Baldassare, Mark. 1979. *Residential Crowding in Urban America*. Berkeley: University of California Press.

Ball, Michael. 1973. "Recent Empirical Work on the Determinants of Relative Housing Prices." *Urban Studies* 10:213–233.

————. 1976. "Owner Occupation." In M. Edwards, F. Gray, S. Merrett, and J. Swann (eds.), *Housing and Class in Britain*. London: Political Economy of Housing Workshop of the Conference of Socialist Economists (pp. 24–29).

Bartlet, David, and Ronald Lawson. 1982. "Rent Control and Abandonment: A Second Look at the Evidence." *Journal of Urban Affairs* 4:4.

Beckman, M. 1976. "Building for Everyone: The Disabled and the Built Environment in Sweden." Information provided to U.N. Conference on Human Settlements (HABITAT). Stockholm: Ministry of Housing and Physical Planning.

Belcher, J. C. 1970. "Differential Aspirations for Housing between Blacks and Whites in Rural Georgia." *Phylon* 31:231–243.

Berger, Bennett. 1960. *Working Class Suburb*. Berkeley: University of California Press.

Betz, J. 1981. "Rental Housing Crisis Called Calamity." *Los Angeles Times*, Oct. 4, Sec. VIII-23.

Beyer, Glen. 1958. *Housing: A Factual Analysis*. New York: Macmillan.

————. 1966. *Housing and Society*. New York: Macmillan.

Bickert, Browne, Coddington, and Associates. 1976. "An Analysis of the Impact of State and Local Government Intervention on the Homebuilding Process in Colorado, 1970–1975." Denver: Association of Housing and Building.

Black, J. Thomas, and Frank R. Dunau. 1981. "The Effect of Regulations on Residential Land Prices." Washington, D.C.: Urban Land Institute.

Blank, D. and L. Winnick. 1953. "The Structure of the Housing Market." *Quarterly Journal of Economics* LXXVII:2:181–208.

Blum, Terry C., and Paul William Kingston. 1984. "Homeownership and Social Attachment." *Sociological Perspectives* 27:2:159–180.

Blumberg, Richard, Brian Q. Robbins, and Kenneth Baar. 1974. "The Emergence of Second Generation Rent Control." *Clearinghouse Review* (Aug.), pp. 240–249.

Booth, Alan, and John N. Edwards. 1976. "Crowding and Family Relations." *American Sociological Review* 41:308–321.

Booth, Heather. 1981. "Left with the Ballot Box." *Working Papers for a New Society* 8:3.

Boston. 1986. "Making Room: Comprehensive Policy for the Homeless." Boston: Office of Mayor.

Boston. 1983. *The October Project: Seeing the Obvious Problem.* Boston: Emergency Shelter Commission Report.

Boudreau, John, Quon Kwan, William Faragher, and Genevieve Denault. 1977. *Arson and Arson Investigation.* Washington, D.C.: National Institute for Law Enforcement and Criminal Justice.

Bourne, Larry S. 1977. "The Housing Supply and Price Debate: Divergent Views and Policy Consequences." Toronto: University of Toronto Centre for Urban and Community Studies, Research Paper No. 86.

Box, G. E. P., and Gwilyn Jenkins. 1976. *Time Series Analysis: Forecasting and Control.* San Francisco: Holden Day.

Box, G. E. P., and G. C. Tiao. 1965. "A Change in Level of a Non-Stationary Time Series." *Econometrica* 52:181–192.

———. 1975. "Interventions Analysis with Application to Economic and Environmental Problems." *Journal of the American Statistical Association* 70:70–92.

Boyarsky, Bill. 1980. "Will Los Angeles' Future Make Room for the Poor?" *Los Angeles Times* (Sunday), May 25, Part V, p. 3.

Boyer, Richard, and David Savageau. 1981. *Places Rated Almanac.* New York: Rand McNally.

Bradbury, K., and Anthony Downs. 1981. *Do Housing Allowances Work?* Washington, D.C.: Brookings Institution.

Brady, James. 1983. "Arson, Urban Economy, and Organized Crime: The Case of Boston." *Social Problems* 31:1.

Bratt, Rachel G., Chester Hartman, and Ann Meyerson (eds.). 1986. *Critical Perspectives on Housing.* Philadelphia: Temple University Press.

Brigham, E. F. 1965. "The Determinants of Residential Land Values." *Land Economics* (Nov.).

Brooks, Andree. 1982. "Foreclosing on a Dream." *New York Times Magazine,* Sept. 12.

Brown, H. James, and John Yinger. 1986. *Home Ownership and Housing Affordability in the United States: 1963–1985.* Cambridge, Mass.: Joint Center for Housing Studies of Massachusetts Institute of Technology and Harvard University.

Browning, Harley, and Nestor Rodriguez. 1985. "The Migration of Mexican *Undocumentados* as a Settlement Process: Implications for Work." In George Borgas and Marta Tienda (eds.), *Hispanics in the U.S. Economy.* New York: Academic Press.

Bruss, Robert J. 1979. "Real Estate Mailbag." *Philadelphia Inquirer,* Aug. 4, p. 13C.

Bullard, Robert D. 1984. "The Black Family: Housing Alternatives in the '80s." *Journal of Black Studies* 14:3:341–351.

Burgess, Ernest W. 1925. "The Growth of the City: An Introduction to a Research Project." Reprinted in Robert E. Park, Ernest W. Burgess, and R. D. McKenzie (eds.), *The City*. Chicago: University of Chicago Press (pp. 47–62).

Burns, Leland, and Frank Mittelbach. 1968. "Efficiency in the Housing Industry." In *A Decent Home* (vol. 2 of Presidents' Commission on Housing). Washington, D.C.: Government Printing Office.

Business Week. 1985. "How Tax Laws Pushed Apartment Owners into Overdrive." May 13, pp. 124–125.

Butler, Katy. 1986. "Surge in Street Deaths Among San Francisco's Homeless." *San Francisco Chronicle*, Dec. 22, sec. 1, p. 1.

California Construction Industry Research Board. 1975. "Cost of Delay prior to Construction." Los Angeles: CCIRB.

California Department of Housing and Community Development. 1977. *California Statewide Housing Plan*. Sacramento: State Department of Housing and Community Development.

California Housing Task Force. 1979. *Major Housing Legislation for 1979: Recommendations to the Governor and Legislature*. Sacramento: State of California Office of Planning and Research.

CALPIRG [California Public Interest Research Group]. 1980. *Speculation and Housing Crisis: A CALPIRG Investigation of Real Estate in San Diego*. San Diego: CALPIRG.

Capek, Stella. 1985. "Urban Progressive Movements: The Case of Santa Monica." Ph.D. dissertation, University of Texas, Dept. of Sociology, Austin.

Carroll, Jerry. 1981. "High-priced Housing: Causing College Brain Drain?" *San Francisco Chronicle*, Sept. 18, p. 23.

Carter, Robert. 1980. "Arson and Arson Investigation in the United States." *Fire Journal* 74:40–47.

Castells, Manuel. 1975. "Advanced Capitalism, Collective Consumption and Urban Contradictions: New Sources of Inequality and New Models for Change." In Robert Linberg, Robert Alford, Colin Crouch, and Claus Offe (eds.), *Stress and Contradiction in Modern Capitalism*. Lexington, Mass.: Lexington Books.

———. 1980. *The Urban Question*. Cambridge, Mass.: MIT Press.

———. 1983. *The City and the Grassroots*. Berkeley: University of California Press.

Cherry, R., and E. J. Ford. 1975. "Concentration of Rental Housing Property and Rental Housing Markets in Urban Areas." *American Real Estate and Urban Economics Association Journal* 3:1:7–16.

Chicago Tribune. 1982. "Housing Prices Hold Individual Mysteries." Nov. 3, Sec. 3, p. 19.

Christian, J., and T. J. Parliment. 1982. *Home Ownership: The American Dream Adrift*. Chicago: U.S. League of Savings Associations.

Clark, William, and Alan Heskin. 1982. "The Impact of Rent Control on Tenure Discounts and Residential Mobility." *Land Economics* 58:1:109–117.

Clark, William, Alan Heskin, and Louise Manuel. 1980. *Rental Housing in the City of Los Angeles*. Los Angeles: Institute for Social Science Research, University of California.

Clemer, Richard B., and John C. Simonson. 1983. "Trends in Substandard Housing,

1940–1980." *Journal of American Real Estate and Urban Economics Association* 10:442–464.

COACT. 1979. *Residential Property Turnover Study: A Report to the City of Madison, Wisconsin.* Madison: COACT Research Associates.

Cockburn, Alexander, and James Ridgeway. 1981. "Tenant Coalition Sweeps Local Elections." *Village Voice,* Apr. 22–28.

COIN [Consumers Opposed to Inflation in the Necessities]. 1979. *There Are Alternatives: A Program for Controlling Inflation in the Necessities of Life.* Washington, D.C.: COIN.

Collins, Randall. 1986. "Sociology in the Doldrums?" *American Journal of Sociology* 91:6:1336–1355.

Community Development Project. 1976. *Profits against Houses: An Alternative Guide to Housing Finance.* London: Community Development Project Information and Intelligence Unit.

Consortium for the Homeless. 1983. "The Homeless of Phoenix: Who Are They? And What Should Be Done?" Phoenix: CFTH.

Cooper, Clare. 1971. "The House as Symbol of Self." Working Paper No. 120. Berkeley: University of California Institute of Urban and Regional Development.

Cox, Kevin. 1982. "Housing Tenure and Neighborhood Activism." *Urban Affairs Quarterly* 18:1:107–129.

Cranston, Alan. 1986. *Santa Barbara News Press,* Oct. 21.

Cronin, Francis J. 1983. "Market Structure and Price of Housing Services." *Urban Studies* 20:365–375.

Cubbin, J. S. 1970. "A Hedonic Approach to Some Aspects of the Conventional Housing Market." Warwick, Eng.: Warwick Economic Research Papers.

Cullingworth, John B. 1981. "Rent Control and Redistribution: A Report to the Ontario Ministry of Housing" (mimeo). Toronto: University of Toronto Centre for Urban and Community Studies.

Cummings, Scott. 1986. "Urban Policy Research and the Changing Fiscal Focus of the State: Sociology's Ambiguous Legacy and Uncertain Future." In Mark Rosentraub (ed.), *Urban Policy Problems: Federal Policy and Institutional Change.* New York: Praeger (pp. 167–200).

Currier, Chet. 1983. "Experts Predict Rent Will Climb." *Green Bay Press Gazette,* Aug. 2, p. A-10.

Daugherbaugh, Debbie. 1975. "Anchorage Rent Review Program." Anchorage: Alaska Public Interest Group.

Daun, Ake. 1979. "Why Do Swedish Suburbs Look the Way They Do?" *Human Environment in Sweden* 9 (Feb).

de Jouvenel, Bertrand. 1948. *No Vacancies.* Irvington-on-Hudson, N.Y.: Foundation for Economic Education.

Devine, Richard J. 1986. "Who Benefits from Rent Control?" Oakland: Center for Community Change.

Division of State and Regional Planning. 1972. "New Jersey Municipal Profiles of Intensity of Urbanization." Trenton: Department of Community Affairs.

Dolbeare, Cushing N. 1983. "The Low-Income Housing Crisis." In Chester Hartman (ed.), *America's Housing Crisis: What Is to Be Done?* Boston: Routledge and Kegan Paul (pp. 29–75).

Doling, J. 1983. "British Housing Policy 1974–1983: A Review." *Regional Studies* 17 (Dec.): 475–478.

Dorfman, Dan. 1983. "Apartments Gaining as Investments." *Green Bay Press Gazette,* Jan. 23, p. A-10.

Dowall, David. 1980a. "The Effects of Land-Use and Environmental Regulations on Housing Costs." In Roger Montgomery and Dale Marshall (eds.), *Housing Policy for the 1980's.* Lexington, Mass.: D. C. Heath.

———. 1980b. "An Examination of Population Growth-Managing Communities." *Policy Studies* 9:3:414–427.

——— and John Landis. 1980. "Land-Use Controls and Housing Costs: An Examination of San Francisco Bay Area Communities." Center for Real Estate and Urban Economics Working Paper No. 81-24. Berkeley: University of California.

———. 1982. "Land-Use Controls and Housing Costs: An Examination of San Francisco–Bay Area Communities." Berkeley: University of California Institute of Urban and Regional Development. Reprint No. 196.

Downs, Anthony. 1980. "Too Much Capital for Housing?" *Brookings Bulletin* 17(Summer):1–5.

———. 1983. *Rental Housing in the 1980's.* Washington, D.C.: Brookings Institution.

Dreier, Peter. 1979. "The Politics of Rent Control." *Working Papers* 6: 55–63.

———. 1982a. "Dreams and Nightmares." *The Nation* 235:141–146.

———. 1982b. "The Status of Tenants in the United States." *Social Problems* 30:2:179–198.

——— and John Atlas. 1980. "The Housing Crisis and the Tenants' Revolt." *Social Policy* (Jan.), pp. 13–24.

Dreier, Peter, John I. Gilderbloom, and Richard P. Appelbaum. 1980. "Rising Rents and Rent Control: Issues in Urban Reform." In Pierre Clavel, John Forrester, and William Goldsmith (eds.), *Urban Planning in an Age of Austerity.* New York: Pergamon Press (pp. 154–176).

Drummond, James. 1986. "Rent Decline Continues in Houston." *Houston Chronicle,* Nov. 4, Sec. 1, p. 1.

Duncan, S. S. 1981. "Housing Policy, the Methodology of Levels, and Urban Research: The Case of Castells." *International Journal of Urban and Regional Research* 5:2.

Eckert, Joseph. 1977. "The Effect of Rent Controls on Assessment Policies, Differential Incidence of Taxation and Income Adjustment Mechanisms for Rental Housing in Brookline, Massachusetts." Ph.D. dissertation, Tufts University.

Economist. 1977. "The Arsonists" (editorial). London, May 27, p. 11.

Edel, Matthew. 1982. "Home Ownership and Working-Class Unity." *International Journal of Urban and Regional Research* 6:205–221.

Edelman, Murray. 1967. *The Symbolic Use of Politics.* Chicago: University of Illinois Press.

Elliot, Michael. 1981. "The Impact of Growth Control Regulations on Housing Prices in California." *Journal of American Real Estate and Urban Economics Association* 9:2:115–133.

Erickson, Jon, and Charles Wilhelm (eds.). 1986. *Housing the Homeless.* New Brunswick, N.J.: Rutgers University Center for Urban Policy Research.

Esping-Andersen, Gosta, and Roger Friedland. 1980. "Class Coalitions in the Making of Western European Economics." Mimeograph. Santa Barbara: University of California at Santa Barbara, Department of Sociology.

Evans, A. W. 1971. *The Economics of Residential Location*. New York: St. Martin's Press.

Feagin, Joe. 1983. *The Urban Real Estate Game*. Englewood Cliffs, N.J.: Prentice-Hall.

―――. 1986a. "Toward a New Urban Ecology." *Contemporary Sociology* 15:4:531–533.

―――. 1986b. "Urban Real Estate Speculation in the U.S.: Implications for Social Science and Urban Planning." In Rachel Bratt, Chester Hartman, and Ann Meyerson (eds.), *Critical Perspectives on Housing*. Philadelphia: Temple University Press.

Ferguson, C. E., and S. C. Maurice. 1974. *Economic Analysis*. Homewood, Ill.: Richard D. Irwin.

Field, Mervin. 1979. "Mervin Field Poll of California Views on Rent." *San Francisco Chronicle*, June 13, p. 3.

Fire and Arson Investigator. 1981. "Analysis of Arson and Socio-economic Backgrounds" (editorial). 31:3:3–16.

Fisch, Oscar. 1983. "The Impact of Rent Control on Effective Tax Bias and on Structural Changes of Residential Buildings." Paper delivered at Lincoln Land Institute Colloquium on Rent Control. Boston: Lincoln Land Institute.

Fischer, Claude. 1982. *To Dwell Among Friends: Personal Networks Among Town and City*. Chicago: University of Chicago Press.

Fischer, Claude, R. Jackson, C. Stueve, K. Gerson, and L. Jones, with M. Baldassare. 1977. *Networks and Places*. New York: Free Press.

Fisher, Ernest M. 1951. *Urban Real Estate Markets: Characteristics and Financing*. New York: National Bureau of Economic Research.

―――. 1966. "Twenty Years of Rent Control in New York City." In *Essays in Urban Land Economics*. Berkeley: Real Estate Research Program, University of California (pp. 31–67).

Fitch, R. 1977. "Planning New York." In Roger Alcaly and David Mermelstein (eds.), *The Fiscal Crisis of American Cities: Essays on the Political Economy of Urban America with Special Reference to New York*. New York: Vintage (pp. 246–284).

Flanigan, William H., and Nancy H. Zingale. 1979. *Political Behavior of the American Electorate*. Boston: Allyn and Bacon.

Foley, Donald L. 1980. "The Sociology of Housing." In Alex Inkeles (ed.), *Annual Review of Sociology* 6:457–478.

Form, William H. 1954. "The Place of Social Structure in the Determination of Land Use: Some Implications for a Theory of Urban Ecology." *Social Forces* 32:4:317–323.

Frankena, Mark. 1975. "Alternative Models of Rent Control." *Urban Studies* 12:303–308.

Franklin, James J., and Thomas Muller. 1977. "Environmental Impact Evaluation, Land Use Planning, and the Housing Consumer." *Journal of American Real Estate and Urban Economics Association* 5:3:279–301.

Franklin, Scott B. 1981. "Housing Cooperatives: A Viable Means of Home Ownership for Low-Income Families." *Journal of Housing* (July), pp. 392–398.

Frech, H. E., III. 1982. "The California Coastal Commission's Economic Impacts."

In M. Bruce Johnson (ed.), *Resolving the Housing Crisis: Government Policy, Decontrol, and the Public Interest*. San Francisco: Pacific Institute for Public Policy Research.

Freeman, Howard, and Peter Rossi. 1984. "Furthering the Applied Side of Sociology." *American Sociological Review* 49 (Aug.): 571–580.

Freeman, Richard, and Brian Hall. 1986. "Permanent Homeless in America?" Cambridge, Mass.: National Bureau for Economic Research, working paper #2013 (Aug.).

Fried, Marc. 1963. "Grieving for a Lost Home." In L. J. Duhl (ed.), *The Urban Condition*. New York: Basic Books.

Frieden, Bernard J. 1979a. *The Environmental Protection Hustle*. Cambridge, Mass.: MIT Press.

———. 1979b. "The New Regulation Comes to Suburbia." *The Public Interest* 55:15–27.

———. 1982. "The Exclusionary Effect of Growth Controls." In M. Bruce Johnson (ed.)., *Resolving the Housing Crisis*. San Francisco: Pacific Institute for Public Policy Research.

——— and Authur P. Solomon. 1977. "The Nation's Housing: 1975 to 1985." Cambridge, Mass.: Joint Center for Urban Studies.

Friedland, Roger. 1976. "Class Power and the Central City: The Contradictions of Urban Growth." Ph.D. dissertation, University of Wisconsin at Madison.

———. 1982. *Power and Crisis in the City*. London: Macmillan.

Friedman, Milton, and George Stigler. 1946. "Roofs or Ceilings? The Current Housing Problem." *Popular Essays on Current Problems* 1:2.

Furlong, Tom. 1986. "Real Estate Industry Finds Changes Devastating." *Los Angeles Times*, Aug. 20, Pt. 1, p. 16.

Gabriel, Stuart A., Lawrence Katz, and Jennifer Wolch. 1979. "Local Land-Use Regulation and Proposition 13: Some Findings from a Recent Survey." Berkeley: University of California Institute of Business and Economic Research. Working Paper No. 80-4.

Gabriel, Stuart, and Jennifer R. Wolch. 1980. "Local Land-Use Regulation and Urban Housing Values." Berkeley: University of California Institute of Business and Economic Research. Working Paper No. 80-18.

Gans, Herbert. 1982. *The Urban Villagers* (rev. ed.). New York: Free Press.

Garrigan, Richard. 1978. "The Case for Rising Residential Rents." *Real Estate Review*, G:2:36–41.

Gilderbloom, John I. 1976. "Report to Donald E. Burns, Secretary of Business and Transportation Agency, on the Validity of the Legislative Findings of A.B. 3788 and the Economic Impact of Rent Control." Sacramento: California Department of Housing and Community Development.

———. 1980. *Moderate Rent Control: The Experience of U.S. Cities*. Washington, D.C.: National Conference on Alternative State and Local Public Policies.

———. 1981a. "Moderate Rent Control: Its Impact on the Quality and Quantity of the Housing Stock." *Urban Affairs Quarterly* 17:2:123–142.

———. 1981b. *Rent Control: A Source Book*. San Francisco: Foundation for National Progress.

———. 1982. "Toward an Understanding of Inter-City Rent Differential: A Sociological Contribution." Ph.D. dissertation, University of California, Santa Barbara.

———. 1983. "The Impact of Moderate Rent Control in New Jersey: An Empirical Study of 26 Rent Controlled Cities." *Urban Analysis* 7:2:135–154.

———. 1984. "Redistributive Impacts of Rent Control in New Jersey." Paper presented at American Sociological Meeting, San Antonio.

———. 1985a. "Hispanic Housing in the United States: A Review of the Literature." *Housing Needs of Hispanics*. Also, Hearing before Subcommittee on Housing and Community Development of Committee on Banking, Finance and Urban Affairs, House of Representatives, 99th Congress, 1st Sess. (Sept. 18). Washington, D.C.: Government Printing Office.

———. 1985b. "Houston's Rental Housing Conditions: A Longitudinal and Comparative Analysis." *Public Housing Needs and Conditions*. Also, Hearing before Subcommittee on Housing and Community Development of Committee on Banking, Finance and Urban Affairs, House of Representatives, 99th Congress, 1st sess. (Sept. 18). Washington, D.C.: Government Printing Office.

———. 1985c. "Social Forces Affecting Landlords in the Determination of Rent." *Urban Life* 14:2:155–179.

———. 1985d. "Toward a Sociology of Rental Housing Markets." Paper presented at American Sociological Association Meeting, Washington, D.C.

———. 1986a. "The Impact of Rent Control on Rent in New Jersey Communities." *Sociology and Social Research* 71:1.

———. 1986b. "Trends in the Affordability of Rental Housing: 1970 to 1983." *Sociology and Social Research* 70:4.

——— and Richard Appelbaum. 1984. "Rent Control in the United States: A Brief Summary of Recent Studies." Paper presented at American Association of Housing Educators Conference, Washington, D.C.

———. 1987. "Toward a Sociology of Rent." *Social Problems* (Feb.) 34:3:401–416.

Gilderbloom, John I., and Stella Capek. 1988 (forthcoming). *The Tenants' Movement and American Democracy*. Albany, N.Y.: State University of New York Press.

Gilderbloom, John I., Simon Gottschalk, and Nora Amory. 1986. "The Impact of Housing Status on Political Beliefs." Paper presented at American Sociological Association Annual Meeting, New York.

Gilderbloom, John I., and Mike Jacob. 1981. "Consumer Price Index Rent Increases." In John I. Gilderbloom (ed.), *Rent Control: A Source Book*. San Francisco: Foundation for National Progress (pp. 35–40).

Gilderbloom, John I., and Dennis Keating. 1982. "An Evaluation of Rent Control in Orange." San Francisco: Foundation for National Progress, Housing Information Center.

Gilderbloom, John I., Mark Rosentraub, and Robert Bullard. 1987. *Financing, Designing, and Locating Housing and Transportation Services for the Disabled and Elderly*. Houston: University of Houston Center for Public Policy.

Gleeson, Michael E. 1979. "Effects of an Urban Growth Management System on Land Values." *Land Economics* 55:3:350–365.

Glennon, Wink, and Richard P. Appelbaum. 1980. "Housing Opportunities for All." *Santa Barbara News-Press*, June 5, 16-page insert.

Gordon, David. 1977. *Problems in Political Economy: An Urban Perspective* (2d ed.). Washington, D.C.: Heath.

Gove, Walter, Michael Hughes, and Omar Galle. 1979. "Overcrowding in the Home:

An Empirical Investigation of Possible Pathological Consequences." *American Sociological Review* 44 (Feb.):59–80.

Granger, C. W. J., and Paul Newbold. 1977. *Forecasting Economic Time Series*. New York: Academic Press.

Grant, Gary. 1976. "Speech to the Sacramento Apartment Owners' Association." In John I. Gilderbloom (ed.), "Report to Donald E. Burns, Secretary, Business and Transportation Agency, on the Validity of the Legislative Findings of A.B. 3788 and the Economic Impact of Rent Control." Sacramento: California Department of Housing and Community Development.

Gray, Thomas. 1979. "Student Housing and Discrimination: An Empirical Approach." Mimeograph. Santa Barbara: University of California Department of Economics.

Green Bay Press Gazette. 1983. "Homeless Jam New York Shelters." Jan. 23, p. A-10.

Greve, J. 1971. *Voluntary Housing in Scandinavia*. Birmingham, England: Centre for Urban and Regional Studies.

Grigsby, William. 1973. "Housing Markets and Public Policy." In Daniel Mandelker and Roger Montgomery (eds.), *Housing in America: Problems and Perspectives*. Indianapolis: Bobbs-Merrill (pp. 51–55/226–228).

Groller, Ingrid. 1978. "Kids Keep Out." *Parents' Magazine* 53 (Aug.), p. 63.

Gruen, Paul, and Nina Gruen. 1977. *Rent Control in New Jersey: The Beginnings*. Sacramento: California Housing Council.

Guenther, Robert. 1982. "Rate of Homeownership Falls, Possibly Signalling Big Change." *Wall Street Journal*, Aug. 11, p. 25.

Gulino, Denis. 1983. "Mortgage Delinquency Rate Surges." *Washington Post*, Mar. 29.

Gupta, Dipka, and Louis Rea. 1984. "Second Generation Rent Control Ordinances: A Quantitative Comparison." *Urban Affairs Quarterly* 19:3:395–408.

Guterbock, T. 1980. *Machine Politics in Transition: Party and Community in Chicago*. Chicago: University of Chicago Press.

Hall, Peter. 1981. "Squatters' Movement Solidifies." *Rolling Stone*, Sept. 17.

Hanushek, E.A., and J.E. Jackson. 1979. *Statistical Methods for Social Scientists*. New York: Academic Press.

Harloe, Michael. 1977. *Captive Cities*. London: John Wiley.

———. 1985. "Landlord/Tenant Relations in Europe and America—The Limits and Functions of the Legal Framework." *Urban Law and Policy* 7:359–383.

Harper's. 1985. "Who Pays for Economic Change? Debating the Need for an Industrial Policy." *Harper's Magazine* (Feb.), pp. 35–48.

Harrison, Bennett, and Barry Bluestone. 1984. "Ready-Made Issue for the Democrats." *Houston Chronicle*, June 22, Sec. 1, p. 29.

Hartman, Chester. 1975. *Housing and Social Policy*. Englewood Cliffs, N.J.: Prentice-Hall.

———. 1979. "Landlord Money Defeats Rent Control in San Francisco." *Shelterforce* 5:3.

———. 1983. *America's Housing Crisis: What Is to Be Done?* Boston: Routledge and Kegan Paul.

———. 1984. *The Transformation of San Francisco*. Totowa, N.J.: Rowman and Allanheld.

————. 1986. "Housing Policies under the Reagan Administration." In Rachel G. Bratt, Chester Hartman, and Ann Meyerson (eds.), *Critical Perspectives on Housing*. Philadelphia: Temple University Press.

———— and Michael Stone. 1980. "A Socialist Housing Program for the United States." In Pierre Clavel, John Forester, and William M. Goldsmith (eds.), *Urban and Regional Planning in an Age of Austerity*. New York: Pergamon.

————. 1986. "A Socialist Housing Alternative for the United States." In Rachel G. Bratt, Chester Hartman, and Ann Meyerson (eds.), *Critical Perspectives on Housing*. Philadelphia: Temple University Press.

Hartman, Chester, Dennis Keating, and Richard LeGates. 1981. *Displacement: How to Fight It*. Berkeley: National Housing Law Project.

Harvey, David. 1973. *Social Justice and the City*. Baltimore: Johns Hopkins University Press.

————. 1978. "Labor, Capital and Class Struggle around the Built Environment in Advanced Capitalist Societies." In Kevin Cox (ed.), *Urbanization and Conflict in Market Societies*. Chicago: Maaroufa Press.

————. 1979. "Rent Control and a Fair Control." *Baltimore Sun*, Sept. 20.

————. 1981. "Rent Control and a Fair Return." In John I. Gilderbloom (ed.), *Rent Control: A Source Book*. Santa Barbara: Foundation for National Progress, Housing Information Center.

Hayden, Delores. 1979–80. "Charlotte Perkins Gilman and the Kitchenless House." *Radical History Review* 21:225–247.

————. 1984. *Redesigning the American Dream: The Future of Housing, Work, and Family Life*. New York: W. W. Norton.

Hayek, F. A. 1972. "Austria: The Repercussions of Rent Restrictions." In A. Seldon (ed.), *Verdict on Rent Control*. Worthing, Eng.: Cormorant Press.

Haywood, Ian. 1984. "Denmark." In Martin Wynn (ed.), *Housing In Europe*. London: Croom Helm.

Headey, Bruce B. 1978. *Housing Policy in the Developed Economy*. London: Croom Helm.

Heer, David M., Robert W. Hodge, and Marcus Felson. 1985. "The Cluttered Nest: Evidence that Young Adults Are More Likely to Live at Home than in the Recent Past." *Sociology and Social Research* 69:3:436–441.

Heffley, Dennis, and Rex Santerre. 1985. "Rent Control as an Expenditure Constraint: Some Empirical Results." Paper presented at Annual Meetings of Eastern Economic Association, Pittsburgh, Pa., March 21–23.

Heimburger, Peter. 1976. "Land Policy in Sweden." Information provided to U.N. Conference on Human Settlements (HABITAT). Stockholm: Ministry of Housing and Physical Planning.

Hendershott, Patric H. 1981. "The Rental Housing Crisis." In John C. Weicher, Kevin E. Villani, and Elizabeth A. Roistacher (eds.), *Rental Housing: Is There a Crisis?* Washington, D.C.: Urban Institute Press.

———— and Sheng-Cheng Hu. 1980. "Government Induced Biases in the Allocation of the Stock of Fixed Capital in the United States." In G. M. Von Furstenberg (ed.), *Capital, Efficiency, and Growth*. New York: Ballinger.

Henretta, John C. 1984. "Parental Status and Child's Home Ownership." *American Sociological Review* 49:131–140.

Herbers, John. 1985. "Housing-Aid Debate Focuses on Question of United States Duty to Poor." *New York Times,* May 4, Sec. 1, p. 1.

Heskin, Allan D. 1981a. "A History of Tenants in the United States: Struggle and Ideology." *International Journal of Urban and Regional Research* [special issue on housing], 5:2:178–204.

———. 1981b. "Is the Tenant a Second Class Citizen?" In John I. Gilderbloom (ed.), *Rent Control: A Source Book.* Santa Barbara: Foundation for National Progress, Housing Information Center.

———. 1981c. "Tenants and the American Dream: The Ideology of Being a Tenant." Mimeograph. Los Angeles: University of California, Los Angeles School of Urban Planning and Architecture.

———. 1983. *Tenants and the American Dream.* New York: Praeger.

Hoch, Irving. 1972. "Income and City Size." *Urban Studies* 9:3:294–328.

Hohm, Charles F. 1984. "Housing Aspirations and Fertility." *Sociology and Social Research* (Apr.).

Hombs, Mary Ellen, and Mitch Snyder. 1982. *Homelessness in America: Forced March to Nowhere.* Washington, D.C.: Community For Creative Non-Violence.

Housing and Development Reporter. 1986. "Apartments Should Continue to Be Good Investments, Study Predicts" (June 30).

Houston Post. 1985. "Housing Shortage Foreseen." October 15, p. 14C.

HPP [Ministry of Housing and Physical Planning]. 1976. "Swedish Experiences of Self-Building, Co-operation, Consumer Research, Participation." Information provided to U.N. Conference on Human Settlements (HABITAT). Stockholm: Ministry of Housing and Physical Planning.

———. 1980. "Housing, Building, and Planning in Sweden." Information provided to 41st Session of ECE Committee on Housing, Building, and Planning. Stockholm: Ministry of Housing and Physical Planning, in cooperation with National Housing Board, National Board of Physical Planning and Building, and National Institute for Building Research.

HSB. 1975. *HSB's Riksforbund, HSB Sweden.* Stockholm: HSB.

Ingram, G. K., H. Leonard, and R. Schafer. 1976. "Simulation of the Market Effects of Housing Allowances." In National Bureau of Economic Research, *Development of the Supply Sector* (vol. III). New York: National Bureau of Economic Research.

Inman, Bradley. 1985. "Affordability Gap." *Los Angeles Times,* May 5, Part VIII, p. 20.

Ipcar, Charles. 1974. "The Student Ghetto Housing Market." Mimeograph. Lansing, Mich.: Lansing Community College, Social Sciences Division.

IUT [International Union of Tenants]. 1982. "The Scandinavian States Support Ownership." *International Information* 4:1–2.

Jacob, Mike. 1977. "Understanding Landlording." Oakland: California Housing Action and Information Network.

———. 1979. "How Rent Control Passed in Santa Monica, California." Oakland: California Housing Action and Information Network.

James, Franklin J., and Thomas Muller. 1977. "Environmental Impact Evaluation, Land Use Planning and the Housing Consumer." *Journal of American Real Estate and Urban Economics Association* 5:279–301.

Janczyk, J. 1980. "The Potential Impacts of High Interest on the Housing Industry." *Growth and Change* 11 (Jan.).

Jenkins, Gwilym. 1979. *Practical Experiences with Modeling and Forecasting Time Series.* Jersey, Eng.: CJP Ltd.

Johnson, M. Bruce. 1982. *Resolving the Housing Crisis.* Cambridge, Mass.: Ballinger.

Jussil, Suny. 1975. "Steering Mechanisms." In Hans-Erland Heineman (ed.), *New Towns and Old.* Stockholm: Swedish Institute.

Kadushin, C. 1976. *Introduction to the Sociological Study of Networks.* New York: Columbia University Press.

Kain, J., and J. M. Quigley. 1970. "Measuring the Value of Housing Quality." *Journal of American Statistical Association* 65:532–606.

Kaish, Stephen. 1981. "What Is Just and Reasonable in Rent Control?" *American Journal of Economics and Sociology* 40:2:129–136.

Karlin, Norman. 1982. "Zoning and Other Land Use Controls." In M. Bruce Johnson (ed.), *Resolving the Housing Crisis.* San Francisco: Pacific Institute for Public Policy Research.

Karter, Michael. 1982. "Fire Loss in the United States during 1981." *Fire Journal* 76:68–86.

Katz, Lawrence, and Kenneth T. Rosen. 1980. "The Effects of Land-Use Controls on Housing Prices." Berkeley: University of California, Center for Real Estate and Urban Economics, Working Paper No. 80-13.

Kearl, J. R., Clayne Pope, Gordon Whiting, and Larry Wimmer. 1979. "A Confusion of Economists?" *American Economic Review* 69:2:28–37.

Keating, W. Dennis. 1976. "Rent and Eviction Controls: An Annotated Bibliography." Monticello, Ill.: Council of Planning Librarians, Exchange Bibliography No. 1136, October 1976.

————. 1980. "Rent Control as a Response to the Rental Housing Crisis: Policy Alternatives for California." Mimeograph. Berkeley: University of California Department of City and Regional Planning.

Kelley, E. N. 1975. "How to Get Your Manager to Raise Rents." Chicago: Institute of Real Estate Management (Reprinted from *Journal of Property Management,* Mar./ Apr. 1975).

Kelley, Jonathan, Ian McAllister, and Anthony Mughan. 1984. "The Decline of Class Revisited: Class and Party in England, 1964–1979." Paper presented to Annual Meeting of American Sociological Association, San Antonio.

Kemeny, Jim. 1977. "A Political Sociology of Homeownership in Australia." *Australian and New Zealand Journal of Sociology* 13:47–52.

————. 1978. "Urban Home-ownership in Sweden." *Urban Studies* 15:313–320.

————. 1980. "Homeownership and Privatization." *International Journal of Urban and Regional Research* 4:3:372–387.

Kennedy, Declan. 1984. "West Germany." In Martin Wynn (ed.), *Housing in Europe.* London: Croom Helm.

Kent, J. 1978. "Examining the Ventura Housing Market via Linear Regression Techniques." Santa Barbara: University of California Urban Economics Program.

Kimball, Larry J., and David Shulman. 1980. "Growth in California: Prospects and Consequences." *Public Affairs Report.* Berkeley: University of California Institute of Governmental Studies.

Kinchen, David M. 1982. "Real Estate Predictions Coming True?" *Los Angeles Times,* July 11, Pt. VIII, p. 30.

———. 1985. "Bush Defends Reagan Policies on Housing." *Los Angeles Times,* Nov. 17, VIII-I.

King, A. T., and P. Mieszcowski. 1973. "Racial Discrimination, Segregation, and the Price of Housing." *Journal of Political Economy* 81:590–606.

Kingston, Paul William, John L. P. Thompson, and Douglas M. Eichar. 1984. "The Politics of Homeownership." *American Politics Quarterly* 12:2:131–150.

Kirschman, Mary Jo. 1980. "Winning Rent Control in a Working Class City." Mimeograph. Baltimore: Rent Control Campaign.

Kjellberg, C., and T. Burns. 1981. "Hyrestratter blir bostadstratter it Goteborg." Preliminary report to Stockholm University.

Klein, Joe. 1981. "The State of the Democratic Party." *Rolling Stone,* Sept. 17, p. 21.

Koenig, Tom, and Robert Gogel. 1981. "Interlocking Corporate Directorships as a Social Network." *American Journal of Economics and Sociology* 40:1:37–50.

Kondratas, S. Anna. 1986. "A Strategy for Helping America's Homeless." In Jon Erickson and Charles Wilhelm (eds.), *Housing the Homeless.* New Brunswick, N.J.: Rutgers University Center for Urban Policy Research.

Krinsky, Steve. 1981. "Tenant Activist Wins City Council Seat." *Shelterforce* 6, no. 2.

——— and John Atlas. 1981. "Tenant Vote Can Win Political Power." *Shelterforce,* vol. 6, no. 2.

Krohn, Roger, and Berkeley Fleming. 1972. "The Other Economy and the Urban Housing Problem: A Study of Older Residential Neighborhoods in Montreal." Cambridge, Mass.: Joint Center for Urban Studies, Working Paper 11.

——— and Marilyn Manzer. 1977. *The Other Economy: The Internal Logic of Local Rental Housing.* Toronto: Peter Martin Associates.

Kutner, Robert. 1985. "The Tax Law that Really Needs Reform." *Business Week,* June 24.

Lamb, H. Richard. 1986. "Deinstitutionalization of the Homeless Mentally Ill." In John Erickson and Charles Wilhelm (eds.), *Housing the Homeless.* New Brunswick, N.J.: Rutgers University Center for Urban Policy Research.

Lane, R. 1970. "Some Findings on Residential Location, House Prices and Accessibility." Paper given to Research and Intelligence Unit, Department of Planning and Transportation, Greater London Council.

Lauber, Daniel, and Jesus Hinojosa. 1984. "Viewpoint." *Planning* (April), p. 18.

Lawson, Ronald (n.d.). "Labor Unions and Tenant Organizations: A Comparison of Resource Mobilization, Strategic Leverage and Impact." Mimeograph. Flushing, N.Y.: Queens College Urban Studies Department.

———. 1980. "The Political Face of New York's Real Estate Industry." *New York Affairs* 6:2:85–96.

———. 1983. "A Decentralized but Moving Pyramid: The Evolution and Consequences of the Structure of the Tenant Movement." In Jo Freeman (ed.), *Social Movements of the Sixties and Seventies.* New York: Longman.

———. 1984. "Owners of Last Resort: An Assessment of the Track Record of New York City's Early Low Income Cooperative Conversions." New York: New York City Department of Housing Preservation and Development.

————. 1986. *The Tenant Movement in New York City, 1904–1984*. New Brunswick, N.J.: Rutgers University Press.

LeBlanc, Paul, and Donald Redding. 1982. "Large Loss Fires in the United States: 1981." *Fire Journal* 74:32–52.

Leight, Claudia, Elliot Lieberman, Jerry Kurtz, and Dean Pappas. 1980. "Rent Control Wins in Baltimore." *Moving On*. Chicago: New America Movement.

————. 1981. "Rent Control Wins in Baltimore." In John I. Gilderbloom (ed.), *Rent Control: A Source Book*. San Francisco: Foundation for National Progress.

Leijonhufvud, S. 1982. "Election Year '82: New Exits from the Middle Road." *Political Life in Sweden* 15 (Dec.).

Lett, Monica. 1976. *Rent Control: Concepts, Realities and Mechanisms*. New Brunswick, N.J.: Center for Urban Policy Research.

Levee, Richard. 1979. "Projections of Investment Returns for a Four Bedroom House in Santa Barbara." Mimeograph. Santa Barbara: California Time Sharing.

LIHIS [Low Income Housing Information Service]. 1987. "The 1988 Low Income Housing Budget." Washington, D.C.: LIHIS.

Linson, Neal. 1978. "Concentration of Ownership in Santa Barbara." Mimeograph. Santa Barbara: Santa Barbara Tenants' Union.

Lipsky, Michael. 1970. *Protest in City Politics: Rent Strikes, Housing and the Power of the Poor*. Chicago: Rand McNally.

Logan, John, and Harvey Molotch. 1986. *Urban Fortunes: The Political Economy of Place*. Berkeley: University of California Press.

Longman, Phillip. 1986. "The Mortgaged Generation: Why the Young Can't Afford a House." *Washington Monthly* 18:3:11–20.

Los Angeles Community Development Department. 1979. *Rent Stabilization Study, City of Los Angeles*. City of Los Angeles.

Los Angeles RSD [Rent Stabilization Division]. 1985a. *Rental Housing Study: Housing Production and Performance under Rent Control*. Los Angeles: Rent Stabilization Division.

————. 1985b. *Rental Housing Study: The Rent Stabilization System: Impacts and Alternatives*. Los Angeles: Rent Stabilization Division.

Los Angeles Times. 1979. "State Boosts Brown's Rent 36% to $375." May 2.

————. 1980. "Los Angeles Times Poll." Aug. 13, I:32.

————. 1982. "Figures on Vacancy Rates for City Rental Units Differ." Mar. 16, II.

————. 1985a. "Affordability Gap." May 5, VIII:20.

————. 1985b. "Rent Control Makes No Sense." May 23, II-6.

Lowe, Carey, and Richard Blumberg. 1981. "Moderate Regulations Protect Landlords, as Well as Tenants." In John I. Gilderbloom (ed.), *Rent Control: A Source Book*. San Francisco: Foundation for National Progress (pp. 72–75).

Lowry, D., and L. Sigelman. 1981. "Understanding the Tax Revolt: Eight Explanations." *American Political Science Review* 75:963–974.

Lowry, Ira. S. 1960. "Filtering and Housing Standards." *Land Economics* 36 (Nov.):362–370.

————. 1981a. "Inflation Indexes for Rental Housing." Santa Monica: Rand Corporation.

————. 1981b. "Rental Housing in the 1970s: Searching for the Crisis." In Weicher et al. (eds.), *Rental Housing: Is There a Crisis?* Washington, D.C.: Urban Institute Press.

Lundevall, Owe. 1976. "Swedish Experience of Co-Operative Housing: Information to the United Nations Conference on Human Settlement HABITAT." Stockholm: Ministry of Housing and Physical Planning.

Lundqvist, L. J. 1981. *Housing Tenures in Sweden.* Gavle: National Swedish Institute for Building Research.

Malone, M. E. 1986. "Activists Say Estimate of 350,000 Homeless in US Is Too Low." *Boston Globe,* Sept. 6, p. 24.

Mandelker, D., and R. Montgomery. 1973. *Housing in America: Problems and Perspectives.* Indianapolis: Bobbs-Merrill.

Manzer, Marilyn, and Roger Krohn. 1973. "Private Redevelopment and Older Low Rent Housing: A Conflict of Economies." Mimeograph. Montreal: McGill University.

Marcuse, Peter. 1975. "Residential Alienation, Homeownership and the Limits of Shelter Policy." *Journal of Sociology and Social Welfare* 3:181–203.

———. 1979. *Rental Housing in the City of New York: Supply and Conditions, 1975–1978.* New York: New York City Department of Housing Preservation and Development.

———. 1981a. *Housing Abandonment: Does Rent Control Make a Difference?* Washington, D.C.: Conference on State and Local Policies.

———. 1981b. "The Strategic Potential of Rent Control." In John Gilderbloom (ed.), *Rent Control: A Source Book.* Santa Barbara: Foundation for National Progress, Housing Information Center.

———. 1982. "Determinants of State Housing Policies: West Germany and the United States." In Norman I. Fainstein and Susan Fainstein (eds.), *Urban Policy under Capitalism.* Beverly Hills: Sage.

———. 1986. "The Uses and Limits of Rent Regulations: A Report to the Division of Housing and Community Renewal." Albany: State of New York Division of Housing and Community Renewal.

Mariano, Ann. 1983. "Home Foreclosures Jump Sharply." *Washington Post,* Feb. 24.

Markusen, James R. 1979. "Elements of Real Asset Pricing: A Theoretical Analysis with Special Reference to Urban Land Prices." *Land Economics* 55:2:153–166.

Martin, Phillip. 1976. "The Supreme Courts' Quest for Voting Equality on Bond Referenda." *Baylor Law Review* 28:25–37.

Massachusetts Department of Corporations and Taxation. 1974. "A Study of Rent and Eviction Controls for the Commonwealth of Massachusetts." Boston: Joint Legislative Committee on Local Affairs, State of Massachusetts.

Massell, B. F., and J. M. Stegart. 1971. "The Determinants of Residential Property Values." Stanford: Stanford University Programme in Urban Studies, Institute for Public Policy Analysis.

Maxwell, David O. 1986. "Still the American Dream." *Houston Chronicle,* Nov. 3, Sec. 1, p. 15.

McCleary, Richard, and Richard A. Hay. 1980. *Applied Time Series Analysis for the Social Sciences.* Beverly Hills, Calif.: Sage Publications.

McGuire, Chester. 1981. "Urban Revitalization & Rent Control in the District of Columbia." *Real Estate Issues* (Summer), pp. 32–40.

McKee, Cindy. 1981. "Tenants Help Elect Progressive Mayor." *Shelterforce* 6:2.

Mercer, Lloyd J., and W. Douglas Morgan. 1982. "An Estimate of Residential Growth Controls' Impact on House Prices." In M. Bruce Johnson (ed.), *Resolving the Housing Crisis*. San Francisco: Pacific Institute for Public Policy Research.

Merton, Robert. 1948. "The Social Psychology of Housing." In Wayne Dennis et al. (eds.), *Current Trends in Social Psychology*. Pittsburgh: University of Pittsburgh Press.

Michelson, William. 1966. "An Empirical Analysis of Urban Environmental Preferences." *Journal of American Institute of Planners* 32:355–360.

———. 1977. *Environmental Choice, Human Behavior and Residential Satisfaction*. New York: Oxford University Press.

Mills, C. Wright. 1959. *The Sociological Imagination*. New York: Oxford University Press.

Mills, Edwin. 1972. *Urban Economics*. Glenview, Ill.: Scott, Foresman.

Minneapolis Star and Tribune. 1983. "Two Studies Show Rise in Income Inequality." Dec. 12, p. 4A.

Moberg, David. 1984. "The Poor Still Getting Poorer." *In These Times* (Aug. 12–Sept. 4), pp. 6–7.

Mollenkopf, John, and Jon Pynoos. 1973. "Boardwalk and Park Place: Property Ownership, Political Structure and Housing Policy at the Local Level." In Jon Pynoos, Robert Schaffer, and Chester Hartman (eds.), *Housing Urban America*. Chicago: Aldine (pp. 56–74).

Molotch, Harvey L. 1976. "The City as a Growth Machine: Toward a Political Economy of Place." *American Journal of Sociology* 82:2:309–332.

Molotch, Harvey, and Joey Kasof. 1982. "The Impacts of Land Use Constraint: Environmentalism, Speculation and the Housing Crisis." Mimeograph. Santa Barbara: University of California Sociology Department.

Monroe, E. 1931. *Value and Income*. Cambridge, Mass.: Harvard University Press.

Moore, Joan, and Harry Pachon. 1985. *Hispanics in the United States*. Englewood Cliffs, N.J.: Prentice-Hall.

Morris, Earl W., S. R. Crull, and M. Winter. 1976. "Housing Norms, Housing Satisfaction and the Propensity to Move." *Journal of Marriage and the Family* 38:309–320.

Morris, Earl W., Mary Winter, and Mary Ann Sward. 1984. "Reporting Error and Single-Family Home Ownership Norms and Preferences." *Housing and Society* 11:2:82–97.

Moskovitz, Myron, Ralph Warner, and Charles Sherman. 1972. *California Tenants' Handbook*. Occidental, Calif.: Nolo Press.

Muth, Richard. 1969. *Cities and Housing*. Chicago: University of Chicago Press.

——— and Elliot Wetzler. 1976. "The Effect of Constraints on House Costs." *Journal of Urban Economics* 3:57–67.

Muwakkil, Salim. 1986. "HUD Closing Door on Commitment to Affordable Shelter." *In These Times* (Jan.), p. 5.

Myers, Dowell. 1983. "The Impact of Rising Homeownership Costs on Family Change." Paper presented at Annual Meeting of Population Association of America, Pittsburgh.

——— and Katherine Baillargeon. 1985. "Deriving Place-Specific Measures of the

Rental Housing Crisis from the 1980 Census: An Application from Texas." *Journal of Urban Affairs* 7:3:63–74.

National Association of Home Builders. 1982. "Land Use and Construction Regulations: A Builder's View." Washington, D.C.: NAHB.

———. 1985. *Land Use and Construction Regulations: A Builder's View*. Washington, D.C.: NAHB.

National Housing Law Project. 1981. *Alternative Approaches to the Management of Subsidized Housing*. Washington, D.C.: National Housing Law Project, Multifamily Demonstration Program (August).

Nesslein, T. S. 1982. "The Swedish Housing Model: An Assessment." *Urban Studies* 19:235–246.

New Jersey Department of the Treasury. 1970–77. "Crime in New Jersey." Trenton: Division of State Police, Uniform Crime Reporting Unit.

———. 1970–77. "Summary: New Jersey Residential Permits and Demolitions." Trenton: New Jersey Department of Labor and Industry.

Newman, Oscar. 1980. *Community of Interest*. Garden City, N.Y.: Anchor/Doubleday.

Nicholas, James C. 1981. "Housing Costs and Prices under Regional Regulations." *Journal of American Real Estate and Urban Economics Association* 9:4:384–396.

Nie, Norman, C. Hadlai Hull, Jean Kenkins, Karin Steinbrenner, and Dale Bent. 1975. *SPSS: Statistical Package for the Social Sciences* (2nd ed.). New York: McGraw-Hill.

Niebanck, Paul, Milton Lifschitz, et al. 1976. "Appellants vs. City of Miami Beach, Florida, Appellee: Appellee's Brief." Kansas City, Mo.: E. L. Mendenhall.

Oakland Tribune. 1985. "The Rent Control Illusion." June 16, p. N-P (editorial).

O'Connor, James. 1981. "Rent Control Is Absolutely Essential." In John Gilderbloom (ed.), *Rent Control: A Source Book*. San Francisco: Foundation for National Progress, Housing Information Center.

Ohls, James, Richard Weisberg, and Michelle White. 1974. "The Effects of Zoning on Land Value." *Journal of Urban Economics* 1:428–444.

Olsen, Edgar. 1973. "A Competitive Theory of the Housing Market." In Jon Pynoos, Robert Shafer, and Chester Hartman (eds.), *Housing in Urban America*. Chicago: Aldine (pp. 228–238).

Orange County Cost of Housing Committee. 1975. "The Cost of Housing in Orange County." Orange, Calif.: OCCHC.

Orbell, J. M., and T. Uno. 1972. "A Theory of Neighborhood Problem Solving: Political Action vs. Residential Mobility." *American Political Science Review* 61:471–489.

Oswald, Rudy. 1979. "Inflation: Tracing the Causes." Washington, D.C.: AFL-CIO.

Padovani, Liliana. 1984. "Italy." In Martin Wynn (ed.), *Housing in Europe*. London: Croom Helm.

Pahl, Ray E. 1975. *Whose City?* Middlesex, Eng.: Penguin.

Paish, F. W. 1950. "The Economics of Rent Restriction." London: Lloyd's Bank Review.

Pearsall, John. 1984. "France." In Martin Wynn (ed.), *Housing in Europe*. London: Croom Helm.

Pennance, F. G. 1969. *Housing Market Analysis and Policy*. London: Simon-Wherry Press.

————. 1972. "Introduction." In Arthur Seldon (ed.), *Verdict on Rent Control.* Worthing, Eng.: Cormorant Press.

Percy, Charles. 1966. "A New Dawn for Our Cities." *Congressional Record* (Oct. 17), 89th Congress, 2nd sess., vol. 112, part 20:2725B–2726B.

Perrin, Constance. 1977. *"Everything in Its Place."* Princeton: Princeton University Press.

Pindyck, R. S., and D. L. Rubinfeld. 1976. *Econometric Models and Economic Forecasts.* New York: McGraw-Hill.

Piven, Francis Fox, and Richard Cloward. 1971. *Regulating the Poor.* New York: Pantheon.

Popenoe, D. 1977. *The Surburban Environment: Sweden and the United States.* Chicago: University of Chicago Press.

President's Commission on Housing. 1981. *Interim Report.* Washington, D.C.: Government Printing Office.

————. 1982. *Report of the President's Commission on Housing.* Washington, D.C.: Government Printing Office.

————. 1983. *Final Report.* Washington, D.C.: Government Printing Office.

Priest, Donald E. 1980. "Regulatory Reform, Housing Costs, and Public Understanding." *Urban Land* 39:4:3–4.

Proxmire, William. 1978. "The Destructive Folly of Rent Control." *Congressional Record* 124 (Sept. 18), pt. 22, p. 29735.

Pynoos, Jon, Robert Schafer, and Chester Hartman. 1973. *Housing Urban America.* Chicago: Aldine.

Rakoff, Robert M. 1977. "Ideology in Everyday Life: The Meaning of the House." *Politics and Society* 7:85–104.

Renters' Alliance. 1980. "Analysis of a Campaign." *Shelterforce* 5:3.

Revenue and Rent Study Commission (Brookline, Mass.). 1974. "Minutes of Meeting" (Apr. 19).

Rex, J. 1968. "The Sociology of a Zone of Transition." In Ray Pahl (ed.), *Readings in Urban Sociology.* London: Pergamon.

———— and R. Moore. 1967. *Race, Community and Conflict.* Oxford: Oxford University Press.

Rich, Jonathan M. 1984. "Municipal Boundaries in a Discriminatory Housing Market: An Example of Racial Leapfrogging." *Urban Studies* 21:31–40.

Ridker, R., and J. Henning. 1967. "The Determination of Residential Property Values with Special Reference to Air Pollution." In Harvard University Committee on Economic Research, *Review of Economics and Statistics.* Cambridge, Mass.: Harvard University Press.

Rocky Mountain News. 1982. "Apartment Rents Ready to Soar?" Sept. 4, p. 19-H.

Rodgers, Harrell R., Jr. 1984. "American Housing Policy in a Comparative Context: The Limits of the Positive State." In Harrell R. Rodgers, Jr. (ed.), *Public Policy and Social Institutions.* Greenwich, Conn.: JAI Press (pp. 155–182).

Roistacher, Elizabeth. 1972. "The Distribution of Tenant Benefits under Rent Control." Ph.D. dissertation, University of Pennsylvania (Philadelphia).

Ronmark, K. 1981. "Housing Management." Swedish monograph for Economic Commission for Europe Committee on Housing, Building, and Planning (U.N.).

Ropers, Richard H. 1986. "Living on the Edge: The Sheltered Homeless, an Empirical

Study of Los Angeles Single Room Occupancy Residents." Cedar City, Utah: Department of Behavioral and Social Sciences, Southern Utah State College.

Rose, Daniel. 1985. "Rent Control vs. Real World" (letter to editor). *Journal of American Planning Association* 51:1:96.

Rosen, Harvey S. 1978. "Housing Decisions and the U.S. Income Tax." *Journal of Public Economics* II:1–23.

———— and Kenneth T. Rosen. 1980. "Federal Taxes and Homeownership: Evidence from Time-Series." *Journal of Political Economy* 88:59–75.

Rosen, Kenneth T., and Lawrence Katz. 1981. "Growth Management and Land Use Controls: The San Francisco Bay Area Experience." *Journal of American Real Estate and Urban Economics Association* 9:4:321–343.

Rosentraub, Mark, and Robert Warren. 1986. "Tenants' Associations and Social Movements: The Case of the United States." Paper presented at Urban Affairs Association Meeting, Fort Worth, March 8.

Rothblatt, Donald, Daniel J. Garr, and Jo Sprague. 1979. *The Suburban Environment and Women*. New York: Praeger.

Rudel, Thomas K. 1984. "Female Income, Fertility, and the First Home Purchase." Paper presented at 79th Annual Meeting of American Sociological Association, Aug. 27–31, San Antonio.

Rybeck, Rick. 1982. *Meeting America's Housing Needs: A Progressive Agenda*. Public Policy Report, Conference on Alternative State and Local Policies, Washington, D.C.

Rydell, Peter. 1977. "Effects of Market Conditions on Prices and Profits of Rental Housing." Santa Monica: Rand Corporation.

————. 1981. "The Impact of Rent Control on the Los Angeles Housing Market." Santa Monica: Rand Corporation.

Rydenfelt, Sven. 1949. "Rent Control Thirty Years On." In *Human Action: A Treatise on Economics*. New Haven: Yale University Press.

Saegert, Susan. 1981. "Masculine Cities and Feminine Suburbs: Polarized Ideas, Contradictory Realities." In Catherine Stimson et al. (eds.), *Women and the American City*. Chicago: University of Chicago Press.

Samuelson, Paul. 1967. *Economics: An Introductory Analysis*. New York: McGraw-Hill.

San Francisco Chronicle. 1979. "Mervin Field Poll of California Residents: Views on Rents Charged Are . . ." June 13.

————. 1985. "A Rent Bill Deserves Support." May 5.

Santa Barbara News Press. 1978. "Raise Rents." Dec. 3, p. 1.

Santa Monica Rent Control Board. 1979. "Proposed General Rent Adjustment." Santa Monica: Rent Control Office.

Saunders, Peter. 1978. "Domestic Property and Social Class." *International Journal of Urban and Regional Research* 2:233–51.

————. 1979. *Urban Politics: A Sociological Interpretation*. London: Hutchinson.

————. 1981. *Social Theory and the Urban Question*. New York: Holmes and Meier.

Schifferes, Steve. 1986. "The Dilemmas of British Housing Policy." In Rachel Bratt, Chester Hartman, and Ann Meyerson (eds.), *Critical Perspectives on Housing*. Philadelphia: Temple University Press.

Schoonmaker, Mary Ellen. 1987. "The Real Estate Story: Hard News or Soft Sell?" *Columbia Journalism Review* (Jan.–Feb.), pp. 25–31.

Schorr, Alvin. 1963. *Slums and Social Insecurity.* Washington, D.C.: Government Printing Office.

Schwartz, Seymour I., David E. Hansen, Richard Green, William G. Moss, and Richard Belzer. 1979. *The Effect of Growth Management on New Housing Prices: Petaluma, California.* Davis: University of California Institute of Governmental Affairs, Environmental Quality Series.

Seidel, Stephen R. 1978. *Housing Costs and Government Regulations: Confronting the Regulatory Maze.* New Brunswick, N.J.: Center for Policy Research.

Seldon, Arthur. 1972. "Preface." In A. Seldon (ed.), *Verdict on Rent Control.* Worthing, England: Cormorant Press.

Selesnick, Herbert L. 1976. *Rent Control: A Case For.* Lexington, Mass.: Lexington Books.

Shearer, Derek. 1982. "Planning and the New Urban Populism: The Case of Santa Monica, California." *Journal of Planning Education and Research* 2:1.

Shipnuck, Leslie, Dennis Keating, and Mary Morgan. 1974. "The People's Guide to Urban Renewal." Berkeley: A Community Defense Manual.

Shlay, Ann. 1983. "Castles in the Sky: Measuring Housing and Neighborhood Ideology." Paper presented at American Sociological Association Annual Meeting, Detroit, Sept. 3.

Shulman, David. 1980. "Real Estate Valuation under Rent Control: The Case of Santa Monica." Mimeograph. Los Angeles: University of California, Business Forecasting Project.

SI [Swedish Institute]. 1980. *Fact Sheet on Sweden.* Stockholm: SI.

Smith, Barton. 1976. "The Supply of Urban Housing." *Quarterly Journal of Economics* XC:3:389–406.

———. 1986. "The Houston Housing Market: 1986 Update." Houston: University of Houston Center for Public Policy.

Smith, Roger. 1984. "Great Britain." In Martin Wynn (ed.), *Housing in Europe.* London: Croom Helm.

Smith, W. F. 1973. "Filtering and Neighborhood Change." In Daniel Mandelker and Roger Montgomery (eds.), *Housing in America: Problems and Prospects.* Indianapolis: Bobbs-Merrill.

Solomon, Arthur P. 1981. "Flawed Analysis of Market Trends Fuels Assaults on Housing Expenditures." *Journal of Housing* (Apr.), pp. 194–200.

——— and K. D. Vandell. 1982. "Alternative Perspectives on Neighborhood Decline." *Journal of American Institute of Planners* 45:1:81–91.

Sorenson, Baerbel. 1983. "The Alaska Emergency Residential Rent Regulation and Control Program." Paper presented at Lincoln Land Institute Colloquium on Rent Control.

Squires, Gregory. 1981. "Housing in America: Shelter or Social Control." *Contemporary Sociology* 10:6:755–757.

Starr, Paul, and Gosta Esping-Anderson. 1979. "Passive Intervention." *Working Papers for a New Society* VII:2:14–25.

Stegman, Michael A. 1972. *Housing Investment in the Inner City: The Dynamics of Decline*. Cambridge, Mass.: MIT Press.

———. 1982. *The Dynamics of Rental Housing in New York City*. New York: New York City Department of Housing Preservation and Development.

——— and H. Sumka. 1976. *Nonmetropolitan Urban Housing: An Economic Analysis of Problems and Policies*. Cambridge, Mass.: Ballinger.

Steinberger, P. 1981. "Political Participation and Community: A Cultural/Interpersonal Approach." *Rural Sociology* 46:7–19.

Sternlieb, George. 1966. *The Tenement Landlord*. New Brunswick, N.J.: Rutgers University Press.

———. 1974. "The Realities of Rent Control in the Greater Boston Area." New Brunswick, N.J.: Rutgers University Center for Urban Policy Research.

———. 1975. "Fort Lee Rent Control." New Brunswick, N.J.: Rutgers University Center for Urban Policy Research.

———. 1980a. *America's Housing: Prospects and Problems*. New Brunswick, N.J.: Rutgers University Center for Urban Policy Research.

——— and James W. Hughes. 1980b. "The Post-Shelter Society." In George Sternlieb and James Hughes (eds.), *America's Housing: Prospects and Problems*. New Brunswick, N.J.: Rutgers University Center for Urban Policy Research.

———. 1981. *The Future of Rental Housing*. New Brunswick, N.J.: Center for Urban Policy Research.

Stone, Lorene Hemphill. 1986. "Shelters for Battered Women: A Temporary Escape from Danger or the First Step toward Divorce?" In Jon Erickson and Charles Wilhelm (eds.), *Housing the Homeless*. New Brunswick, N.J.: Rutgers University Center for Urban Policy Research.

Stone, Michael. 1973. "Housing, Mortgages and the State." In Daniel Mandelker and Roger Montgomery (eds.), *Housing in America: Problems and Perspectives*. Indianapolis: Bobbs-Merrill (pp. 69–81).

———. 1975. "The Housing Crisis, Mortgage Lending, and Class Struggle." *Antipode* 7:2:22–37.

———. 1980a. "Housing and the American Economy: A Marxist Analysis." In Pierre Clavel, John Forester, and William W. Goldsmith (eds.), *Urban Planning in an Age of Austerity*. New York: Pergamon Press (pp. 81–116).

———. 1980b. "The Housing Prospect in the United States: Origins and Prospects." *Socialist Review* 52:65–119.

———. 1983. "Housing and the Economic Crisis: An Analysis and Emergency Program." In Chester Hartman (ed.), *America's Housing Crisis: What Is to Be Done?* Boston: Routledge and Kegan Paul.

Stoner, Madelaine R. 1986. "The Plight of Homeless Women." In Jon Erickson and Charles Weilhelm (eds.), *Housing the Homeless*. New Brunswick, N.J.: Rutgers University Center for Urban Policy Research.

Stull, William J. 1974. "Land Use and Zoning in an Urban Economy." *American Economic Review* 64:3:337–347.

Stutz, Frederick P., and Auther E. Kartman. 1982. "Housing Affordability and Spatial Price Variations in the United States." *Economic Geography* 58:3:221–235.

Susser, Ida. 1982. *Norman Street: Poverty and Politics in an Urban Neighborhood*. New York: Oxford University Press.

Svenska Riksbyggen [SR]. 1980. *Facts on Swedish Housing.* Stockholm: SI.

Svensson, R. 1976. *Swedish Land Policy in Practical Application.* Stockholm: Swedish Council for Building Research.

Sykes, G. 1951. "The Differential Distribution of Community Knowledge." *Social Forces* 29:376–382.

Tabb, William K., and Larry Sawers. 1978. *Marxism and the Metropolis.* New York: Oxford University Press.

Taeuber, Karl. 1975. "Racial Segregation: The Persisting Dilemma." *Annals of the American Academy of Political and Social Science,* no. 87.

Tagge, C. 1976. "The Effects of Public Regulation on the Costs of New Single Family Units." University of Texas M.A. Thesis, Austin.

Task Force on Housing Costs. 1979. *Final Report of the Task Force on Housing Costs.* Washington, D.C.: U.S. Department of Housing and Urban Development.

Thorsberg, Frank. 1985. "Bay City Housing Costs Drive Residents Away." *Los Angeles Times,* July 28, VIII-22.

Thurow, Lester. 1982. "High Interest and the Public Weal: Why Rates Must Fall." *Los Angeles Times,* July 4, V-3.

———. 1984. "The Disappearance of the Middle Class." *New York Times* (Sunday), Feb. 5, Sec. 3, p. 3.

Turner, Bengt. 1981. "Fair Rents in Sweden—Market Adapted Prices or . . .?" Presented at Swedish Institute for Building Research National Housing Conference, Stockholm, June.

Turpin, Dick. 1985a. "California Median Home Price Now Tops $120,000." *Los Angeles Times,* Oct. 27, VII-1.

———. 1985b. "Solving State's Housing Needs Deemed Critical." *Los Angeles Times,* Apr. 23, Part VIII, p. 1.

Urban Institute. 1986. "Income Squeeze." *Time* Magazine, May 19, p. 37.

Urban Land Institute [ULI]. 1977. *Effects of Regulation on Housing Costs: Two Case Studies.* Washington, D.C.: ULI.

———. 1980. "Housing Costs and Land Use Regulations: A Statement of ULI Concern." *Urban Land* 39:1:24–25.

Urban Planning Aid. 1975. "Critique of the Rental Housing Association Rent Control Study: An Analysis of the Realities of Rent Control in the Greater Boston Area." Cambridge, Mass.: Urban Planning Aid.

USA Today. 1985. "USA's Homeless Face More Health Problems." Dec. 16, p. 9A.

U.S. Bureau of the Census. 1962. *County and City Data Book, 1962 (A Statistical Abstract Supplement).* Washington, D.C.: Government Printing Office.

———. 1963a. *Census of Housing (Volume I, General Housing Characteristics).* Washington, D.C.: Government Printing Office.

———. 1963b. *1960 Census of the Population (Volume I, Number of Inhabitants and General Social and Economic Characteristics).* Washington, D.C.: Government Printing Office.

———. 1970. *Census of Housing: New Jersey.* Washington, D.C.: Government Printing Office.

———. 1972. *1970 Census of Housing (Volume I, Detailed Housing Characteristics).* Washington, D.C.: Government Printing Office.

———. 1973a. *County and City Data Book, 1972 (A Statistical Abstract Supplement)*. Washington, D.C.: Government Printing Office.

———. 1973b. *1970 Census of Population (Volume I, Number of Inhabitants and General Social and Economic Characteristics)*. Washington, D.C.: Government Printing Office.

———. 1975. *Historical Statistics*. Washington, D.C.: Government Printing Office.

———. 1977. *Annual Housing Survey, 1977*. Washington, D.C.: Government Printing Office.

———. 1978. *Statistical Abstract of the United States*. Washington, D.C.: Bureau of Commerce.

———. 1979. *Current Population Reports* (Series P-20, no. 344). "Voting and Registration in the Election of November 1978." Washington, D.C.: Government Printing Office.

———. 1980. *Census of Housing: New Jersey*. Washington, D.C.: Government Printing Office.

———. 1981a. *Current Housing Reports, Annual Housing Survey: 1980, Part C, Financial Characteristics of the Housing Inventory, U.S. and Regions* (Series H-15—80). Washington, D.C.: Government Printing Office.

———. 1981b. *Statistical Abstract of the United States*. Washington, D.C.: Government Printing Office.

———. 1982a. *Census of Population and Housing, Supplementary Report: Provisional Estimates of Social, Economic, and Housing Characteristics for States and Selected SMSA's* (PHC 80-S1-1). Washington, D.C.: Government Printing Office.

———. 1982b. *Current Housing Reports, Annual Housing Survey: 1979, Part B, Indicators of Housing and Neighborhood Quality by Financial Characteristics, U.S. and Regions* (Series H-150—79). Washington, D.C.: Government Printing Office.

———. 1982c. *Current Housing Reports, Annual Housing Survey: 1980, Part A, General Housing Characteristics, U.S. and Regions* (Series H 150-80). Washington, D.C.: Government Printing Office.

———. 1983a. *Characteristics of New Housing, 1982. Construction Reports* (Series C25). Washington, D.C.: Government Printing Office.

———. 1983b. *Housing Starts. Construction Reports* (Series C20-83-2). Washington, D.C.: Government Printing Office.

———. 1983c. *Annual Housing Survey, 1983, Houston, Texas SMSA Housing Characteristics for Selected Metropolitan Areas*. Washington, D.C.: Government Printing Office.

U.S. Comptroller General. 1979. *Rental Housing: A National Problem that Needs Immediate Attention*. General Accounting Office report to Congress. Washington, D.C.: Government Printing Office.

———. 1978. *Housing Abandonment: A National Problem Needing New Approaches*. Washington, D.C.: Government Printing Office.

U.S. Congressional Budget Office. 1981. *The Tax Treatment of Homeownership: Issues and Options*. Washington, D.C.: Government Printing Office.

U.S. Department of Housing and Urban Development. 1977. *Preliminary Report of the Task Force on Multifamily Property Utilization*. Washington, D.C.: Government Printing Office.

————. 1978a. *Final Report of the Task Force on Multifamily Property Utilization.* Washington, D.C.: Government Printing Office.

————. 1978b. *The 1978 HUD Survey on the Quality of Community Life.* Washington, D.C.: Government Printing Office.

————. 1979. *Final Report of the Task Force on Housing Costs.* Washington, D.C.: Department of Housing and Urban Development.

————. 1980. *1980 Housing Production Report,* Appendix A. Office of the Secretary of the Treasury, Office of Tax Analysis. Washington, D.C.: Government Printing Office.

————. 1981. *Residential Displacement: An Update.* Office of Policy Development and Research, Report to Congress. Washington, D.C.: Government Printing Office.

————. 1982. *Recent Evidence on the Cost of Housing Subsidy Programs.* Office of Policy Development and Research. Washington, D.C.: Government Printing Office.

————. 1983a. *Annual Housing Survey: General Housing Characteristics for the United States and Regions.* Washington, D.C.: Government Printing Office.

————. 1983b. *Evaluation of the Urban Homesteading Demonstration Program: Final Report. Vol. 1, Summary Assessment.* Washington, D.C.: Government Printing Office.

————. 1984. *A Report to the Secretary on the Homeless and Emergency Shelters.* In U.S. House of Representatives, Joint Hearing before the Subcommittee on Housing and Community Development and the Subcommittee on Manpower and Housing (May 24), and *HUD Report on Homelessness.* Banking Committee. Serial No. 98-91. Washington, D.C.: Government Printing Office.

U.S. Department of Labor. 1982. *The Employment Situation: November 1982.* Washington, D.C.: Bureau of Labor Statistics (Release No. 82-454, Dec. 3).

USGAO [U.S. Government Accounting Office]. 1986. *Housing Allowances: An Assessment of Program Participation and Effects.* Washington, D.C.: General Accounting Office.

————. 1978. *Housing Abandonment: A National Problem Needing New Approaches.* Washington, D.C.: General Accounting Office.

U.S. House of Representatives. 1984. *Congressional Record,* Banking Committee Serial No. 98-91. Washington, D.C.: Government Printing Office.

————. 1985. *Congressional Record,* Banking Committee Serial No. 99-56. Washington, D.C.: Government Printing Office.

U.S. League of Savings Association. 1982. *Homeownership: The American Dream Adrift.* Chicago: League of Savings Associations.

Vaughan, Roger. 1972. "Landlord-Tenant Relations in a Low-Income Area." In Stephen Burghardt (ed.), *Tenants and the Urban Housing Crisis.* Dexter, Mich.: New Press (pp. 77–88).

Vestbro, D. U. 1979. "Collective Housing Units in Sweden." *Current Sweden* (a publication of the Swedish Institute, Stockholm).

Vitaliano, D. F. 1983a. "The Economic Consequences of Rent Control: Some Evidence from New York State." Presented at Lincoln Land Institute's Colloquium on Rent Control.

————. 1983b. "Public Housing and Slums: Cure or Cause?" *Urban Studies* 20:173–183.

Wabe, J. S. 1971. "A Study of House Prices as a Means of Establishing the Value of Journey Time, the Rate of Time Preference and the Valuation of Some Aspects of Environment in the London Metropolitan Region." *Applied Economics* 3:4:247–255.

Walsh, Joan. 1985. "Are City Shelters Now Open Asylums?" *In These Times* 9:9.

Wechsler, H. 1961. "Community Growth, Depressive Disorders, and Suicide." *American Journal of Sociology* 67:9–16.

Weicher, John C. 1979. "Urban Housing Policy." In Peter Mieszkowski and Mahlon Straszheim (eds.), *Current Issues in Urban Economics.* Baltimore: Johns Hopkins University Press.

———, Kevin E. Villani, and Elizabeth A. Roistacher. 1981. *Rental Housing: Is There a Crisis?* Washington, D.C.: Urban Institute Press.

———. 1982. *Metropolitan Housing Needs of the 1980s.* Washington, D.C.: Urban Institute Press.

Weintraub, Robert E. 1982. "Private Housing Starts and the Growth of the Money Supply." In M. Bruce Johnson (ed.), *Resolving the Housing Crisis.* San Francisco: Pacific Institute for Public Policy Research.

Wheeler, D. R. 1974. "Economic Control and Urban Growth." Ph.D. Thesis, Massachusetts Institute of Technology.

Whitte, A. D. 1975. "The Determination of Inter-urban Residential Site Price Differences: A Derived Demand Model with Empirical Testing." *Journal of Regional Science* 15:351–364.

Wiktorin, M. 1982. "Housing Policy and Disadvantaged Groups in Sweden." *International Journal of Urban and Regional Research* 6:2:246–255.

Wilkinson, R. K. 1971. "The Determinants of Relative House Prices." Paper presented to C.E.S. Urban Economics Conference, Keele, Great Britain, July.

Williams, J. A. 1971. "The Multifamily Housing Solution and Housing Type Preference." *Social Science Quarterly* 52:543–559.

Williams, O. P. 1971. *Metropolitan Political Analysis.* New York: Macmillan.

Willis, John W. 1950. "Short History of Rent Control Laws." *Cornell Law Quarterly* 36:54–92.

Wilson, Dick. 1986. "Real Estate May Be Only 'Loophole' Under New Tax Law." *Santa Barbara News-Press,* Sept. 19.

Wilson, James Q. (ed.). 1966. *Urban Renewal: The Record and the Controversy.* Cambridge, Mass.: MIT Press.

Wingo, L. 1973. "The Quality of Life: Toward a Microeconomic Definition." *Urban Studies* 10:3–18.

Winograd, Kenneth. 1982. "Street People and Other Homeless—A Pittsburgh Study." Pittsburgh: Emergency Shelter Task Force.

Wirth, Louis. 1947. "Housing as a Field of Sociological Research." *American Sociological Review* 12:2:137–142.

Witt-Stromer, Holly. 1977. "Owner-Building of Smallhouse-Areas and the Owners Participating in Administration and Use of Those Areas" (report). Stockholm: Smahusavdelningen.

Wolfe, Marian F. 1983. "An Empirical Examination of Landlord Behavior and Implications for Rental Housing Policies." Paper presented at 25th Annual Conference of Association of Collegiate Schools of Planning, San Francisco.

Wright, Gwendolyn. 1981. *Building the Dream: A Social History of Housing in America*. Cambridge, Mass.: MIT Press.

Wynn, Martin. 1984. "Introduction." In Martin Wynn (ed.), *Housing in Europe*. London: Croom Helm.

Yankelovich, Clancy, and Shulman. 1986. "Portrait of a Generation." In *Time* Magazine, May 19, p. 35.

Zald, Mayer N., and J. D. McCarthy (eds.). 1979. *The Dynamic of Social Movements*. Cambridge, Mass.: Winthrop Publishers.

Zigas, Barry. 1987. [Zigas is president of the National Low Income Housing Coalition.] Personal communication (January 28).

AUTHOR INDEX

SUBJECT INDEX